Purity and Pollution in the Hebrew Bible

In this book, Yitzhaq Feder presents a novel and compelling account of pollution in ancient Israel, from its emergence as an embodied concept, rooted in physiological experience, to its expression as a pervasive metaphor in social-moral discourse. Feder aims to bring the biblical and ancient Near Eastern evidence into a sustained conversation with anthropological and psychological research through comparison with notions of contagion in other ancient and modern cultural contexts. Showing how numerous interpretive difficulties are the result of imposing modern concepts on the ancient texts, he guides readers through wide-ranging parallels to biblical attitudes in ancient Near Eastern, ethnographic and modern cultures. Feder demonstrates how contemporary evolutionary and psychological research can be applied to ancient textual evidence. He also suggests a path of synthesis that can move beyond the polarized positions that currently characterize modern academic and popular debates bearing on the roles of biology and culture in shaping human behavior.

Yitzhaq Feder is a lecturer at the University of Haifa. His research integrates textual study with advances in psychological and anthropological research. He has received numerous prizes, including the 2012 SBL David Noel Freedman Award for Excellence and Innovation in Biblical Studies. His most recent research focuses on biblical and ancient Near Eastern notions of taboo and their implications for understanding the emergence and historical development of morality.

T0370953

Purity and Pollution in the Hebrew Bible

From Embodied Experience to Moral Metaphor

YITZHAQ FEDER

University of Haifa

Shaftesbury Road, Cambridge CB2 8EA, United Kingdom

One Liberty Plaza, 20th Floor, New York, NY 10006, USA

477 Williamstown Road, Port Melbourne, VIC 3207, Australia

314–321, 3rd Floor, Plot 3, Splendor Forum, Jasola District Centre, New Delhi – 110025, India

103 Penang Road, #05–06/07, Visioncrest Commercial, Singapore 238467

Cambridge University Press is part of Cambridge University Press & Assessment, a department of the University of Cambridge.

We share the University's mission to contribute to society through the pursuit of education, learning and research at the highest international levels of excellence.

www.cambridge.org
Information on this title: www.cambridge.org/9781009045650

DOI: 10.1017/9781009042642

First published 2022
First paperback edition 2024

A catalogue record for this publication is available from the British Library

Library of Congress Cataloging-in-Publication data
NAMES: Feder, Yitzhaq, 1977– author.
TITLE: Purity and pollution in the Hebrew Bible : from embodied experience to moral metaphor / Yitzhaq Feder, University of Haifa, Israel.
DESCRIPTION: Cambridge, United Kingdom ; New York, NY, USA : Cambridge University Press, [2022] | Includes bibliographical references and index.
IDENTIFIERS: LCCN 2021024930 (print) | LCCN 2021024931 (ebook) | ISBN 9781316517574 (hardback) | ISBN 9781009042642 (ebook)
SUBJECTS: LCSH: Bible. Old Testament – Criticism, interpretation, etc. | Pollution – Biblical teaching. | Purity, Ritual – Biblical teaching. | BISAC: RELIGION / Biblical Studies / Old Testament / General
CLASSIFICATION: LCC BS1171.3 .F43 2022 (print) | LCC BS1171.3 (ebook) | DDC 221.6/6–dc23
LC record available at https://lccn.loc.gov/2021024930
LC ebook record available at https://lccn.loc.gov/2021024931

ISBN   978-1-316-51757-4   Hardback
ISBN   978-1-009-04565-0   Paperback

Contents

MATING

PART III IMAGES, CODES AND DISCOURSE

Figures

Tables

Preface

When I began to write this preface in January 2020, the coronavirus pandemic had just begun to capture the world's news headlines, which reported China's frantic efforts to control its spread by restricting the mobility of approximately 50 million citizens in the most affected cities. Within weeks, the virus was no longer "over there." Suddenly, the populations of the world (myself included) were engulfed by the virus, under strict quarantine restrictions, put in place in a desperate effort to slow the pace of infection.

Approximately 4,000 years ago, similar quarantine attempts were instituted by the leaders of Mari in northern Syria, as reported from letters from times of epidemics. Consider the following letter from the eighteenth century BCE:

The god is striking in the upper district, so I without delay took a bypass. Furthermore, my lord should give orders that the residents of the cities that have been touched [*laptūtu*] not enter cities that are not touched, lest they touch [*ulappatū*] the whole land.[1]

With minor changes, these words could have been written today. Even the apparently strange idiom "touched" (Akkadian *lapātu*) for infected cities is in fact an exact semantic parallel of the word "contagion," from Latin *com-tangere* ("touched with").[2] Aside from the historical significance of this being the earliest written evidence pertaining to infectious disease, there is a more fundamental point, which is, in fact, the *leitmotif* of this

---

[1] ARM 26/1 17 (my translation). See further the discussion below, p. 84.
[2] See Chapter 3.

book: our ability to understand these ancient texts (and any linguistic expression, for that matter) is defined by our ability to relate its content to our own personal experience. As a case in point, we can better understand the ancients' fear of impurity if we understand that it corresponds, in part, to today's fear of disease.

The fact that these preventative measures, including quarantine, were often expressed in the idiom of *purity* should alert us to the fact that the fear of pollution (i.e., defilement) was imminently real. Yet, scholars continue to write about "ritual" purity as if the cultures of the ancient world shared modern Western attitudes regarding the strict separation of science and religion. The point of this book is to argue that the idea of pollution in ancient Israel and as represented in the Hebrew Bible, like other ostensibly religious concepts, was firmly grounded in everyday experience.

The "contagion" described in this book is not limited to disease. It encompasses the transfer of *uncleanness* and, indeed, any invisible essence that has been transferred. It can also include the transfer of holiness and even the transfer of femininity. Even more interestingly, a key theme to be examined here is how the physiological sources of contagion are translated into an idiom of moral pollution in the Bible and beyond.

At the heart of this book is the challenge of describing a phenomenon that was perpetually just outside the threshold of language. Humans have always encountered contagion in its various forms and have struggled to understand it. Today we have an elaborate toolbox of concepts to describe both the physical processes underlying actual contagion (e.g., epidemiology in the case of infectious disease) as well as the psychological responses, particularly in the multidisciplinary study of human emotions. Yet, these concepts cannot be forcibly retrofitted onto the experience of previous generations, which need to be first understood in their own terms and historical contexts. Accordingly, the central task of this book is to mediate the experience of contagion in ancient Israel to the modern reader. This task requires that we acknowledge the fluidity of terms in ancient texts, but also that we recognize that our analytic discourse is also based on words. These terms are sometimes slippery and sometimes sticky; in any case, they cannot be viewed as products of *pure* reason.

The present study is devoted to understanding what the development of notions of pollution (which I will henceforth use interchangeably with "impurity") in ancient Israel, the ancient Near East and other cultures can teach us about the evolution of human thought as a historical process. As with the study of any aspect of human behavior and psychology, a comprehensive examination of pollution requires consideration of at least three key elements: (1) innate cognitive and emotional capacities and predispositions; (2) embodied experience; and (3) culture. Since experience is predicated on certain psychological capacities, the first two of these elements will be combined under the single term "experience," which will serve as the key to understanding the universal aspects of pollution. In making sense of pollution, it will be helpful to view its experiential, embodied basis as the raw materials which are given a defined form by the linguistic constructions of a specific culture.

Different aspects of this dynamic relationship between experience and language will be highlighted in the chapters that follow. Part I of this study ("Setting the Stage") will examine the embodied origins of purity and pollution. Chapter 1 introduces the concept of "contagion" from a psychological perspective and lays out some of the theoretical foundations for an embodied account of pollution in the Hebrew Bible. It will set forth a three-tier model for the analysis of pollution in ancient Israel, to be elaborated upon in the chapters that follow, based on a distinction between embodied images, normative codes and cultural discourse. The chapter provides a brief application of embodied cognition to the terminology of purity. Here the semantics of purity demonstrate how the structure of experience supplies the implicit rationale for otherwise unintelligible semantic relationships. The excursus that concludes this chapter presents a more detailed overview of the approach called "embodied cognition" as it is applied in this book.

Chapter 2 constitutes the DNA for the rest of the book, introducing its general approach to pollution and the various problems that will be examined in subsequent chapters. Contrary to accounts which have attempted to explain defilement as a system of abstract symbols, this chapter will argue that two basic types of pollution can be identified, a moderate form arousing disgust and conceptualized as uncleanness, and a more severe form arousing fear and associated with infectious disease, alongside a further extension of impurity into the domain of morality in the form of a "stain of transgression."

Part II ("Embodying Pollution through the Life Cycle") constitutes the core of the book. It examines the role of pollution as it bears on the life cycle, including disease, diet, death, birth and sexuality. Considerable attention is given to the role of pollution as a folk theory of infectious disease. Chapter 3 focuses on the biblical skin disease called *ṣaraʿat* and its conventional translation "leprosy" as a test case for probing the complex relationship between the experience of disease and language. Situated within a cross-cultural history of medicine, this chapter highlights the fallacy of the commonplace scholarly distinction between "ritual" impurity and disease; indeed, they can be one and the same.

Chapter 4 examines in further detail the possibility, raised in previous chapters, that the depiction of disease in the Priestly source of the Torah has deliberately obscured the dangers associated with infectious disease. This suspicion is confirmed by means of comparisons with Mesopotamian ritual texts which serve to highlight the idiosyncrasies of the Priestly treatment of disease. These include an absence of healing rites, an apparent lack of concern for the infectiousness of disease as a threat to individuals and an attempt to obscure the once commonplace connection between sickness and sin (Chapter 5). This latter characteristic, which might suggest that disease is a physiological occurrence free of moral implications, is examined in Chapter 6, where these developments are compared to the stance of ancient Greek and medieval Islamic texts that deemphasize the threat of infection as a part of their polemics against popular beliefs and practices. This discussion provides an additional perspective on how cultural discourse can reconstrue the role of pollution as a causal theory of the infectiousness of disease.

Chapters 7 and 8 further develop the idea that pollution is directly related to folk biology, relating it to the biblical concept of the soul (*nepeš*) in the domains of diet and death. These chapters explore how Priestly rules of pollution relate to the partially dualistic concept of self reflected in these sources, specifically how the *nepeš* can be both defiled and defiling. Through the consumption of impure animal flesh and blood – essentially merging the person's *nepeš* with that of the animal – the person's spirit is defiled. In the context of death, contact with the spirit of the deceased constitutes a source of pollution, specifically in the transitional phase when the spirit separates from the body.

Chapters 9 through 11 engage the topic of sexual pollution, which provides the opportunity to examine the socio-moral implications of pollution. Chapter 9 evaluates the wide spectrum of sexual pollutions in the Hebrew Bible, distinguishing between physiological (genital emissions) and moral pollution; the latter category being associated with prohibited sexual behaviors such as adultery and incest. Of particular interest is the fact that the biblical evidence for "moral pollution" is disproportionately associated with the sexual domain. These observations will be examined in light of developments in moral psychology examining how the evolved physiological functions of emotions could give rise to their communicative role in the social and moral domains. Chapter 10 deals with the contagiousness of femininity, including the possible association of pollution with sexual antagonism. Chapter 11 tackles an ambiguity regarding the procedure for women's purification, probing the implications of the seeming absence of an obligation for female impurity-bearers to wash.

The final part of this book ("Images, Codes and Discourse") examines the broader ramifications of the previous chapters. Chapter 12 examines how the embodied approach can be applied to the notion of holiness. Due to its close association with divinity, this concept would appear to be completely detached from mundane experience and hence pose a challenge to an embodied approach. Yet, even the depictions of the sacred prove to be deeply rooted in embodied imagery. Moreover, this chapter explores how sacred objects may themselves exhibit the characteristics of contagion. Chapter 13 brings the conclusions of the present study to bear on some pressing issues in today's study of religions. In particular, it will deal with whether the role of embodied cognition in shaping ancient Israelite notions of pollution vindicates naturalistic accounts of religion.

Finally, a word to readers who are not native to the territory of biblical studies: shalom! Though the focus of this book is on the notion of pollution in ancient Israel, its aims are more expansive. A central goal has been to bring biblical materials into a dialogue with the numerous disciplines that have helped me to make sense of these ancient documents, most prominently anthropology and psychology, including the interdisciplinary field called the cognitive science of religions. This aim builds on the realization that the evidence of ancient civilizations (the ancient Near East, in this case) constitutes a largely unexploited resource for social scientific (not to mention life-science) investigation. There are numerous factors that have, in the past, stifled this conversation, which need not detain us here.[3] For now, let it be stressed that I have sought to relegate the more technical philological and source-critical issues to the footnotes, leaving more detailed discussion to the original articles from which these chapters have developed. Hopefully, by foregrounding the issues of interdisciplinary interest, this book will serve as a platform for further debates, where the positions will not be predetermined by disciplinary boundaries.

So, with no further ado . . .

---

[3] See Chapter 13.

Acknowledgments

As this book goes to press, my disbelief gives way to gratitude, in acknowledgment of all who have helped me bring this project to fruition.

This research has benefited immensely from several research fellowships and grants. The development of these ideas began during my fellowship at the W. F. Albright Institute of Archaeological Research in winter 2012, and their crystallization in the present form would not have been possible without the opportunity provided by a Robert Carrady Fellowship at the Katz Center for Advanced Judaic Studies (University of Pennsylvania) in spring 2018. I thank the director Steven Weitzman and associate director Natalie Dohrmann for this stimulating experience. The final stages of revising this manuscript at the University of Haifa have benefited from a generous grant (1589/18) from the Israel Science Foundation.

For their encouragement and support over the years, I thank the colleagues and teachers who have remained in my corner, most notably: Gershon Galil, Ed Greenstein, Christophe Nihan, Takayoshi Oshima, Tania Notarius and Ziony Zevit. I would also like to express my appreciation to colleagues in psychology for welcoming me, an outsider to their field, with hospitality and interest. These include Joshua Rottman, Nina Strohminger and especially Paul Rozin. Here I must also mention my teacher, Itamar Singer z"l, who passed away during the early stages of this research, but whose unwavering support has remained a continuing source of inspiration.

Previous drafts of these chapters have benefited from the incisive comments of David Frankel and Matt Susnow. I also thank Fern Reis for her valuable insights in the presentation of this research to a broader audience. Several of the topics discussed in this book have appeared on the website thetorah.com, and I am grateful to the editors Marc Brettler and Zev Farber for numerous thought-provoking interactions and to David Steinberg for his ongoing friendship.

My experience working with Cambridge University Press has been a pleasure. I am grateful to the editors, Beatrice Rehl and Katherine Tengco Barbaro, for their care and efficiency in facilitating this volume's publication. Furthermore, I must express my deep appreciation to Frances Tye for her diligence and professionalism in copyediting the manuscript. I also thank Yoel Halevi for his help preparing the bibliography.

A sweet debt of gratitude belongs to my partner in life, Esty, who keeps me out of trouble and shares with me the challenges and wonders of embodiment. In raising our children together, she has helped me to appreciate that the foundations of knowledge and faith are one: to see behind what is immediately perceived.

Finally, by way of introducing the various unseemly topics that follow, it is an honor and privilege to dedicate this book to the outcasts:

"The slab despised by the builders has become the corner stone."

Psalm 118:22

Several of the chapters that follow are revised and updated versions of published articles. I thank the publishers for permission to reuse these materials:

Chapter 2: "Contagion and Cognition: Bodily Experience and the Conceptualization of Pollution (*tum'ah*) in the Hebrew Bible," *JNES* 72 (2013): 151–168.

Chapter 4: "Behind the Scenes of a Priestly Polemic: Leviticus 14 and its Extra-Biblical Parallels." *JHS* 15.4 (2015): 1–26 (https://doi.org/10.5508/jhs.2015.v15.a4).

Chapter 8: "Death, Afterlife and Corpse Pollution: The Meaning of the Expression *ṭāmēʾ la-nepeš*," *VT* 69 (2019): 408–434.

Chapter 9: "Defilement and Moral Discourse in the Hebrew Bible: An Evolutionary Framework" *Journal of Cognitive Historiography* 3 (2016): 157–89.

Notes on Transcriptions and Translations

In transcriptions of Hebrew and Akkadian, the sign š designates the sound /sh/ as in "sheep."

All translations of Hebrew, Akkadian and Hittite are my own, unless otherwise specified.

Abbreviations

AB	Anchor Bible
AfO	*Archiv für Orientforschung*
AHw	Wolfram von Soden, *Akkadisches Handwörterbuch*, vols. 1–3, Wiesbaden: Harrasowitz, 1965–1981
Akk	Akkadian
ALASP	Abhandlungen zur Literatur Alt-Syren-Palästinas und Mesopotamiens
Am	Amos
ANE	Ancient Near East
AOAT	Alter Orient und Altes Testament
AoF	*Altorientalische Forschungen*
ANET³	J. B. Pritchard (ed.), *Ancient Near Eastern Texts Relating to the Old Testament*. Princeton: Princeton University Press, 1969
ARM	Archives royales de Mari
BASOR	*Bulletin of the American Schools of Oriental Research*
BBSt	L. W. King, *Babylonian Boundary-Stones and Memorial Tablets in the British Museum* (London: Longmans & Co., 1912)
BF	Baghdader Forschungen
BiOr	Bibliotheca Orientalis
CAD	*The Assyrian Dictionary of the Oriental Institute of the University of Chicago*

CAT	M. Dietrich et al., *The Cuneiform Alphabetic Texts from Ugarit, Ras Ibn Hani and Other Places*. Münster: Ugarit Verlag, 2013
CBQ	*Catholic Biblical Quarterly*
CHD	*The Hittite Dictionary of the Oriental Institute of the University of Chicago*
Chr	Chronicles
CM	Cuneiform Monographs
CoS	W. W. Hallo (ed.), *The Context of Scripture*, vols. 1–5. Leiden-Boston: Brill, 2003
CTH	Catalogue des textes hittites
Dan	Daniel
DDD	K. van der Toorn, B. Becking and P. W. van der Horst (eds.), *Dictionary of Deities and Demons in the Bible*. Leiden: Brill, 1999
Deut	Deuteronomy
DULAT	Gregorio del Olmo Lete and Joaquín Sanmartín, *A Dictionary of the Ugaritic Language in the Alphabetic Tradition*. Leiden: Brill, 2003
EA	El-Amarna
Esth	Esther
ESV	English Standard Version
Ex	Exodus
Ezek	Ezekiel
FAOS	Freiburger Altorientalische Studien
FAT	Forschungen zum Alten Testament
GBH	P. Joüon and T. Muraoka, *Grammar of Biblical Hebrew*. Rome: Editrice Pontificio Instituto Biblico, 2006
Gen	Genesis
GKC	*Gesenius' Hebrew Grammar*, edited by W. Gesenius and E. Kautsch, translated by A. Cowley. Oxford: Clarendon Press, 1983
H	Holiness Legislation
Hag	Haggai
HALOT	W. Baumgartner et al., *The Hebrew and Aramaic Lexicon of the Old Testament*. Leiden: Brill, 1994
HAT	Handbuch zum Alten Testament
HB	Hebrew Bible
Heb	Hebrew
HeBAI	*Hebrew Bible and Ancient Israel*

Hos	Hosea
HSS	Harvard Semitic Studies
HTR	*Harvard Theological Review*
HUCA	*Hebrew Union College Annual*
ICC	International Critical Commentary
IDB	*Interpreter's Dictionary of the Bible*
IEJ	*Israel Exploration Journal*
Isa	Isaiah
JAAR	*Journal of the American Academy of Religion*
JAJ	*Journal of Ancient Judaism*
JANER	*Journal of Ancient Near Eastern Religion*
JANES	*Journal of the Ancient Near Eastern Society*
JAOS	*Journal of the American Oriental Society*
JBL	*Journal of Biblical Literature*
JCS	*Journal of Cuneiform Studies*
Jer	Jeremiah
JJS	*Journal of Jewish Studies*
JNES	*Journal of Near Eastern Studies*
Josh	Joshua
JPS	Jewish Publication Society
JSS	*Journal of Semitic Studies*
JSOT	*Journal for the Study of the Old Testament*
JSOTSup	Journal for the Study of the Old Testament: Supplement Series
Judg	Judges
KAI	*Kanaanäische und aramäische Inschriften*. Edited by Herbert Donner and Wolfgang Röllig, 5th ed. Wiesbaden, Germany: Harrassowitz, 1966–2002
KBo	*Keilschrifttexte aus Boghazköy*
Kgs	Kings
KHC	Kurzer Handkommentar zum Alten Testament
KJV	King James Version
KUB	*Keilschrifturkunden aus Boghazköy*
Lam	Lamentations
Lev	Leviticus
LKA	E. Ebeling, *Literarische Keilschrifttexte aus Assur*. Berlin: Akademie Verlag, 1886–1955
LXX	Septuagint (Greek translation of the Hebrew Bible)
m	Mishna
Mic	Micah

MT	Masoretic Text
Msk	Tablet siglum of texts from Meskene (Emar)
NA	Neo-Assyrian
NABU	*Nouvelles Assyriologiques Brèves et Utilitaires*
NB	Neo-Babylonian
NEB	New English Bible
Neh	Nehemia
NICOT	New International Commentary on the Old Testament
NJPS	New Jewish Publication Society Translation
Num	Numbers
OB	Old Babylonian
OBO	Orbis Biblicus et Orientalis
OrNS	*Orientalia New Series*
OTL	Old Testament Library
P	Priestly source
PEQ	*Palestine Exploration Quarterly*
Prov	Proverbs
Ps	Psalms
RA	*Revue d'Assyriologie et Archéologie orientale*
RB	*Revue biblique*
RINAP	Royal Inscriptions of the Neo-Assyrian Period
RlA	*Reallexikon der Assyriologie und vorderasiatischen Archäeologie*
RS	Ras Shamra
RSV	Revised Standard Version
SAA	State Archives of Assyria
SAACT	State Archives of Assyria Cuneiform Texts
Sam	Samuel
SANE	Sources of the Ancient Near East
SB	Standard Babylonian
SJOT	*Scandinavian Journal of the Old Testament*
SpTU	*Spätbabylonische Texte aus Uruk*
StBoT	*Studien zu den Boğazköy-Texten*
TDOT	*Theological Dictionary of the Old Testament*, edited by G. J. Botterweck et al., translated by J. T. Wills and D. E. Green. Grand Rapids, MI: Eerdmans, 1977–2006
THeth	*Texte der Hethiter*
TLOT	*Theological Lexicon of the Old Testament*, edited by E. Jenni and C. Westermann, translated by M. E. Biddle. Peabody, MA: Hendrickson, 1997

Ṭoh	*Ṭohorot*
TUAT	*Texte zur Umwelt des Alten Testaments*, edited by O. Kaiser. Gütersloher Verlagshaus Gerd Mohn: Gütersloh 1982–1997, Supplement 2001
UF	*Ugarit-Forschungen*
VAT	Vorderasiatisches Museum, Berlin
VT	*Vetus Testamentum*
WAW	Writings from the Ancient World
WO	*Die Welt des Orients*
ZA	*Zeitschrift für Assyriologie*
ZAH	*Zeitschrift für Althebraistik*
ZAW	*Zeitschrift für die Alttestamentliche Wissenschaft*
Zeb	*Zebaḥim*

PART I

SETTING THE STAGE

I

Introduction

A survey of pollution beliefs from cultures around the world over the span of recorded history reveals a remarkable commonality in the types of phenomena viewed as causing impurity. These tend to include corpses, genital emissions (ordinary and pathological), certain animals and disease. How is this striking commonality in disparate cultures to be explained? Before attempting to answer, let us frame the object of investigation in more familiar terms.

Imagine the following scenario: you are staying in a hotel room and wake up to find your bed infested with swarming insects. Fortunately, the front desk assures you that they are perfectly harmless, and, in any case, you were fully clothed. Under these circumstances, would you:

A. Bathe or shower immediately
B. Promptly check out of the hotel and then find a place to bathe or shower
C. Go back to sleep

If you answered A or B to this question, then the notion of pollution should not seem so strange. This psychological response of "contagion" can be defined as the perceived transfer of a negative essence from a source to a target.[1] As several mundane examples can show, there is nothing

[1] Carol Nemeroff and Paul Rozin pioneered the research on the "contagion" response in the 1990s, as summarized in these more recent summaries: "The Makings of the Magical Mind: The Nature and Function of Sympathetic Magical Thinking," in *Imagining the Impossible: Magical, Scientific and Religious Thinking in Children*, eds. K. S. Rosengren, C. N. Johnson and P. L. Harris (Cambridge: Cambridge University Press, 2000), 1–34; "Sympathetic Magical Thinking: The Contagion and Similarity 'Heuristics,'" in *Heuristics*

particularly mystical about the spread of an invisible essence. We experience *actual* contagion in numerous domains: the handling of a smelly object transfers its odor, interaction with a sick individual leads to infection and so on. It is hardly surprising, therefore, that these everyday experiences shape our expectations when interacting with our environment.

The word "contagion" is meaningfully ambivalent, bearing important implications for human psychology. In its everyday usage, it usually refers to the infectiousness of disease. In modern psychological research, however, contagion (also known as "contamination") refers to the "interpretation or response to situations in which *physical contamination* may have occurred."[2] For example, psychological contagion refers to the fact that many people feel a need to wash their hands after touching an animal carcass. As you may have noticed, this definition is illicit: the term is reused in its definition. Though violating a cardinal rule of dictionaries, this definition captures a fascinating aspect of psychological contagion: one's internal response seems to be perfectly attuned to external reality. Contagion seems to emerge at the point where the boundary between mind and world all but dissolves.[3] This startling phenomenon has not eluded evolutionary psychologists. For example, one group of researchers has commented on how disgust "amounts to an implicit germ theory."[4] How did this vital tendency to avoid sources of pathogens emerge in us? Is our aversion to pollution based on Darwinian self-protective instincts? And if so, how were the triggers determined?

This book is dedicated to solving the puzzle of contagion. Its point of departure is the Hebrew Bible, but the scope of the question pertains to all

and Biases: The Psychology of Intuitive Judgment, eds. T. Gilovich, D. W. Griffin and D. Kahneman (Cambridge: Cambridge University Press, 2002), 201–216. This response is often termed "contamination appraisals" in current research.

[2] Paul Rozin and April E. Fallon, "A Perspective on Disgust," *Psychological Review* 94.1 (1987): 29 (emphasis added).

[3] This subtle point was articulated by Gregory Bateson as follows: "In the natural history of the living human being, ontology and epistemology cannot be separated. His (commonly unconscious) beliefs about what sort of world it is will determine how he sees it and acts within it, and his ways of perceiving and acting will determine his beliefs about its nature. The living man is thus bound within a net of epistemological and ontological premises which – regardless of ultimate truth or falsity – become partially self-validating for him" (*Steps to an Ecology of Mind* [Chicago: University of Chicago Press, 1972], 314).

[4] Megan Oaten, Richard J. Stevenson and Trevor I. Case, "Disgust as a Disease Avoidance Mechanism: A Review and Model," *Psychological Bulletin* 135 (2009): 303–332 (313); see also Paul Rozin, Jonathan Haidt and Clark R. McCauley, "Disgust," in *Handbook of Emotions*, eds. M. Lewis, J. M. Haviland-Jones and L. F. Barrett, 3rd ed. (New York: Guilford Press, 2008), 757–776.

humans and all times. The rest of this chapter is dedicated to introducing the key theoretical principles which guide my approach. The next section will situate the current study in relation to previous trends in the investigation of pollution. The discussion will present a central theme of this book, the relation between language and experience, examining how each of these dimensions needs to be confronted in dealing with biblical pollution. As an initial illustration, these principles are applied to understanding semantics of purity in the ancient Near East. The final sections survey the bodies of evidence that will serve as the basis for this study and set forth its broader aims as a synthesis of sciences and humanities. The chapter closes with an appendix which offers a more detailed overview of the key insights of embodied cognition as they are applied in this book.

POINT OF DEPARTURE

Whenever the topic of purity is mentioned in academic discourse in general, and in relation to ancient Israel in particular, discussion turns quickly to anthropologist Mary Douglas' groundbreaking study *Purity and Danger*, published in 1966. As a theoretical work that maintains a pervasive influence in multiple disciplines over fifty years after its publication, it was clearly a rare scholarly achievement.

From the outset, a rather surprising point needs to be stated plainly. The *Purity and Danger* that pops into scholars' minds when the word "purity" is mentioned is usually based on a few selected passages from the book. Douglas' literary executor and intellectual biographer Richard Fardon makes the following revealing observations:

Being so well known, I had thought that *Purity and Danger* would yield to succinct summary; but rereading it several times, two decades after I last read it cover to cover, I realized how selective my memory of it had become. This would not be worth mentioning, except that other accounts of how to read *Purity and Danger* (including some by Mary Douglas herself) also dwell upon elements of the book's argument to the detriment of the book as a whole.[5]

Remarkably, the modern reception of *Purity and Danger* has tended to focus on a few key passages, while ignoring the complexity, equivocation and problematic aspects of the book as a whole.[6] Furthermore, as far as

[5] *Mary Douglas: An Intellectual Biography* (London/New York, NY: Routledge, 2001), 79.
[6] In Fardon's sympathetic sequential reading of the text, the critical issue of the book is not the topic of impurity but rather a reflection on the role of anthropological discourse in framing "the question of the differences between 'them' (primitives) and 'us' (moderns)"

the Hebrew Bible is concerned, Douglas abandoned many of her own lines of interpretation in her later books.[7]

One of the most enduring contributions of *Purity and Danger* is the possibility that the grimy details of impurity rules can be sublimated to an abstract symbolic discourse on order and disorder. Indeed, a provocative offshoot of this general approach is the view that death, bodily emissions and impure animals have significance beyond bare materialistic concerns, serving as means to represent and maintain social and intellectual boundaries. Yet, it should be recognized that Douglas never even attempts to explain how this symbolic discourse unconsciously emerges. In her efforts to see beyond the nitty-gritty details of purity practices, Douglas never fully accounted for the fact that they remain seated in the body, specifically those less pleasant aspects of it, and that it is precisely in these details that one finds a startling degree of commonality between disparate cultures.

In recent decades, evolutionary psychologists have addressed this lacuna with their etiology of bodily disgust. According to these accounts, disgust serves an adaptive function in protecting individuals against pathogen threats.[8] This evolutionary explanation offers a plausible account for the universality of disgust elicitors, such as disease, vermin, corpses and the like.[9] In recent years, Thomas Kazen is to be credited for applying these insights to pollution in the Hebrew Bible and ancient Judaism, arguing compellingly that naturalistic (evolutionary) and cultural modes of explanation need not be viewed as contradictory.[10]

(ibid., 83). The key point here is that *Purity and Danger* was not necessarily intended to be a systematic treatise on purity as much as a commentary on anthropological method.

[7] As Fardon incisively points out, "Scholars who continue to refer to the thirty-year-old analysis of *Purity and Danger* as if it were Douglas's last word on the subject should at least recognize that the famous 'abominations' of Leviticus are, in Douglas's later view, not abominations at all, and that the 'message' of the editors of Leviticus is not one of ethnic exclusivity" (ibid., 204).

[8] Steven Neuberg, Douglas T. Kenrick and Mark Schaller, "Human Threat Management Systems: Self-Protection and Disease Avoidance," *Neuroscience and Biobehavioral Reviews* 35.4 (2011): 1042–1051; Mark Schaller and Justin H. Park, "The Behavioral Immune System (and Why It Matters)," *Current Directions in Psychological Science* 20.2 (2011): 99–103.

[9] Rozin, Haidt and McCauley, "Disgust"; Daniel Kelly, *Yuck! The Nature and Moral Significance of Disgust* (Cambridge, MA: MIT Press, 2011); Oaten, Stevenson and Case, "Disgust as a Disease Avoidance Mechanism"; Valerie Curtis, Mícheal de Barra and Robert Aunger, "Disgust as an Adaptive System for Disease Avoidance Behavior," *Philosophical Transactions of the Royal Society B: Biological Sciences* 366 (2011): 389–401; Valerie Curtis, *Don't Look, Don't Touch, Don't Eat: The Science Behind Repulsion* (Oxford: Oxford University Press, 2013).

[10] Thomas Kazen, "Impurity, Ritual, and Emotion: A Psycho-Biological Approach," in *Issues of Impurity in Early Judaism* (Winona Lake, IN: Eisenbrauns, 2010), 13–40; Eve

Yet, questions remain. Is it really disgust that can account for all of the types of defilement? How does disgust develop into fully articulated notions of pollution? As will be seen, an attempt to address these broad theoretical questions can lead to striking new understandings of the ancient textual sources. To refine the discussion further, it is necessary to address the relation between language and experience. First, however, it is necessary to examine more closely each side of the equation: the language of pollution and the phenomenon of contagion.

LINGUISTIC PITFALLS OF PURITY

In studying the phenomena of purity and pollution, the potential for terminological confusion is twofold. First of all, it is necessary to recognize that our (etic) analytic vocabulary is fluid and often lacks any criteria delineating what distinguishes purportedly scientific anthropological concepts from the semantics of the relevant terms in our everyday language. Just as products boasting of their "purity" beckon to us from every shelf of the supermarket, on the packages of anything from toilet cleaners to spearmint chewing gum, so too the language of pollution is found in a wide array of domains (most obviously the environmental) which have little bearing on the question at hand. This fluidity would not pose a problem if it were not for the fact that academic conferences and volumes on purity and pollution are often structured by these vernacular usages.

The obvious remedy is to pay attention to the correspondence between our analytic terminology and the emic terms of the culture being studied, but here a second, subtler, source of confusion awaits. The frustrating fact is that even the "native" terminologies are imprecise, serving as generic terms for a heterogeneous group of phenomena. For example, the Biblical Hebrew term for pollution *ṭum'ah* is relatively rare (36 x in the Hebrew Bible) and constitutes a reification of the much more common adjective *ṭam'e* (87 x). In other words, the noun is derivative from the adjective, just as the English "im/purity" and German "un/reinheit" are derivative of their respective adjectives ("im/pure"; "un/rein").[11] This lexicographical observation has important semantic implications, since *ṭum'ah* can have different usages, referring to the source of pollution as well as the state

---

Levavi Feinstein, *Sexual Pollution in the Hebrew Bible* (Oxford: Oxford University Press, 2014), 11–41.
[11] The priority of the adjectival form is evident from the nominalizing suffixes -ity in English and -*heit* in German.

transferred to the recipient of pollution. Moreover, even when referring to the causes of pollution, this term serves as a generic umbrella category for a heterogeneous array of sources, including disease, impure animals and corpses, each of which operates according to very different rules.[12]

Here we might keep in mind Ludwig Wittgenstein's famous discussion of "games":

Consider, for example, the activities we call "games." I mean board-games, card-games, ball-games, athletic games, and so on. What is common to them all? – Don't say: "They *must* have something in common, or they would not be called 'games'" – but *look and see* whether there is anything common to all.[13]

Similarly, we cannot take terms like "purity" and "pollution" as being self-understood. Even Mary Douglas herself, reflecting on *Purity and Danger* thirty-eight years later, came to realize the danger of the word "purity":

"Purity" is one of those traps for the scholarly that Wittgenstein warned us about, a typical philosophical problem about words. Sometimes the screen of my PC goes blank and a little box appears with the message: "You have done an illegal action," then appears an error number and a penalty. It is often like this when we use the word "purity": we get into trouble when we seem to assign it some specific existence.[14]

When seeking to reconstruct native conceptions based on texts, it is necessary to ask whether they are systematic or even coherent. The situation becomes even more complicated when one seeks to address additional crucial variables, such as multiplicity of viewpoints within a culture and changing attitudes over time. These problems bear also on the distinction between literal and rhetorical usages: is it possible to distinguish "real" impurity from "metaphorical" impurity? In order to answer questions such as this, it is necessary to clarify what in the world of experience was referred to by terms like *ṭum'ah*.

CONTAGION AND EXPERIENCE

As pointed out above, disgust research has made a significant contribution to the study of pollution. One aspect of disgust that is highly relevant is its "domain-specificity," referring to the fact that participants in these studies

---

[12] See next chapter for further discussion of these points.
[13] Ludwig Wittgenstein, *Philosophical Investigations*, trans. G. E. M. Anscombe, P. M. S. Hacker and J. Schulte (Chichester: Wiley-Blackwell, 2009), 36e (§66).
[14] *Jacob's Tears: The Priestly Work of Reconciliation* (Oxford: Oxford University Press, 2006), 159.

respond differently to different types of contamination, be it excrement, tuberculosis or bedbugs.[15] In particular, these various contaminants are treated differently in their modes of transmission, their perceived ramifications and the means for their cleansing.[16] Where do these intuitions come from? Are we born with this capability to identify different types of threat and respond accordingly? To claim that "disgust" can explain this sophisticated capability is little more than hand-waving.

Accordingly, one may ask whether "disgust" is the best term to describe the contagion response. One way to solve this problem is to define "disgust" broadly, as does Valerie Curtis, who identifies it with "the system in brains that drives parasite-avoidance behavior."[17] Still, expanding the scope of "disgust" does not amount to an explanation. A more accurate point of departure is to admit that contagion relates to avoidance emotions more generally, including disgust and fear. To appreciate this last point, it is worth pointing out that the analytic term "disgust" and its designation as a basic emotion entails imposing a somewhat arbitrary boundary onto the emotional landscape.[18] Can either label – "disgust" or "fear" – by itself do justice to the feeling of waking up in an insect-infested bed?

In psychological research, avoidance emotions – and disgust in particular – serve to curb the individual's appetite in the domains of eating and sexuality. It is the possibilities of close contact and oral ingestion of an unwanted entity that elicit vigilant expressions of these emotions. Here it is necessary to stress the primal character of these avoidance emotions, which is most evident in the central role of the olfactory system of the brain, responsible for smell.[19] Theoretical neuroscientist Walter J. Freeman III writes: "The nose was and is the final arbiter of what we

[15] E.g., Bunmi O. Olatunji, Craig Ebesutani, Jonathan Haidt and Chad N. Sawchuk, "Specificity of Disgust Domains in the Prediction of Contamination Anxiety and Avoidance: A Multimodal Examination," *Behavior Therapy* 45.4 (2014): 469–481.
[16] For more detailed discussion, see Yitzhaq Feder, "Contamination Appraisals, Pollution Beliefs and the Role of Cultural Inheritance in Shaping Disease Avoidance Behavior," *Cognitive Science* 40.6 (2016): 1561–1585.
[17] Curtis, *Don't Look*, 34.
[18] James A. Russell, "Core Affect and the Psychological Construction of Emotion," *Psychological Review* 110.1 (2003): 145–172; See Lisa Feldman Barrett, "Are Emotions Natural Kinds?" *Perspectives on Psychological Science* 1.1 (2006): 28–58; Giovanna Colombetti, *The Feeling Body: Affective Science Meets the Enactive Mind* (Cambridge, MA: MIT Press, 2014), 25–82.
[19] Kai Qin Chan et al., "Disgust and Fear Lower Olfactory Threshold," *Emotion* 16.5 (2016): 740–749; Martin Kavaliers, Klaus-Peter Ossenkopp and Elena Choleris, "Social Neuroscience of Disgust," *Genes, Brain and Behavior* 18.1 (2019): e12508.

ingest and of what we are afraid."[20] These observations can go a long way toward explaining the relationship between foul odors and pollution in the Hebrew Bible and elsewhere.[21] As will be seen in the chapters that follow, smell seems to play a key role in detecting sources of impurity in relation to foods, corpses and sex. Still, one cannot dismiss the role of other sensory modalities through which disgust and fear can be elicited.

Even recognizing the importance of these affective mechanisms, they can only go so far in explaining how humans respond to different sources of contamination. As this book will argue, any plausible explanation must acknowledge three partners which together produce this capacity: innate predispositions, experience (learning) and culture. Of these three inputs, the role of experience is the most difficult to isolate in experimental situations, and for this reason has been left out of scholarly discussion, but its contribution is no less significant.

EMBODIMENT AND LANGUAGE

A basic premise of this study is that embodied experience provides the foundation for cultural discourse. In the natural world, the emergence of verbal language among humans is an anomaly that is responsible, more than any other capacity, for their cognitive and technological superiority over other animals. Surprisingly enough, the basis for this system of seemingly unlimited potential is the arbitrary coupling of acoustic signs with ideas, conventional to every language.[22]

This valid insight served as the foundation of Ferdinand de Saussure's *Course on General Linguistics*, but in a distorted form that would have catastrophic ramifications for the humanities:

The linguistic fact can therefore be pictured in its totality – i.e. language – as a series of contiguous subdivisions marked off on both the indefinite plane of jumbled ideas (A) and the equally vague plane of sounds (B). The following diagram gives a rough idea of it:

---

[20] *How Brains Make Up Their Minds* (New York: Columbia University Press, 2000), 20.
[21] Following Darwin and building on etymology, most disgust research has focused on taste (e.g., Rozin, Clark and McCauley, "Disgust," 637). For an account that emphasizes smell, see Aurel Kolnai, *On Disgust* (Chicago and La Salle, IL: Open Court, 2004 [1929]). See also Kazen, "Dirt and Disgust," 52–53; Curtis, *Don't Look*, 11–17.
[22] Eva Jablonka and Marion J. Lamb, *Evolution in Four Dimensions* (Cambridge, MA: MIT Press, 2005), 193–204.

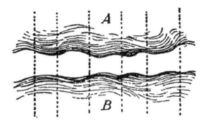

The characteristic role of language with respect to thought is not to create a material phonic means for expressing ideas but to serve as a link between thought and sound, under conditions that of necessity bring about the reciprocal delimitations of units. Thought, chaotic by nature, has to become ordered in the process of its decomposition.[23]

This scheme provided the foundations for the notion of linguistic relativity, as articulated by Benjamin Whorf: "We dissect nature along lines laid down by our native languages. The categories and types that we isolate from the world of phenomena we do not find there because they stare every observer in the face; on the contrary, the world is presented in a kaleidoscopic flux of impressions which has to be organized by our minds – and this means largely by the linguistic systems in our minds."[24] In other words, thought is dependent on arbitrary distinctions imposed by language. This implication is expressed clearly by de Saussure himself: "In the language itself, there are only differences ... the language includes neither ideas nor sounds existing prior to the linguistic system, but only conceptual and phonetic differences arising out of that system."[25] This overly simplistic scheme leads to many absurdities, especially when serving as the springboard for structuralist and poststructuralist cultural theories in which language is endowed with an unbounded power to construct social phenomena.[26]

Rather than viewing the linguistic system as autonomous, the alternative approach is to view language as inextricably connected with extralinguistic experience. One of the major contributions of cognitive linguistics has been to illuminate the relationship between human experience and semantic structure. This connection is commonly formulated in the

[23] *Course in General Linguistics*, trans. W. Baskin (London: Peter Owen, 1959), 112.
[24] Benjamin Lee Whorf, *Language, Thought and Reality*, ed. J. B. Carroll (Cambridge, MA: MIT Press, 1956), 213.
[25] Saussure, *Course*, 120.
[26] See Edward Slingerland, *What Science Offers the Humanities* (Cambridge University Press, Cambridge, 2008), 74–147.

assertion that word meaning is encyclopedic. William Croft summarizes this view as the recognition that "everything you know about the concept is part of its meaning."[27] In communication, the exchange of linguistic meanings by communicating parties is dependent on their shared world knowledge. In her book *Meaning and Experience*, Patrizia Violi offers a systematic program for relating lexical semantics to experience, claiming that "all language is intrinsically indexical, referring to the extralinguistic dimension of our experience."[28]

These observations provide a coherent framework for understanding the long-standing observation in the field of Semitic lexicography that the abstract uses of a term can often be traced back to an original concrete sense. Ludwig Koehler expresses this assumption in the preface to the Koehler–Baumgartner *Lexicon*:

> [I]t may be readily understood that the theological rendering of Hebrew words and phrases received the greatest amount of attention, and was given pride of place … But the theological, and also the more far reaching religious, world of ideas grew out of the non-theological, the common, world of ideas; whatever one wished to say theologically was expressed in language drawn from the common world of ideas.[29]

Embodied cognition offers an account which can explain the necessity for this process of scaffolding, whereby abstract (experientially distant) concepts emerge from concrete (experientially proximate) ones.[30] These principles find striking realization in the ancient Near Eastern terminology for "purity," as it relates to concrete experience.

AN ILLUSTRATION: THE SEMANTICS OF PURITY

Though the primary topic of the present study is pollution, it is necessary to take a quick look at its more attractive counterpart, purity.[31] An interesting point which pertains to ancient and modern languages alike

---

[27] William Croft, "The Role of Domains in the Interpretation of Metaphors and Metonymies," in *Metaphor and Metonymy in Comparison and Contrast*, eds. R. Dirven and R. Pörings (Berlin: de Gruyter, 2003), 163.

[28] *Meaning and Experience*, trans. J. Carden (Bloomington, IN: Indiana University Press, 2001), 46.

[29] Ludwig Koehler and Walter Baumgartner, *Lexicon in Veteris Testament Libros* (Leiden: Brill, 1958), xiv.

[30] For further discussion, see the appendix at the end of this chapter.

[31] The following is a highly abbreviated summary of my article: "The Semantics of Purity in the Ancient Near East: Lexical Meaning as a Projection of Embodied Experience," *JANER* 14.1 (2014): 87–113.

is that the meaning of "purity" (and comparable terms) is distinct from "cleanness." For example, try to substitute "clean" for "pure" in expressions such as "pure-blooded Irishman" and "pure nonsense," and it is evident that the terms are not interchangeable. As a point of reference, the American Heritage Dictionary offers the following definitions for "pure":

1. Having a uniform composition; not mixed
2. Free of adulterants or impurities
3. Free of dirt, defilement or pollution
4. Complete; utter
5. Having no faults; perfect
6. Chaste; virgin[32]

This set of senses is remarkably similar to those represented in ancient Near Eastern languages, accentuating the question: What is purity and how did this cross-cultural concept originate?

In attempting to reconstruct the conceptual prehistory of "purity," it will be necessary to move beyond the standard structuralist definition of purity as the opposite of impurity. The latter approach (still influential in modern lexicographical works) is based on Ferdinand de Saussure's programmatic attempt to distinguish language as an object of analysis from extralinguistic experience. As noted above, de Saussure offered a mentalistic definition of the linguistic sign as a relation between a concept (e.g., dog) and an acoustic image (the sound /d-o-g/), leaving aside the dimension of reference (i.e., to an actual dog in a particular speech context). Second, and more importantly, he defined meaning as value, such that the sense of a term is *solely* determined by its relationship with the other terms in the linguistic system. Stated in his words: "The conceptual side of value is made up solely of relations and differences with respect to the other terms in language."[33] In this vein, one might be led, as was even the great lexicographer of Biblical Hebrew, James Barr, to define the meaning of Hebrew *ṭahor* as "(ritually) clean" as opposed to *ṭame'* "unclean."[34] As indicated above, such an understanding of "purity" is superficial and, in fact, imprecise. Without denying that these two terms can operate as antonyms (e.g., in Leviticus 11), it remains necessary to

---

[32] The dictionary also includes: "of unmixed blood or ancestry" and "theoretical" (e.g., "pure science"), but these are clearly derivative of senses 1–2 and 4, respectively.
[33] Saussure, *Course*, 117.
[34] "Semantics and Biblical Theology – A Contribution to the Discussion," in *Congress Volume: Uppsala 1971*, VTSupp 22 (Leiden: Brill, 1972), 15.

take into consideration the distinct domains of embodied experience from which these terms originated. Whereas the root *ṭ-m-'* relates to contagion, the etymology of *ṭ-h-r* leads in a different direction entirely, as will be seen presently.

A survey of the lexical evidence from the ancient Near East leads to a striking and unambiguous conclusion. In diverse languages (Sumerian, Akkadian, Hittite, Ugaritic and Biblical Hebrew), the primary terms for purity used in ritual and cultic contexts refer to radiance, not cleanness. This observation is particularly striking in light of the fact that Hittite and Sumerian are not Semitic languages, and that even the terms in Akkadian are etymologically distinct from those in Ugaritic and Hebrew, showing that this phenomenon occurred in these languages independently. As an illustration, consider the use of the Hebrew term *ṭahor*, as it appears in the description of the divine throne in Exodus 24: "They saw the God of Israel and beneath his feet was like a brick-work of lapis lazuli and like the very heavens in its brilliance (*la-ṭohar*)." The Ugaritic cognates of this term (*ṭhr/ẓhr*) also link the brilliance of lapis lazuli to the sky and are employed exclusively in this concrete sense.[35] Similarly, terms such as Sumerian *kug*, Akkadian *ellu* and *ebbu* and Hittite *parkui* all share this general range of meanings, including the brightness, shininess and radiance of physical objects, including metals, precious stones and oil. These terms were applied to the cultic and ritual domains only secondarily. What is the reason for this ubiquitous semantic transition from radiance to purity?

The background for this transition is the fact that certain substances – especially metals like silver and gold – are most radiant in their pure and polished forms. Likewise, the golden hue of pure olive oil from a ripe fruit and the bright white appearance of processed wool provided salient images for understanding the notion of purity and could also be exploited in ritual acts. These cultures viewed radiant substances such as precious metals and stones as revealing an otherworldly or numinous character. For this reason, most of these terms could also be used to designate a state of holiness. For example, the Akkadian terms *ellu* and *ebbu*, like their Sumerian counterpart *kug*, were often ambiguous in their reference to purity or sanctity, designating an object or person ritually prepared for an encounter with the gods.[36]

---

[35] See further James N. Ford, "The Ugaritic Letter RS 18.038 (KTU2 2.39) and the Meaning of the Term spr 'lapis lazuli' (= BH sappīr 'lapis lazuli')," *UF* 40 (2008): 302–304.
[36] See Chapter 12.

Even from this brief example, it can be seen that an ostensibly meta-physical concept such as purity can be traced back to its origins in a world of embodied meanings. These images provide the raw materials – the repertoire of signs – that serve as the basis for linguistic codes, which in turn provide the substance for cultural discourse and practice.[37] The invisible hand guiding this process of cultural cognitive development is the necessity to establish a collectively recognizable currency for the articulation of religious intuitions, based in its initial stages upon mutually perceptible concrete symbols. As Emile Durkheim aptly commented: "Logical thought is possible only when man has managed to go beyond the fleeting representations he owes to sense experience and in the end to construct a whole world of stable ideals, the common ground of intelligences."[38]

No less importantly, etymology often continues to guide usage,[39] as is illustrated by the following diagram (Figure 1.1) of the semantic transitions of Akkadian purity terms:

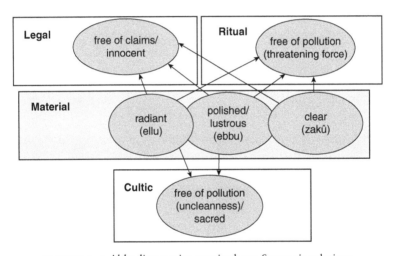

FIGURE 1.1 Akkadian purity terminology: Semantic relations

---

[37] See Jordan Zlatev, "Embodiment, Language and Mimesis," in *Body, Language and Mind. Volume 1: Embodiment*, eds. T. Ziemke, J. Zlatev and R. M. Frank (Berlin: de Gruyter, 2007), 297–337.

[38] See E. Durkheim, *The Elementary Forms of Religious Life*, trans. K. E. Fields (New York: Free Press, 1995 [1912]), 437.

[39] Compare Barr's warning: "Etymology is not, and does not profess to be, a guide to the semantic value of words in their current usage, and such a value has to be determined from the current usage and not the derivation" (*The Semantics of Biblical Language* [London: Oxford University, 1961], 107). Without denying this point, a balanced perspective should acknowledge that the origins of words often continue to guide actual usage.

This diagram depicts the semantic development of Akkadian terms for purity. The rectangular frames represent experiential domains, both material and nonmaterial (legal, ritual and cultic). Here the "cultic" domain refers to sacrificial service of the gods to show them homage, as opposed to the "ritual" domain, which refers to therapeutic rituals that seek to eliminate metaphysical threats to an individual. The circles represent particular terms, which in the material domain correspond to experiential images pertaining to radiance (*ellu*), lustrousness (*ebbu*) or clarity (*zakû*).

Using this diagram, we see how the terminology for radiance in the material domain served as a resource for describing more abstract situations of being "pure" in the legal and cultic domains. It can be seen that only *ellu* and *ebbu*, whose concrete senses are "radiant" and "lustrous" (respectively), were employed also in the cultic sense of "sacred," whereas *zakû*, whose concrete sense was "clear" (i.e., free of adulterants), could refer to being "clear" of legal responsibility but did not serve as a productive image for cultic purity. The phenomena of radiance (*ellu*) and lustrousness (*ebbu*), perceived as manifestations of a numinous quality, were much more appropriate for cultic purity, which involves the possibility of interacting with the world of the gods. As can be seen, the concrete image on which each term is based continued to exert influence on its semantic trajectory.

BODIES OF EVIDENCE

Having discussed the broader theoretical point of departure of the present study, it is now necessary to define the set of data which will be subject to analysis. As noted, the study of pollution in ancient Israel requires a dual perspective, recognizing both universal and culture-specific aspects of this phenomenon. The focus of the study is the Hebrew Bible (HB), a heterogeneous collection of texts composed between 1000 and 300 BCE. This evidence will be contextualized by extensive use of ancient Near Eastern (ANE) documents, which exhibit a large degree of similarity in terminology and worldview. These should be dated roughly between 2000 and 500 BCE and represent an array of cultures and languages, including Sumerian, Akkadian, Hittite, Ugaritic and Aramaic. In addition, some discussions will engage ancient Greek literature from the mid-to-late first millennium BCE. In some cases, pollution discourse in ancient Israel will be traced into later (Jewish) sources, including the Dead Sea Scrolls from Qumran and rabbinic literature.

In parallel, recognition of the embodied foundations of pollution requires a consideration of the universal aspects of human psychology and experience. Accordingly, this study makes selective use of ethnographic literature from contemporary (or near-contemporary) traditional cultures located in Africa, Asia, Melanesia and North America. It also incorporates psychological research, usually based on experiments with WEIRD participants, that is, from Western educated industrialized rich and democratic societies.[40] Taken together, the diversity of these data sets serves to reinforce the remarkable unity of the psychological phenomenon of contagion.

Further specification is required regarding the biblical texts since the distinction between various textual sources provides the basis for tracing developments and internal polemics within ancient Israel. Critical biblical scholarship has identified several distinct layers and sources from which the Torah (Pentateuch) is composed. The key source of information bearing on the present study is the Priestly source, a body of traditions which describes the divine origins of the cultic institutions and their laws in the wilderness of Sinai. Though these Priestly traditions manifest a largely homogenous style and ideology, they are not cut from a single cloth. In particular, it will be helpful to distinguish the Priestly traditions (P) that dominate the first part of the book of Leviticus (chapters 1–16) from the Holiness Legislation (H) that is found in chapters 17–27.[41] The present study will take as its point of departure the view of a growing consensus of scholars that H is later than P and constitutes the final redaction of the book of Leviticus. Likewise, it is recognized that several Priestly texts outside of Leviticus, including Exodus, Lev 1–16 and Numbers, exhibit a style and ideology similar to that found in Lev 17–27; hence they will be identified as H, though they may be later than the redaction of Leviticus.[42]

In terms of dating the Priestly traditions, the authors have been successful at thwarting the efforts of modern scholars to give them an absolute date, since they refer to an ideal wilderness situation that allows few if any historical anchors. Generally, a *longue durée* approach is warranted that recognizes that many of the ritual traditions may stretch back into the Late Bronze Age (fifteenth to twelfth centuries BCE), while also acknowledging that the final editing of these texts may have taken place in the Persian era (fifth century BCE), perhaps later. For the purposes of this

[40] Joseph Heinrich, J., Steven J. Heine and Ara Norenzayan, "The Weirdest People in the World," *Behavioral and Brain Sciences* 33.2–3 (2010): 61–83.

[41] For a detailed discussion of the current state of research, see Julia Rhyder, *Centralizing the Cult*, FAT 134 (Tübingen: Mohr Siebeck, 2019), 25–64.

[42] See Christoph Nihan, "The Priestly Laws of Numbers, the Holiness Legislation, and the Pentateuch," in *Torah and the Book of Numbers*, FAT 2/62; eds. C. Frevel, T. Pola and A. Schart (Tübingen: Mohr Siebeck, 2013), 109–137.

study, it will be sufficient to recognize the *relative* lateness of certain Priestly texts, such as H and most found in the book of Numbers, which will enable crucial insights differentiating earlier and later stages of Priestly thought. In reconstructing the history of pollution, it will be crucial to compare these Priestly texts with other non-Priestly biblical texts. The latter sources often reveal notions that are at odds with the ideology of the Priestly texts, specifically in their final redaction (H). As such, they shed light on the latter's rhetorical tendencies and reveal implicit polemics within ancient Israel.

Finally, in light of these comments, a word regarding the potential ambiguity of the term "Priestly." In most cases, this term will refer to the Priestly traditions in general, to be contrasted with non-Priestly biblical texts. However, when distinguishing layers within this body of traditions, "Priestly" (usually through the abbreviation P) will be set in contrast with H. These cases should be obvious from the context.

ANCIENT TEXTS AND THE HISTORY OF HUMAN THOUGHT

To summarize this wide-ranging introduction, the study of pollution in the Hebrew Bible and in other cultures requires a framework that can disentangle the respective roles of experience and language in shaping pollution beliefs. Such a framework, building on the insights of embodied cognition, can help account for both universal and culturally contingent aspects of pollution.

To confront these challenges, we will need to track the evolution of pollution in ancient Israel as a dynamic concept. Considering the numerous methodological pitfalls described above, this goal can be achieved only by carefully following the trajectory of pollution from an embodied concept, rooted in universal human psychology, to its culturally specific, flexible permutations in biblical and post-biblical discourse. More specifically, I will advance a three-tiered approach, isolating the following discrete levels or stages in the analysis of pollution: **images** – recurrently meaningful bodily experiences (not necessarily visual) and gestures;[43]

[43] This usage is largely compatible with Michael Kimmel's characterization of "image schemas." It is important to keep in mind that the pollution schema is primarily a pattern of active response, not a mental representation. See M. Kimmel, "Culture Regained: Situated and Compound Image Schemas," in *From Perception to Meaning: Image Schemas in Cognitive Linguistics*, ed. B. Hampe (Berlin: de Gruyter, 2005), 285–312; and "Properties of Cultural Embodiment: Lessons from the Anthropology of

codes – incorporating these images, and making up a culture's conventional linguistic and behavioral repertoires; and **discourse** – the entirety of a culture's verbal and nonverbal capacity for interaction, which incorporates these codes in both traditional and novel ways.[44]

Until now, the possibility of such a synthetic account has been encumbered by disciplinary tensions between evolutionary psychology and its emphasis on innate affective mechanisms and other disciplines (especially anthropology and the humanities) which tend to place greater emphasis on the role of cultural construction. This tension took on explosive proportions in the sociobiology debate of the 1970s in the wake of Edward O. Wilson's book *Sociobiology: The New Synthesis,* whose final chapter argued that human psychology and behavior should be understood within a common evolutionary framework together with that of other animals.[45] This potentially hegemonic view of biology over the humanities aroused fierce opposition from both scientists and humanists.[46] The integrative approach of the present work seeks to overcome the unhelpful dichotomy of biological and cultural approaches to human behavior. As a unified account which incorporates both biological and cultural factors, this analysis offers a test case of "consilience" – the potential offered through a synthesis of naturalistic and humanistic cultural investigation.[47] Not only will it aim to show how life sciences, anthropology and psychology can contribute to the study of ancient texts, it will also argue that these ancient documents can fill in crucial gaps for reconstructing the cognitive development of human civilizations.

---

the Body," in *Body, Language and Mind. Volume 2: Sociocultural Situatedness,* ed. T. Ziemke, J. Zlatev and R. M. Frank (Berlin: de Gruyter, 2008), 77–108.

[44] It is tempting to compare the latter two tiers to de Saussure's well-known distinction between *langue* (the linguistic system) and *parole* (instantiated speech), which corresponds respectively to the distinction between semantics and pragmatics. At the same time, as pointed out by linguists and philosophers of language alike, one must not press these theoretical distinctions too far. See further Ronald W. Langacker, *Cognitive Linguistics: A Basic Introduction* (New York: Oxford University Press, 2008), 40–42; Ruth Garrett Millikan, *Beyond Concepts* (Oxford: Oxford University Press, 2017), 167–183.

[45] *Sociobiology: The New Synthesis* (Cambridge, MA: Belknap Press, 2000 [1975]), 547–576.

[46] Ullica Segerstråle, *Defenders of the Truth: The Sociobiology Debate* (Oxford: Oxford University Press); Kevin N. Laland and Gillian R. Brown, *Sense and Nonsense: Evolutionary Perspectives on Human Behaviour* (New York: Oxford University Press, 2011). We will return to this topic in Chapter 13.

[47] Edward O. Wilson, *Consilience: The Unity of Knowledge* (New York: Alfred Knopf, 1998); Edward Slingerland, *What Science Offers the Humanities* (Cambridge: Cambridge University Press, 2008); Edward Slingerland and Mark Collard (eds.), *Creating Consilience: Integrating the Sciences and the Humanities* (Oxford: Oxford University Press, 2012). Some scholars use the designation "vertical integration."

It is now time to embark on this archaeology of the mind. In carrying out this excavation, there is no choice but to get our hands dirty.

APPENDIX: WHAT IS EMBODIED COGNITION?

Embodied cognition, like many things, is easiest to define by what it is not. It is a rejection of an extreme dualism that views human cognition as a mind that can operate entirely independently from a body, like a computer that manipulates symbols without any need for direct sensory-motor experience of the things that these symbols represent.[48] One need not deny that minds can manipulate abstract concepts: they can solve mathematic equations, play chess and perform a whole host of other tasks which seem to take place in a disembodied virtual reality. Regarding such capacities, embodied cognition makes two reservations. First, such abstract manipulations constitute a small fraction of the intellectual activities in which humans engage on a daily basis. Second, and more importantly, these abstract capacities are based on experientially grounded concepts.

The following discussion will highlight two key premises of embodied cognition as they apply to the present study:

Premise 1: Cognition Is Inextricably Tied to the Needs of the Organism in Adapting Itself to Its Environment

Embodied cognition argues that the unique cognitive capacities of humans are outgrowths of the biological needs and resources that govern the evolution of cognition in other creatures.[49] Its point of departure is the evolutionary assumption that humans for all of their uniqueness share a common biological – and neurological – origin with "lower" mammals. This shared origin is evident, inter alia, by the shared structure of mammalian brains, with the unique abilities of humans predicated on the latest phase of neuro-anatomical development, fittingly named the "neocortex."[50] An important implication of this approach is that the

---

[48] See John Searle, "Can Computers Think?" in *Philosophy of Mind: Classical and Contemporary Readings*, ed. D. J. Chalmers (New York: Oxford University Press, 2002), 669–675.

[49] Louise Barrett, "The Evolution of Cognition: A 4E Perspective," in *The Oxford Handbook of 4E Cognition*, eds. A. Newen, L. de Bruin and S. Gallagher (Oxford: Oxford University Press, 2018), 719–734.

[50] See, e.g., Mark F. Bear, Barry W. Connors and Michael A. Paradiso, *Neuroscience: Exploring the Brain* (Philadelphia, PA: Lippincott Williams & Wilkins, 2007), 167–200.

most basic levels of embodiment – which serve as the foundation for linguistically formulated concepts such as pollution – can be found in the nonverbal experience of other animals. It also enables us to recognize that minds coevolved with bodies, not for the purpose of playing chess or other abstract computations as ends unto themselves, but for the adaptive control of action within the organism's natural environment.[51]

This perspective will enable us to see the fallacy, common to much psychological research, of drawing a sharp distinction between emotions and judgment. Giovanni Colombetti dissolves this distinction as part of her "enactivist" view of mind, arguing that "cognition is both 'embodied' (realized, enacted, or 'brought forth' not just by the brain but by the whole organism) and 'embedded' (realized by the organism in interaction with the environment)." This perspective enables a reassessment of the role of affect (emotions, moods, etc.) in cognition:[52]

What is distinctive about enactivism is that it provides a theory of biological organization and of its relation to the mind that entails that not just emotions, moods, motivational states, etc., are affective, but that *cognition* is too. More precisely, as we are about to see, enactivism claims that the hallmark of cognition is "sense-making," and a close look at this notion reveals that sense-making is simultaneously a cognitive and an affective phenomenon.[53]

To apply this theoretical point, imagine the feeling of an unidentified creature slowly crawling up your arm. Is your response determined by the identification "this is an insect," or is the feeling itself also key to shaping your reaction? Recognizing that our affective predispositions are an important part of our ability to make sense of our environment offers a holistic and more plausible account of the role of affect in shaping one's judgments. Accordingly, linguistically defined concepts are grounded in experience in the deepest sense, deriving their significance from the types of drives and emotions that facilitate the organism's attunement to its environment. This evolutionary approach suggests a simple and intuitive understanding of embodiment as referring to the holistic synthesis of mind and body in the service of realizing the organism's needs.

[51] Gün R. Semin and Eliot R. Smith, "Introducing Embodied Grounding," in *Embodied Grounding: Social, Cognitive, Affective and Neuroscientific Approaches*, eds. G. R. Semin and E. R. Smith (Cambridge: Cambridge University Press, 2009), 1.
[52] "Enacting Affectivity," in *The Oxford Handbook of 4E Cognition*, eds. A. Newen, L. de Bruin and S. Gallagher (Oxford: Oxford University Press, 2018), 571–572.
[53] Ibid., 574.

Premise 2: Symbolic Modes of Communication Are Grounded in Experience

As noted above, influential approaches to semantics, based on structuralist principles, have tended to divorce the linguistic system from experience. In contrast, an embodied approach to language views its "digital" (conventional) aspects as grounded in "analog" images, grounded in embodied experience.

A compelling framework showing how to incorporate these two dimensions is Daniel Dor's monograph *The Instruction of Experience*, which outlines a comprehensive linguistic theory based on the recognition of the interaction between individualized experience and the semantic system ("the symbolic landscape"). In this account, the organization of the semantic system is in part autonomous, yet it remains inextricably tied to the world of experience to which it refers.[54] This relation is depicted as follows:[55]

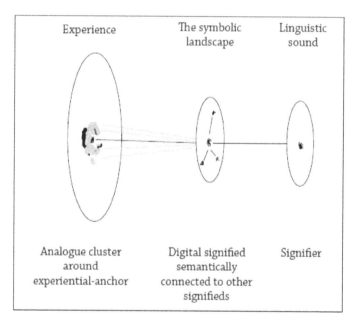

Experience	The symbolic landscape	Linguistic sound

| Analogue cluster around experiential-anchor | Digital signified semantically connected to other signifieds | Signifier |

---

[54] Daniel Dor, *The Instruction of Imagination: Language as a Social Communication Technology* (Oxford: Oxford University Press, 2015), 34–59.

[55] Ibid., 45 (Figure 3.1), used with permission.

In his example, the signifier "chair" (acoustically /tʃɛər/) interacts with related terms in the semantic landscape (such as "stool," "armchair," "upholstery," "legs," "table," "furniture," "comfortable," "sit") as well as the individual's personal experience involving chairs.

Dor's account of how this semantic knowledge is acquired by the language learner is highly relevant for the present discussion:

> As our experiences accumulate in our embodied minds (leaving their traces in our nervous system), we detect similarities and analogies between them, and construct generalizations – experiential generalizations, always analogue, holistic, fuzzy, and context-dependent – which then color, shape, and sometimes determine the way we further experience. This is how we learn. This does not deny the possibility that our nervous systems might be innately biased, in different ways, toward certain ways of experiencing and accumulating experiences … What it does deny, and very strongly so, is the idea that our general cognition can be described – let alone explained – in terms of the manipulation of abstract symbols.[56]

This account is highly compatible with the "Perceptual Symbol Theory" outlined by Lawrence Barsalou, which seeks to reconcile digital and analog aspects of language. According to his model, perceptual images are stored in memory and can be activated in the form of "simulations" by linguistic cues.[57] A related body of research argues that the processing of action verbs activates the motoric regions of the brain, not only those traditionally associated with general language processing. For example, brain imaging studies seem to indicate that an action word involving the legs (e.g., "kick") activates the corresponding region in the motor cortex, distinguishable from the region corresponding to the hands.[58] Similar insights have been applied to the processing of metaphors. Brain imaging

---

[56] Ibid., 18–19. For a detailed account for how the world structures language around experiential anchors (called "unicepts"), see Millikan, *Beyond Concepts*.

[57] Lawrence Barsalou, "Perceptual Symbol Systems," *Behavior and Brain Sciences* 22 (1999): 577–660 (with responses); Lawrence Barsalou, "Grounding Symbolic Operations in the Brain's Modal Systems," in *Embodied Grounding: Social, Cognitive, Affective and Neuroscientific Approaches*, eds. G. R. Semin and E. R. Smith (Cambridge: Cambridge University Press, 2009), 9–42; and his excellent survey of related research: "Grounded Cognition," *Annual Review of Psychology* 59 (2008): 617–645. See also: Andrew J. Bauer and Marcel A. Just, "Neural Representations of Concept Knowledge," in *Oxford Handbook of Neurolinguistics*, eds. G. I. de Zubicaray and N. O. Schiller (Oxford: Oxford University Press, 2019), 518–547.

[58] Friedemann Pulvermüller, "Brain Embodiment of Category-Specific Semantic Memory Circuits," in *Embodied Grounding: Social, Cognitive, Affective and Neuroscientific Approaches*, eds. G. R. Semin and E. R. Smith (Cambridge: Cambridge University Press, 2009), 71–97.

and other experimental techniques have demonstrated that the processing of metaphoric language may activate loci of the brain pertinent to the source domain of the metaphor.[59]

Alongside these expanding fields of experimental research, another important body of evidence substantiating the primacy of experience can be found in ancient languages. This aspect is often overlooked by cognitive scientists who lack familiarity with ancient languages and their dependency on concrete imagery. Nevertheless, the role of experience in shaping the linguistic repertoire has not been entirely ignored. Anticipating evolutionary theory and psychological research of recent decades, the eighteenth-century Scottish philosopher Thomas Reid derived this point logically, based on his distinction between "artificial" and "natural" languages: "An artificial sign has no meaning except what is attached to it by contract or agreement among those who use it; a natural sign is one which (independently of any contract or agreement) has a meaning that every man understands through the drives in his nature." On this basis, he proposed a scaffolding process by which artificial language emerged from natural language:

Having premised these definitions, I think it is demonstrable, that if mankind had not a natural language, they could never have invented an artificial one by their reason and ingenuity. For all artificial language supposes some compact or agreement to affix a certain meaning to certain signs; therefore there must be compacts or agreements before the use of artificial signs; but there can be no compact or agreement without signs, nor without language; and therefore there must be a natural language before any artificial language can be invented.[60]

The basis of communication is first and foremost reference – a focus of shared attention.[61] To a large extent, this principle informs both the acquisition of language by infants and the development of language on

---

[59] Raymond W. Gibbs, Jr., *Embodiment and Cognitive Science* (Cambridge: Cambridge University Press, 2006), 158–207; George Lakoff, "The Neural Theory of Metaphor," in *The Cambridge Handbook of Metaphor and Thought*, ed. R. Gibbs Cambridge: Cambridge University Press, 2009), 17–38. For a meta-analysis of relevant studies, see Alexander Michael Rapp, "Comprehension of Metaphors and Idioms: An Updated Meta-Analysis of Functional Magnetic Resonance Imaging Studies," in *Oxford Handbook of Neurolinguistics*, eds. G. I. de Zubicaray and N. O. Schiller (Oxford: Oxford University Press, 2019), 710–735.

[60] T. Reid and D. R. Brookes, *Thomas Reid, an Inquiry into the Human Mind on the Principles of Common Mind* (Edinburgh: Edinburgh University Press, 1997), p. 51.

[61] Terrance W. Deacon, *The Symbolic Species: The Co-Evolution of Language and the Brain* (New York: W. W. Norton, 1997), 47–101.

the scale of societies. Indeed, Michael Tomasello, building on his extensive research in primatology and developmental psychology, argues that

the first forms of uniquely human cooperative communication were the natural gestures of pointing and pantomiming used to inform others helpfully of situations relevant to them. Pointing and pantomiming are human universals that even people who share no conventional language can use to communicate effectively in contexts with at least some common ground.[62]

Only once such correlations between acoustic signs and experience are established is it possible to employ the repertoire of signs independently of experience, making it possible to refer to past, future, hypothetical and even impossible situations.

A useful analogy can be taken from the emergence of human writing systems, including Egyptian hieroglyphics, Mesopotamian cuneiform and even the alphabet. The visual signs on which all of these systems are based originated as iconic symbols (pictures), which were only secondarily appropriated to "represent" sounds (syllables and phonemes) by virtue of convention.[63]

In sum, the various forms of human communication, including bodily gestures and linguistic signs (visual and acoustic), originated by means of an intersubjective moment which enables the establishment of consensus, an agreement that a given sign is to be correlated with a particular communicative function. Once this has been established, it becomes available for a diverse array of additional communicative functions, limited only by the associative capacities of the communicating partners.

Overall, the account of pollution in this book can be viewed as an extended application of these principles of embodied cognition, showing that:

---

[62] *A Natural History of Human Thinking* (Cambridge, MA: Harvard University Press, 2014), 32–79 (49–50), building on his systematic argumentation in *The Origins of Human Communication* (Cambridge, MA: MIT Press, 2008). There he argued, "If we want to understand human communication, therefore, we cannot begin with language. Rather, we must begin with unconventionalized, uncoded communication, and other forms of mental attunement, as foundational" (59).

[63] For the origin and development of the cuneiform system, see Jerrold S. Cooper, "Sumerian and Akkadian," in *The World's Writing Systems*, eds. P. T. Daniels and W. Bright (New York: Oxford University, 1996), 37–57; Piotr Michalowski, "Origin," in *The World's Writing Systems*, eds. P. T. Daniels and W. Bright (New York: Oxford University, 1996), 33–36; J.-M. Durand, "Cuneiform Script," in *A History of Writing*, ed. A.-M. Christin (Paris: Flammarion, 2002), 20–32.

1. The discourse on pollution is rooted in concerns that are thoroughly embodied, pertaining to affective processes of sense-making that enable the organism to survive and thrive in its environment;
2. This embodied repertoire of meanings provided the raw materials for extending this imagery into the socio-moral domain.

In the following analysis of textual materials which deal with aspects of the life cycle as represented in the biblical sources, the first principle will be most evident in the sections that deal with disease, diet and death. The second principle will rise to the fore in the discussions of sexuality and holiness.

2

What Is Pollution?

Certain aspects of our everyday bodily existence – like sex, and excreting waste – are deemed best to conceal from the public view. These functions are relegated to the margins and recesses of household architecture, the relevant body parts are covered and their linguistic signifiers protected by euphemisms (going to the *bath*room; sleeping together). The biblical rules of pollution seem to revel in the details of these kinds of experiences, casting a spotlight on these domains, where silence seems more appropriate.

Scholarly discourse on pollution often serves (probably unknowingly) to cover up this exposed body, thereby restoring our comfort zone. "Purity" – the more congenial and marketable counterpart of "pollution" – becomes a discourse on abstract category oppositions such as order and disorder or life and death, allowing one to forget that the relevant textual materials prefer to get down and dirty with the details of dead rodents, sexual discharges and the symptomology of skin disease. One may get the impression that this branch of scholarship is written for and by androids, oblivious to the messiness of lived experience, and exceptionally capable of manipulating categories of purity in the form of abstract, disembodied symbols. Admittedly, this portrayal of scholarship is an unfair caricature, but it's intended to raise a crucial question: Should an account of pollution be based on an abstract explanation that sees *beyond* the textual details dealing with bodily experience? Or should the explanation emerge from an engagement with these grisly details? If the latter, what would such an account look like?

This chapter will explore the relationship between pollution and the experiences of uncleanness and disease. Are pollution, uncleanness and disease the same? How are they different, or how are they connected? Although the similarity of purity regulations to hygienic practices and fear of infection is obvious, it has yet to be adequately explained. In fact, due to the recognition that pollution cannot be simply reduced to a concern for bodily cleanliness and health, this relationship has often been dismissed categorically. In my view, this rejection is overhasty, based on faulty methodological premises.

My discussion will be divided into four sections. The first section focuses on different approaches to interpreting pollution and their theoretical background, emphasizing the distinction between the abstract rationality implicit in symbolic interpretations and the notion of embodied cognition advocated here. The second section examines a possible relationship between pollution and the perceptions of infectious disease in the ancient world. The aim here is to provide an appropriate context for analyzing ancient notions of disease and their relation to the biblical notion of pollution. The third section builds upon the methodological and historical considerations of the previous sections in order to elucidate biblical texts in which a relationship between pollution and infection is suggested, specifically Leviticus 15 (genital discharges), Numbers 19 (death pollution) and Lev 13–14 (skin disease). The fourth and final section explores the logic underlying the conceptualization of pollution, elucidating the psychological mechanism by which this unseen force was modeled after phenomenal experience.

POLLUTION AS ABSTRACT RATIONALITY: THE SEARCH FOR A UNIFYING LOGIC

One of the challenges of studying *ṭum'ah,* ordinarily translated as "pollution" or "impurity," is the fact that this concept is neither wholly concrete nor wholly abstract. Though some scholars have suggested that the term may be etymologically related to "dirt" or "mud,"[1] it needs to be

---

[1] Wilfried Paschen, *Rein und Unrein: Untersuchung zur biblischen Wortgeschichte* (Munich: Kösel-Verlag, 1970), 27. This sense finds cognates in Syriac, Mandaic, early South Arabian inscriptions and Egyptian Arabic. See also G. André, "טמא" *TDOT* 5:330–331; *HALOT*: 375. Thomas Kazen accepts this etymology: "The original source domain for *ṭāmē'* can be construed as the experience of being sullied by some dirty substance, an experience associated with feelings of discomfort and disgust and with a wish to have the dirt removed, which in the case of literal dirt would be effected by scraping or washing" ("The Role of Disgust in Priestly Purity Law: Insights from Conceptual Metaphor and Blending Theories," *Journal of Law, Religion and State* 3.1 [2014]: 77–78).

recognized that this concrete sense is unattested in the Bible.[2] Furthermore, as pointed out in the Introduction, the nominal form *ṭum'ah*, ("pollution") is quite rare in the Hebrew Bible when compared with the hundreds of related adjectival and verbal forms.[3] More importantly, even within these few instances of the noun *ṭum'ah*, it has at least two distinct meanings, referring to both cause and effect. The first refers to the metaphysical cause of pollution. For example, in Judges 13:7, the future mother of Samson is instructed by an angel: "don't eat any pollution [*ṭum'ah*]," that is, any food causing a state of impurity.[4] The second usage pertains to the technical state of being impure, as in Lev 15:25, where the impure status of the female gonorrheic is compared to that of a

---

[2] Still, this proposal seems preferable to other suggestions. For example, another possible etymology suggests a derivation from the word for bones, which appears in Aramaic as *ṭmy* (so already Rashi on Num 5:2). It would be cognate with Hebrew *'ṣm*, having lost the initial guttural. Developing this suggestion, Karel van der Toorn has compared Akkadian word for ghost *eṭemmu*, which in certain textual contexts refers to bones. See "Family Religion in Second Millennium West Asia (Mesopotamia, Emar, Nuzi)," in *Household and Family Religion in Antiquity*, eds. J. Bodel and S. M. Olyan (Malden, MA: Blackwell, 2008), 20–36. It may be added that this point is valid for the Sumerogram GIDIM corresponding to *eṭemmu*, which is also used in Middle Babylonian texts to refer to the dead's physical remains, that is, bones. Daniel Fleming has objected that the Akkadian term for bones is *eṣemtu* ("The Integration of Household and Family Religion," in *Household and Family Religion in Antiquity*, eds. J. Bodel and S. M. Olyan [Malden, MA: Blackwell, 2008], 37–59). However, it is possible that the *eṭemmu/ eṣemtu* distinction is the result of a phonetic and semantic dissimilation. Nevertheless, there remain several problems with this suggestion. First, the Hebrew term is based on the root *ṭ-m-'*, which assumes a consonantal aleph in the third position, whereas the alleged Aramaic cognate loses the initial consonant (*ṭ-m-' ≠ '-ṭ-m*). Second, Toorn's suggestion would assume that death pollution is the prototypical category of pollution from which all other types are derived, but there is little substantiation for this assumption in the textual evidence. An additional possibility, unlikely but nevertheless tantalizing, is to view *ṭamē* ("impure") as a loanword from Akkadian *tamû* ("cursed"; CAD T 159), which appears repeatedly as a contagious force in Standard Babylonian incantations (see citations from Šurpu below). Though a transition t > ṭ is rare, it is attested in loans between Akkadian and Aramaic, for example the phonetically similar *temēru* (Akkadian: "bury"/ "conceal") > *ṭ-m-r* (Aramaic "conceal") > Hebrew *ṭ-m-n* (see Michael Sokoloff, *A Dictionary of Jewish Babylonian Aramaic* [Ramat Gan: Bar-Ilan University, 2002], 506–507). I thank Ronnie Goldstein for this example.

[3] As pointed out in the introduction, like the English term "impurity," derived from the adjective "impure," the Hebrew noun seems to derive from the more widely attested adjective *ṭam'e* ("impure"), which appears eighty-seven times. The various verbal forms (over 160 times: stative, factitive and reflexive in function) also appear to be semantically derivative from the adjective.

[4] As a Priestly example, Lev 5:3 employs *ṭum'ah* twice as the source of pollution: "Or when he touches human uncleanness (*ṭum'at 'adam*) – any such uncleanness (*ṭum'ato*) whereby one becomes unclean."

menstruant: "When a woman has had a discharge of blood for many days, not at the time of her menstruation, or when she has a discharge beyond her period of menstruation, all of the days of her flow impurity [*zob ṭum'atah*; literally: the flow of her impurity] are like the days of her menstrual impurity [*niddatah*], she shall be impure."[5]

This ambiguity of subject (agent) and object (recipient) is hardly surprising, since the state of being impure usually involves the power to make something else impure (Lev 15:31), and it is doubtful that the audience would distinguish such nuances. Nevertheless, it is significant that certain usages highlight the causal aspect of pollution, whereas others highlight the effect of pollution, the state of being impure. In the former case it is reified as a "force"; in the latter, it is treated as a legal status. Correspondingly, one finds ambivalence regarding whether pollution is "on" the person (Lev 7:20; 22:3), or whether a person is "in" (a state of) pollution (15:31; 18:19). This fluidity of usage is characteristic of natural language, but it somewhat undermines the efforts of the Priestly authors to establish a precise formal vocabulary. These findings suggest that hesitance is warranted when expecting to find a systematic view of pollution in ancient Israel.[6]

The recognition of this fluidity will be highly significant for the following discussion in where it will be shown that, even when referring to the causes of pollution, this term serves as a generic umbrella category for a heterogeneous array of sources, with each operating according to very different rules. Blurring the domains of hygiene and morality, and encompassing disparate situations such as genital emissions (normal and abnormal), death, bloodshed, sexual misconduct and idolatry, *ṭum'ah* seems to resist systematic analysis. In reality, however, the main obstacle that stands in the way of making sense of this category is a lexicographic predisposition toward abstract, disembodied logic, particularly the assumption that linguistic categories are defined by necessary and sufficient membership criteria.

This latter approach, which has guided innumerable studies in biblical semantics until this day, can be traced back at least to Aristotle. However, as pointed out by Wittgenstein and discussed in the previous chapter,[7] the

[5] See also Lev 7:20; 15:3 (twice); 22:3. Compare also Ezekiel 36:17, where God complains that "their ways were in my sight like the uncleanness of a menstruous woman (*kᵉṭum'at ha-niddah*)."
[6] A lexical evidence for the root *ṭ-h-r* ("pure") leads to a similar conclusion (compare the discussion of this root in the previous chapter).
[7] See above, p. 8.

inadequacy of this approach becomes apparent when confronted with categories such as "games" (e.g., baseball, solitaire, ring-around-the-rosy) that cannot be reduced to a set of fixed characteristics. In the case of "games," characteristics such as amusement and competition do not apply to all cases.[8] One may argue that these games share some common characteristics (e.g., they have rules), but these are insufficient, taken by themselves, for inclusion in the category.[9]

Such linguistic considerations have led to the emergence of alternative theories, which emphasize the role of family resemblances and prototypes in shaping the semantic development of languages.[10] These modern approaches are more consistent with the recognition that languages develop through localized innovations (through principles of association such as metonymy and analogy) which need not conform to any single rigid propositional logic. Whereas the classical approach expects linguistic categories to be homogeneous, governed by a pervasive and comprehensive order (criteria of inclusion and exclusion), modern approaches recognize that many linguistic categories are heterogeneous, structured around several distinct prototypical examples. In short, one can distinguish between a "top-down" model of semantics, whereby the lexicon of a given language is governed by rules dictated by the rational mind, and a "bottom-up" model, whereby the linguistic system is the result of countless localized instances of semantic development. While the former model may serve as the ideal for a formal language (an artificial language created for the sake of mathematics, computer programming, philosophical inquiry, etc.), only the latter model is appropriate for a natural language.[11] As Daniel Dor points out, semantic development "is the product of a haphazard, unplanned, evolutionary process, in which signs and relations are added to the symbolic landscape [i.e., the linguistic

---

[8] Ludwig Wittgenstein, *Philosophical Investigations*, trans. G. E. M. Anscombe, P. M. S. Hacker and J. Schulte (Chichester: Wiley-Blackwell, 2009), 36e (§66).

[9] See P. Violi, *Meaning and Experience*, trans. J. Carden (Bloomington, IN: University of Indiana Press, 2001), 152–154.

[10] For a more detailed overview, see George Lakoff, *Woman, Fire and Dangerous Things: What Categories Reveal About the Mind* (Chicago, IL: University of Chicago Press, 1987), 5–154, with special attention given to the work of Eleanor Rosch.

[11] Generally, the aim of creating formal languages is to eliminate ambiguity by attributing a univalent definition to each term. A notable example would be the attempt to establish an ideal philosophical language, pursued by Bertrand Russell and Wittgenstein in the early twentieth century. Ultimately Wittgenstein abandoned this project to delve into the complexities of natural language.

repertoire – Y.F.], in order to meet the growing communicative needs of certain communities of speakers, in certain specific social settings."[12]

With respect to these considerations, the heterogeneous content of the biblical category of pollution is hardly exceptional. What is necessary to make sense of the different types of *ṭum'ah* and their characteristics is a proper appreciation of experiential images or models upon which they are based. Not only will this approach provide a more accurate understanding of the lexical data, but it will also offer a key to the exegesis of the purity laws.

So far, I have discussed the rationality of semantic categories as it pertains to the concept of *ṭum'ah*. A similar tendency to assume a coherent rational structure also finds expression in the analysis of pollution-related practices. Whether based in the symbolist tradition of Émile Durkheim or the structuralist tradition of Claude Lévi-Strauss, these analyses tend to assume an underlying logical scheme, whereby the practices represent either social or cognitive categories.

Though attempts to understand this concept allegorically can be traced back to late antiquity, the modern tendency to interpret purity regulations as a symbolic system is largely indebted to the influential work of Mary Douglas. Starting from the premise that dirt is "matter out of place," she shows the potential for using impurity customs and beliefs as keys to deciphering the symbolic system of the culture:

> Dirt then, is never a unique, isolated event. Where there is dirt, there is system. Dirt is the by-product of a systematic ordering and classification of matter, in so far as ordering involves rejecting inappropriate elements. This idea of dirt takes us straight into the field of symbolism and promises a link-up with more obviously symbolic systems of purity.[13]

According to this framework, before one can account for why a given act is defiling, one must first identify the classificatory system that is being violated. In this manner, Douglas argued that the designation of animals such as camels and rock badgers as impure in Lev 11 and Deuteronomy 14 stems from their anomalous characteristics, their out-of-placeness (e.g., as is also the case for aquatic creatures lacking fins and scales). These deviations caused them to be perceived as threatening the biblical notion of holiness, equated with wholeness: "To be holy is to be whole, to

---

[12] *The Instruction of Imagination: Language as a Social Communication Technology* (Oxford: Oxford University, 2015), 76–77.

[13] Mary Douglas, *Purity and Danger: An Analysis of the Concepts of Pollution and Taboo* (Routledge: London, 1992 [1966]), 35.

be one; holiness is unity, integrity, perfection of the individual and the kind."[14]

This approach has been refined and adapted in subsequent studies, including those by Douglas herself, and its working assumption continues to inspire research. In particular, biblical scholars have enthusiastically developed the premise that the body can serve as a medium of expression onto which social ideals and patterns are projected. For example, Howard Eilberg-Schwartz writes: "The fluids of the body turn out to be a kind of language in which various religious themes find their voice."[15] Even more forcefully, Jon Berquist views the laws of bodily fluids as implying an aspiration for bodily wholeness, itself a microcosm for the ideal Israelite society:

The whole body, for Israel, was not only a construction of how culture expected the physical body to operate and perform; the body was also a representation of how the society should organize itself and function, in the smallest units (the family or household) as well as the largest (the tribe, the nation, the colony, or any other form of the "body politic").[16]

With all due respect for the ingenuity required for such homologies, these studies raise several difficulties. For instance, since there is no evidence that the ancient Israelites were aware of such interpretations when observing their ritual practices, it must be assumed that they were external to their conscious motives. Yet, these studies fail to explain by what mechanism these symbolic schemes unconsciously emerged. Furthermore, these interpretations assume a questionable mind–body dualism in which the body serves as a vehicle of expression which can effectively be disregarded once the encoded message is comprehended.[17] While authors disagree as to how to interpret the hidden logic of the

---

[14] Ibid., 54.

[15] Howard Eilberg-Schwartz, *The Savage in Judaism: An Anthropology of Israelite Religion and Ancient Judaism* (Bloomington, IN: Indiana University Press, 1990), 179.

[16] Jon L. Berquist, *Controlling Corporeality: The Body and the Household in Ancient Israel* (Piscataway, NJ: Rutgers University Press, 2002), 45. This view takes its inspiration from Douglas's assertion: "The threatened boundaries of [the Israelites'] body politic would be well mirrored in their care for the integrity, unity, and purity of the physical body" (*Purity and Danger*, 124). However, it should be noted that Douglas later retracted this statement in light of the fact that Lev and Num do not employ these rules to separate Israelites from foreign races (*In the Wilderness: The Doctrine of Defilement in the Book of Numbers* [Sheffield: JSOT Press, 1993], 20).

[17] See Michael Jackson, *Paths Toward a Clearing: Radical Empiricism and Ethnographic Inquiry* (Bloomingfield, IN: University of Indiana Press, 1989), 122–123.

"purity system,"[18] they rarely address the possibility that the project itself is fundamentally ill-conceived.[19]

For example, a common view which finds expression among traditional and modern exegetes alike is that impurity symbolizes death.[20] Proponents of this theory point to the explicit connections between the skin disease *sara'at* (conventionally translated as "leprosy")[21] and references to death (Num 12:12) and mourning (Lev 13:45–46). These scholars also construe menstrual impurity (Lev 15:19–24) as stemming from the loss of life-fluid and as constituting a period of infertility. Unfortunately, this view is ill-equipped to explain why sexual relations defile (Lev 15:18).[22] Notwithstanding the counterintuitive claim that the loss of seed (even in coitus) is a kind of death,[23] it seems that the only death involved in the procreative act is that of ill-begotten theories. These theories suffer from the endemic weakness of Aristotelian categories: the assumption that category membership is defined by fixed criteria.

An alternative approach has been to explain the impurity of certain discharges as being a result of their uncontrollable nature. For example, to clarify the biblical distinction between the minor impurity of semen and the more serious impurity of other genital discharges, Eilberg-Schwartz argues: "Since semen is ejaculated from the body through orgasm, its loss is symbolically associated with direct action and conscious thought. Nonseminal discharge and menstrual blood, on the other hand, are

---

[18] For an insightful survey, see Christophe Nihan, *From Priestly Torah to Pentateuch*, FAT 2/25 (Tübingen: Mohr Siebeck, 2007), 301–339.

[19] See, however, Walter Houston's extensive critique of Douglas's view as it bears on the dietary laws (*Purity and Monotheism: Clean and Unclean Animals in Biblical Law*, JSOTSup 140 [Sheffield: JSOT Press, 1993], 93–123), and more comprehensively Tracy M. Lemos, "Where There Is Dirt, Is There System? Revisiting Biblical Purity Constructions," *JSOT* 37.3 (2013): 265–294.

[20] This interpretation has been advanced forcefully by Jacob Milgrom, *Leviticus* (AB; 3 vols.; New York: Doubleday, 1991), 1.766–768; 1000–1003. See also Saul M. Olyan, *Rites and Rank* (Princeton, NJ: Princeton University Press, 2000), 143–144, n. 15; Nihan, *From Priestly Torah*, 304, n. 158.

[21] "Leprosy" is the conventional translations for the biblical term *sara'at*, which seems to conflate several different types of skin diseases (see Milgrom, *Leviticus*, 1.816–820). See next chapter for further discussion.

[22] Nor can this "anomaly" be swept under the rug, since it appears consistently cross-culturally. See e.g., Robert Parker, *Miasma: Pollution and Purification in Early Greek Religion* (Oxford: Clarendon Press, 1983), 74; Karl van der Toorn, *Sin and Sanction in Israel and Mesopotamia: A Comparative Study* (Assen: Van Gorcum, 1985), 22.

[23] See e.g., Gordon J. Wenham, "Why Does Sexual Intercourse Defile (Lev 15, 18)?" *ZAW* 95 (1983): 432–434. For further discussion, see Chapters 9 and 10.

passively released from the body."[24] But this theory is hard-pressed to explain why the impurity of a deliberate sexual act is the same as that of an accidental seminal emission (Lev 15:16).[25] Upon reading these attempts, one is struck by the intensity of effort expended to derive the concrete rules pertaining to bodily conditions from abstract categories. When the originally proposed dichotomy (life/death, control/lack of control) fails to fit the data, further distinctions are added – male versus female, upper versus lower orifices and so on – with the aim of preserving the abstract category distinctions.[26] If adding more detailed parameters based on embodied experience contributes to a better understanding of the data, perhaps we should consider the possibility that the logic is embodied through and through and unrelated to abstract schemes.

POLLUTION AS EMBODIED RATIONALITY

I have suggested above that the semantics of the term *ṭum'ah* and the practices associated with it may be better explained as an expression of a "bottom-up" (situated and embodied) mode of rationality.[27] In referring to embodiment in the present context, I wish to demonstrate that the ancient Israelite conception of pollution was grounded in concrete experience, manifesting the principles of embodied cognition.

As a first step, let us begin with an anthropological account of pollution which encapsulates many of the emphases of embodiment theory. In an important critique of Douglas's theory that is based on fieldwork in Papua New Guinea, Meigs points out that not every disordered phenomenon is considered defiling. Whereas a toy boat on the kitchen table may be "messy," it is not considered defiling like shoes on the kitchen table. The

---

[24] Eilberg-Schwartz, *Savage in Judaism*, 186–189, esp. 187.

[25] Meir Malul, who substitutes his notion of "epistemic control," is still unable to offer a satisfactory explanation (*Knowledge, Control and Sex: Studies in Biblical Thought, Culture and Worldview* [Tel-Aviv-Jaffa: Archaeological Center Publication, 2002], 387–390.

[26] Ibid., 386–394. These efforts are reminiscent of early attempts to create a disembodied artificial intelligence by means of abstract rules and propositions, despite the fact that human intelligence is situated and embodied. See Herbert L. Dreyfus, *What Computers Still Can't Do: A Critique of Artificial Reason* (Cambridge, MA: MIT Press, 1992); Andy Clark, *Being There: Putting Brain, Body and World Together Again* (Cambridge, MA: MIT Press, 1997). For a relevant set of studies in which participants intuitively distinguished the disgust potential of different orifices, see Paul Rozin et al., "The Borders of the Self: Contamination Sensitivity and Potency of the Body Apertures and Other Body Parts," *Journal of Research in Personality* 29.3 (1995): 318–340.

[27] See Chapter 1.

reason for this discrepancy, Meigs suggests, is that shoes are potential carriers of substances such as feces, urine and saliva from the street. More generally, she relates notions of defilement to a visceral sense of disgust regarding decay and waste matter, particularly when these threaten to access another person's body, such as through eating or sexual relations.[28] For our purposes, the important point is the difference between Meigs's emotional/intuitive account of defilement and that of Douglas and others, who relate the notion to category violations or ambivalent states. Unlike the abstract explanations of pollution which invoke goals foreign to the motives of the actors, Meigs's account is consistent with their conscious concerns.[29]

As the work of Meigs suggests, one need not travel to Papua New Guinea in order to study pollution, as this notion finds parallels much closer to home. In a large-scale research program spanning decades, Carol Nemeroff and Paul Rozin examined the notion of contagion, particularly as experienced by academically educated Americans. In a general formulation, they describe contagion as the assumption that "physical contact between the source and the target results in the transfer of some effect or quality (essence) from the source to the target."[30] In some cases, the assumption of a transfer of essence is corroborated by science (e.g., in germ theory), but frequently it is based on an emotional bias that overwhelms cold reason. As a simple illustration, a person who picks up a piece of feces or cockroach by means of a plastic bag is usually inclined to wash his or her hands afterwards, despite the absence of actual contact.

The modes of transfer involved in schemas of contagion are modeled after those perceived in phenomenological experience. Among the numerous experiments carried out by Nemeroff and Rozin, a particularly relevant study was their inquiry into mental models associated with contagion, first published in 1994.[31] This study was based on interviews and questionnaires given to adult Americans who were asked about their

---

[28] Anna S. Meigs, "A Papuan Perspective on Pollution," *Man* 13.2 (1978): 304–318.

[29] See ibid., 317, n. 9.

[30] Carol Nemeroff and Paul Rozin, "The Makings of the Magical Mind: The Nature and Function of Sympathetic Magical Thinking," in *Imagining the Impossible: Magical, Scientific and Religious Thinking in Children*, eds. K. S. Rosengren et al. (Cambridge: Cambridge University Press, 2000), 3.

[31] Carol Nemeroff and Paul Rozin, "The Contagion Concept in Adult Thinking in the United States: Transmission of Germs and Interpersonal Influence," *Ethos* 22.2 (1994): 158–186, and "Sympathetic Magical Thinking: The Contagion and Similarity 'Heuristics,'" in *Heuristics and Biases: The Psychology of Intuitive Judgment*, eds. T. Gilovich et al. (Cambridge: Cambridge University Press, 2002), 211–213. The

reaction to wearing a sweater after it had been in contact with various types of negative influence. Participants were also questioned as to whether they felt certain "purificatory" procedures could undo the negative effects of contagion. In analyzing these responses, Nemeroff and Rozin detected a clear distinction between physical and nonphysical models of contagion.

The physical model of contagion included sources such as feces and disease, whereby the sweater could be "purified" by acts such as washing and boiling. The nonphysical model, by contrast, applied to moral and social sources, that is, a sweater worn by an enemy or mass-murderer, which could be best "purified" by exposure to an opposing valence (i.e., being worn by a person with positive social or moral attributes). Granted, responses were not as systematic as the categories employed by Nemeroff and Rozin might imply, often blurring the distinction between physical and nonphysical sources of contagion. Nevertheless, the results of this study clearly support the conclusion that contagion schemas operate according to domain-specific assumptions regarding the nature of the essence transmitted within the framework of accepted cultural beliefs, though, when questioned, respondents would admit (with embarrassment) that their responses were not entirely consistent with purely scientific reasoning. As noted in the previous chapter, this domain-specific aspect of disgust has been substantiated subsequently by a vast body of experimental research.

DEFILEMENT AND DISEASE: REGAINING A HISTORICAL PERSPECTIVE

The psychological definition of "contagion" suggested by Nemeroff and Rozin is remarkably similar to the one given by Thomas Lodge in his "Treatise on Plague," published in 1602: "*Contagion*, is an evil quality in a body, communicated unto another by touch, engendering one and the same disposition in him to whom it is communicated."[32] This similarity is not coincidental. As will be argued, the experience of infection was central to the conceptualization of pollution in the ancient world, but this straightforward claim has been obscured by a lack of appreciation for how disease was experienced in premodern societies.

---

following summary is necessarily much abbreviated; the reader should consult the original publication for further details.
[32] English modernized (Y. F.).

The momentous advances in our understanding of infectious disease from the past century and a half have revolutionized medicine and immunology, but this radically new vantage poses numerous pitfalls for reconstructing the history of disease. In particular, one notes the widespread yet problematic tendency to identify diseases of the past in light of modern diagnoses, leading to a situation in which "the past of medicine is being rewritten to accord with the laboratory model of disease."[33] Even more importantly, it distorts our understanding of how disease was experienced, mediated by culture-specific models which informed understandings of causes and the appropriate means of prevention.[34] A history of pollution that fails to take these issues into consideration cannot avoid being anachronistic.

The need for a proper historical perspective can be illustrated by the treatment of the relationship between purity and hygiene in modern scholarship. Despite the common recognition of the similarity between practices motivated by hygiene and those pertaining to "ritual purity," the relationship between them has yet to receive an adequate explanation. Mary Douglas was largely dismissive of what she labeled "medical materialism," attempts to rationalize purity rules in terms of promoting public health.[35] More recently, the social historian Virginia Smith emphatically stressed the need to distinguish between these categories of behavior:

Religious purity has a distinct role in the history of personal hygiene. It was not functional, not rational, and more often than not completely illusory; but it was a key cultural component that determined the lives and cleansing behaviour of very large numbers of people.[36]

The arguments for this separation of domains – the practical and the religious – often appear quite logical in themselves. The discussion of the dietary laws (Lev 11) offers a helpful illustration. When the biblical rules are consistent with medical knowledge, for example the relationship between trichinosis and uncooked pork, the question raised is how the Israelites could have known. When scientific data contradict the rules, that

---

[33] Andrew Cunningham, "Transforming Plague: The Laboratory and the Identity of Infectious Disease," in *The Laboratory Revolution in Medicine*, eds. A. Cunningham and P. Williams (Cambridge: Cambridge University Press, 1992), 209.

[34] Cunningham, "Transforming Plague," 213.

[35] *Purity and Danger*, 31–32, though she qualifies: "There is no objection to this approach unless it excludes other interpretations" (32).

[36] V. Smith, *Clean: A History of Personal Hygiene and Purity* (Oxford: Oxford University, 2007), 29–30.

is taken as even stronger grounds for rejecting a hygienic rationale.[37] Most forcefully, the medieval rabbinic commentator Abravanel points out that there is no evidence that Jews were healthier than gentiles, thus dismissing the assumption of health as a basis for the dietary laws.[38]

Since the anachronism implicit in these arguments is seldom recognized, it is necessary to begin our discussion with a historical survey in order to establish a more fitting interpretive context by which to understand the biblical evidence.[39] Premodern conceptions of infectious diseases were invariably structured by metaphors.[40] Nutton writes: "It is important first to remember that in all this we are dealing with descriptions of the invisible, with hypothetical reconstructions of how things are or act, based only on the observance of 'macrophenomena.'"[41] Although Galen's references to "seeds of disease" in the second century CE may have prefigured germ theory to some degree, this potential was left virtually unexplored for the next 1,600 years. In the meantime, Western medicine was dominated by the metaphor of a stain (Greek *miasma*, Latin *infectio*), that could spread corrupting influence either by means of direct contact or through the bad air emitted by putrefaction.[42] These two models for infection persisted as late as the mid-nineteenth century CE, represented by the rival schools of contagionism (by direct contact) and miasmatism (via bad air) which attempted to account for the spread of cholera in London.[43] In fact, these models – based on an assumed correlation between perceptible means of transmission and the spread of infection – severely impeded the emergence of alternative accounts, including the

---

[37] Ibid., 69–70. [38] Commentary on Lev 11.

[39] I thank Markham Geller for suggesting that I explore the history of Western notions of infection.

[40] These expressions frequently persist as "dead metaphors" in our modern lexicon. Referring to expressions such as "cold-blooded," "melancholy" and "hysterical," David Wootton remarks, "Our language is littered with the flotsam and jetsam of a vast historical catastrophe, the collapse of ancient medicine, which has left us with half-understood turns of phrase that we continue to use because metaphorical habits have an extraordinary capacity for endurance" (*Bad Medicine: Doctors Doing Harm Since Hippocrates* [Oxford: Oxford University Press, 2006], 12).

[41] Vivian Nutton, "The Seeds of Disease: An Explanation of Contagion and Infection from the Greeks to the Renaissance," *Medical History* 27.1 (1983): 2.

[42] Owsei Temkin, "An Historical Analysis of the Concept of Infection," in *The Double Face of Janus and Other Essays in the History of Medicine* (Baltimore, MD: Johns Hopkins Press, 1977 [1953]), 157, 161.

[43] See Henk ten Have, "Knowledge and Practice in European Medicine: The Case of Infectious Diseases," in *The Growth of Medical Knowledge*, eds. H. ten Have et al. (Dordrecht, the Netherlands: Springer, 1990), 15–40.

correct one, that cholera was transmitted by imperceptible water-borne germs.[44]

The important point that emerges from this brief historical survey is that we must be careful not to impose anachronistic category distinctions on the evidence, such as that between "religious pollution" and infectious disease. For example, upon noting that Greek notions of pollution could be dependent on the social status of a person, Eireann Marshall comments: "[W]hile ancient Greeks did not necessarily perceive diseases as *infectious*, they thought that *religious pollution* could be spread to other people."[45] Compare Robert Parker's more fitting characterization:

> It is not clear that diseases ever truly became infectious in any other sense than this in Greek thought. Greeks were practically aware, in time of plague, that the disease could be contracted by contact, but in popular perception this may have been no more than an acute instance of the contagiousness of misfortune.[46]

For an accurate insider's understanding of the ancient sources, it is not sufficient merely to recognize that the conflation of the categories "infection" and "defilement" is an inevitable consequence of the nonexistence of a developed scientific approach for studying infectious disease. A full appreciation must acknowledge the existence of metaphysical schemes which assume dynamics such as the contagiousness of misfortune to be ontologically real. In other words, attitudes toward contagion involve metaphysical assumptions; that is, culture-specific understandings of invisible causal forces.[47]

Letters from the city-state of Mari in Syria of the early eighteenth century BCE provide us with the earliest written documentation of how the spread of infection was perceived.[48] These letters describe the epidemic(s) which took place during the reigns of Zimri-Lim and

---

[44] This case of scientific stagnation is all the more disturbing in light of the fact that the existence of micro-organisms had been observed by microscopes already in the late seventeenth century; see Wootton, *Bad Medicine*, 195–210.

[45] "Death and Disease in Cyrene," in *Death and Disease in the Ancient City*, eds. V. M. Hope and E. Marshall (London: Routledge, 2000), 22 (emphasis added).

[46] See Parker, *Miasma*, 219–220.

[47] Similarly: Nemeroff and Rozin, "The Makings of the Magical Mind," 25.

[48] Jean-Marie Durand, "Trois études de Mari," *MARI* 3 (1984): 143–149 (§I/9. Maladies); E. Neufeld, "The Earliest Document of a Case of Contagious Diseasein Mesopotamia (Mari Tablet *ARM* X, 129)," *JANES* 18.1 (1986): 53–66; Walther Farber, "How to Marry a Disease: Epidemics, Contagion, and a Magic Ritual against the 'Hand of a Ghost,'" in *Magic and Rationality in Ancient Near Eastern and Greco-Roman Medicine*, eds. H. F. J. Horstmanshoff and M. Stol (Leiden: Brill, 2004), 119–122. On contagious disease in general, see Joann Scurlock and Burton Andersen, *Diagnoses in*

Yasmaḫ-Adad as a form of divine intervention. In these texts, a plague was referred to as a "devouring by the god" (*ukulti ilim*) or as the god's "placing the hand" (*qātum šaknat*) or "touching" (*ilappat/ulappat*) the affected region. These letters also describe the response to these plagues, which range from containing individual cases through quarantine to mass exodus from affected (*laptum*, literally "touched") cities.

Though the epidemics were attributed to divine anger, the descriptions of quarantine procedures resemble a fairly modern reaction to infectious disease. In a letter from the queen Šibtum to Zimri-Lim, it is related that her servant was placed in an isolated dwelling where she would eat her meals separately from the rest of the palace servants: "[No o]ne will approach her bed or chair."[49] In a letter from Zimri-Lim to Šibtum, the king expresses concern regarding another infected servant who has been freely interacting with the personnel: "Now command that no one will drink from a cup that she drinks from, nor sit in a chair in which she sits, nor sleep on a bed in which she sleeps!"[50]

Scholars have noted that these sources find a striking parallel in Tablet III of the Mesopotamian Šurpu incantation which deals with the dangers of making contact with an "accursed" (*tamû*) person (lines 130–133):[51]

> The curse (*māmītu*) of talking to an accursed man,
> The curse of eating an accursed man's food,
> the curse of drinking an accursed man's water,
> the curse of drinking an accursed man's left-overs.

The term *māmītu*, which originally signified an "oath-curse," is depicted here as a curse that can be transferred through contact with the cursed

---

Assyrian and Babylonian Medicine (Urbana and Chicago, IL: University of Illinois Press, 2005), 17–20.

[49] ARM 10, 14; Durand, "Trois études de Mari," 144; Farber, "How to Marry a Disease," 122.

[50] ARM 10, 129; Durand, "Trois études de Mari," 144; Farber, "How to Marry a Disease," 122.

[51] Text and translation: Erica Reiner, *Šurpu. A Collection of Sumerian and Akkadian Incantations*, AoF Beiheft 11 (Osnabrück: Biblio Verlag, 1970), 22–23 (with adaptations). For a synopsis of alternative readings, see R. Borger, "Šurpu II, III, IV, und VIII in 'Partitur,'" in *Wisdom Gods and Literature: Studies in Assyriology in Honour of W. G. Lambert*, eds. A. R. George and I. L. Finkel (Winona Lake, IN: Eisenbrauns, 2000), 48–49. The resemblance of this text to a notion of infection had been observed already by H. E. Sigrist, *A History of Medicine*, vol. 1 (New York: Oxford University Press, 1951), 446. See also Markham J. Geller, "The Šurpu Incantations and Lev. V. 1–5," *JSS* 25.2 (1980): 188; Farber, "How to Marry a Disease," 126.

person.[52] The following lines repeat these concerns verbatim, but now the dangerous contact is with someone who has committed a sin (*bēl arni*):

> The curse of talking to a transgressor (*bēl arni*),
> The curse of eating a transgressor's food,
> the curse of drinking a transgressor's water,
> the curse of drinking a transgressor's left-overs.

(134–137)

This parallel clearly shows that while the dynamic of contagion was acutely recognized, the precise cause in a given case was often indeterminate. As can be seen from the comparison with the Mari letters, the contagiousness of a curse was indistinguishable from that of a sickness.[53]

These sources are highly relevant for understanding biblical notions of disease and defilement, with "touch" figuring prominently. First of all, like the usage of the Akkadian verb *lapātu*, the Bible employs the verbal root *n-g-ʿ* (whose basic sense is literally "to touch") to describe disease. The derivatives of this verb include the *piel* (causative) verbal form used to describe God afflicting people and lands with disease (e.g., Genesis 12:17; 2 Kgs 15:5) and the nominal form *negaʿ*, used to describe illnesses, especially the skin disease *ṣaraʿat*.[54] Second, like the Mesopotamian sources, the Bible refers to mass afflictions as manifestations of the "hand" of God.[55] It is important to stress that these semantic parallels, as opposed to etymological ones, do not imply intercultural contact or influence, but rather the independent emergence of similar conceptions in both cultures.[56]

---

[52] See Yitzhaq Feder, "The Mechanics of Retribution in Hittite, Mesopotamian and Biblical Texts," *JANER* 10.2 (2010): 127–135.

[53] It is worth adding that elsewhere we find numerous texts portraying *māmītu* as an illness that must be treated by ritualistic medical means. See *CAD* M/I 194; Stefan M. Maul, "Die 'Lösung vom Bann': Überlegungen zu altorientalischen Konzeptionen von Krankheit und Heilkunst," in *Magic and Rationality in Ancient Near Eastern and Greco-Roman Medicine*, eds. H. F. J. Horstmanshoff and M. Stol (Leiden: Brill, 2004), 79–95.

[54] See following chapter. This parallel is noted by Milgrom (*Leviticus*, 1.776), though his interpretation that this term implies either a demonic attack or "contact with the pagan sphere" (following Karl Elliger, *Leviticus*, HAT [Tübingen: Mohr, 1966], 180) is unwarranted and contradicts his subsequent statement: "In the Bible, God is always the author of *negaʿ*." In P and Deut, this term is used exclusively in reference to *saraʿat*.

[55] E.g., Exodus 9:3; 1 Sam 5:6, 9; 2 Sam 24:14–15. A comparable idiom (*yd ʾilm*) is also attested in Ugaritic texts (e.g., *CAT* 2.10 11–13).

[56] The implications of this similarity will be explored in the next chapter.

A similar blurring of boundaries between divine punishment and pathological conditions is reflected in David's curse of Joab for the unjustified killing of Avner:

When David heard afterwards, he said, "I and my kingdom will be forever innocent before Yhwh of the blood of Avner the son of Ner. May it fall on the head of Joab and all of his kinsman. May there never cease to be in the house of Joab a gonorrheic, leper, a holder of the spindle, a victim of the sword or a person lacking bread.["] (2 Samuel 3:28–29)

Among the other unenviable conditions mentioned in this passage, this curse refers to the gonorrheic and the leper, who are among the severe-impurity bearers who must bring a sin offering in Lev 13–15 (as will be explored in the following section). This source explicitly depicts these conditions as divine punishments.[57] If we compare the contagious nature of divine punishment as manifested in the Mesopotamian sources cited above, especially the "curses" described in the Šurpu incantations, we may suspect that the stipulations pertaining to the transfer of "pollution" (*ṭum'ah*) in Lev 13–15 may be rooted in a concern that such pathological conditions may be contagious.

REASSESSING THE BIBLICAL EVIDENCE: BETWEEN INFECTION AND POLLUTION

The previous sections have provided the theoretical and historical background for an embodied account of the biblical concept of pollution, particularly as it relates to infection. The first example to be discussed is Lev 15, which deals specifically with male gonorrheics (*zab*; vv. 3–15),[58] seminal emissions (16–18), menstruants (19–24) and female gonorrheics (25–30). Aside from stipulating the periods of separation and rites of purification necessary in the different cases, the chapter describes the

---

[57] See Saul M. Olyan, *Disability in the Hebrew Bible: Interpreting Mental and Physical Differences* (Cambridge: Cambridge University Press, 2008), 54–56; Yitzhaq Feder, *Blood Expiation in Hittite and Biblical Ritual: Origins, Context and Meaning* (Atlanta: SBL, 2011), 107–108.

[58] The Hebrew term refers to a man with a (genital) "flow." The identification of the biblical condition with gonorrhea is an approximation, considering the problematic enterprise of diagnosing ancient diseases. Nevertheless, it is worth noting that, against some claims to the contrary (e.g., Milgrom, *Leviticus*, 1.907), there is no reason to deny an awareness of venereal diseases in the ancient Near East. See now Scurlock and Andersen, *Diagnoses in Assyrian and Babylonian Medicine*, 88–97.

manner by which pollution was spread, thereby revealing the ontological assumptions underlying the ritual prescriptions.

Throughout the chapter, one finds a repeated distinction between a severe degree of defilement requiring bathing and laundering and a lesser degree of defilement requiring only bathing. The following are cases of the severe form. Those pertaining to gonorrheics include: one who has touched the gonorrheic's bedding (v. 5); one who has sat in the gonorrheic's seat (6); one who has touched his "flesh" (7, see discussion later in this section); a person who has been spat upon by the gonorrheic (8); one who has lifted the gonorrheic's riding seat and other seating implements (10b); and whoever the gonorrheic has touched with unwashed hands (11). Regarding defilement by semen, laundering is required for any fabric or leather with semen on it (17). Severe defilement by menstruants was transferred to one who touched their bedding or seats (21–22), and so too regarding the bedding or seats of female gonorrheics (26–27).

Although many exegetes assume that the person experiencing the discharge would bear the most severe degree of impurity,[59] this assumption is at odds with the text. Throughout Lev 15, we observe that people who suffered from prolonged genital emissions conveyed, by means of their sitting and laying on implements, a degree of defilement which was equivalent to or more severe than the defilement caused by touching the defiling persons themselves. Clearly, the rationale for these laws is the entirely concrete concern that if the emission were to drip on the furnishings, an unsuspecting person who sits or lies on them may accidently touch the emission itself. This concern for leakage was very real in its ancient context (as in developing societies today), before undergarments – not to mention hygienic supplies like tampons – were available.[60] Nevertheless, it is important to recognize that defilement is operating here as a heuristic, whereby the mere possibility that an emission may have dripped on the object becomes a foregone conclusion, at least from the standpoint of preventing the further transfer of defilement.[61] However, this reaction is

---

[59] This assumption is fundamental to the rabbinic understanding of these laws, as well as that of D. Wright and J. Milgrom among modern commentators (see later in the chapter).

[60] E.g., Thérèse Mahon and Maria Fernandes, "Menstrual Hygiene in South Asia: A Neglected Issue for WASH (Water, Sanitation And Hygiene) Programmes," *Gender & Development* 18.1 (2010): 99–113; Tracey Crofts and Julie Fisher, "Menstrual Hygiene in Ugandan Schools: An Investigation of Low-Cost Sanitary Pads," *Journal of Water, Sanitation and Hygiene for Development* 2.1 (2012): 50–58. For this reason, Rachel refuses to stand up for her father, claiming "the way of women is upon me" (Gen 31:35).

[61] For a treatment of contagion as a heuristic (an emotionally biased rule of thumb), see Nemeroff and Rozin, "Sympathetic Magical Thinking," 201–216. Steven Neuberg,

not a mere calculation but produces a nonreflective belief that takes the possibility that the impurity has spread to be a certainty, requiring the appropriate avoidance and – if necessary – purificatory behavior.[62] It is thus comparable to the commonplace repulsion from putting shoes on the kitchen table due to the fear that *perhaps* the person wearing them has stepped in something objectionable. A similar heuristic is well attested in ethnographic data, as reflected by the common fear of a menstruant stepping over one's food.[63]

So far, so good. We will now proceed to see how some purported difficulties in the text can be overcome by following this same logic. In particular, commentators have pointed out the discrepancy between the rule that touching the bedding or seat of the female menstruants or gonorrheics required one to launder one's clothes afterwards (vv. 21–22; 26–27) and the rule that contact with the discharger herself demanded only bathing (19, cf. 25). Some commentators apply *a fortiori* logic to resolve the tension: if these implements, defiled by secondary contact, required laundering, then so much more so the discharger herself, the source of the impurity.[64] Though this argument is perfectly logical, it misconstrues the rationale of the contagion schema by which the possibility of touching the discharge itself was of greater concern than touching the person.

But we must also consider the seemingly anomalous case of touching the "flesh" of the gonorrheic (7), which did require laundering and washing: "The one who touches the *flesh* (*basar*) of a gonorrheic will launder his clothes, wash and be impure until the evening." Here the problem surrounds the polyvalent term *basar*, which was used in two distinct senses within the chapter: in the sense of "body" (vv. 13, 16) and as a euphemism for the male (vv. 2–3, 3x) and female (19) genitalia. Most

Douglas T. Kenrick and Mark Schaller, "Human Threat Management Systems: Self-Protection and Disease Avoidance," *Neuroscience and Biobehavioral Reviews* 35.4 (2011): 1042–1051.

[62] On "nonreflective beliefs," see Chapter 6. The Samaritan halakha recognizes that the danger of direct contact with the defiling fluids is central to understanding purity laws and elaborates on this point in some detail. See Iain R. Bóid, *Principles of Samaritan Halachah* (Leiden: Brill, 1989), 141, 148, 150–151, 154; Thomas Kazen, "Explaining Discrepancies in the Purity Laws on Discharges," *RB* 14.3 (2007): 362.

[63] See e.g., Anna S. Meigs, *Food, Sex, and Pollution: A New Guinea Religion* (New Brunswick, NJ: Rutgers University Press, 1984), 102–103.

[64] So already the Rabbis: *Sipra, Pereq Zabim*, Par. 4:9 (ed. I. Weiss, *Sifra with Rabad's Commentary* [New York, 1946], 78a); m. *Zabim* 5:6. See also David P. Wright, *The Disposal of Impurity: Elimination Rites in the Bible and in Hittite and Mesopotamian Literature* (Atlanta, GA: Scholars Press, 1987), 189.

commentators read the verse in the former sense, such that any contact with the gonorrheic's body required laundering.[65] Once again, some employ *a fortiori* logic: if touching the menstruant's body defiled (19), did it not stand to reason that touching the more severe gonorrheic also defiled?[66]

However logical this argument may have been, it is difficult to reconcile with the language of v. 7. First, we should note that *basar* in the sense "body" appears only in the context of washing, whereas the euphemistic sense appears in the context of defiling contact, as in the present verse. Second, all of the other cases which required laundering involved situations which put the person at risk of touching the emission itself. The only exception was the spit of the gonorrheic (8), which was still a form of direct contact with the impurity bearer's bodily fluid. Indeed, as noted above, contact with the menstruant only required bathing (19b), a comparison which supports understanding *basar* in the more stringent law of v. 7 as referring to the gonorrheic's genitalia.[67]

Moreover, this interpretation is necessary to account for the stipulation in v. 11 that anyone whom the gonorrheic touched without washing his hands would have to launder their clothes and bathe. According to the understanding of v. 7 that any contact with the gonorrheic's body required laundering, one faces the difficulty of explaining why the text specifically refers to his unwashed hands. However, the localized defilement described in this verse is quite understandable if we assume that the concern was that his discharge may have defiled his hands.[68] Since men touch their genitals when urinating, we can understand why this stipulation is not mentioned regarding female dischargers.[69]

As a result, verse 7 is best understood as referring to direct contact with the genitals of the gonorrheic. Though one may be initially surprised that the law would deal with such a possibility, it should be pointed out that

[65] Ibn Ezra; Gordon J. Wenham, *The Book of Leviticus*, NICOT (Grand Rapids, MI: Eerdmans, 1979), 219; Wright, *Disposal of Impurity*, 183; Milgrom, *Leviticus*, 1.914; Kazen, "Purity Laws on Discharges," 358.

[66] Wright, *Disposal of Impurity*, 181, 183, n. 34. Milgrom attributes a similar deduction to the Rabbis, but I was unable to find the midrash cited (*Leviticus*, 1.914). In any case, this understanding leads Milgrom to prefer the reading בה in v. 27 (along with 2 MSS and LXX) against the MT and other versions (1.943). However, since the structure of vv. 26–27 follows that of 21–22, MT should be retained.

[67] Arnold Ehrlich, *Randglossen zur hebräischen Bibel*, vol. 2 (Leipzig: J. C. Hinrichs, 1909), 52; Elliger, *Leviticus*, 191, 197.

[68] So the Samaritan "Book of Insight" (Bóid, *Principles*, 145, 219).

[69] Wright, *Disposal of Impurity*, 183, n. 35; Kazen, "Purity Laws on Discharges," 363.

the chapter deals elsewhere with defilement through sexual relations (18), including those with a menstruant (24).[70] Unlike the minor defilement caused by ejaculation, which takes place only in the course of the sexual act, the discharge of the gonorrheic is continuous. Thus, even aside from sexual relations, contact with the gonorrheic's penis demanded laundering.

This line of interpretation allows us to offer a more precise explanation for the requirement of laundering. This requirement is often taken to be a merely formal indication of the distinction between severe and less severe forms of defilement.[71] However, in light of the fact that the situations which demanded laundering involved potential contact with the emission itself, it would appear that the underlying concern was that the discharge may also have gotten on the person's clothing.[72] Thus, this rule was essentially an extension of the same heuristic which construed the possibility of a "stain" as a foregone conclusion.

A similar dynamic is implied by the biblical depiction of corpse impurity. Num 19:14–15 states that a corpse defiles objects found together with it in an enclosure (*'ohel*, literally a "tent"): "This is the instruction: In the event a person dies inside a tent, anyone who enters the tent and anyone inside the tent shall be impure for seven days. Any open vessel that does not have a lid fastened around it is impure." The underlying conception seems to have been that this defilement would spread like a gas.[73] As Baruch Levine points out, this mode of pollution is particularly clear from the law of the open vessel in v. 15: "The operative principle is that the impurity present within the structure invades all of its interior air, or space, and only sealed vessels are protected."[74] This conceptualization seems to have shaped, at least in part, the rabbinic elaboration of these laws. The conceptualization of corpse impurity as a gas is evident in various principles, including the assumption that corpse impurity spread in all directions inside a tent and the notion that it tended to escape through openings, that "it is the nature of impurity to exit and not to

---

[70] This is the most severe case mentioned in the chapter, transferring a week-long state of impurity equivalent to that of the menstruant herself.

[71] E.g., Milgrom, *Leviticus*, 1.913: "Touching the bedding of the *zāb* requires laundering because of the intensity of the impurity."

[72] However, intensity of contact may perhaps explain other cases of laundering which are not related to genital discharges (e.g., Lev 11:39–40; 14:46–47). See Wright, *Disposal of Impurity*, 185–186, n. 39.

[73] So Jacob Neusner, *The Mishnaic System of Uncleanness: Its Context and History*, vol. 22 of A History of the Mishnaic Law of Impurities (Leiden: Brill, 1977), 72.

[74] Baruch A. Levine, *Numbers 1–20*, AB (New York: Doubleday, 1993), 467.

enter."[75] Why did corpse impurity spread like a gas within an enclosure, unlike the forms of defilement described in Lev 15, which required contact? The answer is simple: the spread of this form of defilement was modeled after the dissemination of the stench of a decomposing corpse.[76]

A similar correlation between phenomenal experience (odor) and the conceptualization of death pollution is found in other cultures. For instance, classical sources from ancient Greece and Rome attest to the belief that the house in which a corpse was found required purification and should be marked with a pine or cypress branch on its entrance to warn outsiders.[77] Unfortunately, these references tend to be anecdotal, precluding further analysis. Modern ethnographic evidence, however, provides striking parallels which bear directly on the biblical case. Note, for example, the Indonesian custom of scrupulously sealing all of the cracks in a dead individual's coffin due to a concern that death will be spread with the odors. Robert Hertz writes: "The reason [Indonesians] consider it so highly desirable that the putrefaction should take place in a sealed container is that the evil power which resides in the corpse and which is linked to the smells must not be allowed to escape and strike the living."[78] A comparable view is attested among the Cantonese who fear the "killing airs" (*sat hei*) emitted by the corpse, which are thought to permeate the house of the deceased. Watson cites a local informant who describes the danger that the killing airs – associated with the departing spirit of the deceased – will cling to mourners "like an invisible cloud."[79]

---

[75] For a discussion of "realistic" aspects of the tannaitic characterization of corpse impurity, see Vered Noam, "Ritual Impurity in Tannaitic Literature: Two Opposing Perspectives," *JAJ* 1 (2010): 81–86.

[76] For discussion of the underlying conception, specifically the relationship between pollution and the departing spirit (*nepeš*), see Chapter 9 below.

[77] See Parker, *Miasma*, 35, 38; Eireann Marshall, "Death and Disease in Cyrene," in *Death and Disease in the Ancient City*, eds. V. M. Hope and E. Marshall (London: Routledge, 2000), 10; Hugh Lindsay, "Death-Pollution and Funerals in the City of Rome," in *Death and Disease in the Ancient City*, eds. V. M. Hope and E. Marshall (London: Routledge, 2000), 155, 166, 169. One wonders if these branches also served a function in dispelling (or covering up) the odor. See also the fifth-century BCE house purification ritual from Keos: Collection of Greek Ritual Norms (CGRN) 35 (http://cgrn.philo.ulg.ac.be/file/35/, accessed on 8/1/2019).

[78] Robert Hertz, *Death and the Right Hand*, trans. R. and C. Needham (Aberdeen: Cohen & West, 1960 [1907–1909]), 32.

[79] See James L. Watson, "Of Flesh and Bones: The Management of Death Pollution in Cantonese Society," in *Death and the Regeneration of Life*, eds. M. Bloch and J. Parry (Cambridge: Cambridge University Press, 1982), 155–186, esp. 158. Among Native Americans, a similar idea is widely documented, for example, among the Navajo: "Traditionally, if a death occurred in a hogan, a hole was broken in the north side (the

These parallels reflect a similar conceptualization of the power of death to spread in a manner corresponding to sense experience.

A final example is that of the "leper" described in Lev 13–14. The numerous biblical references to the banishment of people suffering from the skin disease ṣara'at provides the strongest evidence for a concern with infectiousness. This topic will be discussed in further detail in the following chapters.

It is significant that the leper and the gonorrheic were required to bring expiatory offerings, which was not the case with normal bodily discharges.[80] The leper was required to bring a sin offering together with a burnt offering (Lev 14:19, 31), and the blood of a guilt offering was daubed on his right ear, thumb and big toe (12–14, 21–25). Similarly, both male and female gonorrheics were required to bring sin offerings (Lev 15:15, 30). The need for expiatory offerings in these cases was consistent with David's curse that explicitly referred to leprosy and gonorrhea as divine punishments (2 Sam 3:29).

However, the peculiar fact is that Priestly sources tended to draw a clear distinction between disease and sin. For example, unlike non-Priestly sources which frequently depict leprosy as a punishment (e.g., Num 12; 2 Kings 5:26–27; 2 Chronicles 26:16–21), P makes no inference of this sort.[81] Moreover, the rationales given in the sin-offering instructions clearly distinguish between offerings brought on account of transgressions (Lev 4; 16; Num 15: 22–31) and those brought on account of impurities (Lev 12; 14–15). Whereas the sin offering in the former cases serves to expiate sin and gain forgiveness, in the latter cases it merely removes defilement.[82] This distinction would seem to differentiate P's perspective from the conflation of sin and disease implied by David's curse. On this background, the requirement that the leper and gonorrheic bring expiatory offerings (Lev 14–15) is best understood as reflecting the conservatism of cult practice.[83]

---

north being the direction in which spirits travel), and the house was abandoned" (David F. Aberle, "Navaho," in *Matrilineal Kinship*, ed. D. M. Schneider and K. Gough [Berkeley, CA: University of California, 1974], 136).

[80] For discussion of these offerings, and the relation between disease and sin more generally, see Chapter 5 below.

[81] Joel S. Baden and Candida R. Moss, "The Origins and Interpretation of ṣāra'at in Leviticus 13–14," *Journal of Biblical Literature* 130 (2011): 643–653.

[82] See Roy Gane, *Cult and Character: Purification Offerings, Day of Atonement, and Theodicy* (Winona Lake, IN: Eisenbrauns, 2005), 112–124.

[83] For further discussion, see Chapter 5 below.

Aside from distinguishing between pollution and sin, Priestly materials also seem to distinguish pollution from infection. It is striking that the priests play no role in healing the leper; the text limits their function to his purification after the condition has healed on its own (Lev 14:3).[84] This tendency is particularly striking in H's redaction of the purity rules, which emphasize the fear of defiling the sanctuary, and implicitly reject any inherent danger associated with these conditions (Lev 15:31; Num 5:1–4; 19:13, 20). The rationale for these Priestly tendencies will be examined in more detail in chapters 4 and 5.

In summary, the Priestly depiction of these conditions presents us with a paradox. On one hand, the characterization of the spread of pollution as well as the isolation and expiatory offerings required of the impurity bearer hint at an underlying concern with the spread of infection or curse. On the other hand, the biblical materials display an effort to de-emphasize or even deny the danger of infection. Despite these efforts to depict pollution as posing a threat only in relation to the sacred domain, the behaviors associated with these forms of impurity indicate that these conditions were not always perceived to be innocuous. The rationale and ramifications of this transformation will be explored in the chapters which follow.

POLLUTION AS A CONCEPTUAL BLEND

Although the notion of an unseen force exhibiting physical properties may seem obscure initially, its inner logic can be elucidated by reference to the cognitive linguistic notion of "blending" (also known as "conceptual integration").[85] Unlike work on conceptual metaphor (e.g., "argument is a war") that assumes a unidirectional mapping from a concrete source domain to a more abstract target domain,[86] research on blending

---

[84] See Yehezkel Kaufmann, *The Religion of Israel*, trans. M. Greenberg (Chicago, IL: University of Chicago, 1960), 107–108; Milgrom, *Leviticus*, 1.887–889; cf. Baruch A. Levine, *In the Presence of the Lord* (Leiden: Brill, 1974), 83–85. Interestingly, a similar tendency is also attested outside the Priestly materials, particularly in the story of Naaman's leprosy (2 Kgs 5), in which the contraction of the disease by Gehazi is portrayed as a consequence of his disobedience to Elisha and not as an immediate result of contagion. See below, p. 87.

[85] For an elaborate application of blending theory to biblical pollution with different emphasis, see Kazen, "Role of Disgust."

[86] For a brief introduction to this theory and its application to biblical studies, see Job Jindo, "Toward a Poetics of the Biblical Mind: Language, Culture and Cognition," *VT* 59.2 (2009): 222–243.

focuses on how two distinct domains can merge. One type of blending which is particularly relevant to our discussion is that of experiential correlation, as elucidated through the theory of "primary metaphors." According to this theory, the inherent correlation between two or more units of experience (subscenes) in a recurrent primary scene can serve as the basis for primary metaphors.[87] For example, a statement such as "You *saw* the logic of my argument" can be taken as based on a metaphor: "seeing is understanding." In this case, the primary metaphor "seeing is understanding" originates in the fact that the state of understanding (a cognitive subscene) often correlates with visual recognition (a perceptive subscene). In such situations, to visually detect X is tantamount to becoming aware of X.

This analytic framework can be adapted to elucidate the biblical notion of bloodguilt, which is depicted in terms similar to pollution (e.g., Num 35:33–34; Deut 21:1–9). The biblical corpus gives abundant expression to the view that the spilling of innocent blood results in a stain that will invoke a divine punishment on the entire community unless proper action is taken against the murderer. While some sources depict a personified conception in which the blood of the victim remains in a state of distress as long as the perpetrator goes unpunished (Gen 4:11; Job 16:18),[88] most sources depict retribution as an automatic mechanical process in which references to "blood" (*damim*) denote an invisible taint which threatens to invite punishment until the blood debt is paid off.[89] The important point for our purposes is that the guilt is conceptualized as a bloodstain, which can stain the perpetrator's body and pollute the land. This synthesis is represented in Table 2.1.

Though one might be tempted to say that the blood *symbolizes* (i.e., represents) the culpability, this formulation distorts the fact that we are dealing with a single concept. In this case, the blood spilled is merely the

---

[87] See Joseph Grady and Christopher Johnson, "Converging Evidence for the Notions of Subscene and Primary Scene," in *Metaphor and Metonymy in Comparison and Contrast*, eds. R. Dirven and R. Pörings (Berlin: De Gruyter, 2003), 533–555. For "primary metaphors" as a source of conceptual integration, see Joseph Grady, "Primary Metaphors as Inputs to Conceptual Integration," *Journal of Pragmatics* 37.10 (2005): 1595–1614. Many of the examples, including those below, could also potentially be described as metonymy-based metaphor, specifically the "effect for cause" metonymy (but cf. Grady and Johnson, "Converging Evidence," 540).

[88] See also Isa 26:21; Ezek 24:7–8. This scheme should probably be related to the belief that the blood contains a person's animating spirit (e.g., Gen 9:4; Deut 12:23).

[89] E.g., Deut 21:1–9; 2 Sam 3:28; 21:1–6; 1 Kgs 2:33. See Feder, "The Mechanics of Retribution," 138–149, and *Blood Expiation*, 173–189.

TABLE 2.1 *Bloodguilt as a conceptual blend*

Experiential subscenes	Metaphysical concept (synthesis)
physical bloodstain	bloodguilt as an invisible stain
culpability (causing retribution)	

TABLE 2.2 *Genital pollution as a conceptual blend*

Experiential subscenes	Metaphysical concept (synthesis)
physical stain of abnormal discharges	pollution (*ṭum'ah*) spread through contact
spread of misfortune (infection)	

perceptible aspect of a deed which has unseen, yet nevertheless inevitable, ramifications. This phenomenon of conceptual integration is also manifested in the characterization of sexual misdeeds (especially incest) as polluting.[90] As in the case of bloodshed, the guilt entailed by illicit sexual intercourse is depicted as defiling, a taint that can cause the land to vomit out its inhabitants (Lev 18: 26–28). The significance of this application of pollution terminology to social norms will be examined further in Chapter 9.

In a comparable fashion, the Israelite conception of pollution as it applies to genital disorders is depicted in Table 2.2. A similar model could be used for corpse impurity (Num 19), but in this case, the correlation is between the odor of the corpse and the perceived spread of misfortune.

We can now integrate these insights in identifying a set of base images of *ṭum'ah* in the Hebrew Bible. These separate models involve a clear correspondence between an experiential image and the emotional response and normative cultural implications involved with it. Though these models should not be taken rigidly (see my caveats below), they seem

---

[90] E.g., Gen 34:5, 13, 27; Lev 18; Num 5:12–31. See Tikva Frymer-Kensky, "Pollution, Purification and Purgation in Biblical Israel," in *The Word of the Lord Shall Go Forth: Essays in Honor of David Noel Freedman in Celebration of his Sixtieth Birthday*, eds. C. L. Meyers and M. O'Connor (Winona Lake, IN: Eisenbrauns, 1983), 408.

TABLE 2.3 *Experiential grounding of pollution schemas*

Experiential image	Uncleanness	Infection	Stain of Transgression
Core emotion	Disgust[1]	Fear	Outrage[2]
Examples	Normal genital discharges	Abnormal genital discharges, corpse impurity, leprosy	Bloodguilt Sexual immorality
Normative implications/ concerns	Separation from sacred	Spread of misfortune	Defilement of person/land, divine retribution
Methods of purification	Passage of time, washing[3]	Banishment, passage of time, washing and sacrifice	Expiatory act (if possible), punishment

[1] "Disgust" as used here may vary from a mild sense of dirtiness following contact with semen to a more intense repulsion, e.g., as a reaction to menstrual blood, as reflected in the more serious ramifications associated with the latter (Chapter 10).

[2] Cf. Kazen's reference to "sense of justice" ("Impurity, Ritual and Emotion").

[3] Regarding the sin offering of the parturient, see Chapter 6.

to reflect fundamental distinctions between different types of pollution (see Table 2.3).

Forms of *ṭum'ah* which fit the characterization of being "unclean" are the least severe, requiring only that the person or object be distanced from the sacred realm. The governing factor here is the need to be pure when approaching God.[91] This basic attitude toward approaching the divine realm is probably universal and finds vivid expression in the Mesopotamian concern not to approach the gods in anything less than a state of total cleanliness; even bad breath was deemed unacceptable.[92]

The "infection" model has been discussed earlier in this chapter. It pertains to a selected group of conditions which were associated with a fear of contagion. This fear element can account for the more complex

[91] See Lev 12:4. This consideration is at work also in the law of the war camp in Deut 23:10–15. Alongside the demand that soldiers who experience a seminal emission must be excluded, the soldiers are required to relieve themselves outside the camp, so as not to offend the divine presence in their midst.

[92] See van der Toorn, *Sin and Sanction*, 21–36.

purificatory process and need for sacrificial offerings. As noted above, the manner of infection is modeled after the concrete expression of this defilement (e.g., genital emission, odor).

The "stain of transgression" pertains to violations of cultural norms, specifically those of murder and sexual misconduct. Since these are analogous to the sources of infection in that they involve a release of bodily fluids (stains) and a fear of imminent danger (threats of punishment), the stain of transgression might be viewed as derivative of the cleanliness and infection models, which are more directly grounded in bodily experience. Unlike the other models, however, these forms of pollution are described as defiling the land, and they cannot be rectified by ritual cleansing or even sacrifice. These stains invariably lead to retribution: murder demands payback for the blood spilled (Num 35:34), and the perpetrators of sexual misdeeds are subject to the death penalty and divine punishment, the "cutting off" (*karet*) of oneself and one's lineage (Lev 18; 20).[93] The extension of pollution into the moral domain will be examined in Chapter 9.

As in the models analyzed by Nemeroff and Rozin, the distinct characteristics of each image, and particularly the distinct means of purification for each, supports the assumption that they were taken as separate models, despite the fact that they were incorporated into a common category: *ṭum'ah*.[94] To be more specific, it appears that the basic experience which governs the various uses of *ṭum'ah* is that of contagion. Hence, the distinct images of uncleanness and infection could be included under a single term. A related psychological phenomenon was recognized by Daniel Kelly in his study of disgust. He explains the "elicitor neutral" aspect of contamination sensitivity as follows: "Any elicitor of disgust, regardless of the actual nature of the elicitor or which 'domain' of disgust

---

[93] Frymer-Kensky, "Pollution, Purification and Purgation," 406–409. To an extent, the distinction between bodily sources of pollution from the "stain-of-transgression" model resembles the distinction between "ritual" and "moral" impurity advocated by some scholars; see Adolph Büchler, *Studies in Sin and Atonement in the Rabbinic Literature of the First Century* (New York, NY: Ktav, 1967), 212–269; Jonathan Klawans, *Impurity and Sin in Ancient Judaism* (New York, NY: Oxford University Press, 2000), 21–42. For further discussion, see Chapter 9.

[94] Interestingly, Kelly has advanced the "Entanglement Thesis," arguing that human notions of disgust are comprised of two evolutionarily distinct responses, the "affect program" which reacts to ingesting potentially toxic substances and "core disgust" which is an adaptive response to disease and parasites (*Yuck! The Nature and Moral Significance of Disgust* [Cambridge, MA: MIT Press, 2011], 43–60). Whether or not this theory is correct, it offers a suggestive model for how two similar but distinct experiences could converge under a common terminology.

it falls in (physical, social, moral), has contamination potency of the same basic sort."[95] That is to say, the notion of contagion was sufficiently generic to warrant the usage of a common term to describe both uncleanness and infection.[96] However, as noted above, the stain-of-transgression image should probably be viewed as a secondary development, modeled after aspects of uncleanness and infection.[97]

It should be stressed, however, that the biblical treatment of pollution in all of its heterogeneity captures a richness of embodied experience which cannot be adequately represented in a schematic chart. In particular, it is not possible to determine a priority between the experiential schema and the emotion evoked by it. As noted above, emotional response is an inherent part of the perception of contagion.[98] Furthermore, some sources of pollution do not conform so neatly to this analytic framework. In particular, though menstrual and puerperal blood are normal discharges, they had implications even outside the sacral sphere, namely in the strict ban on sexual relations.[99] Since sex with a menstruant involves the violation of the acceptable norms of conduct – being listed together with abominable sexual acts such as bestiality and incest – and entails divine punishment (Lev 18:19, 20:18), it fits the stain-of-transgression model in this regard. But rather than contradicting the existence of distinct

---

[95] Ibid., 19; see also 33–34, 39.

[96] Hence, "pollution" should be viewed as a "classifier," a linguistically constructed category which can refer to several distinct types of experience (see Violi, *Meaning and Experience*, 132).

[97] The same would apply to the usage of pollution terminology to describe idolatry, which is further removed from bodily experience. For discussion of the latter, see Frymer-Kensky, "Pollution, Purification and Purgation," 406; André, "אמט," TDOT 5:330–331; Wright, "Unclean and Clean," 734.

[98] This is a complex topic which requires further discussion. For the view that normative and affective content is built into concepts and schemas, see Roy G. D'Andrade, "Schemas as Motivation," in *Human Motives and Cultural Models*, eds. R. G. D'Andrade and C. Strauss (Cambridge: Cambridge University Press, 1992), 23–44; Richard A. Shweder, "Ghost Busters in Anthropology," in *Human Motives and Cultural Models*, eds. R. G. D'Andrade and C. Strauss (Cambridge: Cambridge University Press, 1992), 45–58; Patrizia Violi, "Beyond the Body: Towards a Full Embodied Semiosis," in *Body, Language and Mind. Volume 2: Sociocultural Situatedness*, eds. R. M. Frank et al. (Berlin: de Gruyter, 2008), 66–71. See also p. 21. above.

[99] For discussion of the "menstrual taboo" in Israel and cross-culturally, see Eilberg-Schwartz, *Savage in Judaism*, 177–194; Malul, *Knowledge, Control and Sex*, 379–394; and more generally Meigs, *Food, Sex, and Pollution*; see also Thomas Buckley and Alma Gottlieb, "A Critical Appraisal of Theories of Menstrual Symbolism," in *Blood Magic: The Anthropology of Menstruation*, eds. T. Buckley and A. Gottlieb (Berkeley, CA: University of California Press, 1988), 3–53.

types suggested above, this case should serve as a reminder that the various types of pollution are ultimately derived from attitudes toward the body in all of its multifarious possibilities – not from a rigid disembodied logic.

CONCLUSION

In this chapter, I have outlined a framework for understanding the embodied logic of pollution as depicted in the Hebrew Bible. Contrary to the dominant tendency to search for a unified abstract logic which underlies the purity laws, I have aimed to show that these rules were based on a series of distinct models of contagion, including uncleanness, infection and the stain of bloodshed and sexual misdeeds. These models were based on schemas of recurrent human experiences and involved a correlation between a perceptible phenomenon (stain, odor, etc.) and an unseen essence (pollution). In particular, I have focused on the laws of abnormal genital discharges in Lev 15, corpse impurity in Num 19 and leprosy in Lev 13–14, all of which were based on folk conceptions of infection. Though this model makes sense of this evidence to a considerable degree, it also exposes inconsistencies within the biblical evidence. The task of the following chapters will be to grapple with these issues.

PART II

EMBODYING POLLUTION THROUGH THE LIFE CYCLE

Disease

3

The "Touch" of Leprosy: Diagnosing Disease between Language and Experience

In the previous chapter, it was argued that a key experiential schema governing the use of *ṭum'ah* is that of infection. In this chapter, this relationship will be examined in more detail, highlighting the complications involved when articulating the experience of disease in language. These difficulties will be demonstrated through an examination of biblical *ṣara'at* and its common translation as "leprosy." This specific case will serve as a point of entry for examining the awareness of contagion more generally in ancient Israel and neighboring cultures, particularly as expressed in the terminology of pollution. This line of inquiry will provide the necessary background to reevaluate attempts to downgrade the severity of biblical diseases as sources of mere "ritual" impurity.

PITFALLS IN DIAGNOSING ANCIENT DISEASES: THE CASE OF "LEPROSY"

Insatiable scholarly interest has been attracted to the diagnosis of ancient diseases. The case of biblical *ṣara'at* and its possible identification with "leprosy" (Hansen's disease) epitomize this line of research.[1] Despite the erudition of these studies (to which the present discussion is deeply indebted), both philological and medical, they often underestimate the magnitude of the methodological challenges to be surmounted. These studies generally seek to correlate the name of a disease as defined by

---

[1] Still one of the most comprehensive studies to date, with references to earlier literature: E. V. Hulse, "The Nature of Biblical 'Leprosy' and the Use of Alternative Medical Terms in Modern Translations of the Bible," *PEQ* 107.2 (1975): 87–105.

modern medicine with the descriptions and symptomology (when available) of illnesses recorded in ancient texts. The tacit assumption, though sometimes explicitly posed as a question, is that the same viral or bacteriological causes of disease were present in the historical context under investigation. This assumption can in some cases find remarkable validation today by means of DNA testing of bone remains from earlier centuries and even millennia.

So, what's the problem? One problem is the anachronistic imposition of a laboratory model of disease which only emerged in the mid-nineteenth century (CE) on earlier societies whose understanding of disease was radically different.[2] Put differently, one cannot impose an understanding of disease that is defined by precise criteria contingent on laboratory instruments upon the vaguer experience of premodern cultures.[3] One may compare the more circumspect viewpoint that informs some more recent medical histories, as in the following introduction: "This is a history of the French Disease; or, in the English vernacular, the pox. It is not a history of syphilis."[4] In contrasting the pre-bacteriological understanding with the modern, the authors explain:

But all of this did not represent confusion, for confusion is a muddling of extant categories, and our categories did not yet exist. In solving their own problems in their own ways these doctors serve to highlight the great change that came over medicine after the laboratory and germ theory. Their perceptions were so different that we cannot insist on the identity of diseases before and after. We are simply unable to say whether they were the same, since the criteria of "sameness" have been changed.[5]

In other words, it is not just a question of them not knowing from what disease patients of an earlier epoch were suffering; they suffered from different diseases.

---

[2] See Andrew Cunningham, "Transforming Plague: The Laboratory and the Identity of Infectious Disease," in *The Laboratory Revolution in Medicine*, eds. A. Cunningham and P. Williams (Cambridge: Cambridge University Press, 1992), 209–244.

[3] Some attempts to overcome this problem include Temkin's influential distinction between "ontological" (=diseases existed as discrete entities) and "physiological" (=diseases are idiosyncratic to the person), discussed in the chapter "The Scientific Approach to Disease: Specific Entity and Individual Sickness," in *The Double Face of Janus and Other Essays in the History of Medicine* (Baltimore, MD: John Hopkins Press, 1977 [1953]), 441–455. Cf. also Arthur Kleiman's distinction between illness as understood by the world of medicine and illness as experienced by the patient, discussed in *The Illness Narratives: Suffering, Healing, and the Human Condition* (New York, NY: Basic Books, 1988).

[4] Jon Arrizabalaga, John Henderson and Roger French, *The Great Pox: The French Disease in Renaissance Europe* (New Haven, CT: Yale University Press, 1997), 1.

[5] Ibid., 2. The quote is taken from Cunningham, "Transforming Plague," 242 (see also 210).

What may seem to be an exaggerated and unlikely conclusion proves to be unavoidable when one confronts the actual research seeking to identify ancient diseases. First, the symptoms in ancient texts (e.g., those attributed to ṣara'at in Leviticus 13) often defy any single modern diagnosis. Second, historical studies can show that frequently a single term for an ancient disease (e.g., Greek *lepra*) is applied in different periods or contexts to different diseases. Therefore, it is hardly surprising that the hundreds of attempts to address the question whether "real leprosy" existed in ancient Israel, defined by the presence of *Mycobacterium leprae* or *Mycobacterium lepromatosis*, have failed to attain conclusive results.

ETYMOLOGY AND EXPERIENCE

Against the dominant tendency to pin a bacteriological diagnosis on ancient descriptions, the following discussion will explore the terminology of several skin diseases from the ancient Near East and Mediterranean, focusing on how the terminology of disease can serve as a window onto experience. It will also show the fluidity of disease terminology, with the case of biblical "leprosy" serving as a paradigm case.

As a point of entry into this discussion of ṣara'at, it is helpful to compare it with a Mesopotamian skin disease called saḫaršubbû, which shares numerous characteristics with its biblical counterpart,[6] and which will also set the stage for the discussion of a ritual for the healing of saḫaršubbû in the next chapter. This Akkadian term is a loan from Sumerian saḫar.šub.ba: "covered with dust."[7] Most likely, this name refers to the appearance of scaly skin on the patient, such as is characteristic of modern psoriasis. Interestingly, Exodus 9:8–9 describes an inflammation (šeḫin) of boils ('ababu'ot) afflicting the Egyptians: "Then Yhwh said to Moses and Aaron, 'Each of you take handfuls of soot from the kiln, and let Moses throw it toward the sky in the sight of Pharaoh. *It shall become a fine dust all over the land of Egypt, and cause an inflammation breaking out in boils* on man and beast throughout the land of Egypt'"

---

[6] See *CAD* S 36–37; Marten Stol, "Leprosy: New Light from Greek and Babylonian Sources," *Jaarbericht van het Vooraziatisch-Egyptisch Genootschap (Ex Oriente Lux)* 30 (1989), 22–31; JoAnn Scurlock and Burton Andersen, *Diagnoses in Assyrian and Babylonian Medicine* (Urbana and Chicago, IL: Illinois University Press, 2005), 70–73, 231–233, 723–724, nn. 139–140.

[7] See Stol, "New Light," 30–31; Jacob Klein, "Leprosy and Lepers in Mesopotamian Literature," *Korot* 21 (2011–2012), 9–24 (in Hebrew), esp. 11, n. 4.

(NJPS, adapted). Like the Mesopotamian etymology, this narrative explicitly relates this skin condition to a dust that causes the boils on the skin. This Mesopotamian disease covered the body of its victim like a garment and lead to stigmatization and banishment from the community, reflecting a perception that it was contagious. Like *ṣara'at*, it was often viewed as a divine punishment or curse.[8] Often the victim was forced to literally roam the steppe, as in the following boundary-stone (*kudurru*) inscription from the eleventh century BCE: "May Sîn clothe his whole body in *saḫaršubbû* which will never lift so that all the days of his life he will be impure and, like a wild ass, wander outside his city."[9] In one incantation text, the patient of this disease is mentioned alongside the *musukku* (ú.ka), a term which refers to an outcast, derived from the verb *masāku*, which is associated with disgust, disease and banishment.[10] Like the *musukku*, the person suffering from *saḫaršubbû* was an outcast, physically isolated from society. For this reason, Karl van der Toorn defended the translation "leprosy" for both the biblical and Mesopotamian skin diseases, even while recognizing it to be medically inaccurate: "We must rid ourselves of the fixation on a single scientifically proven disease, since the terms *saḫaršubbû* and *ṣāra'at* cover in fact several diseases all of which manifested themselves in unpleasant, often scaly skin conditions."[11] As implied by the German term for leprosy *Aussatz* (equivalent to "outcast"), the victims of these diseases were literally banished from society.[12] This implication is stated in equally explicit terms in a Mesopotamian omen text regarding an unspecified

---

[8] For a detailed analysis of these curse formulas attested in documents from the fourteenth to seventh centuries BCE see Kazuko Watanabe, "Die literarische Überlieferung eines babylonisch-assyrischen Fluchthemas mit Anrufung des Mondgottes Sîn," *Acta Sumerologica* 6 (1984), 99–119.

[9] Text: Leonard W. King, *Babylonian Boundary-Stones and Memorial Tablets in the British Museum* (London: Longmans & Co., 1912), 41 (kudurru 7, col. 2, ll. 16–18). See also Kathryn E. Slanski, *The Babylonian Entitlement narûs (kudurrus)*, ASOR Books 9 (Boston, MA: American Schools of Oriental Research, 2003), 225–226; Ann Marie Kitz, *Cursed Are You! The Phenomenology of Cursing in Cuneiform and Hebrew Texts* (Winona Lake, IN: Eisenbrauns, 2014), 148–149.

[10] *CAD* M/1 322 renders *masāku* "to be ugly, bad"; *mussuku:* "to spoil, make disgusting, revile." For discussion, see Yitzhaq Feder, "Defilement, Disgust and Disease: The Experiential Basis for Akkadian and Hittite Terms for Pollution," *JAOS* 136.1 (2016): 106–107.

[11] Karl van der Toorn, *Sin and Sanction in Israel and Mesopotamia: A Comparative Study* (Assen: Van Gorcum, 1985), 72–75.

[12] See Luke Demaitre, *Leprosy in Premodern Medicine* (Baltimore, MD: Johns Hopkins University Press, 2007), 82.

skin condition characterized by white spots and marks covering the body: "this man is rejected by his deity (and) rejected by humanity."[13]

Much scholarly literature has been preoccupied with whether ṣara'at can be identified with leprosy (Hansen's disease), though other possible diagnoses have been entertained. One of the most systematic discussions in recent decades, and oft quoted for good reason, is that of E. V. Hulse, who finds the closest resemblance to psoriasis.[14] Like *lepra*, from which "leprosy" derives, the usage of *psora* and *psoriasis* was fluid and applied to various skin conditions. Indeed, there is a consensus that Galen's description of "psoriasis" is not the modern disease of that name. Hence, it is hardly surprising that these terms were used interchangeably in the premodern period, as one reviewer points out: "In total, the confusion between psoriasis and leprosy lasted about two thousand years!"[15] These words are a sobering reminder for modern scholars seeking a concrete bacteriological referent for ancient terminology. From a purely bacteriological perspective, the question of when *Mycobacterium leprae* first arrived in the Mediterranean region is still debated. Though some scholars viewed the late arrival in Hellenistic times as proved by its absence in bone remains, this lack of osteoarchaeological evidence now seems less than conclusive. Numerous scholars in recent decades have drawn the opposite conclusion, that terms for ancient skin diseases including Hebrew ṣara'at and Akkadian *saḫaršubbû* were used

[13] VAT 7525 II 42–45; Cited by J. V. Kinnier Wilson, "Leprosy in Ancient Mesopotamia," *RA* 60.1 (1966): 49; Kitz, *Cursed Are You!*, 148. For the symptoms described, see also Scurlock and Andersen, *Diagnoses*, 218, 220. As this book was going to press, I discovered another striking parallel to biblical ṣara'at in a disease designated *sḫt* in Demotic papyri from Ptolemaic Egypt, attested from the late third century BCE. This Egyptian disease involved a whitening of the skin, was stigmatized as a divine punishment and could require banishment. See Amber Jacob, "Demotic Pharmacology: An Overview of the Demotic Medical Manuscripts in the Papyrus Carlsberg Collection," in *Parlare la medicina: fra lingue e culture, nello spazio e nel tempo*, eds. N. Reggiani and F. Bertonazzi (Milan: La Monnier Università, 2018), 57–79 (67–69). This parallel warrants further investigation.

[14] "Nature of Biblical 'Leprosy,'" 96–101. Incidentally, it is tempting to draw a connection between the Greek term *psora*, which is listed as a skin disease in Herodotus (fifth century BCE), and the Hebrew ṣara'at, considering that the guttural consonant that has no parallel in Greek. However, since the Greek term has a native etymology ψάω ("itch"), it appears that this phonetic similarity is coincidental. I thank Jonathan Price for his help evaluating this possibility and for further pointing out to me that the Septuagint uses *psora* as a translation for biblical גרב.

[15] Franklin S. Glickman, "Lepra, Psora, Psoriasis," *Journal of the American Academy of Dermatology* 14.5 (1986): 863–866.

in reference to Hansen's disease among several other conditions, which were not sharply differentiated from it.[16]

In any case, from Hellenistic times two key Greek terms, *lepra* and *elphas*, play a key role in the discourse on this disease. Mirko Grmek and others have observed that *lepra*, which was ultimately adopted as the designation for Hansen's disease as "leprosy," was applied to more benign skin conditions in Hippocratic texts.[17] Sources from the beginning of the Common Era begin to refer to a skin disease named *elephas* that offers a more likely candidate for Hansen's disease, as noted by Luke Demaitre:

> There is no need to reach for retrospective diagnosis in order to realize that descriptions of this newly noted affliction corresponded, individually and cumulatively, far more closely to the manifestations of Hansen's disease than to the skin condition in biblical and Hippocratic sources. Described symptoms ranged from discolored or darkened embossments over the whole body to facial deformities and loss of extremities.[18]

The translators of the Septuagint adopted *lepra* as the translation for *ṣaraʿat*, perhaps preferring a more familiar term than that used for the more serious condition *elephas*, which was gaining attention in Alexandria during this period.[19] This choice of translation would become a source of considerable confusion. On the one hand, the frequent presence of *lepra* in the Septuagint led to the widespread identification of biblical *ṣaraʿat* with "leprosy." On the other hand, more recently, the Greek translation has served as a key argument that "real" leprosy was unknown in biblical times; otherwise, one cannot explain why the translators chose the comparatively benign term for the biblical disease.

Most ironic, however, is the fact that it was the biblical translation itself that influenced the official acceptance of *lepra* as the name for the

---

[16] Stol, "Leprosy," 21–31; Scurlock and Andersen, *Diagnoses*, 70–73, 231–233, 723–724, nn. 139–140.

[17] Aphorism 3.20. See Demaitre, *Leprosy*, 83.

[18] *Leprosy*, 85. See also Mirko D. Grmek, *Diseases in the Ancient Greek World*, trans. M. and L. Muellner (Baltimore, MD: Johns Hopkins University Press, 1989), 168–171. Martin Stol has argued that the relation to elephants is based on a folk etymology and suggests that this term is derived from *epaphe* ("touch"), which appears elsewhere in the context of disease, as noted above. "Leprosy," 25–26, citing the efforts of Aretaeus to relate to elephants [IV.13; ed. Hude, *Corpus Medicorum Graecorum*, II, 2nd ed.; Berlin: Akademie Verlag, 1958), 85–90]. See further Vivian Nutton, "Did the Greeks Have a Word for It?" In *Contagion: Perspectives from Pre-Modern Societies*, edited by L. I. Conrad and D. Wujastyk, 137–162 (Aldershot: Ashgate, 2000), 138–140, citing also Karl Sudhoff's view that *epaphe* referred to leprosy: "Ἐπαφή der Aussatz?" *Sudhoffs Archiv für Geschichte der Medizin* 21 (1929): 204–206.

[19] Grmek, *Diseases*, 169.

debilitating disease in the Middle Ages. Medical authorities yielded to the influence of popular and liturgical usage over the more precise diagnostic traditions of Hippocrates and Galen, such that *elephantiasis* was left to be reused for the condition now known by that name.[20] In other words, whether or not *ṣaraʿat* was real leprosy (Hansen's disease), the main reason that the name *lepra* was adopted for the latter was the influence of the Greek translation of *ṣaraʿat*. As can be seen from this short survey, the very possibility of retelling the history of "leprosy" requires that we unravel the entangled threads of bacteriology, experience and nomenclature. Having addressed some of the terminological issues pertaining to ancient disease as they pertain to the case of *ṣaraʿat*, it is now possible to address the more fundamental question of contagion, particularly as reflected in Lev 13–14.

CONTAGION AND INFECTION: PENETRATING THE METAPHORS

As noted in the previous chapter, the shared terminology for disease in Mesopotamia and the HB, specifically Akkadian *lapātu* and Hebrew *n-g-ʿ*, suggests a common conceptual framework. Further investigation reveals that this idiom of "touch" is attested even beyond the ancient Near East, including the word "contagion" itself, derived from Latin *com* + *tangere* ("touched with") and Greek *epaphe*, also meaning "touch."[21] These related semantic parallels seem to reflect an intuition shared by ancient Mesopotamian, biblical, Latin and Greek authors. Does this, however, directly relate to the phenomenon that we today call "contagion"?

In many ancient languages, including those of the Mediterranean and the Near East, the terminology of disease suggests the idea of being stricken by the gods. The term "plague" itself is a salient example, derived from Latin *plaga*, referring to a blow or wound.[22] In the ancient

---

[20] Grmek, *Diseases*, 172–173.

[21] Vivian Nutton elaborates that *epaphe* "and its verb *ephaptein* simply mean 'touch'; the prefix *epi-* intensifies the touching" ("Did the Greeks," 139). For a helpful survey of primary sources from the classical world, see Saul Jarcho, *The Concept of Contagion: In Medicine, Literature, and Religion* (Malabar, FL: Krieger Publishing, 2000), 1–20. The clearest example of knowledge of contagion in early Greek writings is Thucydides' discussion of the Athenian plague (2.47.4), where it is observed that the doctors were among the most numerous to die due to their extensive contact with the sick.

[22] Margaret Healy, "Anxious and Fatal Contacts: Taming the Contagious Touch," in *Sensible Flesh: On Touch in Early Modern Culture*, ed. E. D. Harvey (Philadelphia, PA: University of Pennsylvania, 2003), 24.

conception, disease is a result of the person being struck by deities, whose touch renders the person sick.[23] The biblical term for plague, *maggepa* (e.g., Num 26:11; 1 Sam 6:4), is derived from the root *n-g-p* ("strike"), which is frequently used to describe a divine punishment in the form of illness.[24] A similar usage is found with the root *n-g-ʿ*, which can mean both "touch" and "hit," as in the divine punishment of Pharaoh for taking Sarai: "But Yhwh struck (*waynaggaʿ*) Pharaoh and his household with mighty plagues on account of Sarai, the wife of Abram" (Gen 12:17). Similarly, in taunting God to test Job's piety, the Adversary (Satan) argues: "If you send forth your hand and *touch* [Job's] bones and flesh, he will surely 'bless' (curse) you to your face" (Job 2:5). This root also provides the etymology for *neggaʿ* ("affliction"), which is ubiquitous in the discussion of *ṣaraʿat* in Lev 13–14 (see below). Ostensibly, this view of the divine origins of an affliction has nothing to do with the phenomenon of contagion, understood as a process of interpersonal transmission. For this reason, one might raise doubts that the biblical (and Akkadian) terminology is related to what we call "contagion."

Yet, further examination suggests that the use of this idiom does in fact relate to interpersonal transmission. The broader usage of "touch" terminology in both Semitic and Indo-European languages (Akkadian *lapātu*; Hebrew *n.g.ʿ*; Latin *contagio;* Greek *epaphe*) suggests that this idiom reflects a vague awareness of the contagiousness of disease, regardless of the precise mechanisms of transmission, which were not known. The British medical historian, Vivian Nutton, comments regarding the Greek and Latin evidence:

> In all this it is perhaps foolish to seek to distinguish between degrees of propriety in the application of a metaphor, or to differentiate medical from non-medical. Many of those who talked of the contagion of illness or of heresy would not have been able to explain in what way they thought that the "common touch" worked, and few, if any, would have restricted the touch to the mere physical person-to-person transmission of a noxious substance. What mattered was the consequence, the "sharing" of the disease, rather than the action of touching itself.[25]

[23] For numerous Mesopotamian examples, see Scurlock and Andersen, *Diagnoses*, 429–528. Note also Laws of Hammurabi §249, which refers to an ox that a god has stricken down. For the Hebrew Bible, see Ex 9:3; 1 Samuel 5:6, 9; 2 Sam 24:14–15. For the idiom *yd ʾilm* in Ugarit, see, e.g., *CAT* 2.10 11–13.

[24] E.g., 2 Sam 12:15; 2 Chronicles 21:18. Compare Akkadian *nakāpu* "to butt; to gore, to abut" (*CAD* N/1 156–158).

[25] Nutton, "Did the Greeks," 154.

Granting the fact that the mechanisms for the cause and transfer of disease remained mysterious, how can we explain this ambiguity between the "touch" of gods (divine punishment) and interpersonal contagion, caused by physical interpersonal touching?

It seems that the choice of this idiom cross-linguistically reflects the fundamental perception of an external catalyst responsible for the cause and spread of disease. Here a useful analogy is the English term "infection," which can be used to describe the multiplication of bacteria within a person (e.g., "his wound got infected") and the interpersonal spread of disease (what we call "infectious disease"). The ambiguity of "infection" is not accidental. It reflects the practical difficulty of determining whether the cause is internal or external and is rooted in the Latin etymology of the term *inficere,* which refers to the dyeing of fabrics, that is, the *spread* of the dye's influence.[26] Accordingly, "infection" can refer to the spreading of diseases within the body as well as between bodies. Similarly, alongside the use of the language of contagion (*contagio*) in late antiquity as reference to interpersonal transmission,[27] one finds this terminology used throughout the Middle Ages to describe infection, corruption and putrefaction that spread *within* the body.[28]

These considerations help explain the ambiguity of "touch": a disease may start with a person being struck by a deity, but once one person contracts the disease, it can spread from that person to others. The "touch," whether a god's or a person's, is the catalyst. This understanding finds striking confirmation in the letter from Mari (ARM 26/1 17) which opened this study.[29] At the beginning of that passage, the author observes

---

[26] The same image governs the Greek term for pollution, *miasma*. See Owsei Temkin, "An Historical Analysis of the Concept of Infection," in *The Double Face of Janus and Other Essays in the History of Medicine* (Baltimore, MD: Johns Hopkins, 1977 [1953]), 157, 161; Mirko D. Grmek, "Les vicissitudes des notions d'infection, de contagion, et de germe dans la médicine antique," *Textes médicaux latins antiques (Mémoires 5)*, ed. G. Sabbah (St. Etienne: Centre Jean Palerne, 1984), 53–66; Danielle Gourévitch, "Peut-on employer le mot d'*infection* dans les traductions françaises de textes latins?," *Mémoires du Centre Jean Palerne* 5 (1984): 49–52.

[27] Jarcho, *Concept of Contagion*, 12–13.

[28] See François-Olivier Touati, "Contagion and Leprosy: Myth, Ideas and Evolution in Medieval Minds and Societies," in *Contagion: Perspectives from Pre-Modern Societies*, eds. L. I. Conrad and D. Wujastyk (Aldershot: Ashgate, 2000), 188, citing Gregory of Tours (sixth century) and Giles of Corbeil (late twelfth century).

[29] For this text, see also Walther Farber, "How to Marry a Disease: Epidemics, Contagion, and a Magic Ritual against the 'Hand of a Ghost,'" in *Magic and Rationality in Ancient Near Eastern and Greco-Roman Medicine*, eds. H. F. J. Horstmanshoff and M. Stol (Leiden: Brill, 2004), 119–120.

that "the god is striking/touching (*ulappat*) in the upper district," depicting a god as the agent. Yet, several lines later, the writer demands that the king issue a decree that the "residents of the cities that have been touched not enter cities that are not touched, lest they touch (*ulappatū*) the whole land." Here the residents of the infected city are the subject of this verb, posing the threat of spreading the plague to the entire land.

Returning to the biblical evidence, it is significant that the key diagnostic characteristic of a *negga'* is its spreading, as expressed by the verb *paśah*. This latter term appears twenty-two times in Lev 13–14 and nowhere else in the Bible, for example (Lev 13:5–8):

[5]On the seventh day the priest shall examine him, and if the affliction has remained unchanged in color and the disease has not spread (*paśah*) on the skin, the priest shall isolate him for another seven days. [6] On the seventh day the priest shall examine him again: if the affliction has faded and has not spread (*paśah*) on the skin, the priest shall pronounce him pure. It is a rash; he shall wash his clothes, and he shall be pure. [7] But if the rash should spread (*paśah*) on the skin after he has presented himself to the priest and been pronounced pure, he shall present himself again to the priest. [8] And if the priest sees that the rash has spread on the skin, the priest shall pronounce him impure; it is *ṣara'at*.

The presence or absence of spreading is what determines whether or not the condition is diagnosed as "impure." Once the diagnostic importance of spreading is taken into consideration, it becomes less strange that *negga'* is applied to a type of mold or fungus that spreads on the walls of a house (Lev 14:33–53) alongside its use in reference to a disease affecting humans.

These observations can explain the repeated close association of *negga'* with *ṣara'at,* the former appearing over sixty times in Lev 13–14, including the compound expression *negga' ṣara'at* (11 x). This disease, more than any other, was treated as contagious, as suggested by both biblical and Second Temple Period writings.[30] Before examining this evidence, however, it will be helpful to take a closer look at *ṣara'at* and the attempts to identify the condition in modern medical terminology. As will be seen, our inability to pin a modern diagnosis onto the biblical ailment often plays into arguments to downgrade *ṣara'at* to a mere "ritual" concern.

---

[30] Temple Scroll 48:14–17; Josephus, *Against Apion* I 281 (ed. Thackeray, 276–277). For evidence of exclusion in the New Testament, see Thomas Kazen, *Jesus and Purity Halakhah* (Stockholm: Almqvist & Wiksell, 2002), 116–118. Note also that the Aramaic rendering of *ṣara'at* in the Targumim is *segurata*, clearly suggesting seclusion (from s-g-r).

THE CASE OF *ṢARAʿAT*: REAL OR RITUAL?

So far, this chapter has examined the fluidity of the ancient terminology used to describe the general phenomenon of infection and in reference to specific diseases, particularly the case of biblical *ṣaraʿat*. This fluidity, compared with the more rigorous and systematic use of terms in modern medicine, has been used to substantiate claims that *ṣaraʿat* was only a ritual concern, bearing important ramifications for understanding to what extent "pollution" (*ṭumʾah*) had consequences outside the sacred domain. Indeed, some modern scholars have taken this as a point of departure to assert a strict distinction between the problems of "ritual impurity" and disease. As such, it is worthwhile to examine more closely the role of purity terminology, especially as it pertains to this disease.

Aside from the detailed procedures for the diagnosis and purification of *ṣaraʿat* recorded in Lev 13–14, the treatment of pollution in general and *ṣaraʿat* in particular scattered throughout the HB provide important glimpses of attitudes that are sometimes at odds with P.[31] As mentioned, whereas P (more precisely: H) seems to limit the ramifications of impurity to the sacred domain (Lev 15:31; Num 5:1–4; Num 19:13, 20), a few non-P sources suggest that the relationship between disease and pollution was related to infection, not sanctity. More pertinent to the case of *ṣaraʿat*, 2 Kings 7 relates a story of four "lepers" (*meṣoraʿim*) that were banished from the city:

> [3]There were four men, lepers, outside the gate. They said to one another, "Why should we sit here waiting for death? [4]If we decide to go into the town, what with the famine in the town, we shall die there; and if we just sit here, still we die. Come, let us desert to the Aramean camp. If they let us live, we shall live; and if they put us to death, we shall but die."

This banishment, carrying the threat of starvation, has no discernable connection to sanctity. Rather, it seems motivated by the danger posed by the "lepers" to the society at large.[32] As a further example, David's curse of Joab in 2 Samuel 3:28–29 treats abnormal genital flows (*zab*) and skin disease (*ṣaraʾat*) as divine punishments resulting in ostracism.

---

[31] For many of these sources, see the summary in Thomas Kazen, "Purity and Persia," in *Current Issues in Priestly and Related Literature: The Legacy of Jacob Milgrom and Beyond*, eds. R. E. Gane and A. Taggar-Cohen (Atlanta, GA: SBL, 2015), 435–462.

[32] See also Numbers 12:10; 2 Kgs 15:5; 2 Chr 26:21; see Jacob Milgrom, *Leviticus*, AB; 3 vols. (New York, NY: Doubleday, 1991), 1:805–808.

While not explicitly mentioning contagion, even the laws of ṣara'at in P suggest that the ostracism was not motivated only by cultic concerns: "As for the person with a leprous affliction, his clothes shall be rent, his head shall be left bare, and he shall cover over his upper lip; and he shall call out, 'Impure! Impure!' He shall be impure as long as the disease is on him. Being impure, he shall dwell apart; his dwelling shall be outside the camp" (Lev 13:45–46). Despite the fact that the text makes no allusion to the possibility of infection, the requirement that the leper warn others of his condition and his isolation from the camp suggest a fear of contagion. Moreover, the requirement to cover the mustache (or upper lip) of the leper has been explained as reflecting the fear that he would spread his condition through his breath.[33] This interpretation finds support among interpreters of the Second Temple Period who warned against being downwind of the leper, which correlates suggestively with the fact that actual leprosy (Hansen's disease) is contracted via the respiratory system.[34] Even without equating the biblical disease with leprosy, this point shows that transmission via breath was a justifiable concern.

Moreover, the purifying leper was to perform an elimination rite in which the pollution was transferred to a bird and sent off into the open country. Although this rite took place after he had already healed (Lev 14:3), it is highly reminiscent of scapegoat rites carried out in cases of plague.[35] Finally, even after the first stage of purification had been performed and the purifying leper was permitted to reenter the camp, he was still required to dwell outside his tent (14:8). This latter requirement was understood by its early interpreters in the Second Temple Period as implying that he defiled all that was inside an enclosure with him.[36]

---

[33] Ibn Ezra on v. 45; see Milgrom, *Leviticus*, 1.805–806. In fact, the Temple Scroll (46:16–18) and the Rabbis (*Leviticus Rabbah* 16:3) show unease about being downwind from the "leper." See also Yitzhaq Feder, "The Polemic Regarding Skin Disease in 4QMMT," *DSD* 19.1 (2012): 69. Admittedly, in Ezekiel 24:17, 22, covering the upper lip is associated with mourning. However, it is possible that this mourning practice originated from a concern with exposure to the spirit of the dead (see Chapter 8).

[34] The validity of this point depends on the assumption that ṣara'at (in biblical and later usage) included Hansen's disease among other conditions. For discussion, see Feder, "Polemic Regarding Skin Disease," 68–70.

[35] See Kjell Aartun, "Studien zum Gesetz über den grossen Versöhnungstag Lv 16 mit Varianten. Ein ritualgeschichtlicher Beitrag," *Studia Theologica* 34 (1980), 84–86; David P. Wright, *The Disposal of Impurity: Elimination Rites in the Bible and in Hittite and Mesopotamian Literature* (Atlanta, GA: Scholars Press, 1987), 45–57; 65–69.

[36] See Milgrom, *Leviticus*, 1.843; H. Maccoby, *Ritual and Morality: The Ritual Purity System and Its Place in Ancient Judaism* (Cambridge: Cambridge University Press, 1999), 141–148; Feder, "Polemic Regarding Skin Disease," 60, 63.

Yet, the use of the terminology of pure and impure in relation to the leper has been taken by some prominent scholars as grounds for stressing the exclusively religious (or symbolic) significance of purity.[37] For example, Jacob Milgrom writes: "In chaps. 13–14, the verbal statistics underscore this point: *ṭāhēr* 'be pure' occurs thirty-six times; *ṭāmēʾ* 'be impure' thirty times and *nirpāʾ* 'be healed' only four times. Nothing could be clearer: we are dealing with ritual, not medicine."[38] Even the illustrious scholar of ancient medicine, Grmek, ties himself into knots in his attempt to apply the ritual/medical distinction to the biblical evidence:

> To a mind not biased in favor of a purely medical interpretation for any ancient account of a pathological state, one thing is clear: *Ẓaráʿat*, the mark of divine wrath, is not a medical notion but a ritual one. It can be and is applied in the Bible not only to a person but also to clothing or a house . . . To be sure, Leviticus is not a medical handbook; the expulsion of "impure" persons is a matter of tabus, not infections in the medical sense.[39]

However, he immediately erases this distinction in the following sentence: "Still, medicine itself existed only in the shadow of ritual and without distinction from it. It is hard to believe that such a radical social rejection of a person infected with a certain disease is simply the result of mistaken religious ideas about completely benign symptoms."[40]

A similar forced distinction between ritual and medicine has been expressed regarding the pathological genital flows described in Lev 15. For example, Dorothea Erbele-Küster has observed that the use of a common term (*zob*; "flow") for both male and female discharges "makes clear that the Hebrew text operates with physiological categories that are incompatible with modern medical concepts."[41] While this statement is true, it implies an expectation that the biblical symptomology

---

[37] Milgrom, *Leviticus*, 1.816–820; Henning G. Reventlow, "Krankheit – ein Makel an heiliger Vollkommenheit. Das Urteil altisraelitischer Priester in Leviticus 13 in seinem Kontext," in *Studies on Ritual and Society in the Ancient Near East: Tartuer Symposien 1998–2004*, ed. T. R. Kämmerer (Berlin: de Gruyter, 2007), 282–290. Even Scurlock and Andersen, in their compendium of Assyrian diagnostic texts, attempt to distinguish the biblical disease from its Mesopotamian counterparts on the following basis: "The point is that *ṣaraʾat* is not a cognate of *saḫaršubbû*, *epqu*, or *garābu*, and that *ṣaraʾat* is inextricably linked with concepts of cultic purity and impurity that most scholars would à priori assume to be peculiar to ancient Israel" (*Diagnoses*, 724, n. 139).
[38] *Leviticus*, 1.817.   [39] *Diseases*, 160–161.   [40] Ibid., 161.
[41] *Body, Gender and Purity in Leviticus 12 and 15* (London: T&T Clark, 2017), 62. Later in the book, she argues for the literary rather than practical nature of these regulations, describing Leviticus's "utopian, eschatological character" as a reading space (160).

would somehow prognosticate modern medicine. Despite the vagueness of the biblical text, there is nothing contrary to medical reality about the fact that male and female discharges can be described by a common term, "flow," all the more so since a single disease (e.g., gonorrhea) can be characterized by discharges of pus for males and discharges of blood for females. Indeed, in addressing the question "I was treated for gonorrhea. When can I have sex again?", the gonorrhea fact sheet of the United States' Centers for Disease Control and Prevention (CDC) advises someone cured of gonorrhea to "wait seven days after finishing all medications before having sex."[42] Apparently, the seven-day waiting period for purification prescribed by Lev 15 (vv. 13–15, 29–30) is not so detached from medical reality.

Admittedly there is a polemical aspect of the Priestly source's treatment of pollution and disease, and this topic will be addressed in detail in the chapters that follow. Still, the use of purity terminology in this context is not distinctive. For example, Mesopotamian texts that deal with *saḫaršubbû* also employ the terminology of purity and impurity (usually *ebēbu*) to designate the healing or incurability of the disease. Note the following curse, similar to the one cited above:[43] "May Sîn cover his entire body with incurable *saḫaršubbû* so that he will not be pure/healed (*ay ibbib*) until the end of his days!"[44] Within the HB, it is worth stressing that even Naaman, the Aramean general stricken with leprosy, seeks a cure for the disease using the terminology of purification (2 Kgs 5:12): "Are not the Amanah and the Pharpar, the rivers of Damascus, better than all the waters of Israel? I could bathe in them and be clean (*wᵉ-ṭaharti*)!" This statement, attributed to the "pagan" general, can hardly be expressing a uniquely Israelite conception of disease.

This recognition invites us to reexamine the use of purity language in relation to disease in Lev 13–15. Focusing on the biblical evidence, the roots *ṭ-h-r* and *ṭ-m-'* have several instances which would correspond to a medical diagnosis, specifically whether the patient is "pure" (= healed) or "impure" (= bears the disease in question). For example, Lev 13 requires the priest to determine, expressed in the *piel* forms of these

---

[42] "Gonorrhea: CDC Fact Sheet" (CDC, 2014). www.cdc.gov/std/gonorrhea/stdfact-gonorrhea.htm (accessed 2/16/2020). There is no reason to suspect that this government organization, whose mission statement includes "putting science and advanced technology into action to prevent disease," is basing its directives on Leviticus.

[43] See n. 9 above.

[44] See *CAD* E 4. For a more comprehensive treatment of relevant Akkadian and Hittite evidence, see Feder, "Defilement, Disgust and Disease."

roots, whether the person is diagnosed with *ṣaraʿat* (e.g., vv. 3, 6, 8, 11 passim). Verse 8 epitomizes this usage: "And if the priest sees that the rash has spread on the skin, the priest shall pronounce him impure (*va-ṭimm'o ha-kohen*); it is *ṣaraʿat*." The implications of the priestly diagnosis of whether the symptoms constituted actual *ṣaraʿat* were far-reaching, determining whether or not the patient needed to be quarantined from the community. Hence the determination that the patient was "impure" was imminently real, just as the equivalent determination in the Middle Ages that a person bore the "disease known by the name of *lepra*" or, for that matter, in the twenty-first century, that a person bears COVID-19.[45]

Another distinct but related usage pertains to the use of the term "pure" to designate that a person has healed from either skin disease or abnormal genital discharges. For example, the rules for the man with a discharge in Lev 15 read as follows (13): "When one with a discharge is healed (*yiṭhar*) of his discharge, he shall count off seven days for his purification, wash his clothes, and bathe his body in fresh water; then he shall be pure (*ve-ṭaher*)." This verse employs the root *ṭ-h-r* in two distinct senses. The first designates the cessation of flow, enabling him to begin the seven-day process of purification; the second appears at the end of this verse and designates the purification or cleansing. The first refers to the physiological situation which enables the purification to take place. The second refers to the state of purity that results from the completion of the purification rites. As can be seen, the usage of purity terminology is not confined to ritual concerns.

Despite the explicit association of pollution with infectious disease, biblical scholars have tended to overlook this important aspect in favor of viewing it in theological terms. Here they are accurately following the emphasis in the Priestly source itself, which foregrounds the concern with defiling the wilderness sanctuary (Lev 15:31; Num 5:3; Num 19:13, 20) at the expense of any attention to the danger of infection posed to society. Nevertheless, in reconstructing the origins of this discourse, it needs to be recognized that the association of pollution with the contagiousness of disease is the rule rather than the exception as far as cross-cultural evidence is concerned. For example, in his ethnographic work on the East African Kikuyu tribes, Louis Leakey points out that smallpox was understood to leave *mūrimu*-pollution and writes regarding purification of a patient from this disease:

---

[45] For a document of such a determination regarding *lepra* from October 9, 1411, see Demaitre, *Leprosy*, 75.

Even after this, for the duration of one moon he had to keep to himself, sleep by himself, and eat by himself, after which he might resume normal life. Although the purification for a *mūrimu* was thus a ceremonial one from the Kikuyu point of view, it provided a reasonably good way of disinfecting and isolating a person who had a serious disease, until his freedom from it was certain.[46]

Rahul Peter Das draws a similar conclusion from classical Indian texts, namely that for the avoidance of disease "the so-called 'ritual purity', so often mentioned in connection with India, makes eminent sense, though clearly the adjective 'ritual' is, in the light of what we have seen so far, quite out of place here."[47]

More recently, the medical anthropologist Edward Green has stated categorically in his monograph *Indigenous Theories of Contagious Disease*:

Pollution . . . is not so mystical when examined closely. In the anthropological sense, pollution denotes a belief that people will become ill as a result of contact with, or contamination by, a substance or essence considered dangerous because it is unclean or impure . . . They involve an impersonal process of illness through contact or exposure. Polluted individuals are not singled out for illness or misfortune by a human or superhuman force; they typically become polluted from mere contact, from being in the wrong place at the wrong time.[48]

For this reason, Green argues that the belief in pollution as a medium for disease transmission is largely compatible with Western germ theory, noting: "Illnesses believed caused by pollution seem to be those biomedically classified as infectious and contagious."[49] Significantly, he points out that a certain class of diseases is the most likely to elicit the explanation of pollution, namely "illnesses whose cause-and-effect relationship between exposure or contact and illness is most apparent (e.g., syphilis, measles, leprosy, and cholera)."[50] In light of this observation, it seems hardly coincidental that the most severe sources of *ṭum'ah* in P include sexually transmitted diseases (Lev 15) and skin disease (Lev 13–14).

CONCLUSION

As part of the broader challenge this book attempts to meet, that of grappling with the difficulty of mediating between ancient and modern

---

[46] *The Southern Kikuyu Before 1903*, vol. 3 (London: Academic Press, 1977), 1265.

[47] "Notions of 'Contagion' in Classical Indian Medical Texts," in *Contagion: Perspectives from Pre-Modern Societies*, eds. L. I. Conrad and D. Wujastyk (Aldershot: Ashgate, 2000), 76.

[48] *Indigenous Theories of Contagious Disease* (Walnut Creek, CA: AltaMira, 1999), 13–14.

[49] Ibid., 57.   [50] Ibid., 248–249.

conceptions of contagion, this chapter has examined the concept of "contagion" itself and its expression in relation to the biblical disease *ṣaraʿat*. It was seen that the idiom of "touch" was widespread throughout the ancient world to express the awareness of interpersonal transmission, though it was used without scientific rigor. The fluidity of terminology relating to *ṣaraʿat* (including its Greek translation *lepra*) and disease in general has misled scholars into imposing an anachronistic distinction between ritual and medical prescriptions, leading them to underestimate the role of pollution as a theory of infection. In short, as demonstrated by cross-cultural parallels, ancient and modern, the fact that these texts appear remote from *our* understanding of medical reality does not warrant the conclusion that pollution was remote from *their* medical reality.

Despite explicit emphasis on the sanctuary in the Priestly texts, one only needs to scratch their surface to reveal that the explicit rhetoric conceals a more down-to-earth role for purity in ancient Israel, related to the control and treatment of contagious disease. What remains to be examined in probing the relationship between disease and pollution is why this connection is obscured in the Priestly source in its near-exclusive focus on the cultic implications of impurity. This puzzle will be addressed in the following chapters.

4

The Missing Ritual for Healing Skin Disease

As was seen in the previous chapters, the recognition that the concept of pollution (*ṭum'ah*) provided an account for the infectiousness of disease may resolve some problems in interpreting biblical texts related to this topic, but it also exposes new riddles, especially the seeming reluctance to openly address the infectiousness of disease. The purpose of this chapter and the ones that follow is to demonstrate that this silence is not accidental and to explore the far-reaching implications of this recognition for understanding the implicit worldview of the Priestly source.

The treatment of disease in the Priestly writings presents a formidable puzzle. In particular, the relationship between disease, pollution and sin raises several questions. Regarding the effects of disease, why are skin diseases (Lev 13–14) and genital disorders (15:2–15, 25–30) treated as sources of pollution, with next to no mention of illness or healing? Regarding the cause of disease, does the absence of explicit statements relating disease to sin like those found elsewhere in the HB presuppose that this relationship is taken for granted or that it is rejected? Were defilement and disease understood as being synonymous or was defilement a secondary effect of disease?

None of these questions has a simple answer that can be found in explicit statements in Priestly texts. One reason is that the issue of disease as a problem unto itself is not dealt with directly in these chapters, and is always subordinated to the concern for the divine presence in the camp. This silence is particularly striking in light of the abundance of ancient Near Eastern rituals and diagnostic texts which openly address bodily disorders and their treatment. However, to judge from ancient and modern interpreters of the biblical texts who take P's focus on purification

76

(not healing) for granted,[1] it appears that the Priestly authors have succeeded at disguising the elephant (and the *elephantiasis*) in the room.

The previous chapter mentioned the Mesopotamian disease called *saḫaršubbû*, which bears numerous points of similarity to biblical *ṣaraʿat*. While this comparison has been widely recognized, there is an important text pertaining to *saḫaršubbû* whose significance for biblical studies has not been fully appreciated. This ritual for treating *saḫaršubbû*, the only one of its kind discovered to date, has profound implications for understanding the tacit ideology of the Priestly texts.

THE EMAR RITUAL FOR TREATING *SAḪARŠUBBÛ*

In 1999, Akio Tsukimoto published a medical text apparently composed in Emar (located on the bend of the Euphrates River in Syria) in the thirteenth century BCE.[2] Lines 37–84 of this tablet contain a ritual for the treatment of *saḫaršubbû*, also designated *epqannu* in the text.[3] This section contains an incantation (ll. 37–42), a treatment (43–84) and a rite following recovery (85–93). The medical treatment section distinguishes between different types of the disease and offers specific instructions for treating each one. Interestingly, like Leviticus 13, lines 50–84 of this text focus on skin discolorations (white, yellow, red, black and different combinations), and the appropriate treatment is determined accordingly. For example, the text states that if "the *saḫaršubbû* is yellow and red, it is

---

[1] The Rabbis codified the purity laws as focusing almost exclusively on contact with the sacred realm (e.g., m. Kelim 1:7–10), following the implications of sources like Leviticus 15:31 and Numbers 5:1–4. Likewise, modern scholars employing a synchronic approach have been led to a similar understanding of disease as impurity, e.g., David P. Wright's categorization of "tolerated impurities": "The Spectrum of Priestly Impurity," in *Priesthood and Cult in Ancient Israel*, JSOTSup, 125, eds. G. A. Anderson and Saul M. Olyan (Sheffield: JSOT Press, 1991), 152–158; likewise Jonathan Klawans, *Impurity and Sin in Ancient Judaism* (New York, NY: Oxford University, 2000), 21–25, employing the designation "ritual impurity." For the distinction between "ritual" and "moral" impurities, see Chapter 9.

[2] "'By the Hand of Madi-Dagan, the Scribe and *Apkallu*-Priest' – A Medical Text from the Middle Euphrates Region," in *Priests and Officials in the Ancient Near East*, ed. K. Watanabe (Heidelberg: Winter, 1999), 187–200. The question regarding its provenance derives from the fact that it belonged to a private collector. Nevertheless, its provenance appears fairly certain based on external characteristics. For discussion, see Yoram Cohen, *The Scribes and Scholars of the City of Emar in the Late Bronze Age* (Winona Lake, IN: Eisenbrauns, 2009), 217–219, 232.

[3] For this later term, see JoAnn Scurlock and Burton R. Andersen, *Diagnoses in Assyrian and Babylonian Medicine* (Urbana and Chicago, IL: Indiana University Press, 2005), 232.

the hand of Sîn. To remove it, you should anoin[t him] with human semen for seven days [and he will recover]" (60).

Most striking, however, is the section dealing with the recovery of the patient. The bandages used in healing the patient are to be removed and thrown in a fire. An incense altar and table with offerings are presented to the sun god, Šamaš. Then the following rite takes place (ll. 87–89):

ˡᵘGIG BI *ana* IGI ᵈUTU ʿi ʾ-*za-az* 1 MUŠEN *ḫur-ri u al-lu-ut-ta ana* IGI ᵈUTU *ta-qa -al-lu iš-tu* MUŠEN *ḫur-ri ra-ma-an-šu tu-kap-pár-ma ú-maš-šar*

This patient stands before Šamaš. You shall burn one partridge and a crab before Šamaš, [and] with [another] partridge you shall wipe his body and he will let [it] go.[4]

This Emar rite is highly reminiscent of the bird rite in Leviticus 14 (vv. 1–9):

¹Yhwh spoke to Moses, saying: ²This shall be the ritual of the leper at the time of his purification. When it is reported to the priest, ³the priest shall go outside the camp. The priest shall make an examination, and if the disease has abated from the patient, ⁴the priest shall order that two pure live birds, a cedar wood, crimson (yarn) and hyssop be brought to the person being purified. ⁵The priest shall order one bird to be slaughtered into an earthenware vessel over spring water. ⁶He shall take the live bird, the cedar wood, the crimson yarn and the hyssop, and he shall dip them and the live bird in the blood of the bird that had been slaughtered over spring water. ⁷He shall sprinkle seven times onto the one being purified from "leprosy," thus purifying him, and he shall release the live bird in the open country. ⁸The one being purified shall launder his clothes, shave off all of his hair and bathe in water, thus becoming pure. Then he may enter the camp, but he must dwell outside his tent for seven days. ⁹On the seventh day, he shall shave off all of his hair – of his head, chin and eye-brows – indeed, he shall shave off all of his hair. He will launder his clothes and wash his body in water; then he shall be pure.

In both of these texts, we find the use of two birds, one of which is killed while the other is used to carry the pollution away from the community. More precisely, the rubbing of the partridge on the body of the patient in the Emar ritual finds its functional equivalent in the sprinkling of blood on the patient in the biblical ritual, serving to transfer the impurity from the

---

[4] For further discussion of this translation, which differs markedly from Tsukimoto's edition, see Yitzhaq Feder, "Behind the Scenes of a Priestly Polemic: Leviticus 14 and Its Extra-Biblical Parallels," *JHS* 15.4 (2015): 1–26, https://doi.org/10.5508/jhs.2015.v15.a4 (6–8). Two other recent translations of the text offer similar renderings. See Daniel Schwemer, "Akkadische Texte des 2. und 1. Jt. V. Chr. 2: Therapeutische Texte," *TUAT* 5: 41–45 (2.2.2); JoAnn Scurlock, "'Supernatural' Causes: The Moon God Sîn (4.88G): Leprosy," *CoS* 4: 291–293. Schwemer recommends emending the second-to-last verb so that the patient is the subject of both actions: "Mit einem (anderen) ›Höhlen-Vogel‹ wischt er sich selbst ab und lässt (ihn) frei" (45).

patient to the released bird, which had been previously dipped in the blood. Since these rituals pertain to the same type of disease, these similarities are quite significant.[5]

Having demonstrated the close similarity in subject matter and content relating the Emar ritual and Lev 13–14, a comparison of the overall structure of these texts leads to the most important point (see Table 4.1).

The elaborate diagnostic procedures outlined in Leviticus 13 parallels the detailed symptomology of *saḫaršubbû* recorded in ll. 50–84 of the Emar tablet, with the primary diagnostic criteria in both texts being

TABLE 4.1 *Treatment of Mesopotamian and biblical skin diseases: Structural parallels*

	Saḫaršubbû	Sara'at
Diagnostic procedures	"If a person has *saḫaršubbû* and there is white color on his body . . . " (53) "Likewise if the *saḫaršubbû* is yellow and red . . . " (55) (Emar tablet, ll. 50–84)	"And the priest shall see, and look, there is a white lesion in the skin, and it has turned the hair white . . . " (10) "And if the flesh on his skin has a burn by fire and the healthy part of the burn on his skin becomes bright, shiny reddish-white or white . . ." (25) (Lev 13:1–59)
Treatment of illness	" . . . you should take *ašāgu* plant, salt, barley, flour . . . and anoint him and he will get well" (53–54) " . . . with human semen you should anoin[t him] for seven days" (60) (Emar tablet, ll. 50–84)	

(continued)

[5] Nevertheless, one should not ignore the differences between the two rituals, particularly the use of blood in Leviticus 14, which seems to reflect a separate tradition related to the sin offering, as is apparent from the analogous goat rite in Leviticus 16. For a related Hurro-Hittite ritual of Syrian origin involving a blood rite, see Yitzhaq Feder, *Blood Expiation in Hittite and Biblical Ritual* (Atlanta, GA: SBL, 2011), 125–134. Incidentally, there is no indication that the bird slaughtered in Leviticus 14:5 is considered an offering, contra Rudiger Schmitt, *Magie im Alten Testament*, AOAT, 313 (Münster: Ugarit Verlag, 2004), 31.

TABLE 4.1 *(continued)*

	Saharšubbû	Saraʿat
Ritual after recovery	"You shall burn one partridge and a crab before Šamaš, [and] with (another) partridge you shall wipe his body and he will let (it) go." (87–89) (Emar tablet, ll. 85–89)	"⁵The priest shall order one bird to be slaughtered into an earthenware vessel over spring water. ⁶He shall take the live bird, the cedar wood, the crimson yarn and the hyssop, and he shall dip them and the live bird in the blood of the bird that had been slaughtered over spring water. ⁷He shall sprinkle seven times onto the one being purified from 'leprosy,' thus purifying him, and he shall release the live bird in the open country." (Lev 14:4–7)

skin discolorations. In turn, Leviticus 14 parallels the section in ll. 85–89 dealing with the leper "after he recovers" (*kîmê iblut* [TI-*ut*]). From this comparison, it becomes clear that the main difference between the two texts is the striking absence of any treatment for the leper in the biblical text. The comprehensive similarity between the two texts makes the absence of a corresponding healing rite in Leviticus 14 highly significant. Hence, it is difficult to avoid the conclusion that similar healing rites were known to the Israelite priesthood but that they were deliberately omitted.[6] As a result, this comparison brings into sharp relief the fact that the rites preserved in Leviticus 13–14 have been carefully selected from a larger body of ritual traditions to which the priests and the Israelite population in general were privy. In the following sections, we will examine additional Mesopotamian parallels to Leviticus 13–14, which will strengthen the impression

---

[6] Though some scholars might question how this thirteenth-century tradition could have found its way into the much later Priestly writings, it is now well established that Late Bronze Age Syria was a melting pot of ritual traditions of varied origins, many of which are recognizably preserved in P. For further examples, references and discussion, see Feder, *Blood Expiation*, 123–125, 243–252. The Emar tablet is itself representative of this cross-cultural ritual koiné, with links to Mesopotamian, Hittite and Ugaritic traditions. See Tsukimoto, "By the Hand," 189; Irving L. Finkel, "Magic and Medicine at Meskene," *NABU* (1999), 28–30; Cohen, *Scribes and Scholars*, 217–219.

that the Priestly authors deliberately transformed and censored the ritual traditions that they appropriated.

NEVER MIND THE FUNGUS ON THE WALL

The rules for *ṣara'at* in houses (Lev 14:33–53) provide an additional opportunity to compare the Priestly view with extra-biblical parallels. Several ancient Near Eastern rituals for the purification of houses have been identified and discussed in modern scholarship. Of particular interest are the Mesopotamian namburbi rituals which seek to counteract the threats portended by ominous signs in a house.[7] Though these traditions seem to have originated in an earlier period, the vast majority of the existing documents were composed in Babylonia and Assyria during the first millennium BCE.[8] A Hurro-Hittite ritual for the purification of a house also seems to originate from this body of tradition, with ominous signs being taken as indications that impurity, bloodshed, curses, witchcraft and other evil forces have "infected" the house.[9]

Of these purification rituals, the most similar to Leviticus 14:33–53 is the namburbi ritual dealing with *katarru* fungus. Like Lev 14, the treatment of *katarru* focuses on discoloration in the walls of the house, requiring removal and purification. The potential danger portended by this fungus is outlined in the twelfth tablet of the omen series *Šumma ālu*, which is devoted to different manifestations.[10] Aside from the case of a black fungus, which is viewed as a sign of success, other possible colors, including white, red and green, portend calamity. Similarly, Lev 14:37 specifies that *ṣara'at* expressed in red or green discoloration requires purification.

Measures to thwart the danger of *katarru* fungus are provided in a specific namburbi ritual.[11] The danger posed to a particular family member is determined by the precise location of the fungus in the house. For example, it specifies: "[If] there is fungus on a man's house on the outer northern side, the owner of the house will die and his [house] will be

---

[7] See Stefan M. Maul, *Zukunftsbewältigung*, BF, 18 (Mainz: Zabern, 1994), 97–101.

[8] Ibid., 159.

[9] CTH 446; edition: Heinrich Otten, "Eine Beschwörung der Unterirdischen aus Boğazköy," *ZA* 54 (1961): 116–117, 142–143; English translation: Billie Jean Collins, "Purifying a House: A Ritual for the Infernal Deities," *CoS* 1:168.

[10] See Samuel Meier, "House Fungus: Mesopotamia and Israel (Lev 14: 33–53)," *Revue Biblique* 96 (1989), 187; Maul, *Zukunftsbewältigung*, 174.

[11] See Maul, *Zukunftsbewältigung*, 354–366.

scattered."[12] If it is on the east, the victim will be his wife, and so on. In order to counteract this threat, the namburbi ritual requires that the priest observe the fungus, scrape it off with a special tool and dispose of it. Without engaging in a detailed comparison,[13] it is clear that the biblical rite follows the same basic contours, involving diagnosis of the fungus and removal of the contaminated stones. However, the biblical text also includes a purification rite involving two birds, which is clearly based on the analogy of ṣara'at for a human being (vv. 4–7 // 49–53).

There are clear indications that the pericope on house purification is a later addition to Leviticus 13–14.[14] Whether it is assumed to have been composed in the exilic or post-exilic period, the late provenance of Leviticus 14:33–53 strengthens the assumption of Babylonian influence, which is independently supported by the similarities to the namburbi rituals for *katarru* fungus. While the exact provenance of this tradition is not crucial to the present discussion, the fact that such a tradition was secondarily incorporated into Leviticus 14 illustrates the modularity of ritual traditions. That is to say, ritual traditions were exchanged throughout the ancient Near East and adapted by local practitioners to their needs. Even more importantly, once one acknowledges that the biblical and extra-biblical texts draw on a common body of tradition, several of the differences between them become highly significant. The first major distinction between Leviticus 14:33–53 and its Babylonian parallels is that the biblical text shows no indication that ṣara'at is dangerous. As far as can be seen, it is a case of pollution, but nothing more.

[12] Maul, *Zukunftsbewältigung*, 358, l. 28. English translation: Richard Caplice, "Namburbi Texts in the British Museum," *OrNS* 40 (1971): 144, l. 23; Richard Caplice, *The Akkadian Namburbi Texts: An Introduction*, SANE 1/1 (Los Angeles, CA: Undena, 1974), 18.

[13] See Meier, "House Fungus."

[14] The secondary nature of this section is demonstrated clearly by the chapter's colophon in vv. 54–57. As noted by Michael Fishbane and others, v. 55, which deals with ṣara'at of clothing and houses, is an obvious interruption between vv. 54 and 56, which follow the order of ṣara'at in humans as outlined in 13:1–46. From this interpolation to the colophon, one can identify the section on clothes (13:47–58) and houses (14:33–53) as later additions ("Biblical Colophons, Textual Criticism, and Legal Analogies," *Catholic Biblical Quarterly* 42.4 [1980], 440–442). For further arguments, see also M. Noth, *Leviticus. A Commentary*, OTL, trans. J. E. Anderson (London: SCM Press, 1965), 104; Karl Elliger, *Leviticus*, HAT (Tübingen: Mohr, 1966), 177; also Jacob Milgrom, *Leviticus*, AB 3 vols. (New York, NY: Doubleday, 1991–2000), 1:886–887, who notes stylistic affinities to H. For a comprehensive discussion of the composition of these chapters, see Christophe Nihan, *From Priestly Torah to Pentateuch*, FAT 2/25 (Tübingen: Mohr Siebeck, 2007), 271–281.

An additional point of interest in the biblical text is the specification in v. 36 that all of the residents' belongings be removed from the house before the priest make his diagnosis:

The priest will order the house cleared before the priest comes to inspect the plague, so that nothing in the house will be made impure. Afterwards, the priest will inspect the plague.

The rationale for this concession, as is explicitly stated, is to enable the house owner to save his possessions from needing to be discarded (or at least purified) as carriers of pollution. Already the rabbis of the Mishnah noted this example of the Torah making a special dispensation to avoid material loss, allowing the determination of impurity to be contingent on the priest's declaration.[15] This particular example reveals a much broader tendency to downgrade the perceived seriousness of pollution. Here I can only agree with Milgrom's conclusion that "we are dealing with an impurity that has been eviscerated of its principal potency."[16]

AN IMPLICIT POLEMIC?

Having demonstrated in the foregoing examples that Leviticus 13–14 reveals a shared heritage with bodies of tradition attested in texts from Mesopotamia and the Levant, a close comparison of these rituals can serve to focus attention on the points where the biblical rites differ from their Mesopotamian counterparts. In comparison with the Mesopotamian parallels, the rituals in Leviticus 13–14 reveal several striking characteristics. As was seen, P's treatment of disease focuses only on pollution, not infection, and this tendency is consistent with its explicit statements that this pollution pertains only to the sacred realm, specifically the camp where Yhwh resides (Lev 15:31; Num 5:3; 19:13, 20). Furthermore, these chapters obscure the relationship between disease and sin, as will be elucidated in more detail in the following chapter. Most strikingly, P does not preserve any healing rituals, in a sharp distinction from ancient Egyptian, Mesopotamian and Greek literature.

Do these characteristics indicate an underlying polemic? Nearly a century ago, Yehezkel Kaufmann expressed the view, later developed

---

[15] See m. *Negaim* 12:5; Milgrom, *Leviticus*, 1:869. For a possible Mesopotamian analogy to this concern, see LKA 120; edition: Maul, *Zukunftsbewältigung*, 484–494. English translation adapted from Caplice, *Akkadian Namburbi Texts*, 21, discussed in Feder, "Behind the Scenes."

[16] Milgrom, *Leviticus*, 1:889.

by Jacob Milgrom, that the biblical rituals are predicated on an implicit rejection of "pagan" elements:

Now the distinctive feature of biblical purifications when compared with those of paganism is that they are not performed for the purpose of banishing harm or sickness. The pagan seeks to avert harm; his purgations are in effect a battle with baleful forces that menace men and gods. Biblical purifications lack this aspect entirely. Lustrations play no part in healing the sick. The woman who bears a child, the leper, the gonorrheic, the "leprous" house, are all purified after the crisis or disease has passed.[17]

The above examination of rituals dealing with *saḫaršubbû* disease and *katarru* fungus in a house, which were unknown to Kaufmann, powerfully corroborate his astute observations. These texts, which preserve extra-biblical traditions apparently known in some form to the authors of Leviticus 14, call our attention to the striking absence of any therapeutic or exorcistic activities in Priestly ritual. It is further noteworthy that Kaufmann makes reference here also to Leviticus 12, a source which will be discussed in the following chapter.

Since Kaufmann's arguments were based to a large extent on silences in the Priestly text, they have been justifiably questioned by more recent scholarship. Is Kaufmann reading too much between the lines? May there be a more mundane explanation to the Priestly peculiarities?

IS THERE A DOCTOR IN THE HOUSE?

Before jumping to conclusions, it is worth exploring the possibility that these have a much more practical or political explanation. A helpful attempt to offer an explanation along these lines has been suggested by Isabel Cranz. She proposes that the Priestly authors were concerned with the purity of the temple and that the health of private individuals was not part of their specialization:

To sum up, the Priestly conceptualization of pollution need not be understood as a theological statement. Rather, the fact that the priests in P were not directly involved in the healing process of the individual can be viewed as the result of the Priestly focus on matters relating to the sanctuary. The responsibility of the priests in P lay solely with assuring the purity of the camp and holiness of the sanctuary, which allowed the divine presence to reside in their midst. That the treatment of

---

[17] Yehezkel Kaufmann, *The Religion of Israel*, trans. M. Greenberg (Chicago, IL: University of Chicago, 1960), 107.

physical disorders fell outside the scope of Priestly duties explains why P refrains from addressing these matters in ritual legislation.[18]

These remarks call for caution when making inferences based on P's omissions. However, Cranz's suggestion raises a question: If the Aaronide priests were not involved in ritual healing, who was?

Despite the recent publication of some comprehensive studies on the "health care system" in ancient Israel,[19] the bottom line is that the record for the existence of healing professionals is tellingly slim. The existence of "physicians," the common translation of *rop'e*, is attested by a few sporadic references in the HB as well as a bulla (personal seal) from " . . ., son of Zakkur, the physician."[20] Surprisingly, however, the HB never describes any of these physicians in action. Several scholars have concluded based on this scattered evidence that physicians were "held in low esteem" or even "illegitimate."[21] Most likely, aside from cases of fractures (Ex 21:19) and the like, they were regarded as ineffective. For more serious illnesses, the outcome could only be determined by God and there were two possibilities: he will live, or he will not (e.g., 1 Kgs 14; 2 Kgs 8).[22]

This argument is not based only on lack of evidence. Significantly, the references to human medical treatment in the HB are generally depicted with an attitude of skepticism. In contrast, the use of the root *rp'* in reference to Yhwh emphasizes the Deity's role as the only true healer.

---

[18] Isabel Cranz, *Atonement and Purification*, FAT 2/92 (Tübingen: Mohr Siebeck, 2017), 133.

[19] Hector Avalos, *Illness and Health Care in the Ancient Near East: The Role of the Temple in Greece, Mesopotamia and Israel* (Atlanta, GA: Scholars Press, 1995); Laura M. Zucconi, *Can No Physician Be Found? The Influence of Religion on Medical Pluralism in Ancient Egypt, Mesopotamia and Israel* (diss., University of California, San Diego, 2005).

[20] Jeffrey H. Tigay and Alan P. Millard, "Seals and Seal Impressions" (Hebrew), CoS 2.70. O: 200. For the dating, see Yigal Shiloh, "A Group of Hebrew Bullae from the City of David," *IEJ* 1(2) (1986): 37.

[21] For the former assessment, see Philip J. King and Lawrence E. Stager, *Life in Biblical Israel* (Louisville, KY: Westminster John Knox Press, 2001), 77; for the latter: Avalos, *Illness and Health Care*, 287.

[22] See Avalos, *Illness and Health Care*, 267–270. Truth be told, even Mesopotamian exorcists were forced on occasion to acknowledge the limitations of their craft, as pointed out by Mark Geller in relation to statements that the fate of the patient belonged to the gods: "It is easy to interpret such statements as religious, but they actually express a reality, that much of healing in antiquity was in the lap of the gods and there was little medicine could do to heal or cure" ("Review of Joann Scurlock, Sourcebook for Ancient Mesopotamian Medicine," *JSS* 63.1 [2018]: 262).

For example, in Jeremiah 17, the depiction of God as a healer is contrasted with trust in mortals:

[5]Cursed is one who trusts in man, Who makes mere flesh his strength, And turns his thoughts from Yhwh ... [7]Blessed is he who trusts in Yhwh, Whose trust is Yhwh alone ... [14]Heal me, O Yhwh, and I will be healed; Save me, and I will be saved.

Similarly, Exodus 15:26 presents a divine promise contingent on the Israelites' observance of the commandments that "I will not bring upon you any of the diseases that I brought upon the Egyptians, for I, Yhwh, am your healer (*rop'eka*)." These affirmations together with the near absence of evidence for human physicians elsewhere in the HB suggest a general distrust for this profession.[23]

But that is not the whole story. Biblical narratives describe another group of healers, "men of God" such as Elijah and Elisha, who perform miraculous acts of healing (e.g., 1 Kgs 17:17–24; 2 Kgs 4:17–37).[24] Yet the rhetoric of these passages would seem to emphasize the singularity of these events, certainly not that such healers represented the conventional method of treatment of the time. Moreover, the emphasis of these stories is on the fact that the actual agent of these miracles is Yhwh, who works through the mediation of these healers.[25] In short, the HB is surprisingly silent regarding the healing treatments available, in stark contrast to the literary evidence from ancient Egypt, Mesopotamia and Greece.[26]

The narrative in 2 Kings 5 dealing with the Aramean general Naaman stricken with *ṣaraʿat* can help further situate the peculiarities of Leviticus 13–4 within the broader biblical discourse on disease and healing. The story opens with the general's appeal to the king of Israel for assistance in curing the disease, but the latter responds with a confession of helplessness (7): "Am I God who can kill and bring to life that this one writes to me to heal a man from his leprosy?!" But when the prophet Elisha intervenes and advises Naaman to bathe in the Jordan river, it is the latter who is skeptical and initially refuses to comply: "Are not the Amanah and the Pharpar, the rivers of Damascus, better than all the waters of Israel? I could bathe in them and be healed (*wᵉ-ṭaharti*)!"[27] Ultimately, he accedes

[23] See Avalos, *Illness and Health Care*, 284–295.
[24] These episodes are part of a collection of other miraculous stories: 2 Kings 2:19–22; 2:23–24; 2 Kings 4:1–7; 4:38–41; 4:42–44; 6:1–7; see Schmitt, *Magie im Alten Testament*, 209–301.
[25] See Zucconi, "*Can No Physician*," 87.   [26] See n. 19 above.
[27] For the use of *ṭ-h-r* in the context of healing, see Chapter 3.

to the urgings of his servants, bathes in the Jordan and is healed. At this point, the Aramean general undergoes a dramatic internal transformation: he pledges to worship only Yhwh – and even requests a plot of earth from the Holy Land to this effect – though this new faith will remain "in the closet" when he returns to Aram. This transformation comes full circle when Naaman fervently declares the exclusive ability of the Israelite God to heal *ṣara'at* (15): "Now I know that there is no God in the whole world except in Israel!"

The story takes a twist when Elisha's servant, Gehazi, accepts Naaman's gift of gratitude, which was initially refused by his master. When the fact becomes known to Elisha, the prophet curses Gehazi (27): "The *ṣara'at* of Naaman shall cling to you and your offspring forever!" And so it was. The consequence of accepting the gift and thereby ascribing the miraculous cure to the work of his master and not God is an ironic reversal of fortunes: the healed Aramean returns home to declare the supremacy of Yhwh, while the prophet's helper, who has failed to properly acknowledge God's intervention, is left with Naaman's disease.[28]

At first glance, the treatment of *ṣara'at* in this narrative is quite different from that found in Leviticus 13–14, where little attention is given to Yhwh's role in disease. Upon closer inspection, however, it becomes apparent that points of rhetorical emphasis in 2 Kings 5 correspond to conspicuous points of silence in Leviticus 13–14. First, the simple rite of healing which initially angered Naaman served to emphasize that its efficacy could only be attributed to miraculous divine intervention,[29] and this point corresponds to the absence of a healing rite in Leviticus 14. The second point is that the transmission of leprosy from Naaman to Gehazi is not depicted as the consequence of interpersonal contagion but rather as a divine punishment effected by the prophet's curse. This tacit denial of infection is also reflected in Leviticus 13–14, though the latter differs from 2 Kings 5 in obscuring the notion of *ṣara'at* as divine punishment. From this comparison one may suspect that there is some connection between the absence of a healing ritual in Leviticus 13–14 and the reluctance to admit a fear of infection in these ritual prescriptions. The implications of these silences will be explored in the following

---

[28] Karl van der Toorn, *Sin and Sanction in Israel and Mesopotamia: A Comparative Study* (Assen: Van Gorcum, 1985), 74; Yaira Amit, *Hidden Polemics in the Hebrew Bible*, trans. J. Chipman (Leiden: Brill, 2000), 64–66.

[29] See Milgrom, *Leviticus*, 1: 964–965.

chapters. For the moment, let it suffice to acknowledge that Kaufmann was justified in discerning an implicit polemic in the rituals of Leviticus.

THE IMPLICIT POLEMIC OF LEVITICUS 14: ITS AUDIENCE AND IMPLICATIONS

The fact remains that the closest biblical semblance to ancient Near Eastern healing practices is found in Leviticus 13–14, so that the priests should be regarded as the closest counterpart to ritual healers. The elaborate procedures for diagnosing ṣaraʿat in persons, spanning over forty-six verses (not counting the following instructions for clothing and houses), make the absence of any actual treatment striking. One might suggest that the healing ritual was written on a separate scroll, as is sometimes the case in Mesopotamian literature. Regarding the relationship between separate diagnostic and therapeutic tablets, JoAnn Scurlock makes the following general observation in her *Sourcebook for Ancient Mesopotamian Medicine*: "What all of these therapeutic texts make explicit is what should never have required proof, and that is the close relationship between ancient Mesopotamian diagnostic and therapeutic material."[30] Based on this comparison, one might ask regarding Leviticus 13–14: perhaps the therapeutic section (on a separate scroll) was simply lost? But then, is it by chance that extensive diagnostic material and a ritual for purification *after* recovery have been preserved, but that the therapeutic procedures were not? Together with the other peculiar aspects of P's depiction of disease, the conclusion seems inescapable that this omission was deliberate.

Yet, assuming there is an implicit polemic, it remains to be ascertained: who is the outgroup whose practices are being rejected? Contrary to Kaufmann, it is doubtful that the Priestly authors were interested in debating with "pagans," if the latter are to be identified as their Babylonian counterparts. It seems more likely that Leviticus 13–14 reflect an existing Israelite practice, accepted among worshippers of Yhwh, which was subsequently appropriated and systematically modified to fit the views of the Priestly authors.

---

[30] WAW 36 (Atlanta, GA: SBL Press, 2014), 12. Cf. Markham Geller's more hesitant assessment regarding the relationship between these genres, suggesting that "therapeutic recipes and diagnostic omens were composed in different scribal 'workshops.'" *Ancient Babylonian Medicine: Theory and Practice* (Malden, MA: Wiley Blackwell, 2010), 91; Geller, "Review," 263.

Based on the biblical evidence alone, Priestly and non-Priestly, it may be impossible to identify the other side of this polemic. However, archaeology might also serve as a tool in extracting important information on the matter. Fortunately, the material remains recovered from Iron Age Israel provide crucial evidence for reconstructing the broader context of popular Israelite ritual practice. In particular, an abundance of ritual artifacts, especially figurines and amulets, have been recovered from Late Iron Age and Persian period contexts in Judah, suggesting a widespread use of apotropaic practices, that is, rites to avert malicious forces.[31] On this background, it may be suggested that Leviticus 14 – as elucidated by comparison with the healing ritual from Emar – constitutes a Priestly appropriation of an earlier tradition for treating skin disease that was practiced in Israel. In other words, it seems likely that the Priestly scribes borrowed and adapted elements from popular religious practice.[32]

In fact, it is possible that the Priestly viewpoint reflected in Leviticus 14 was not only elitist but decidedly unpopular. Among the distinctive aspects of this chapter noted above is the absence of any explicit connection between disease and transgression. This attitude contradicts numerous biblical sources and surely went against the grain of popular religious sentiment (see next chapter). More dramatically, the absence of any ritual measures by which diseased individuals (or their family) could seek to overcome illness contradicts the basic human need to seek control over the otherwise uncontrollable forces of disease.[33]

CONCLUSION

This chapter has highlighted some exceptional aspects of Leviticus 13–14, in particular the absence of a healing ritual for *ṣara'at* when compared to

---

[31] See Jeremy D. Smoak, "May YHWH Bless You and Keep You from Evil: The Rhetorical Argument of Ketef Hinnom Amulet I and the Form of the Prayers for Deliverance in the Psalms," *JANER* 12.2 (2012), 202–236; Brian B. Schmidt, "The Social Matrix of Early Judean Magic and Divination: From 'Top Down' or 'Bottom Up,'" in *Beyond Hatti: A Tribute to Gary Beckman*, eds. B. J. Collins and P. Michalowski (Atlanta, GA: Lockwood Press, 2013), 279–294; Eran Darby, *Interpreting Judean Pillar Figurines: Gender and Empire in Judean Apotropaic Ritual*, FAT 2/69 (Tübingen: Mohr Siebeck, 2014).

[32] See further Schmidt, "Social Matrix"; Feder, "Behind the Scenes."

[33] So Bronislaw Malinowski's classic formulation that magic is founded "on the belief that hope cannot fail nor desire deceive" (*Magic, Science and Religion and Other Essays* [Glencoe, IL: Free Press, 1948], 67). For overviews of the therapeutic options available in ancient Israel, see Avalos, *Illness and Healthcare*, 238–420 (see especially the summary diagram on 405); King and Stager, *Life in Biblical Israel*, 68–84.

similar Mesopotamian ritual texts. In part, this difference can be explained as reflecting skepticism regarding the efficacy of ritual healing, which finds expression elsewhere in the HB. At the same time, there are grounds for suspecting an implicit polemic against apotropaic practices that were popular in ancient Israel, as in surrounding cultures.

These tendencies provide a context for interpreting the paradoxical treatment of pollution in P, particularly the apparent tendency to downgrade *ṭum'ah* from a dangerous source of disease to a consideration bearing only on the temple cult. It seems likely that the Priestly editors sought to neutralize pollution so as to remove the impetus for various types of rites aimed at averting and exorcising malicious forces. In other words, to the extent that these diseases were considered to be dangerous, the sick party would be driven to seek some kind of ritual treatment. However, the existing healing options involved the banishment of malicious forces, involving an underlying worldview that was inimical to the Priestly conception. By reframing pollution from a cause of disease to a secondary effect, bearing only on the sanctuary, the temptation to perform such rites was reduced significantly. Rather than focusing on how ritualistic practices had the power to eliminate disease, the Priestly editors preferred to portray the diseases as harmless, thereby discouraging the use of healing rites altogether.

The following chapters will seek to examine this hypothesis in further detail by comparing additional Priestly texts with textual evidence bearing on the relationship between disease and defilement from the ancient Near East and beyond.

5

Diagnosing Sin

As seen in the previous chapter, there are numerous reasons to view the treatment of disease in P as reflecting an implicit polemic against accepted ritual practices. The present chapter will expand this argument to address the role of sin as a cause of disease. Though its point of departure is the rules of ṣara'at in Leviticus 13–14, it will reveal a consistent tension that pervades P.

In stark contrast with other biblical sources dealing with ṣara'at (Numbers 12:10; 2 Samuel 3:29; 2 Kings 5:27; 2 Chronicles 26:19–20), there is no explicit indication in Lev 13–14 that this disease is a divine punishment.[1] Though some scholars have deduced based on extra-biblical parallels the existence of a similar connection between house impurity and sin in Israel,[2] these comparisons only serve to call attention to the absence

---

[1] Joel S. Baden and Candida R. Moss, "The Origins and Interpretation of ṣāra'at in Leviticus 13–14," *JBL* 130 (2011): 643–653.

[2] See Rudiger Schmitt, *Magie im Alten Testament*, AOAT, 313 (Münster: Ugarit Verlag, 2004), 311–316. For the most part, Schmitt's argument is based on inference on the Hittite ritual CTH 446, but he also makes reference to Leviticus 14:34 introducing the laws of house impurity: "When you enter the land of Canaan that I give you (נתן) and I place (ונתתי) 'leprosy' upon a house in the land you possess." However, this verse implies nothing other than that Yhwh is viewed as its source. This view is a standard biblical conception of disease in general – and ṣara'at in particular – which does not inherently imply sin. Indeed, the adjacent use of the same verb (נתן) in the positive context of bestowing the land weighs against interpreting the idiom נתן נגע as expressing divine punishment. Furthermore, one may compare Exodus 4:6–7, where Moses' hand is stricken with this disease and then immediately healed as a display of divine power, not as a punishment. See also Rainer Albertz and Rudiger Schmitt, *Family and Household Religion in Ancient Israel and the Levant* (Winona Lake, IN: Eisenbrauns, 2012), 418. Jacob Milgrom, *Leviticus*, AB 3 vols. (New York, NY: Doubleday, 1991), 1.867–868 and Baden and Moss (ibid.,

of such statements in Lev 13–14, thereby emphasizing the disparity between the attitudes underlying these texts. Yet, such attitudes are not confined to these chapters. With reference to P more generally, Mary Douglas noted the absence of what she called "forensic impurity," that is, disease as an indication of sin, in Leviticus: "I was amazed to find in this book of religious laws that illness and misfortune are not diagnosed as punishments for individual sin . . . Biblical silence about forensic impurity is a major deviation from taboo behavior everywhere else."[3] Before evaluating this attitude as manifested in the biblical texts, it is necessary to situate the question of suffering and sin in a broader context.

MAKING SENSE OF DISEASE

Why am I sick? This question is meaningless from the perspective of the prevalent biomedical view of illness, so it is usually reinterpreted: "*How* did I get sick?*" Was it from that guy that sneezed on me in the train? Was it something I ate?

However, in the ancient world, and in traditional cultures until this day, the distinction between these two questions (how/why) could dissolve in seeking the reason for one's illness. The question may really be: *Why* did I get sick? What did I do? Ultimately, the proximate causes of disease – demonic attack, curses, witchcraft and the like – can be traced back to a misdeed committed by the person. For example, in the Mesopotamian worldview, a person is often protected by a personal god, a kind of guardian angel, who in the context of disease could be viewed as an external immune system.[4] However, various types of misdeeds can cause personal gods to abandon those they protect, thus leaving their devotees susceptible to the countless threats posed by the environment.

Even in the modern world, at a moment of unscientific weakness, a person may ask: why me? The question itself is of tremendous significance as evidence of the complexity of human psychology. This tendency

652–653) are ambivalent on this point, attributing this verse to H, but the comparison to Lev 26:16, 25, which deals with collective violations of the covenant and follows the well-known pattern of vassal treaty curses, is not relevant here.

[3] *Jacob's Tears: The Priestly Work of Reconciliation* (Oxford: Oxford University, 2004), 167.

[4] See Anne Löhnert and Annette Zgoll, "Schutzgott," *RlA* 12 (Berlin: De Gruyter, 2009–2011), 311–314. This idea has biblical parallels, for example: "An angel of Yhwh camps around those who fear him and rescues them" (Psalms 34:8 [7]).

to explain suffering in moralistic terms – and the broader assumption of underlying cosmic justice ("what goes around comes around," "you reap what you sow"), seemingly universal to the world's religions and common even to secular individuals – remains an enigma. From a simple rationalistic perspective, it is difficult to understand why people persistently believe in cosmic justice despite abundant evidence to the contrary.[5]

Though numerous ancient Near Eastern texts grapple with unjust suffering (like the biblical Job), the conventional attitude in Mesopotamia was to assume the inscrutability of the gods. Even if no specific sin was presently known, the existence of sin was taken as a given. Rather than blame circumstances or divine caprice, the petitioners of these texts provide the gods with extensive lists of possible sins that they *might* have transgressed. The phenomenology of this perspective is expressed vividly by Paul Ricoeur:

> This anonymous wrath, the faceless violence of Retribution, is inscribed in the human world in letters of suffering. Vengeance causes suffering. And thus, through the intermediary of retribution, the whole physical order is taken up into the ethical order; the evil of suffering is linked synthetically with the evil of fault; the very ambiguity of the word "evil" is a grounded ambiguity, grounded in the law of retribution . . . If you suffer, if you are ill, if you fail, if you die, it is because you sinned. The symptomatic and detective value of suffering with regard to defilement is reflected in the explanatory, etiological value of moral evil.[6]

The ambiguity of the word "evil" (in the original French: *mal*) is grounded in the blurred distinction between "good" and "bad" as referring to one's (physiological) state of well-being (thriving/suffering) and "good" and "bad" as moral evaluations (right/wrong). According to the conventional ancient Near Eastern worldview, the lexical ambiguity of these terms is motivated by a causal relationship between morality and well-being.

This general attitude finds expression in the terminology of disease. As noted, references to the "touch" (*lapātu*) and "hand" of gods as typical idioms for plague and illness are based on an underlying belief in divine retribution.[7] This relation between illness and retribution is especially characteristic of the ritual literature of the ancient Near East. The transgressions involved are various, including offenses against gods and

---

[5] This point is discussed poignantly in James L. Kugel, *In the Valley of the Shadow: On the Foundations of Religious Belief* (New York, NY: Free Press, 2011), 131–153.

[6] *The Symbolism of Evil*, trans. E. Buchanan (Boston, MA: Beacon Press, 1967), 31.

[7] As discussed in Chapter 3. See also Sylvia Salin, "When Disease 'Touches,' 'Hits,' or 'Seizes' in Assyro-Babylonian Medicine," *Kaskal* 12 (2015): 319–336. See p. 65 above. For later developments in the use of these expressions in diagnostic texts, see n. 46 below.

humans, as well as taboo violations. In several compositions, such as
Šurpu and Dinger.šà.dab₅.ba incantations, the patient is treated by the
recital of litanies which focus on an unknown sin. For example, *Šurpu*
Tablet 2 consists of a litany which spans the whole gamut of transgressions. The patient is described as one

Who has eaten what is taboo to his god, who has eaten what is taboo to his goddess
Who said "no" for "yes," who said "yes" for "no" . . .
He scorned the god, despised the goddess,
His sins are against his god, his crimes are against his goddess.
He is full of contempt against his father, full of hatred against his elder brother.
He despised his parents, offended the elder sister . . .
He entered his neighbor's house,
Had intercourse with his neighbor's wife,
Shed his neighbor's blood

(Šurpu II, lines 5–6, 33–49)[8]

While elsewhere in this tablet the gods feature as punishing agents, it is
interesting to note that Tablet III focuses on the notion of oath-curse
(*māmītu*) as the agent of retribution, suggesting an automatic mechanism
of retribution.[9] More generally, since the precise agent of retribution was
usually obscure, the patient needed to write a "blank check" in claiming
responsibility for any possible transgressions. The Jewish liturgy for Yom
Kippur contains litanies that follow a similar logic, aiming to remove
culpability for any unknown sins or forgotten oaths.[10]

This default assumption that disease is a means of divine retribution
finds ample expression in the HB as well. As was seen above, this presumption is represented in the terminological equivalences to Mesopotamian
expressions such as "touch"/"hit" (*n-g-ʿ*) as the key term for illness, referring to divine retribution, as well as the expression "hand of Yhwh."
Furthermore, biblical narratives frequently depict illness as a divine
punishment.[11]

[8] Erica Reiner, *Šurpu: A Collection of Sumerian and Akkadian Incantations* (Osnabrück: Biblio Verlag, 1970), 13–14.
[9] Yitzhaq Feder, "The Mechanics of Retribution in Hittite, Mesopotamian and Biblical Texts," *JANER* 10.2 (2010): 127–135.
[10] See Markham J. Geller, "The *Šurpu* Incantations and Lev. V. 1–5," *JSS* 25.2 (1980): 188; Margaret Jaques, *Mon dieu qu'ai-je fait?: les diĝir-šà-dab(5)-ba et la piété privée en Mésopotami*, OBO 273 (Fribourg/Göttingen: Academic Press/Vandenhoeck & Ruprecht, 2015), 330–332.
[11] E.g., Numbers 12:10; 2 Samuel 3:29; 2 Chronicles 26:21; likewise covenant curses: Lev 26:16; Deuteronomy 28:20–22.

How does the Priestly source address the relationship between suffering and sin? The obvious place to look for an answer would be in the rules outlining expiatory offerings. Despite the detailed presentation of two separate types, the sin (*ḥaṭṭ'at*) and the guilt (*ašam*) offerings, one finds considerable ambiguity pertaining to the question at hand. Firstly, the relevant texts do not refer to illness. Secondly, the sin offering (*ḥaṭṭ'at*) is used also for the purification of bodily defilement, leading some scholars to suggest that it is more accurately named a "purification offering." Since these difficulties have caused considerable confusion, it is important to confront them here.

THE PRIESTLY SYSTEM OF ATONEMENT: SIN AND POLLUTION

The function of the expiatory offerings has been elucidated by numerous studies in recent decades, and the following brief sketch takes advantage of their numerous insights. The work of Jacob Milgrom and the critique of his student Roy Gane are particularly helpful in understanding these texts as a system.[12] While texts pertaining to these offerings are scattered over numerous chapters in Exodus through Numbers (also Ezekiel 40–48), the key evidence is found in Lev 1–16, where one finds distinct treatments of sin (Lev 4–5) and impurity (11–15), culminating in the sanctuary purgation ritual described in Lev 16.

For example, Lev 4 requires that a sin offering be presented for unknown transgressions, whether committed by the high priest, the whole congregation, a chieftain or a private individual. Omitted from this chapter and explicitly rejected in Num 15 is the possibility of a sin offering for a deliberate crime. The *ḥaṭṭ'at* is also required in cases of purification, as outlined in Lev 12–15, including for a woman who has given birth, lepers and gonorrheics.

Though the circumstances vary, the results of the sin offering are described without exception using the verb *kipper*: "the priest shall *kipper* on his/her behalf." Scholars have struggled to find an adequate modern rendering for this verb. Though the Hebrew root *k-p-r* suggests the "paying-off" (expiation) of guilt,[13] the usage of this verb in the biblical

---

[12] See Milgrom, *Leviticus*, 1.253–288; Roy Gane, *Cult and Character: Purification Offerings, Day of Atonement, and Theodicy* (Winona Lake, IN: Eisenbrauns, 2005).

[13] See Yitzhaq Feder, *Blood Expiation in Hittite and Biblical Ritual: Origins, Context and Meaning* (Atlanta, GA: SBL, 2011), 167–208, where it is shown that the term "expiation"

formulas apply to purification (e.g., Lev 12:7) alongside removing culpability (e.g., Lev 4:20), suggesting a more generic translation such as "clearing."[14] Still, the relevant texts do make a clear distinction between sin and pollution, adding an additional clause distinguishing between whether the individual has been "pardoned" (*nislaḥ*) or "purified" (*ṭaher*).[15] The key point here is that P systematically treats the removal of sin and pollution as distinct processes.

The culmination of this system is the "day of expiation" (*yom ha-kippurim*) ritual described in Lev 16.[16] This complex ritual complements the private sin offering rituals which are performed over the course of the year. The purpose of the blood rites for the purification of the sanctuary are expressed explicitly in v. 16: "Thus he shall purge the shrine of the impurities and transgressions (*peša'im*) of the Israelites, whatever their sins; and he shall do the same for the Tent of Meeting, which abides with them in the midst of their impurities." What are these sins and impurities that have penetrated the most holy precinct of the sanctuary? Commentators generally agree that the term *peša'* refers to an act of rebellion, to be distinguished from the unintentional sins that can be expiated by the ordinary sin offerings. Such "high-handed" (*yad ramah*) sins do not allow forgiveness to their perpetrators under any circumstances (Num 15:30–31), and thus fall on the collective responsibility of the community for their expiation. The pollution described in v. 16 seems to be the exact counterpart of such sins; the verse refers to the impurities caused by Israelites in the camp who failed to undergo the necessary purifications (Lev 15:31; Num 19:13, 20). Even here, when

---

(from Latin *ex-pio*) captures the use of *kipper* as it was used in reference to paying off bloodguilt, which served as a core metaphor for the sin offering and its blood rites.

[14] For the rendering "clearing," see William H. C. Propp, *Exodus 19–40*, AB (New York, NY: Doubleday, 2006), 466–467. Developing this suggestion, Michael Hundley explains: "clearing refers more broadly to the removal of unwanted impediments, while cleansing refers more specifically to the removal of impurity. The ultimate goal of impurity removal is being clean, namely free from impurities, while the ultimate goal of sin removal is forgiveness" (*Keeping Heaven on Earth: Safeguarding the Divine Presence in the Priestly Tabernacle*, FAT 2/50 [Tübingen: Mohr Siebeck, 2011], 135, n. 4). Watts suggests the verb "mitigate," defined as follows: "the alleviation of negative consequences produced by various kinds of problems ranging from legal conflicts to environmental pollution" (*Leviticus 1–10, Historical Commentary of the Old Testament* [Leuven: Peeters, 2013], 345).

[15] For a helpful survey of the evidence, see Gane, *Cult and Character*, 106–143.

[16] The performance of this ritual on a fixed day of the calendar, the tenth day of the seventh month, is determined by the appendix to the chapter (vv. 29–34) and Leviticus 23:26–32.

dealing with the purging of deliberate sins and negligent pollutions from the shrine, the text treats sin and pollution as separate and incommensurable entities.[17]

The systematicity of these rules is evident especially in the manner by which the severity of sin is mapped onto the tripartite division of the Tabernacle. The offerings for private individuals – for unintentional sins and bodily impurities – are performed at the accessible courtyard altar at the entrance to the Tabernacle. The higher severity associated with the collective sins committed by the high priest (Lev 4:3–12) and congregation (13–21) are expiated by the performance of the sin offering blood rites inside the Tent of Meeting. The most severe sins are addressed by the inner-sanctum rites of Lev 16, which focus on deliberate transgressions and the impurities caused by negligent refusal to undergo the prescribed purificatory rites.[18]

To summarize, the presentation of the expiatory offerings in Priestly texts is highly systematic and mutually consistent. The system represented by these texts has been the point of departure for many recent scholarly efforts to elucidate Priestly attitudes regarding disease, sin and pollution. In the texts dealing with diseases (Lev 13–15), illness is explicitly associated with pollution, not sin. In parallel, the sin offerings in cases of sin (Lev 4–5) do not mention disease. Hence, scholars are justified in seeking to remove the stigma of sin from bodily impurities and, by implication, disease. For example, in distinguishing "ritual" from "moral" impurities, Jonathan Klawans has argued that the former are generally natural, unavoidable and not inherently sinful.[19] Yet, the ancient Near Eastern sources reviewed above and a closer inspection of the Priestly terminology raises a suspicion that the distinction between disease and sin was not always so sharply drawn, even in Israel. This possibility will be explored in the remainder of this chapter.

---

[17] Gane, *Cult and Character*, 198–213. Admittedly, Lev 16:30 uses the verb "purify" (*t-h-r*) explicitly in reference to sin, but this exceptional reference to purification in this comprehensive sense should not be taken as obscuring the sharp conceptual distinction between sin and impurity made throughout the sin-offering texts, including Leviticus 16 itself. I thank David Frankel for urging me to clarify this point.

[18] Milgrom, *Leviticus*, 1.253–261, anticipated to some extent by the Rabbis (m. *Shavuot* 1: 2–6).

[19] *Impurity and Sin in Ancient Judaism* (New York, NY: Oxford University Press, 2000), 23–24.

SIN OFFERINGS FOR INDIVIDUAL MISDEEDS

Taking the Priestly texts by themselves, it is possible to accept the sharp separation of disease and sin at face value. However, viewing them in a comparative framework, one can hardly avoid a suspicion that something is amiss. Particularly suspect is Lev 4, whose focus on unknown sins bears an uncanny reminiscence to the Mesopotamian rituals for unknown sins mentioned above. This chapter deals with misdeeds committed inadvertently (4:2) and refers repeatedly to the matter being hidden (*neʿelam dabar*) from the perpetrator (4:13; also 5:2, 17–18), who only later finds out about the misdeed (4:14, 4:23, 4:28). These instructions raise some obvious questions: Why would someone bring an offering for an unknown crime? What were the circumstances in which these previously unknown sins became known?

One possibility is that another member of the community may have played the role of "Big Brother" and rebuked their neighbor for the unknowing misdeed,[20] but it is doubtful that such a case was sufficiently regular to warrant this detailed set of instructions. A more likely situation for implementing Lev 4–5:13 would be in response to illness or personal distress, perhaps leading to an oracular inquiry. In such a scenario, the suffering itself or the results of this inquiry would serve as the impetus for bringing a sin offering. In recent years numerous scholars have made this inference,[21] which is supported by comparisons to extra-biblical rituals

---

[20] Such an explanation could account for the distinction between the passive formulation in v. 14 (נודע החטאת), and the active form הודע אליו חטאתו in vv. 23, 28, whereby the first case refers to a time when the entire community transgressed with no one left to point out the error (cf. Milgrom, *Leviticus*, 1.243). Nevertheless, as the passive formulation in v. 14 itself indicates, rebuke was not the only – and probably not the most common – catalyst for addressing a previously unknown sin. Interestingly, the Qumran scrolls (especially CD 9: 2–8) refer to an institutionalized practice of rebuke with legal sanctions, based explicitly on Leviticus 19:17–18 (see L. Schiffman, *Sectarian Law in the Dead Sea Scrolls: Courts, Testimony and the Penal Code* [Chico, CA: Scholars Press, 1983], 89–109), but which may also be implicitly based on Leviticus 4–5. See A. Shemesh, "Rebuke, Warning and Obligation to Testify – In Judean Desert Writings and Rabbinic Halakha," *Tarbiz* 66 (1997): 154 (in Hebrew), who relates this institution to Leviticus 5:1b.

[21] This line of interpretation is largely consistent with A. Schenker's understanding of אש"ם ("to be liable"), in which misfortune is taken as symptomatic of guilt, as in 1 Samuel 6; see *Recht und Kult im Alten Testament: achtzehn Studien*, OBO 172 (Freiburg: Universitätsverlag, 2000), 107; "Once Again, the Expiatory Sacrifices," *JBL* 116.4 (1997), 697. See also Raymond Westbrook, *Studies in Biblical and Cuneiform Law* (Paris: J. Gabalda, 1988), 27–29; Jay Sklar, *Sin, Impurity, Sacrifice, Atonement: The Priestly Conceptions* (Sheffield: Sheffield Phoenix Press, 2005), 39–41; Hundley, *Keeping Heaven on Earth*, 145; Feder, *Blood Expiation*, 106–108; Isabel Cranz, *Atonement and Purification*, FAT 2/92 (Tübingen: Mohr Siebeck, 2017), 38–49.

like the Mesopotamian Šurpu ritual discussed above,[22] not to mention *ilī ul īdi* ("My god, I did not know") incantations to make amends for unknown sins.[23] Importantly, however, this background is missing from Lev 4–5:13.

These issues raise suspicions that strike at the very heart of the Priestly expiatory system. While disease seems to be comfortably compartmentalized as a source of impurity in Lev 13–15, it is noteworthy that the generic term used to address both sin and impurity is *kipper*, whose etymology links it clearly to appeasement, compensation and expiation – in short, to mitigating misdeeds.[24] In other words, the fact that this term is used for purification as well as expiation suggests that the severe sources of bodily impurity were also once associated with sin. It bears stressing once again that the diseases depicted in P as sources of severe pollution requiring a sin offering are leprosy and gonorrhea, conditions which elsewhere in the HB are explicitly depicted as divine punishments (2 Sam 3:29). These observations call for a reassessment of the prevalent tendency in modern scholarship to refer to this offering as a "purification offering."

SIN OFFERING OR PURIFICATION OFFERING?

As part of his monumental work on Leviticus and the *ḥaṭṭāʾt* offering in particular, Jacob Milgrom has been the leading proponent of the view that the traditional translation of this offering's name as "sin offering" is mistaken and should be replaced with the designation "purification offering."[25] This translation fit well with Milgrom's broader synthesis of the sin-offering texts, specifically Lev 4–5 and 16, which he viewed as *purifying* the sanctuary from sin and pollution. However, it should be noted from the outset that this characterization is imprecise, since these texts do not refer to sin as causing impurity (*ṭ-m-ʾ*) and maintain a clear terminological distinction between sins, requiring pardon (*s-l-ḥ*), and pollution, requiring purification (*ṭ-h-r*).[26] Rather, as pointed out above,

---

[22] See already Geller, "*Šurpu* Incantations," 181–192, and the extensive discussion in Cranz *Atonement and Purification*, 44–50.

[23] W. G. Lambert, "DINGIR.ŠÀ.DIB.BA Incantations," *JNES* 33 (1974), 267–322. See also Watts, *Leviticus*, 303–316, especially 308.

[24] Feder, *Blood Expiation*, 167–208.

[25] See Jacob Milgrom, "Sin-Offering or Purification-Offering," *VT* 21.2 (1971): 237–239; *Leviticus*, 1.253–254, where he argues that the translation "sin offering" is "inaccurate on all grounds: contextually, morphologically, and etymologically."

[26] See Baruch J. Schwartz, "The Bearing of Sin in the Priestly Literature," in *Pomegranates and Golden Bells: Studies in Biblical, Jewish and Near Eastern Ritual, Law, and*

expiation and purification should be viewed as distinct yet parallel processes effected by the *ḥaṭṭaʾt*.[27] Since this issue of translation has implications for understanding the origins and purpose of this offering, it is worthwhile to review Milgrom's key arguments.

The first argument is linguistic and interprets the name of the offering as derived from the *piel* verbal form *ḥiṭṭeʾ*, usually translated "purify." Several problems undermine this claim. Most simply, this interpretation contradicts etymology, which associates the verb with sin, not purity. Scholars had already puzzled over why the verbal form *ḥiṭṭeʾ* would attain the sense "purify" instead of the expected "de-sin."[28] A survey of the usages of the relevant forms reveals that their semantic development has been commonly misunderstood.[29] Put simply, the verbal forms are derivative from the name of the offering. For example, one finds in Lev 6:19: "the priest who *sin-offers* (*meḥaṭṭeʾ*) will eat it," in which the verb means "to offer a sin offering."[30] A secondary development from this usage was "to daub or sprinkle," which appears in numerous sources (e.g., Ex 29:36; Lev 14:49, 52) and is clearly derived from the blood rites associated with the sin offering. This usage underlies the *hitpael* form used throughout Num 19, referring to the patient "being sprinkled" with the waters of the red cow. In these occurrences, the verb refers to the procedure, not the effects.[31] The bottom line of this discussion is that the verbal forms were

Literature in Honor of Jacob Milgrom, eds. D. P. Wright, D. N. Freedman and A. Hurvitz (Winona Lake, IN: Eisenbrauns, 1995), 6–7. Gane, *Cult and Character*, 112–124. For the question of "moral impurity," that is, the reference to sin in terms of pollution, see Chapter 9.

[27] This point need not undermine Milgrom's broader understanding of the operation of the sin offering as removing sin and impurity from the sanctuary (see Feder, *Blood Expiation*, 108–111), though it requires closer attention to the conceptual distinction between them. Regarding the inclusive use of "purify" in Leviticus 16:30, see above, n. 17.

[28] From a strictly linguistic perspective, one would have expected a denominative privative *piel* to bear the sense "de-sin," but this usage is nowhere attested. See *GKC* §52h; Joüon, *GBH* §52d; Ernst Jenni, *Das hebräische Piʿel* (Zurich: EVZ-Verlag, 1968), 274; Bruce K. Waltke and Michael O'Connor, *An Introduction to Biblical Hebrew Syntax* (Winona Lake, IN: Eisenbrauns, 1990), 412.

[29] The following is a simplified presentation of my argument in *Blood Expiation*, 99–108, anticipated already by Menahem Zvi Kaddari, *A Dictionary of Biblical Hebrew* (Ramat-Gan: Bar-Ilan University, 2006), 289 (Hebrew).

[30] So also Leviticus 9:15 and 2 Chronicles 29:24. As Baruch Levine explains, the "denominative from the noun *ḥaṭṭaʾt* itself means 'to perform a sin-offering'" (*Leviticus*, JPS Torah Commentary [Philadelphia, PA: Jewish Publication Society, 1989], 40).

[31] Even Ps 51:9 is best rendered "*Sprinkle* me with hyssop and I will be pure," against the NJPS translation: "*Purge* me with hyssop till I am pure."

derived from the name of the offering, not vice versa, so that Milgrom's linguistic argument collapses.

A second, textual argument for the translation "purification offering" is based on the accurate observation that this offering appears in relation to bodily impurities, where the expressed result of this offering is to purify the beneficiary. As noted, however, since gonorrhea and leprosy were viewed as divine punishments in non-P texts, the translation "sin offering" remains valid. The fact that milder impurities such as sexual intercourse do not require expiatory offerings reinforces this point. The upshot of these observations is that the earliest translators were correct in translating *ḥaṭṭa't* as a "sin offering," meaning a rite for undoing the negative effects of misdeeds.

THE SIN OF GIVING BIRTH

Still, a few more puzzling cases remain, especially the sin offering of a woman who has given birth. Could giving birth be considered sinful? Perhaps, but not by a source that champions being fruitful and multiplying (Gen 1:28; 9:7). Already the Rabbis sensed this problem (b. *Niddah* 31b):

R. Shimon ben Yochai's student asked him: "Why does the Torah ordain that a woman following childbirth (parturient) should bring an offering?"

[R. Shimon] responded: "At the time when she squats to give birth she swears impetuously that she will not have intercourse (again) with her husband. Therefore, the Torah tells her to bring an offering."

This tongue-and-cheek answer did not satisfy the Rabbis, who left the puzzle as is. For his part, Milgrom viewed this example as decisive evidence for the fact that the *ḥaṭṭ'at* was a "purification" offering.

Yet a perusal of ancient Near Eastern texts dealing with birth offers a different, sobering perspective. As in many societies even today, the process of giving birth in the ancient world was rife with dangers to both the mother and the child.[32] While today's pregnant women may vent their "nesting" anxieties by reorganizing their homes, in a cultural

---

[32] E.g., Genesis 35:17–19; 1 Samuel 4:19–20. See JoAnn Scurlock, "Baby-Snatching Demons, Restless Souls and the Dangers of Childbirth: Medico-Magical Means of Dealing with Some of the Perils of Motherhood in Ancient Mesopotamia," *Incognita* 2 (1991): 135–183; Marten Stol, *Birth in Babylonia and the Bible: Its Mediterranean Setting* (CM 14; Gröningen; Styx, 2000), 27–33, 140–141.

context where the stakes are higher, it is hardly surprising that women may concern themselves with possible unatoned sins that may be called into account at the moment of reckoning.

A key piece of evidence for our inquiry comes from the Hittites, specifically from a group of birth rituals from the region of Kizzuwatna (classical Cilicia) in South Eastern Anatolia, bordering on Northern Syria, which can be dated to the fourteenth and thirteenth centuries BCE. These birth rituals contain rites of smearing of blood on the birth seat.[33] Elsewhere, I have argued at length that this blood-smearing rite, sometimes designated by the Hurrian term for blood *zurki*, reflects a shared tradition with the biblical sin offering, the latter involving the smearing of blood on the horns of the courtyard altar. It should be noted that in some other Hittite rituals, the blood-smearing rite is performed on cultic objects, including cult statues.[34]

In the present discussion, it is important to note that at least five of these rituals involve a rite in which blood was smeared on the birthing apparatus.[35] In all of these cases, as in Lev 12, the blood is derived from a bird. In most of these cases, the blood smearing took place before the woman gave birth, though there are examples of this rite taking place after birth.[36] The rationale for this practice, elucidated explicitly in the Papanikri ritual, is to avert potential danger to the woman and child in the birth process, which could be caused by various dangerous influences – especially sins against the gods.[37] This ritual was a response to a case in which the birth seat (comprised of a basin and two pegs) had broken before the woman gives birth, an event that was interpreted as indicating divine anger and as an ominous sign for the upcoming birth. Following the blood-smearing rite, the officiating priest declares:

[33] See Gary Beckman, *Hittite Birth Rituals*, StBoT 29 (Wiesbaden: Harrasowitz, 1983); for the biblical parallels, see Feder, *Blood Expiation*, 125–143.

[34] See *Blood Expiation*, 7–34. Note also the *zukru* ritual from Emar, where blood and oil are smeared on the standing stones; see Emar 373, Msk 7429²ᵃ+ ll. 34, 60, 167. Text and translation: Daniel E. Fleming, *Time at Emar: The Cultic Calendar and the Rituals from the Diviner's House* (Winona Lake, IN: Eisenbrauns, 2000): 234–257 (see also discussion 82–87); also Feder, *Blood Expiation*, 121.

[35] For an analysis of the relationship of these texts to the biblical sin offering, see Feder, *Blood Expiation*, 125–143, especially 140–143.

[36] See Feder, *Blood Expiation*, 141, nn. 101–102.

[37] KBo 5.1 I 1–47; Text edition: Rita Strauß, *Reinigungsrituale aus Kizzuwatna* (Berlin: de Gruyter, 2006), 286–288. For discussion, see also Feder, *Blood Expiation*, 9–13.

If your mother or father have sinned *of late* (i.e., they left over a sin),[38] or you have just committed some sin . . . and the birth stool was damaged or the pegs were broken, O divinity, she has for her part made compensation (*šarninkta*) two times. Let the ritual patron be pure again![39]

This birth ritual explicitly addresses the possibility that the parturient has committed some sin that has aroused divine anger. As such, it fits in with other rituals and prayers from the ancient Near East that view adversity as a divine punishment, which could even be caused by unknown sins. Strikingly, the verb *šarni(n)k*, which describes the effects of the blood rite, here translated "made compensation," is a precise semantic parallel to the Hebrew verb *kipper* employed in the sin offering rituals.[40]

Does this Hittite evidence suggest that the biblical sin offering prescribed in Lev 12 was based on the presumption of an unknown sin? In my opinion, such a claim would be somewhat overstating the case. What the Hittite birth rituals demonstrate is that the tremendous anxiety accompanying birth could lead to such an inquiry,[41] but one may also surmise that the same anxiety could also be expressed as relief and thanksgiving through offerings performed *after* birth. The fact that a sin offering is used for this function and not a well-being offering (Lev 7:12) further suggests an association with expiation. In any case, it is worth mentioning again that a minority of the existing Hittite rituals also include a postnatal blood rite, so that we must keep in mind the fluidity of ritual traditions.

---

[38] For the concern with punishment for parents' sin, compare Hatušili III's prayer: "If before the gods there is some sin of my father and my mother . . . disregard that sin" (Itamar Singer, *Hittite Prayers*, WAW 11 [Atlanta, GA: Society of Biblical Literature, 2002], 100). This concern finds expression in Mesopotamian incantations as well: "Drive out from my body illness from known and unknown iniquity, the iniquity of my father, my grandfather, my mother, [my] grandmother, the iniquity of my elder brother and elder sister, the iniquity of clan, kith and kin" (Lambert, "DINGIR.ŠÀ.DIB.BA," 280–281).

[39] Text edition: Strauß, *Reinigungsrituale*, 286–288; discussion and English translation: Feder, *Blood Expiation*, 9–13.

[40] See Feder, *Blood Expiation*, 167–208.

[41] Similarly, a Mesopotamian ritual for a woman who has experienced miscarriages and hopes to come to term includes a rite by a riverside where she recites: "Receive (evil) from me and so carry away the sin, crime, offense, wrongdoing, evil, (and) weakness from my body downstream with your water" (*SpTU* 5, 248, obv. 13–15). Text and translation: JoAnn Scurlock, *Sourcebook for Ancient Mesopotamian Medicine*, WAW 36 (Atlanta, GA: SBL, 2014), 684, 688. For an interpretation of this ritual, see JoAnn Scurlock, "Translating Transfers in Ancient Mesopotamia," in *Magic and Ritual in the Ancient World*, eds. P. Mirecki and M. Meyer (Leiden: Brill, 2002), 209–223.

To summarize this point, the recent tendency to translate *ḥaṭṭa't* as "purification offering" is problematic in that it obscures the straightforward origins of this ritual, as reflected unambiguously in its etymology and its programmatic instructions outlined in Lev 4. This rationale may or may not account for all the isolated examples of sin offerings,[42] but the same methodological point made regarding pollution is valid here: ritual terminology – like language in general – does not develop according to an Aristotelian logic of necessary and sufficient conditions. For our purposes, the key point – reinforced by the case of the parturient – is that the name *ḥaṭṭa't* serves as a semantic fossil, revealing its origins as a sin offering. More importantly, recognizing the origins of the *ḥaṭṭa't* as a "sin offering" calls attention to P's systematic effort to associate disease with pollution rather than sin, in a dramatic break from the widespread conception in Israel and surrounding cultures.

CONCLUSION

In this chapter, the lack of an explicit association between *ṣara'at* and sin, differentiating Lev 13–14 from other biblical sources, has been placed in a broader context. The evidence reviewed here is complex. On the one hand, there are grounds to assume that P is predicated on a conventional view of suffering and disease as symptomatic of a prior sin. On the other hand, there are indications that P has sought to obscure this connection, as evidenced by the use of the *ḥaṭṭ'at* offering for purification as

---

[42] For instance, one may ask regarding the function of the sin offering in the context of the consecration of the Tabernacle (Ex 29/Lev 8) or in the calendrical offerings (Num 28). As Milgrom notes regarding the parturient (Lev 12), Nazirite (Num 6) and the sanctification of the altar (Lev 8:15), "the *ḥaṭṭā't* is prescribed for persons and objects who cannot have sinned" (*Leviticus*, 1.253). Yet, a partial solution may be suggested in light of the procedural order of the offerings, whereby the sin offering always precedes the other offerings, including the ostensibly more important burnt offering. On this point, Milgrom himself cites approvingly the rabbinic statements that "the *ḥaṭṭa't* always takes priority" (m. *Nazir* 6:5) and that "the blood of the *ḥaṭṭa't* precedes the blood of the burnt offering because it appeases" (m. *Zeb.* 10:2), summarizing that "the *ḥaṭṭā't* by necessity always comes first in any series because the sanctuary must be purged of the impurity caused to it by the offerer" (ibid., 1.488). More generally, these interpretations raise the possibility that the function of the *ḥaṭṭa't* was standardized in the cultic system, so that hairsplitting over a given case may be ill-advised. Regarding the vexed topic of the Nazirite's sin offering, see Roy Gane, "The Function of the Nazirite's Concluding Purification Offering," in *Perspectives on Purity and Purification in the Bible*, eds. N. S. Meshel, J. Stackert, D. P. Wright and B. J. Schwartz. (New York, NY: T&T Clark, 2008), 9–17.

well as expiation, including the purification of the parturient (Lev 12), a rite which may originally have borne expiatory significance.

The comparison with expiatory rituals from surrounding cultures suggests that the obscuring of the traditional causal connection between sin and suffering was deliberate and systematic. More to the point, it appears that the sin offerings which address similar circumstances to those found in Mesopotamian and Hittite rituals should be viewed as a programmatic appropriation of earlier rituals that served to avert and exorcise malicious forces, seeking to incorporate them into the institutionalized framework of the sin offering rituals. One may compare here the enigmatic figure of Azazel in Lev 16, who appears to be a demonic figure that has now been "stripped of his personality."[43] Yet, the transformation described here is much more comprehensive.

To understand the rationale for incorporating localized expiatory rituals into a centralized, systematic framework, one may compare the programmatic decree for cult centralization in Deuteronomy 12, which is grounded on the need to separate Israel from illicit cultic practices. The detailed instructions for cult centralization are framed by commands to destroy all of the cult appurtenances of the previous inhabitants of the land (vv. 1–4) and warnings not to employ similar practices in worship of Yhwh (29–31). Similarly, in the programmatic instruction for cult centralization in Lev 17, the Israelites are prohibited from slaughtering any of the domesticated animals eligible for sacrifice except at the Tabernacle "so that they will no longer offer their sacrifices to the goat-demons (*śeʿirim*) after whom they stray" (7).[44] Like Deut 12, Lev 17 asserts that cult centralization serves to prevent the worship of illicit forces and powers. A similar tendency motivates the repeated references to "the priest" in Lev 13–14, no less than ninety-five occurrences, which seems to reflect a concern that these rites be kept under close supervision.[45]

---

[43] David P. Wright, *The Disposal of Impurity: Elimination Rites in the Bible and in Hittite and Mesopotamian Literature* (Atlanta, GA: Scholars Press, 1987), 25. For broader discussions of the issue of demons in the Hebrew Bible, see Henrike Anthes-Frey, *Unheilsmächte und Schutzgenien, Antiwesen und Grenzgänger: Vorstellungen von "Dämonen" im alten Israel*, OBO 227 (Göttingen: Vandenhoeck-Ruprecht, 2007); Judit M. Blair, *De-Demonising the Old Testament: An Investigation of Azazel, Lilith, Deber, Qeteb and Reshef in the Hebrew Bible*, FAT 2/37 (Tübingen: Mohr Siebeck, 2009).

[44] Regarding these "goat-demons," see the discussion in Julia Rhyder, *Centralizing the Cult*, FAT 134 (Tübingen: Mohr Siebeck, 2019), 205–214.

[45] See Albertz and Schmitt, *Family and Household Religion*, 418.

Likewise, the unification of expiatory and purificatory rites within a single sin-offering system served as a means of excluding illicit practices. Along these lines, the peculiarities of the Priestly treatment of disease may be understood as a programmatic attempt to weed out exorcistic rites. However, these efforts also had far-reaching ramifications which may perhaps have been unintended. In particular, the implicit rejection of the moralization of disease (i.e., that sickness is symptomatic of a prior sin) led inevitably to a recognition of physiological occurrences as "natural," hence amoral processes. Interestingly, scholars have begun to suspect that also in Mesopotamia, traditional expressions such as the "hand" of a certain god were used more as a means of systematizing diagnoses than as an inference of punishment, as emphasized by Markham Geller: "It was clearly taken for granted that the gods were behind this system, but by the first millennium BCE, the process of recording and interpreting omens had become extremely technical and even mechanical, to the extent that the emphasis was upon correct procedure in determining the results rather than pious statements about divine intervention."[46]

For modern readers raised in scientific thinking and accustomed to sharp conceptual distinctions, these inferences may appear far-fetched at first glance. The following chapter will elaborate on this point within a broader theoretical and comparative framework. As will be seen, the explicit polemics pertaining to causes and transmission of disease that can be found in other cultural contexts reinforce the suspicion that the reality of infection can pose a threat not only to bodies but also to certain worldviews.

---

[46] "Review of N. Heessel, Divinatorische Texte II: Opferschau-Omina." *AfO* 53 (2016): 207, citing also the earlier remarks of Karl van der Toorn, *Sin and Sanction in Israel and Mesopotamia: A Comparative Study* (Assen: Van Gorcum, 1985), 78.

6

Naturalizing Disease: Pollution as a Causal Theory

The previous chapter argued in detail that the Priestly source represents a deliberate break with conventional ancient Near Eastern views of disease. Before we can explore the broader significance of this break, it is necessary to first address the more fundamental issue of how notions of causation originate both in the psychological development of individuals (ontogeny) and on the scale of cultures. This framework will provide a basis for situating the Priestly views of disease and pollution in comparison to similar discursive developments outside of ancient Israel, providing an opportunity to test the plausibility of the hypothesis proposed in the previous chapters regarding the polemical tendencies in the Priestly source.

This chapter picks up some of the theoretical threads from Chapters 1 and 2. Those chapters sought to lay the foundations for understanding pollution as based on embodied images, but now it is possible to discuss more comprehensively how pollution can operate as an articulated theory of infection, as well as the possibility for competition between this theory and others. In pursuing this goal, P's treatment of pollution and disease will be juxtaposed with Medieval Islamic approaches to contagion and Hippocratic polemics against ritual healers, providing a new perspective for understanding Leviticus 12 and 15.

STARTING FROM THE BASICS

The discussion of purity and pollution in anthropological discourse since the mid-twentieth century has tended to be drawn into the broader problem of the seeming irrationality of "primitive" cultures. In fact, the theme of the difference between "us" and "them" was arguably more central to Mary Douglas' *Purity and Danger* than the problem of pollution.[1] Carried to its extreme, the question could be formulated as follows: Is the notion of impurity real or imagined? That is, is the distinction between pure and impure determined by essences that exist in the world or are these concepts arbitrary social constructions imposed on the world?[2] One answer to this question would be: For "them," pollution is real; but for "us," it is imaginary. Of course, this assessment is based on the ethnocentric assumption that our *knowledge* enables us to be the ultimate arbiters of other cultures' *beliefs*.[3] Social scientists of the past century and a half have shied away from this implication. An alternative approach that has been advanced in various forms is that "they" never really intended these ideas to be a factual account of reality.[4] This impetus informs, explicitly or implicitly, many of the ritual theories of the last century, to be discussed below. Since such attempts to hedge purity with idioms such as *"ritual purity"* alienate religion from everyday experience (and rationality),[5] one may ask if these attempts are any less patronizing than to label these practices outright as irrational.

The discussion in previous chapters suggests an alternative account, whereby pollution should be viewed as an explicit causal theory with practical implications. In order to understand its role in the broader metaphysical outlook of a culture, it is helpful to examine the relationship between direct experience and underlying causal forces as understood without the aid of elaborate cultural explanations. For the purpose of this discussion, it will be helpful to distinguish between two levels of causal understanding. The first is characterized by *prediction*: the existence of a regular conjunction of Event A and Event B enables one to predict that Event B will occur following Event A. The second level of

[1] Richard Fardon, "Purity and Danger Revisited," in *Mary Douglas: An Intellectual Biography* (London/New York, NY: Routledge, 2001), 74–100.

[2] This tension is also examined in relation to "essentialism" in Chapter 10.

[3] See Byron J. Good, *Magic, Rationality, and Experience: An Anthropological Perspective* (Cambridge: Cambridge University Press, 1994), 17–18.

[4] See Stanley Tambiah, *Magic, Science, Religion, and the Scope of Rationality* (Cambridge, UK: Cambridge University Press, 1990), 54–64 (developing Wittgenstein's remarks on Frazer).

[5] Struggling with this problem, Dan Sperber writes that "when a Dorze friend tells me that pregnancy lasts nine months, I think, 'So, they know that.' When he adds, 'but in some clans it lasts eight or ten months', I think, 'That's symbolic.' Why? Because it is false" (*Rethinking Symbolism*, trans. A. L. Morton [Cambridge: Cambridge University Press, 1975], 3).

causal understanding is characterized by *inference*: to posit the reason why Event A is conjoined with Event B. Whereas prediction can be expressed in behavior and does not necessarily involve reflection, inference is a mental act, mediated by language, and accordingly can be viewed as a theory.

Every organism needs to take into account causal forces which are beyond its comprehension and adjust its behavior accordingly. A cat may not *understand* a highway, but it would be wise to keep its distance from those noisy things zooming by. Similarly, our immediate experience of this world must deal with unseen causal forces. Our expectations of these causal forces inform our behavior and could be viewed as an intuitive metaphysics. For example, preschoolers who see a moving dot obscured by a screen expect to see the dot reemerge at the other side of the screen. These little Newtons have an intuitive sense that an object in motion tends to stay in motion.[6]

These remarks refer to causal understanding as experienced in individual development, but similar observations apply to the understanding of causal forces on the level of cultural discourse. In particular, as pointed out by Geoffrey Lloyd, all cultures have an implicit notion of natural laws, in which "nature" means nothing more than regularity of experience.[7] Farmers know that they cannot grow a crop of wheat unless they first sow seed; hunters take it for granted that their arrows will fly straight without being deflected. Within this domain of invisible causal forces, *we* may distinguish between "natural" and "supernatural" ones, but this distinction itself was a product of our particular intellectual history.

This framework can be depicted as seen in Figure 6.1.

In this diagram, Tier 1 represents the regularity of immediate sensory experience. As noted above, this regularity constitutes the immediately perceivable aspect of the "natural" world, and it provides the basis for inferring the existence of unseen causal forces. Accordingly, the natural world requires that one take into consideration Tier 2 forces that are

[6] See Jean M. Mandler, *Foundations of Mind: Origins of Conceptual Thought* (Oxford: Oxford University, 2004); Susan Carey, *The Origin of Concepts* (Oxford: Oxford University, 2009).

[7] See Geoffrey E. R. Lloyd, *Magic, Reason and Experience* (Cambridge: Cambridge University Press, 1979), 49. For further discussion of the complex pattern of usages of "nature," see Raymond Williams, *Keywords* (Oxford: Oxford University Press, 1983), 219–224, in which Williams comments, "Nature is perhaps the most complex word in the language" (219).

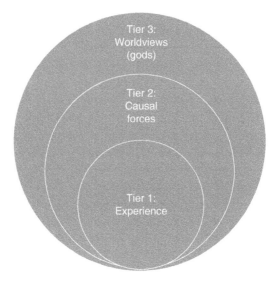

FIGURE 6.1 Levels of causality

outside of immediate sensory apprehension. To the extent that these forces are mysterious, there is no basis for distinguishing between "natural" and "supernatural" forces. Nevertheless, these causal forces may receive explanation by means of Tier 3 cultural theories (theologies, cosmologies, etc.) which often posit a higher level of agency, namely gods, who are able to manipulate the natural world. Within this framework, it may be observed that Tiers 1 and 2 are experienced by any organism with cognitive faculties, whereas Tier 3 would be unique to humans, as it is dependent on language.[8]

THE METAPHYSICS OF HEALING RITUALS

This general framework for understanding levels of causation can serve as a tool for understanding theories of disease causation. As was seen in early

[8] For the emergence of narrative capability as a key turning point in the development of causal reasoning, both phylogenetically and ontogenetically, see respectively Merlin Donald, *Origins of the Modern Mind: Three Stages in the Evolution of Culture and Cognition* (Cambridge, MA: Harvard University Press, 1991): 201–268; Shaun Gallagher and Daniel Hutto, "Understanding Others Through Primary Interaction and Narrative Practice," in *The Shared Mind: Perspectives on Intersubjectivity*, eds. J. Zlatev, T. P. Racine, C. Sinha and E. Itkonen (Amsterdam: John Benjamins, 2008), 17–38.

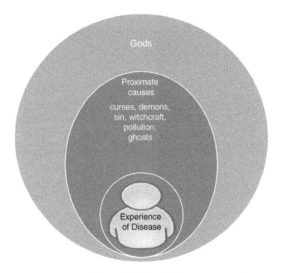

FIGURE 6.2 Metaphysics of disease causation

Mesopotamian sources surveyed in Chapter 2, the infectiousness of certain diseases was understood, but the terminology for articulating the etiologies of disease was fluid, including curse, witchcraft, demons, sins and pollution. This situation can be represented as seen in Figure 6.2.[9]

The middle tier in this hierarchy, referring to the proximate causes of disease, can be conveniently elucidated by means of George P. Murdock's taxonomy based on a survey of 139 ancient and modern cultures.[10] Table 6.1 is a brief summary of Murdock's typology of natural and supernatural causes of disease. As was seen in Chapter 5 in the context of the Šurpu incantations, the ritual practitioner (*āšipu*) did not always bother to seek the precise cause in actual practice, instead employing a laundry list litany to cover all of the possibilities.

Furthermore, it should be stressed that in an ancient Mesopotamian context there is no room for a sharp distinction between natural and supernatural causes. A modern surgeon has offered the following assessment of the role of demons as causes of disease in Mesopotamian rituals:

---

[9] For a strikingly similar schematization of "explanatory and therapy traditions" among Konduru in Southern India, see Paul Hiebert, "Karma and Other Explanation Traditions in a South Indian Village," in *Karma: An Anthropological Inquiry*, eds. C. F. Keyes and E. V. Daniel (Berkeley, CA: University of California Press, 1983), 121.

[10] *Theories of Illness* (Pittsburgh, PA: University of Pittsburgh Press, 1980), 17–21.

TABLE 6.1 *Murdock's causes of illness*

Causality	Characterization
Natural	Illness is a physiological consequence of normal activities that have gone awry (dietary mistakes, climate, accidents, old age).
Mystical	Illness is the *automatic* consequence of an act or experience, brought about by impersonal forces.
Animistic (spirit aggression)	The agent causing the illness is a personalized supernatural being.
Magical	A malicious human being uses covert, magical means to make a person ill.

In other words there is overwhelming evidence that the Babylonians saw disease in great part as resulting from the invasion of the body by a demon. We should add that there is rarely a description of the demon, of its face or its size. No doubt that if the modern doctor would meet an *āšipu* and tell him that we had found out what these demons looked like and that they were exceedingly small, this would perhaps be unexpected but it would hardly be unacceptable to him.[11]

A similar point can be made for ancient Greece: "It seems that fifth century Athenians did recognize the process of contagion, even if they, like Thucydides and all others before the late nineteenth century, did not at all understand the actual causes of contagion in the microscopic world."[12] In parallel, practitioners will often appeal to the gods to ensure the efficacy of their methods. Indeed, it is implicit in the causal hierarchy that the gods can override the lower-level causal forces.

Applying these insights to the HB, the fluidity of terms in describing the cause of disease offers a possible solution to the confusion regarding the interpretation of Exodus 12, where the Israelites are commanded to daub blood on their doorposts and lintels as a signal to God to spare them from the plague of the firstborn. The verses in question read as follows according to the NJPS translation:

[11] Ellis Douek, "Ancient and Contemporary Management in a Disease of Unknown Aetiology," in *Disease in Babylonia*, eds. I. J. Finkel and M. J. Geller (Leiden: Brill, 2007), 217.
[12] Jon Solomon, "Thucydides and the Recognition of Contagion," *Maia* 37 (1985): 122.

And the blood on the houses where you are staying shall be a sign for you: when I see the blood I will pass over you,[13] so that no plague will destroy you (*negep leₘašḥit*) when I strike the land of Egypt. (13)

For when the LORD goes through to smite the Egyptians, He will see the blood on the lintel and the two doorposts, and the LORD will pass over the door and not let the Destroyer (*mašḥit*) enter and smite your home. (23)

According to this widespread understanding of these verses, there is a tension between viewing God as the agent causing the plague in v. 13 and the statement in v. 23b that the "Destroyer" (*mašḥit*) will not be allowed to strike. The term *mašḥit*, a substantivized participle, is often interpreted as a personalized, demonic entity, hence the capital letter in the NJPS translation: "Destroyer." According to the Rabbis, this force is autonomous in carrying out its murderous function: "Once permission has been given to the Destroyer (*mašḥît*), he no longer discriminates between the righteous and the wicked."[14]

This supposed reference to a demonic entity often serves a criterion for distinguishing different layers. Many scholars have assumed that the demonic account was the more original account, which was later modified for theological reasons.[15] In support of reading this verse as a personalized destroyer, the narrative in 2 Samuel 24:16 describes God as sending a "destroying emissary" (*malakh ha-mašḥit*), so that the term in question modifies "emissary."[16] Be that as it may, it is worth noting that the formulation in v. 13, "so that you will not have a plague as a destroyer" (*negep leₘašḥit*; my translation), has the participle in question modifying the term "plague." In light of this verse, it is possible to interpret "Destroyer" (*mašḥit*) in v. 23 as referring to the plague from v. 13. The

---

[13] In modern scholarship, the common translation of the verb *p-s-ḥ* as "pass over" has been challenged. Based on the Aramaic Targumim and Isaiah 31:5, its use in Exodus 12 has been rendered "protect." See Chaim Cohen, "More Examples of 'False Friends': Regular Meanings of Words in Modern Hebrew Which Originated Erroneously," *Language Studies* 11–12 (2008): 188–191 (in Hebrew). My inclination, however, is to maintain the standard translation, since the possibility of a separate homonym of *p-s-ḥ* in Hebrew and other Semitic languages has not been substantiated and in light of other attestations of the root in the sense "skip/jump over" (e.g., 1 Kgs 18:21).

[14] *Mekhilta de-Rabbi Ishmael*, Parshat Bo, 11 (ed. Horovitz-Rabin, 38). See also Baruch Levine, *In the Presence of the Lord* (Leiden: Brill, 1974), 75.

[15] See Martin Noth, *Exodus: A Commentary*, OTL, trans. J. E. Anderson (London: SCM Press, 1965), 91–92; William H. C. Propp, *Exodus 1–18*, AB (New York, NY: Doubleday, 1999), 375–376, 401–402.

[16] Cf. 1 Samuel 13:17 and 14:15, where the substantivized participle *mašḥit* refers to a military force.

implication of this reading is that the Destroyer is nothing other than the plague itself.

Accordingly, the equivocation in the depiction of the agent of destruction (God/plague/destroyer) need not reflect a contradiction between discrete authors.[17] Rather, it reveals the inherent tension in trying to make sense out of disease.[18] The depiction of an impersonal destroyer which passes from house to house, killing its residents, reflects a firsthand familiarity with plague and its indiscriminate path of destruction. At the same time, the command that the sign of blood on the lintels will protect the Israelites appeals to the higher causal plane of divine orchestration, whereby it is Yhwh who ultimately determines the path of the "Destroyer." Hence, there is no real contradiction between these two depictions: they reflect a tension that is inherent to the experience of plague within the context of a belief in divine control. Whether or not these different formulations represent different sources, one thing is clear: the attribution of responsibility for disease to a causal agent is an act of interpretation, and these interpretations have theological ramifications. These ramifications find vivid expression in the polemics surrounding infection that will be explored later in this chapter.

RATIONALITY AND RITUAL

This model offers a new perspective on some vexed issues in ritual studies. From the beginnings of anthropology, scholars have observed in "primitives" a tendency to mistake ideal connections with real ones. In his monumental anthology *The Golden Bough*, James George Frazer views magic as a confused theory of causation and a primitive form of science:

---

[17] For a helpful evaluation of the source critical problems of this passage, see Simon Gesundheit, *Three Times a Year: Studies of Festival Legislation in the Pentateuch*, FAT 2/82 (Tübingen: Mohr Siebeck, 2012), 58–79. While Gesundheit argues convincingly for the Priestly character of Ex 12, I am not convinced by his arguments that vv. 12–14 represent a later revision, which are based largely on the question of agency and its theological ramifications.

[18] Here a modern analogy presents itself: In the face of the coronavirus' sweeping through the populations of nursing homes in the United States, medical officials have referred to it as an "Angel of Death," without anyone questioning their commitment to science. See also Christine H. Legare, "The Coexistence of Natural and Supernatural Explanations Across Cultures and Development," *Child Development* 83.3 (2012): 779–793.

The fatal flaw of magic lies not in its general assumption of a sequence of events determined by law, but in its total misconception of the nature of the particular laws which govern that sequence. If we analyse the various cases of sympathetic magic which have been passed in review in the preceding pages ... we shall find ... that they are all mistaken applications of one or other of two great fundamental laws of thought, namely, the association of ideas by similarity and the association of ideas by contiguity in space or time.[19]

Of course, this "mistaken" attitude is interpreted from Frazer's scientific worldview, which denies that mind could actually affect matter. Such observations gave rise to the postulated existence of "primitive mentalities," the debunking of which has been the focus of great effort in the past century.[20]

In his critique of Frazer's *The Golden Bough*, Ludwig Wittgenstein offered the following compelling account of the causal assumptions involved in healing rites: "In magical healing one *indicates* to an illness that it should leave the patient. After the description of any such magical cure we'd like to add: If the illness doesn't understand *that*, then I don't know how one ought to say it."[21] In other words, ritual constitutes an attempt to communicate directly with metaphysical forces in their own (often nonverbal) language.

Building on Wittgenstein and John Austin, Stanley Tambiah developed a theory of magic in which "performative acts" are built on a persuasive, as opposed to empirical, validity, which are effective only within the specific context ("language game") of ritual.[22] He writes: "Magical acts are ritual acts, and ritual acts are in turn performative acts whose positive and creative meaning is missed and whose *persuasive validity* is misjudged if they are subjected to that kind of empirical verification associated with

---

[19] *The Golden Bough: A Study in Magic and Religion*, 1 vol. abridged ed. (New York: Macmillan, 1952 [1922]), 57.

[20] For this debate, see Geoffrey E. R. Lloyd, *Demystifying Mentalities* (Cambridge: Cambridge University Press, 1990); Tambiah, *Magic, Science*. From a more psychological perspective, see Christopher R. Hallpike, *The Foundations of Primitive Thought* (Oxford: Clarendon Press, 1979), and Hallpike's vitriolic exchange with Richard Shweder reviewed in Michael H. Barnes, *Stages of Thought: The Co-Evolution of Religious Thought and Science* (Oxford: Oxford University Press, 2000), 45–50.

[21] *Remarks on Frazer's Golden Bough*, ed. R. Rhees; trans. A. C. Miles (Gringley-on-the-Hill: Doncaster, 1991), 6e–7e.

[22] Stanley J. Tambiah, *Culture, Thought and Social Action: An Anthropological Perspective* (Cambridge, MA: Harvard University Press, 1985), 60–86; Tambiah, *Magic, Science*; see also Marian W. Broida, *Forestalling Doom: "Apotropaic Intercession" in the Hebrew Bible and the Ancient Near East*, AOAT 417 (Münster: Ugarit-Verlag, 2015), 46–48.

scientific activity."[23] This line of argument was intended as a systematic refutation of the notion of "primitive mentalities." Accordingly, Tambiah resisted the once-commonplace tendency to ascribe to ritualists a belief in a "mysterious magical force" (so-called *mana*) that inheres in objects, stressing the expressive aspect of these rites.[24]

A perhaps unintended side effect of these attempts to avoid attributing metaphysical commitments to other cultures is the severing of the inherent connection between ritual logic and everyday experience. Such tendencies are implicit in ritual theories that eschew the language of belief. For example, in a manner reminiscent of de Saussure's account of language,[25] Jonathan Z. Smith prefers to speak of "difference" in his ritual theory. In the following statement regarding biblical concepts of purity, he seeks to accentuate the arbitrariness of the designations "pure" and "impure":

Here (in the world) blood is a major source of impurity; there (in ritual space) blood removes impurity. Here (in the world) water is the central agent by which impurity is transmitted; there (in ritual) washing with water carries away impurity. Neither the blood nor the water has changed; what has changed is their location.[26]

Leaving aside Smith's characterizations, which cannot withstand scrutiny, the important point is the overall direction of his argument. Liberated from the imputed ontologies imposed by Western observers, cultures no longer need to be held accountable for their metaphysical beliefs – either because they don't have any or because we're not allowed to make inferences regarding them.[27] The only remedy for the ethnocentrism of Taylor or Frazer is to ensure that science and religion occupy "non-overlapping magisteria" – never the twain shall meet.[28] Ironically, this diplomatic solution provides religious beliefs with autonomy, but at the price of relinquishing any claims to rationality.[29]

---

[23] *Culture, Thought and Social Action*, 60 (my emphasis).
[24] *Culture, Thought and Social Action*, 43. For further discussion, see Jonathan Z. Smith, "Manna, Mana, Everywhere and /-/-/," in *Relating Religion: Essays in the Study of Religion* (Chicago, IL: University of Chicago Press, 2004), 117–144.
[25] See Chapter 1.
[26] *To Take Place: Toward Theory in Ritual* (Chicago, IL: University of Chicago Press, 1987), 110.
[27] See Rodney Needham, "Skulls and Causality," *Man* 11.1 (1976): 71–88, critiqued by William James Earle, "Skulls, Causality, and Belief," *Philosophy of the Social Sciences* 15.3 (1985): 305–311.
[28] The expression was coined by Stephen J. Gould, *Rocks of Ages: Science and Religion in the Fullness of Life* (New York: Ballantine Books, 1999), 5.
[29] For a counterargument, see Barnes, *Stages of Thought*.

POLEMICS REGARDING INFECTION AND HEALING: SOME ANALOGIES

While the aforementioned studies are to be credited with adding circum-spection to cross-cultural investigation and establishing checks and balances to ethnocentrism, their claims tend to exaggerate in the direction of social constructivism and relativism. The source of this fallacy, as discussed in Chapter 1, is ascribing an exaggerated power to language at the expense of embodied experience.[30] Returning to the topic at hand, a "symbolic" (with the word "symbolic" hedging, as usual, the rationality of the behavior in question) approach to understanding pollution, how-ever compelling, is inevitably insufficient to account for the cross-cultural evidence. As argued above, it fails to acknowledge the tremendous degree of cross-cultural similarity that bridges local particularities, manifesting that these diverse cultures engage the same types of embodied experience. Truth be told, we live in the same world.

In setting the stage for discussing pollution as a causal theory, it is helpful to draw a distinction between reflective and nonreflective beliefs. The latter refers to the tacit – and usually unconscious – assumptions which serve as the basis for action. For example, one need not contemplate nor (needless to say) understand the law of gravity when throwing a ball to know it will return earthwards. Contagion (or contamination) appraisals can be likewise viewed as nonreflective beliefs based on recurrent experi-ences, for example, "getting dirty," that is, the experience that contact with filth enacts a transfer of substance or odor from the source to the target. These domain-specific contamination appraisals serve as the raw material for culture-specific (reflective) beliefs – explicit and normative formulations regarding which types of pollution are assumed to exist.[31] Reflective beliefs are mediated by language and are thus culturally

---

[30] For example, Rodney Needham's *Belief, Language and Experience* (Blackwell: Oxford, 1972), which is a systematic attempt to deconstruct the anthropological usage of "belief" as an analytic category, makes pervasive reference to Wittgenstein's revised theory of *language*. Non-coincidentally, this leads to a discussion of cultural relativity (176–246).

[31] For the distinction between nonreflective (or intuitive) and reflective beliefs, see Dan Sperber, "Intuitive and Reflective Beliefs," *Mind and Language* 12.1 (1997): 67–83; Justin L. Barrett and Jonathan A. Lanman, "The Science of Religious Beliefs," *Religion* 38.2 (2008): 109–124. However, the present framework places more emphasis on nonverbal embodied experience as the basis for explicit discursively formulated beliefs. For this reason, perhaps a more accurate expression would be Daniel Hutto's "intentional attitude." See his "Why I Believe in Contentless Beliefs," in *New Essays on Belief: Structure, Constitution and Content*, ed. N. Nottelmann (Basingstoke: Palgrave, 2013), 55–74.

transmitted. All kinds of culture-specific theories of pollution fall into this category, from biblical *ṭum'ah* to Western germ theory.

Understanding pollution as a causal theory enables us to make sense of disagreements and historical developments within a given culture's understanding of disease and pollution. Indeed, the preceding chapters have amassed evidence (biblical, extra-biblical and archaeological) that the peculiarities in the Priestly depiction of pollution – the relatively benign characterization of *ṭum'ah*, the absence of healing rituals and the obscuring of a causal connection between sin and suffering – stem from a deliberate attempt to replace popular rites for eliminating malicious forces with a centralized sin-offering ritual. At first glance, it may seem unlikely that the authors would have gone to this extent, but upon deeper inspection, one discovers that similar polemics have informed the discourse on disease in several ancient and medieval societies. These cross-cultural analogies will help flesh out the implications of P's view. As always, such comparisons are limited in their scope, and it will be our task to identify meaningful similarities and differences.

OCCASIONALIST THEOLOGY AND LIMITING "NATURAL" CONTAGION

The first comparison relates to Occasionalist schools in Medieval Islamic theology (*kalām*) regarding the causation of disease. In general, these schools argued "that events have no necessary causal connection and that God creates everything anew at every moment,"[32] and their attitudes regarding the causation of disease epitomized this worldview. Though similar views had been expressed previously, the emergence of a systematic school of thought along these lines is often attributed to al-Ash'ari in the tenth century CE, who denied the existence of natural contagion – attributing all causality to God.[33] The conventional belief in natural contagion, based in everyday observation, was rejected as implying a limit

---

[32] Justin K. Stearns, *Infectious Ideas: Contagion in Premodern Islamic and Christian Thought in the Western Mediterranean* (Baltimore, MD: Johns Hopkins University Press, 2011), 6. See further, Dominik Perler and Ulrich Rudolph, *Occasionalismus: Theorien der Kausalität im arabisch-islamischen und im europäischen Denken* (Göttingen: Vandenhoeck & Ruprecht, 2000).

[33] This general approach had already been expressed in a less systematic form by Ibn Qutayba in the ninth century; see Lawrence Conrad, "A Ninth-Century Muslim Scholar's Discussion of Contagion," in *Contagion: Perspectives from Pre-Modern Societies*, eds. L. I. Conrad and D. Wujastyk (Aldershot: Ashgate, 2000), 163–178.

to Allah's omnipotence and thus was perceived as a potential stumbling block leading to polytheism. As Lawrence Conrad explains:

But as Islam developed as a spiritual system, the old notions concerning contagion could not remain unopposed. First and foremost, in a religious tradition domin-ated by the doctrine of an all-powerful and all ordaining God, there was no place for the concession of devastating powers to minor spirits, or for a conception of disease causation that allowed for the capricious infection of one individual after another regardless of their good or evil deeds.[34]

The debates regarding the question of contagion are recorded in a variety of textual sources. These include exegesis of oral traditions (*aḥadith*) of the Prophet Muhammad's view regarding watering sick and healthy animals together and contact with mangy camels. In legalistic writings, scholars confronted practical dilemmas, such as the treatment of lepers and the question of whether to flee the Black Death of the fourteenth century.[35]

The literature on this topic is vast and beyond the scope of this study. For our purposes, the concern that natural contagion contradicts belief in the absolute hegemony of God suggests an analogy to P's seeming unwillingness to directly address the danger of infection, which, as argued above, is probably motivated by a denial of rituals that eliminate disease-causing forces.[36] The notion that the commonsensical notion of contagion could be theologically problematic may seem illogical to the modern reader. It is here that the Islamic comparison offers a crucial reminder, as Justin Stearns observes:

The danger that a belief in secondary causation – in which God gives his creatures a degree of causative power – could lead to polytheism might not be immediately clear . . . In general, however, it should be remembered that the coalescing Islamic legal and theological tradition of the eighth–ninth centuries depicts Islam as emerging into an intellectual environment characterized by a strong belief in polytheism and thus the causative power of multiple gods. In this context, many scholars . . . were wary of countenancing any hint of a belief in secondary causality, which they depicted as characteristic of bedouin of pre-Islamic Arabia.[37]

Similar anxieties can be found in the assertions of Lev 17 that slaughter outside of the tabernacle is tantamount to the worship of goat-demons.

---

[34] Conrad, "Discussion of Contagion," 166–167. See further, Stearns, *Infectious Ideas*, 13–36.
[35] Stearns, *Infectious Ideas*, 27–36, 106–139, passim.
[36] Compare the assertions that Yhwh is the only true healer (e.g., Ex 15:26; Jeremiah 17:5, 14); see above pp. 85–86.
[37] *Infectious Ideas*, 8 (Islamic dates have been omitted from quote).

Obviously, the point here is not to claim that P anticipated Occasionalist approaches to disease, but rather to view the latter as articulating a tension inherent to disease causation that may be missed by modern readers of the HB. In a theological context of devotion to a single all-powerful deity (monolatry), the existence of "external" causes of disease could be taken as competing with trust in the single God's causal hegemony, especially if these external causes mandated specific types of apotropaic and exorcistic rites to eliminate their influence.

HIPPOCRATIC (PSEUDO-)NATURALISM AND MIASMA

An additional comparison can be made with the Hippocratic critique of ritual healers found in *On the Sacred Disease*. This treatise sets forth a crucial distinction between natural and supernatural causes of disease. The author's central claim is that the appeal to supernatural causes serves as an excuse to cover-up for the inefficacy of the healers' methods:

I am about to discuss the disease called "sacred." It is not, in my opinion, any more divine or more sacred than other diseases, but has a natural cause, and its supposed divine origin is due to men's inexperience, and to their wonder at its peculiar character. Now while men continue to believe in its divine origin because they are at a loss to understand it, they really disprove its divinity by the facile method of healing which they adopt, consisting as it does of purifications and incantations. But if it is to be considered divine just because it is wonderful, there will be not one sacred disease but many, for I will show that other diseases are no less wonderful and portentous, and yet nobody considers them sacred . . . .

My own view is that those who first attributed a sacred character to this malady were like the magicians, purifiers, charlatans and quacks of our own day, men who claim great piety and superior knowledge. Being at a loss, and having no treatment which would help, they concealed and sheltered themselves behind superstition, and called this illness sacred, in order that their utter ignorance might not be manifest.[38]

Importantly, this critique denies only sporadic divine intervention, not the role of the gods in establishing the natural order. The gist of its argument is summarized by Geoffrey Lloyd as follows:

"Nature," for him, implies a regularity of cause and effect. Diseases, like everything else that is natural, have determinate causes and this rules out the idea of

[38] W. H. S. Jones, *Hippocrates*, Loeb, vol. 2 (Cambridge, MA: Harvard University Press, 1923), 139, 141.

their being subject to divine ("supernatural") intervention or influence of any sort. Interestingly enough, however, the writer of *On the Sacred Disease* does not exclude the use of the notion of the "divine" altogether. Indeed his view is not that no disease is divine, but that all are: all are divine and all are natural. For him, the whole of nature is divine, but that idea does not imply or allow any exceptions to the rule that natural effects are the result of natural causes.[39]

These distinctions might give the appearance of intellectual hairsplitting, but they had a practical aim: By negating the validity of supernatural causes, the author negated the main motivation for turning to ritual healers.

A similar tendency seems to have influenced the use of pollution terminology (*miasma*) in relation to disease. In its earliest metaphoric attestations in Greek tragedy, *miasma* referred to the stain of bloodguilt that was the underlying cause of sickness and catastrophe.[40] This miasma was deemed contagious, and its purifications were carried out by ritual acts which sought to banish the source of contagion from the populace. Interestingly, as part of their polemic against magical healing, Hippocratic writers appropriated the term *miasma* for their own naturalistic perspective so that it referred to the environmental cause of disease, specifically bad air.[41] In parallel, the key term for ritual purification, *katharmos*, is appropriated to express physiological purging, situated within a naturalistic etiology of disease. These tendencies are further developed by Galen, who correlates *miasma* with putrefaction. Jacques Jouanna observes that "from the moment that Galen admits the transmission of miasmas through the inhalation of air, he no longer admits the phenomenon of contagion through contact (just like the Hippocratic doctors), despite the fact that Thucydides had implicitly observed it."[42]

---

[39] *Magic, Reason and Experience*, 26.
[40] Robert Parker, *Miasma: Pollution and Purification in Early Greek Religion* (Oxford: Clarendon Press, 1983), 104–143.
[41] See Mirko Grmek, "Les vicissitudes des notions d'infection, de contagion et de germe dans la médecine antique," in *Textes médicaux latins antiques (Mémoires 5)* (St Etienne: Centre Jean Palerne, 1984), 53–70. Likewise, Jacques Jouanna, *Greek Medicine from Hippocrates to Galen: Selected Papers*, trans. N. Allies (Leiden: Brill, 2012), who writes "Thus, *miasma* in the Hippocratic text is a physical and natural cause, whereas in tragedy, *miasma* is a stain resulting from breaking a moral or religious prohibition" (125).
[42] Ibid., 135, referring to Thucydides' discussion of the "Athenian plague" (2.47.4), where it is observed that the doctors were among the most numerous to die due to their extensive contact with the sick. For further discussion of the nonemphasis of contagion in classical medical writings, see Vivian Nutton, "The Seeds of Disease: An Explanation of Contagion and Infection from the Greeks to the Renaissance," *Medical History* 27.1

Ironically, the notion of contagion by contact, despite being the most accurate account of transmission available for many infectious diseases, was marginalized due to its perceived association with ritualistic healing and purifications.[43] It was under the shadow of the great Greek medical authorities that priority was given to "miasmatic" theories of transmission, with the term itself subversively redefined to refer to bad air. Admittedly, the role of transmission by contact was never entirely ignored, so that doctors and laypeople alike needed to reckon with both models of transmission. Nevertheless, it is not an exaggeration to claim that the dogmatic pseudo-naturalism of the Hippocratic tradition effectively suppressed the empirically valid notion of contagion due to its perceived association with "magical" concepts of pollution. The ironic consequence of this plea for naturalism is captured by Jouanna: "Paradoxically, the medical, rational conception of *miasma* is further distanced from the modern understanding of infection than the magico-religious conception of *miasma* that is transmitted through contact."[44] This forced distinction between pollution and infection has haunted research until the present, leading to the strict separation of "religious" practice from biomedicine.

One can hardly ignore the resemblance to the tendency of the biblical sources, especially the Priestly treatments of disease, to obscure the danger of infection. The Hippocratic parallel substantiates in principle the hypothesis that the deemphasis of contagion could be motivated by a programmatic attempt to combat ritual healing practices, particularly those used to banish malicious forces.

Still, there are several obvious differences between the two sources. Whereas the Hippocratic text is explicitly polemical and articulates an unequivocal view denying supernatural causality, the Priestly text is not openly polemical and its broader metaphysical premises can only be discerned by inference. Moreover, whereas the Hippocratic works reject healing rites based on an articulated theory of natural causality, no such theory is found in P. Accordingly, it is possible to interpret P's omission of healing rites as an elaboration of the general skepticism found in the biblical sources regarding the efficacy of (human) healing practices: they

(1983): 14–16, passim; Nutton, "Did the Greeks Have a Word for It?" in *Contagion: Perspectives from Pre-Modern Societies*, eds. L. I. Conrad and D. Wujastyk (Aldershot: Ashgate, 2000), 156–162. In the latter article, additional reasons for the marginalization of contagion, aside from dogmatic adherence to Hippocratic views, are suggested.

[43] Grmek, "Les Vicissitudes"; cf. Nutton's discussion (previous note).

[44] *Greek Medicine*, 126.

simply don't work. Even this minimal reading bears similarity to the Hippocratic critique.

PROTO-NATURALISM IN P?

Yet the analogies between Hippocratic tradition and P have not been exhausted. So far, this comparison might suggest that any apparent naturalism in P is entirely superficial, lacking an underlying conceptual distinction between natural and supernatural causes. However, the Hippocratic texts could be used for a more radical claim that P's purity laws are predicated on *tacit* naturalistic tendencies, which could therefore be termed "proto-naturalistic." With the term "naturalism," I return to Lloyd's commonsense definition of "nature," presented at the beginning of this chapter. "Naturalism" refers to an awareness of the regularity of experience as based on a corresponding regularity of causal forces, excluding sporadic divine intervention. To this effect, P pays considerable attention to the systematization and classification of the phenomenal world. For example, this tendency is reflected in the hierarchal seven-day scheme of creation depicted in Genesis 1, which seeks to account for the emergence of the inanimate world, vegetation, animals and finally humans as a multistaged orderly process of creation. It is also reflected in the detailed laws of pure and impure animals in Lev 11.[45]

A clear example that is relevant to the present study pertains to the organization of Lev 15, which systematically distinguishes pathological and nonpathological genital emissions in a chiastic pattern:[46]

   A. Abnormal male discharges (vv. 2b–15)

      B. Normal male discharges (vv. 16–17)

         C. Sexual intercourse (v. 18)

      B.' Normal female discharges (vv. 19–24)

   A.' Abnormal female discharges (vv. 25–30)

[45] See Richard Whitekettle, "All Creatures Great and Small: Intermediate Level Taxa in Israelite Zoological Thought," *SJOT* 16.2 (2002): 163–183; Naphtali S. Meshel, "Food for Thought: Systems of Categorization in Leviticus 11," *HTR* 101.2 (2008): 203–229.

[46] See Richard Whitekettle, "Leviticus 15.18 Reconsidered: Chiasm, Spatial Structure and the Body," *JSOT* 49 (1991): 31–45; for discussion and slightly different arrangement, see Elizabeth W. Goldstein, *Impurity and Gender in the Hebrew Bible* (Lanham, MD: Lexington Books, 2015), 38–43.

This A-B-C-B'-A' scheme is surprisingly elegant, given the rather inelegant subject matter of genital discharges. There is a structural symmetry between male and female discharges, each one comprised of a distinction between normal and abnormal. Following the definition of "natural" employed in the present discussion, this distinction exemplifies an awareness of "natural" discharges (which we should not have doubted) and distinguishes their lesser degree of pollution from those of abnormal discharges, which require a seven-day waiting period and expiatory offerings.

For a more extended illustration, let us return to the rules of birth impurity in Lev 12:

[1]Yhwh spoke to Moses, saying: [2]Speak to the Israelite people thus: When a woman at childbirth bears a male, she shall be impure seven days; she shall be impure as at the time of her menstrual infirmity. [3]On the eighth day the flesh of his foreskin shall be circumcised. [4]She shall remain in a state of pure blood (*d^emē ṭahora*) for thirty-three days: she shall not touch any consecrated thing, nor enter the sanctuary until her period of purification is completed. [5]If she bears a female, she shall be impure two weeks as during her menstruation, and she shall remain in a state of pure blood (*d^emē ṭahora*) for sixty-six days.

This text depicts the impurity of the mother as passing through two stages: an initial stage of pollution analogous to that of a menstruant (Lev 15:19–24), and a second stage of reduced impurity, designated "pure blood." The duration of each of these stages is determined by the sex of the offspring, lasting 7 + 33 days for a male and 14 + 66 for a female.

The implications of this distinction are not spelled out in Lev 12 and have received conflicting interpretations. According to one reading, the text distinguishes between a severe and moderate degree in the transmission of impurity, so that in the second stage, the woman no longer causes secondary defilement as detailed in Lev 15:19–24 (P). According to a second reading, followed by the Rabbis, the primary implication of this distinction is to determine whether marital relations are forbidden or permitted. They understand the prohibition of sexual relations with a menstruant stated in Lev 18:19 and 20:18 (H) as implicit in Lev 12:2. According to this interpretation, the rule of "pure blood" permits sexual relations despite the presence of lochial discharge. This debate will be discussed further in Chapter 11.

Two main questions can be raised regarding Lev 12. The first has monopolized the attention of ancient and modern exegetes: what is the reason for the differentiation between males and females regarding the duration of impurity?[47] A second question, however, is no less perplexing: why does the text establish a distinction between the initial stage of bleeding and "pure blood" in the first place? This distinction is most striking in the rabbinic interpretation, which permits sexual relations with the mother despite her lochial discharge and thereby exempts her from a severe transgression (Lev 18:19), which carries the penalty of being "cut off" (*karet;* Lev 20:18). This permissive view is quite striking considering the severity of punishment. Indeed, it is instructive to note that all nonrabbinic streams of early Judaism continued to prohibit sexual relations during this period,[48] and ultimately rabbinic tradition also backed down from this leniency.[49]

Plausible interpretations can be given to both of these questions by reference to Greek medical treatises, particularly *The Nature of the Child,* a Hippocratic work dated to the late fifth century BCE. As has been argued in detail recently by Matthew Thiessen, the views expressed in this work represent ideas which were circulating among multiple Greek authors, relating to the differential lengths of formation for male and female embryos.[50] A key passage reads:

Now then, the reason for the discharge (*katharsis*) after birth is this: the earlier period of gestation – up to 42 days for a girl, and 30 for a boy – is the period when the least amount of blood flows to increase the growth of the embryo, while after

---

[47] For discussion, see Jacob Milgrom, *Leviticus,* AB; 3 vols. (New York: Doubleday, 1991–2000), 1.750–751; Jonathan Magonet, "'But If It Is a Girl She Is Unclean for Twice Seven Days . . .': The Riddle of Leviticus 12.5," in *Reading Leviticus: A Conversation with Mary Douglas,* JSOTSup 227, ed. J. F. A. Sawyer (Sheffield: Sheffield Academic Press, 1996), 144–152.

[48] For example, the twelfth-century CE Samaritan work *Kitab al-Khilaf* (*The Book of Differences*) critiques the rabbinic position as follows: "The Jews reckon that *dam tahara* is [the blood of] 'her cleanness' and treat it as clean blood. Their error in this is obvious: there is no kind of blood coming out of the vagina that is clean: all of it is classed as contaminated. Because of this, they let her associate with clean people and let her husband copulate with her. This is a fallacious ruling and contradicts the law of Moses"; translation: Iain Ruairidh mac Mhanain Bóid, *Principles of Samaritan Halachah,* Studies in Judaism in Late Antiquity 38 (Leiden: Brill, 1989), 168. For a helpful survey, see Zev Farber, "The Parturient's 'Days of Purity': From Torah to Halacha," www.thetorah.com /article/the-parturients-days-of-purity-from-torah-to-halacha (accessed 2/2/2020).

[49] See, e.g., Yedidya Dinari, "Customs Related to the Impurity of the Menstruant: Their Origin and Development," *Tarbiz* 49 (1979–1980): 302–324 (in Hebrew).

[50] "The Legislation of Leviticus 12 in Light of Ancient Embryology," *VT* 68.2 (2018): 297–319. See also Richard Whitekettle, "Levitical Thought and the Female Reproductive Cycle: Wombs, Wellsprings, and the Primeval World," *VT* 46.3 (1996): 376–391. For cross-cultural evidence, see Milgrom, *Leviticus,* 1:763–764.

this period the amount increases right up to the time the woman gives birth. We must expect then that the lochial discharge will correspond and flow out in accordance with the number of these days (18.2).[51]

This text explains that, since the gestation of the female embryo takes longer than the male and absorbs more blood during this time, there is a longer duration of lochial discharge following a female birth (a maximum of forty-two days) than that of a male (maximum of thirty days). Without going into a detailed discussion of the presumptions of this text, it is sufficient to recognize that the longer duration of discharge for females offers the most cogent rationale for explaining the differential periods of impurity in Lev 12. No less significantly, the Greek term designating the discharge in this text is *katharsis*, which also serves as the term for purification in ritual contexts.[52] However, this idiom is predicated on the assumption that the release of fluids fulfills a beneficial purging function, based on a conception that emphasizes the need for equilibrium of bodily fluids. This usage suggests a similar understanding of "pure blood" in Lev 12, namely blood that is pure because it is fulfilling a purging function. As Thiessen writes: "The blood that starts at and follows childbirth is, according to the Hippocratic Corpus and Galen, no mere blood, but the most noxious and unhealthy components of blood that the woman's body needs to purge in order for her to live."[53] In fact, these Greek sources invite a reevaluation of the expression *d^emē ṭahora*, which may be rendered "blood of purification."[54] It would then correspond to the use of *ṭahora* in the expression "days (= period) of purification" (*y^emē ṭahora*; vv. 4, 6). Indeed, the parallelism of these two expressions seems deliberate. These comparisons with Greek medical texts suggest that, despite the absence of an articulated distinction

---

[51] Translation: Iain M. Lonie, *The Hippocratic Treatises "On Generation," "On the Nature of the Child," "Diseases IV": A Commentary*, Ars Medica 7 (Berlin: de Gruyter, 1981), 10.

[52] See Parker, *Miasma*, 213–214.

[53] "Legislation," 317. My only quibble with Thiessen here is his later reference to "death-dealing bodily fluid," thereby associating the birth impurity with death. Aside from the unnecessary association of impurity with death, it diverts the emphasis from the remarkable fact that the rule reduces the severity of impurity from this discharge.

[54] See Dorothea Erbele-Küster, *Body, Gender and Purity in Leviticus 12 and 15* (London: T&T Clark, 2017), 37–39, who notes that the LXX renders "impure blood" (ἀκάθαρτος; 50–51). Some scholars have suggested that "pure blood" may refer to the diminished proportion of actual blood in the discharge following the first days after birth. Cf. Parker, *Miasma*, 55, n. 87; Erbele-Küster, *Body, Gender and Purity*, 38.

between natural and unnatural causes, P represents at least a proto-naturalistic awareness of physiological regularity.

CONCLUSION

In this chapter, I have situated the Priestly treatment of pollution in comparison with ostensibly distant bodies of discourse, specifically Occasionalist writings from the Middle Ages and Greek medical writings from late antiquity. These comparisons can be further elucidated in light of the theoretical framework on causality introduced at the beginning of this chapter. According to this model, the experience of suffering may be explained by a plethora of unseen forces (Tier 2). Mesopotamian incantations offer a vivid illustration of the lack of clear distinctions between natural and supernatural agencies in the causation of disease, as well as the corresponding blurring of amoral and moral forces. Occasionalist writers, at least the more extreme proponents of this school, deny any significance to this intermediate level of causality, attributing infection to direct divine orchestration by Allah. Here, theological considerations (in reference to Tier 3) overrule more empirical views of contagion based on experience. The Hippocratic writers also attempt to diminish the concern with contagion, but with a motivation of disparaging the efficacy of ritual healers in favor of their (pseudo-)naturalistic lines of treatment. Regardless of whether these treatments were more successful or not, by diminishing the role of divine intervention, they introduced a crucial distinction between moral and amoral causal forces. As part of their polemic, they saw the need to downgrade the concern with the spread of infection by contact, limiting their use of *miasma* to bad air.

In light of these parallels, it seems more than likely that the peculiarities of P's treatment of disease and pollution were motivated by polemical aims. Such an account can explain its otherwise perplexing tendency to understate the danger of infection and to treat pollution as an exclusively cultic concern. It can also account for the text's obscuring the relationship between sin and disease. Though it may have been motivated by a polemical need to reject popular healing traditions, it seems to incorporate a proto-naturalistic conception of the body. This impression will be reinforced in the following chapters, which examine biblical notions of the soul as they pertain to pollution.

The Soul: From the Table to the Grave

7

You Are What You Eat: Impure Food and the Soul

A fundamental claim of this book has been that pollution, despite being a metaphysical concept (a causal force outside immediate sensory perception), is based on concrete experience and human epistemological capacities. Yet, as an ontological concept – a belief regarding what constitutes reality – it should not surprise us that it is related to other ontological assumptions, including notions of the soul. More precisely, in reference to the model presented in the previous chapter, it will be seen that the soul, like pollution, pertains to Tier 2 in the model, the level of unseen causal forces. The initial step in making this claim will be to show how the biblical *nepeš* functions as a folk-biological concept. Then, in the remaining part of this chapter and in the one following, we will examine how pollution relates to the *nepeš* in the contexts of diet and death, respectively, tracing the effects of *ṭum'ah* on the soul from the table to the grave.

When addressing the biblical concept of "soul," it is necessary to call attention to the intellectual baggage that this term carries from centuries of philosophical and theological discourse in the Western tradition. To facilitate this discussion, we may suggest an escalating scale of characteristics entailed in a soul-belief. These can be viewed as cumulative rather than mutually exclusive:[1]

1. The immaterial essence, animating principle, causing individual life (vitality)

---

[1] This scale is offered as a set of possible interpretations of the biblical evidence. The cross-cultural spectrum of soul concepts would require a much broader scheme.

2. The source of emotion, thought and/or personal identity (personality)
3. The spiritual part of humans as distinct from the physical part (containment)
4. The immortal part of humans having permanent individual existence (separability from the body)

The first of these can be viewed as a minimal characterization, providing a basis for explaining: What is the difference between a living creature and its corpse, even a moment after death? What has changed? What is missing? The second characterization assumes that the vitality which animates the living person is also the seat of his or her personality, the essential self. This assumption provides the basis for more elaborated notions of the soul, that it is a spiritual entity residing in the body that serves as a container (3) and that it can even continue to exist outside the body (4).

These latter characterizations constitute strong *dualistic* conceptions of the relation between body and soul. Plato lionized such a conception, viewing the soul as imprisoned within the body, and similar conceptions have been coupled with beliefs in the immortality of the soul in Western religions. In Western philosophy of the past 500 years (following Descartes), this strong dualism – now articulated as the relation between body and *mind* – has been subject to incessant attack. A key problem with the dualistic position has been its tendency to view the soul (mind) as a tiny person (homunculus) inside one's head. By attributing mental functioning to an empirically untenable homunculus, the theory loses any explanatory power. In short, one might say that the more the concept of the soul has been separated from the body, the more it has been vulnerable to theoretical attack.

Leaving these philosophical debates aside, it should be recognized that the biblical soul concepts are closely tied to bodily existence. At least three terms can be identified in the HB that correspond to the soul as characterized above. The term *nešamah* ("breath") appears already in Genesis 2:7: "Yhwh, God, formed man from the dust of the earth. He blew into his nostrils the breath of life (*nišmat ḥayyim*), and man became a living being." Though *nešamah* became a key term in rabbinic and especially later Jewish mystical writings (*qabbala*) for the divine soul, it is less commonly used in the HB.[2] A second term, *ruaḥ* ("wind" "spirit") often

---

[2] It appears only 24 times in the HB, compared with over 750 instances of *nepeš*.

refers specifically to a mood or disposition that God projects onto a person (Numbers 11:17, 25; Judges 11:29–33; 1 Samuel 10:9–11; 16:14–16). The third term, *nepeš,* is the most common, but its analysis is complicated by its wide semantic range. Like the other terms, it seems to be etymologically related to the breath, which suggests that the spirit was believed to be responsible for a person's breathing.[3] Interesting parallels can also be drawn from Greek soul concepts, many of which are likewise derived etymologically from the terminology of breath or wind, notably the term *psyche.*[4] As James Kugel explains: "'wind,' 'breath,' and 'spirit' all have something in common: they refer to something immaterial and invisible, something you can't point to or hold in your hands . . ., but at the same time something that is active and the *result* of whose doings can indeed be observed."[5] In short, the notion of the soul, as an invisible causal force, provides an example par excellence of metaphysical causal thinking.

---

[3] Compare Akkadian *napāšu* "breathe, become wide" (*CAD* N/1 288). For an association with breathing in Biblical Hebrew, see מפח נפש (Job 11:20: "expiring breath"; also 31:39). See Choon Leong Seow, *Job 1–21: Interpretation and Commentary* (Grand Rapids, MI: Eerdmans, 2013), 597, 617. Also: Exodus 23:12: "Six days you shall do your work, but on the seventh day you shall cease from labor, in order that your ox and your ass may rest, and that your bondman and the stranger *may be refreshed*" (וינפש). Its usage in Semitic cognates and biblical Hebrew to designate the "throat" (e.g., Isaiah 5:14) has tended to dominate the attention of biblical research, at the expense of the etymological connection to "breath." For these cognates, see: *DULAT* 636–637 (Ugaritic *npš*) and *CAD* N/1 296–304 (Akkadian *napištu*). For discussion and refs., see Claus Westermann "נפש nepeš soul," *TDOT* 2: 743–759. The association between "breath" and "throat" via metonymy is straightforward, and the question of which is historically primary need not detain us. The significant point is that the usage as "breath" serves as a more likely source domain for a soul concept than "throat." Note also the similar root *n-š-p,* which refers to blowing out (Ex 15:10; Isa 40:24), whose relation to *n-p-š* can be explained as metathesis. HALOT suggests that *n-š-p* is a by-form of *n-š-m* (Isa 42:14). Sol Cohen (personal communication) suggested to me that these roots are based on bilateral roots with a preformative *nun;* compare also *š-'-p* (Jeremiah 2:24; 14:6; Isa 42:14), which seemingly refers to inhaling. These roots may have been derived from onomatopoeia, as suggested by Thomas Staubli and Silvia Schroer, *Body Symbolism in the Body,* trans. L. Maloney (Collegeville, MN: Liturgical Press, 2001), 62–63.

[4] Likewise Sanskrit *atman.* See David B. Claus, *Toward the Soul: An Inquiry into the Meaning of ψυχή Before Plato* (New Haven, CT/London: Yale University Press, 1981), 93, n. 3; Jan Bremmer, *The Early Greek Concept of the Soul* (Princeton, NJ: Princeton University Press, 1983), 21.

[5] *The Great Shift: Encountering God in Biblical Times* (Boston, MA: Houghton Mifflin Harcourt, 2017), 193, note *. So also Akkadian *zāqīqu,* rendered by Ulrike Steinert as "Windgeist, Freiseele, Traumseele" corresponds to Sumerian líl; see *Aspekte des Menschseins im Alten Mesopotamien: Eine Studie zu Person und Identität im 2. und 1. Jt. v. Chr.* (Leiden: Brill, 2012), 347–365.

Where do the biblical notions of soul stand in light of the gradated scale presented above? Of course, it is necessary to keep in mind that the biblical attitudes on this topic were multifarious and dynamic, changing over the course of the centuries during which the biblical corpus was formed. In general, biblical scholars have been increasingly skeptical of finding a dualistic notion of soul. In twentieth-century research, it was often asserted that the HB asserts a monistic view of the relation between body and soul, whereby the person is an irreducible unity of these two aspects.[6] The key proof text for this contention is Gen 2:7, cited above: "Yhwh, God, formed man from the dust of the earth. He blew into his nostrils the breath of life (*nišmat ḥayyim*), and man became a living being (*nepeš ḥayyah*)."According to this reading, the human *nepeš* is the combination of material (dust) and spiritual (divine breath) components. Yet, as James Barr has cogently pointed out, this widespread interpretation contains several fallacies.[7] In particular, it overlooks the obvious dualism of the dust/breath dichotomy and misinterprets the sense of *nepeš* in this passage. Instead of rendering it correctly as "person" or "human being" (see the lexical survey at the end of this section), they retain the translation "soul" while simultaneously denying the existence of a biblical soul concept.

Kugel has stated his rejection of this possibility – at least in the early biblical period – unequivocally. After reviewing the main "soul" terms and their etymological connection to breath, he writes:

The conclusion to which this leads is, at least at first, quite shocking. It is not, as some have argued, that biblical souls were conceived to be *different* from ancient Greek souls or more modern souls. Rather for much of the biblical period, there simply were no souls. People were people. They had breath that came into their lungs and went out again, and so long as this happened they were alive; it is this that *neshamah* mostly refers to.[8]

---

[6] This view has often been characterized as "totality thinking." For example, Walther Eichrodt writes regarding Genesis 2:7: "Here *nepeš* is obviously not meant as a *tertium quid* between spirit and body, but denotes the totality which has come about through the combination of the body formed out of the earth and the divine breath breathed into it" (*Theology of the Old Testament*, OTL, vol. 2, trans. J. A. Baker [London: SCM Press, 1967], 137).

[7] *The Garden of Eden and the Hope of Immortality* (Minneapolis, MN: Fortress Press, 1992), 36–38. Frequently, the expression here *nepeš ḥayyah* is juxtaposed with *nepeš met* in Numbers 6:6, supposedly expressing the difference between a living and dead being (e.g., Eichrodt, *Theology*, 137). However, despite their initial appearance, these two expressions are not parallel. The term *met* is not an adjective but a noun, hence the expression should be rendered "the soul of the dead" (see below p. 154 for the discussion of *napšot met* in Lev 21:11).

[8] *The Great Shift*, 191.

This skepticism appears to represent a consensus in biblical scholarship, though these sentiments often involve using a Platonic conception as a frame of reference.[9] With all due respect to Plato, there is no reason to grant his soul concept priority over others.

Swimming against this current of opinion, Richard Steiner has argued systematically for viewing the biblical idea of the *nepeš* as implying dualism, and the present discussion will elaborate on this view.[10] There is robust evidence that a conventional view of the *nepeš* in the HB was at least partially dualistic. Linguistically, the *nepeš* is described as being "in" a person's body, employing a schema of containment to conceptualize this relationship.[11] The *nepeš* is depicted as the seat of the emotions, will and even the appetite (Gen 27:4, 25; Micah 7:1; Psalms 107:9). It is also employed as a designation for the seat of individualized personality.[12] Importantly, several sources refer to the *nepeš* as leaving the body at the moment of death (Gen 35:18), and occasionally returning after "near-death" experiences (1 Kings 17:21), first, indicating that the spirit was something that was "in" the body, while also suggesting that the spirit was understood to be separable from the body.[13]

This understanding of the biblical evidence is corroborated by Iron Age Aramaic inscriptions from funerary contexts which depict the *n(a)bš*, a phonetic variant of *nepeš*, as continuing to exist in the burial spot after death. Important evidence comes from the Katumuwa (tentative

---

[9] So even the recent, nuanced discussion of Mathew Suriano problematizes the biblical conception through such a comparison: "The Hebrew Bible's conception of soul (נפש) is inconsistent with the Platonic/Cartesian mapping of a mind–body dichotomy for multiple reasons . . . Yet this dualism did not exist in ancient Israel" (*A History of Death in the Hebrew Bible* [Oxford: Oxford University Press, 2018], 5).

[10] Richard C. Steiner, *Disembodied Souls: The Nefesh in Israel and Kindred Spirits in the Ancient Near East, with an Appendix on the Katumuwa Inscription* (Atlanta, GA: SBL Press, 2015). See also the earlier remarks by James Barr, "Scope and Problems in the Semantics of Classical Hebrew," *ZAH* 6.1 (1993): 6–8, and most recently: Joachim Schaper, "Elements of a History of the Soul in North-West Semitic Texts: npš/nbš in the Hebrew Bible and the Katumuwa Inscription," *VT* 70.1: 156–176.

[11] Corresponding to "containment" (#3) in the scale of soul-beliefs above.

[12] Corresponding to "personality" (#2) in the scale of soul-beliefs above. For the literary technique of dialogues between a person and his *nepeš* (e.g., Ps 104:1), see Steiner, *Disembodied Souls*, 79–80.

[13] Cf. Jacob Licht's illuminating discussion, who struggles with the question of the implicit dualism of these sources: "nefesh," *Encyclopaedia Biblica*, vol. 5 (Jerusalem: Mossad Bialik, 1968), 898–904 (Hebrew). Compare also Ps 146:3–4: "Put not your trust in nobles, in mortal man who cannot save; His spirit departs (תצא רוחו), he returns to the dust." In an anthropogenic conception reminiscent of Genesis 2:7, the spirit/breath (*ruaḥ*) leaves the body, leaving only dust.

vocalization) stele from Zinçirli (ancient Sam'al, near the southern border of modern Turkey) from the late eighth century BCE. This inscription refers to the *nbš* of Katumuwa that continues to live in the stele: "The festal offering of this reception room is a bull for Hadad ... a ram for Kubaba, and a ram for my soul, which is in this stele" (*wybl.lnbšy.zy. bnṣb.zn*).[14] Similar ideas are expressed on the Hadad statue of Panamuwa: "Whoever from among my descendants shall grasp the scepter and sit on my throne ... and sacrifice to this Hadad ... and mention the name of Hadad, let him then say, 'May the soul (*nbš*) of Panamuwa eat with you, and may the soul (*nbš*) of Panamuwa drink with you.' Let him keep mentioning the soul (*nbš*) of Panamuwa with Hadad."[15]

Surveying the biblical evidence, one finds the following uses for *nepeš*:

1. Physiological

    a. "throat"
    b. "breath"

2. Soul

    a. "vitality"
    b. "soul"

3. Person

    a. "individuated life"
    b. "person/human being"
    c. "self" (e.g., Esth 4:13).[16]

It seems fairly straightforward that the usages of *nepeš* in the sense of person (3) are derivative of the notion of *nepeš* as soul (2), which is itself based on a conception whereby the body contains its vital force/spirit, conceptualized as a breath (1b). The important point to stress here is that

[14] Text edition: Dennis Pardee, "A New Aramaic Inscription from Zincirli," *BASOR* 356.1 (2009), 51–71; translation adapted from Steiner, *Disembodied Souls*, 129. See also next chapter, at n. 21.
[15] *KAI* 214: 15–18; see Josef Tropper, *Die Inschriften von Zincirli*, ALASP 6 Münster: Ugarit-Verlag, 1993), 156 (my translation). For further discussion, see Seth L. Sanders, "Naming the Dead: Funerary Writing and Historical Change in Iron Age Levant," *Maarav* 19.1–2 (2012): 11–36; Seth L. Sanders, "The Appetites of the Dead: West Semitic Linguistic and Ritual Aspects of the KTMW Stele," *BASOR* 369.1 (2013): 35–55; Mathew J. Suriano, "Breaking Bread with the Dead: Katumuwa's Stele, Hosea 9:4, and the Early History of the Soul," *JAOS* 134.3 (2014): 385–405.
[16] See also see Horst Seebass, "נפש nepeš," *TLOT* 9: 497–519.

nepeš constitutes the basis for the biblical notion of selfhood, as is reflected in the category 3 usages.[17] From this cursory survey, it can be seen that the biblical evidence supports a partial body–spirit dualism, though it lacked any clearly articulated view of the immortality of the soul as represented in Hellenistic period Judaism and Christianity.

In denying that the biblical concept of *nepeš* constitutes a dualistic concept of soul, scholars have been misled by comparison to the extreme dualism of Plato and propagators of his view in the Western tradition. However, they have rightfully emphasized the fact that the *nepeš* was understood to be flesh as long as the creature lives, constituting the basis of carnal desire and vitality. In this sense, the biblical view is strikingly compatible with many of the fundamental principles of embodied cognition. This conception can be most clearly illustrated by the role of *nepeš* in the dietary restrictions.

DIETARY RESTRICTIONS

A suggestive point of departure from which to introduce the biblical dietary evidence is the following description of pollution among the Yolmo wa in the Nepalese Himalayas:

The body, like the heartmind, should be kept "clean." As with other Himalayan peoples, Yolmo wa typically strive to keep their forms free of pollution . . . Pollution is felt to be an external blemish, manifested in skin rashes and wounds, which causes the afflicted to feel slow-witted and fatigued. The local logic relates to the way in which villagers give spatial form to the link between body and soul: as the defilement derives from material contaminations external to the person, it primarily affects the surfaces of the body. But as a dirty container soils its holdings, so a body's impurities can taint one's spiritual life.[18]

The anthropologist proceeds to explain how various sources of pollution (e.g., feces, menstruation, birth, death) are perceived as a source of bodily harm as well as disqualifying shamans and sacrifices from divine service.

---

[17] Further evidence comes from passages such as Leviticus 5:1–4 and Leviticus 7:20. Even when *nepeš* serves as the subject of these verses, it is treated as both feminine and masculine (Jacob Milgrom, *Leviticus*, AB 3 vols. [New York, NY: Doubleday, 1991–2000], 1:423): the former constitutes the correct gender of *nepeš*, whereas the latter apparently refers to the underlying reference of these rules, the person (*'adam*; masc.). This grammatical point reveals the implicit ontology that the *nepeš* was viewed as the essential component determining personhood.

[18] Robert R. Desjarlais, *Body and Emotion: The Aesthetics of Illness and Healing in the Nepal Himalayas* (Philadelphia, PA: University of Pennsylvania, 1992), 80.

A similar conception in which bodily uncleanness undermines the
capacity to interact with metaphysical or divine forces can also be found
within the broad cultural milieu of ancient Israel. For example, Neo-
Assyrian oracle inquiries include fixed formulas which ask Šamaš (the
sun deity) to disregard any defilement caused when performing the act of
divination: "Disregard that he who touches the forehead of the sheep is
dressed in his ordinary soiled garments (*ginêšu aršāti labšu*), has eaten,
drunk, anointed himself with, touched or stepped upon anything unclean
(*mimma lu"u*)" and so on.[19] Clearly, the implication of these formulas is
that these sources of uncleanness disqualify the offering and undermine
the divinatory process. Likewise, Evans-Pritchard describes the measures
taken by the Azande to avoid defilement to oracles, since "contact of an
unclean person with the oracle is certain to destroy its potency, and even
the close proximity of an unclean person may have this result."[20]

These considerations are particularly relevant for understanding the
biblical dietary laws. Outside of P, several sources suggest that certain
types of meat were inappropriate for divine service. For example, the
non-Priestly flood narrative distinguishes between pure and impure
animals, based on the premise that only the former are admissible offerings to Yhwh. Furthermore, the prohibition of non-slaughtered meat is
followed by the rationale "for you are a holy nation to Yhwh, your God"
(Deuteronomy 14:21; also Exodus 22:30). These non-Priestly sources
suggest that this specific dietary prohibition was originally a priestly
stringency, which was then extended to the entire "kingdom of priests"
(Ex 19:6). This stands to reason, since dietary restrictions are often
limited to priestly classes, posing cumbersome restrictions which can
even be life-threatening in circumstances of drought.[21]

[19] See Ivan Starr, *Queries to the Sungod*, SAA 4 (Helsinki: Neo-Assyrian Text Corpus
Project, 1990), xxiv. For discussion of the Assyrian terminology, see my "Defilement,
Disgust and Disease: The Experiential Basis for Akkadian and Hittite Terms for
Pollution," *JAOS* 136.1 (2016): 104–105.
[20] *Witchcraft, Oracles and Magic among the Azande* (Oxford: Clarendon Press, 1976),
127–134 (132).
[21] Nili Shupak writes regarding food prohibitions in ancient Egypt: "Regarding these
dietary prohibitions, it was primarily the priests and upper classes that were stringent,
not the commoners who were hungry for meat." See "'An Abomination to the Egyptians':
New Light on an Old Problem," in *Marbeh Hokmah: Studies in the Bible and the Ancient
Near East in Loving Memory of Victor Avigdor Hurowitz*, eds. S. Yona, E. L. Greenstein,
M. I. Gruber, P. Machinist and S. Paul (Winona Lake, IN: Eisenbrauns), 271*–294*
(278*; in Hebrew, my translation). One is also reminded of Colin Turnbull's account of
the starving Ik tribe, for whom ritual uses of food could only be viewed as "superfluous

More to the point, an association of the *nepeš* with digestion is attested in Genesis 27. In this non-Priestly narrative, the elderly Isaac requests Esau to bring him meat, so that "my *nepeš* may bless you before I die" (v. 4). This notion, repeated several times in the story, presupposes that meat would invigorate his spirit, which only then would be sufficiently empowered to give a worthy blessing. Here one is reminded again of the Phoenician and Aramaic inscriptions cited above, which speak of meat offerings for the spirit (*nbš*) of the deceased. This narrative, which depicts a positive connection between eating and the *nepeš*, can help explain the polluting power of forbidden foods reflected in P.

Specifically, the prohibition of consuming blood receives considerable attention in P narratives and laws. According to the P narrative of creation, the first humans were forbidden to eat meat, but meat was permitted to Noah after the flood, on the condition that he abstain from consuming the blood. The rationale for the prohibition given here and elsewhere in the Torah is the presence of the *nepeš* of the animal in the blood (Gen 9:4; Lev 17:11; Deut 12:16, 23, 27).[22] This rationale is treated as self-explanatory, though eating the *nepeš* of the animal could be viewed as a source of strength and vitality, considering the existence of cultures who willingly consume blood.[23] Here the explanation of the rabbinic commentator Nachmanides (thirteenth century) is illuminating:

Now it is also known that the food one eats is taken into the body of the eater and they become one flesh. If one were to eat the life of all flesh, it would then attach itself to one's own blood and they would become united in one's heart, and the result would be a thickening and coarseness of the human soul so that it would closely approach the nature of the animal soul which resided in that which he ate, since blood does not require digestion as other foods do, which thereby become changed, and thus man's soul will become combined with the blood of the animal![24]

---

and wasteful" (*The Mountain People* [New York, NY: Simon & Schuster, 1972], 197). See further below, p. 231.

[22] Though the widespread rendering of *nepeš* in these texts is "vitality," Simeon Chavel has recently proposed rendering בנפשו דמו in Genesis 9:4 as "in its throat." He translates: "However, animal-meat, the blood of which is (still) in its throat, you may not eat." See *Oracular Law and Priestly Historiography in the Torah*, FAT 2/71 (Tübingen: Mohr Siebeck, 2014), 73, n. 188, though he accepts the renderings "vitality/life" in related instances (ibid., 78, n. 202).

[23] See, e.g., William Robertson Smith, *Lectures on the Religion of the Semites* (New York, NY: Ktav Publishing, 1969 [1927]), 234, 313–314.

[24] Commentary on Leviticus 17:11. Translation: Charles Chavel, *Ramban (Nachmanides): Commentary on the Torah. Leviticus* (New York, NY: Shilo Publishing, 1971), 240.

Furthermore, the requirement to cover the blood of a hunted animal (Lev 17:13–14) can be elucidated on the background of several non-P texts that express the belief that the unburied blood of a victim calls out for vengeance, as reflected in the story of Abel's blood (Gen 4:10) and Job's plea that his complaint not be subdued (Job 16:18): "Earth, do not cover my blood; Let there be no resting place for my outcry!"[25]

These Priestly rules are based on the presumption that the *nepeš*, responsible for the vitality of a living creature, is located in the blood. This belief is experientially grounded in the observation that loss of blood is tantamount to bodily death. This correlation is represented in linguistic expressions such as "bloodshed" as an expression for murder, which finds abundant analogies in ancient literature and calls attention to the fact that *nepeš* serves as an explanatory biological concept rooted in down-to-earth observation, not abstract theological speculation.[26] Likewise the absence of animacy in objects and plants can be attributed to their lack of blood.

This fear of polluting one's *nepeš* finds even more explicit expression in the holiness rhetoric that concludes the Priestly code of pure and impure animals, Leviticus 11:43–44:

> [43]You shall not draw abomination (*š-q-ṣ*) upon yourselves through anything that swarms; you shall not make yourselves (*napšotekem*) unclean (*ṭ-m-'*) therewith and thus become impure. [44]For I the LORD am your God: you shall sanctify yourselves and be holy, for I am holy. You shall not make yourselves (*napšotekem*) unclean through any swarming thing that moves upon the earth. (NJPS translation)

Most modern translations, like this one, render the term *nepeš* in this passage as "yourselves," to give a reflexive sense to the verbs *š-q-ṣ* ("make disgusting") and *ṭ-m-'* ("defile").[27] However, some scholars have suggested a more concrete, physiological rendering of *nepeš* in light of the

---

[25] See also Ezekiel 24:7–8. For cross-cultural parallels, see e.g., J. G. Frazer and T. H. Gaster, *Myth, Legend and Custom in the Old Testament* (New York, NY: Harper & Row, 1969), 65–69.

[26] Note Akkadian *napišta tabāku* (CAD N/1 299), literally to "pour out" (cognate to Heb. *šapak*) the spirit, as an idiom for bloodshed. Regarding the Greek evidence, Claus writes: "Apart from its use as 'shade', ψυχή is clearly recognizable as a physical 'life-force' in Homeric death contexts: it can be 'destroyed' or 'lost'; it has no decisive physical identification but is ambiguously 'breath'-like and 'blood'-like" (*Toward the Soul*, 97). Cf. Richard Whitekettle, "A Study in Scarlet: The Physiology and Treatment of Blood, Breath and Fish in Ancient Israel," *JBL* 135.4 (2016): 685–704. In my opinion, here Whitekettle overextends the usage of *nepeš* as "breath."

[27] See also NRSV, ESV, KJV among others. This terminology appears again in Lev 20:25.

context of eating, namely "throat" or "gullet."[28] Ostensibly, this translation is corroborated by a similar usage in the book of Ezekiel. When God
demands that Ezekiel eat barley bread baked on human excrement, the
prophet priest protests, "Ah, my lord Yhwh, my throat (*napši*) was never
defiled; nor have I eaten anything that died of itself or was torn by beasts
from my youth until now, nor has foul flesh entered my mouth" (Ezek
4:14). Here *nepeš* in the sense "throat" seems to parallel "mouth" in
the second half of the verse.[29] Even if this rendering of Ezekiel 4:14 is
granted, however, it is more likely that Lev 11:43–44 refer to the Israelites
defiling their selves (not just their gullets).[30]

This point can be clarified by examining additional places in P where
the *nepeš* is associated with eating. Among the relatively numerous
appearances of *nepeš* in P, seven of these feature *nepeš* as the subject of
the verb "eat" in reference to forbidden or defiling foods, including blood,
suet and defiled or spoiled offerings.[31] It is significant that all appearances
of this idiom appear in relation to impure or desecrated meat, including
blood and suet of sacrifices, which may suggest (along the lines of
Nachmanides' interpretation above) that the animal flesh or blood, containing its spirit, pollutes that of its human consumer.

Admittedly, as noted, the term *nepeš* allows for several possible
translations ("gullet," "person," "spirit"). For this reason, it is significant
that the punishment clauses attached to these verses include the "cutting
off" penalty: "that *nepeš* will be cut off from its kinsmen." These idioms
are combined in Lev 7:25 in reference to someone who eats the suet of
an offering: "the *nepeš* who eats it shall be cut off from its kin." Though
the precise meaning of this punishment has been disputed,[32] it seems
to refer to total annihilation of the perpetrator in this life and the afterlife

---

[28] For "throats," see Milgrom, *Leviticus* 1:684, noting that the same expression appears in
20:25b.

[29] See Moshe Greenberg, *Ezekiel 1–20*, AB (New York, NY: Doubleday, 1983), 107.

[30] Note also the seemingly superfluous phrase בם ונטמאתם ("and thus become unclean"),
which clearly refers to the Israelites as persons.

[31] Leviticus 7:18 (*piggul*), 20 (eating sacrificial meat while impure), 25 (blood), 27 (suet);
17:10, 12, 15 (blood). The definition of the *piggul* meat as being three days old (also Lev
19:7–8) supports the common translation "putrid" (see James W. Watts, *Leviticus 1–10,
Historical Commentary of the Old Testament* [Leuven: Peeters, 2013], 417); Cf. David
P. Wright, *The Disposal of Impurity: Elimination Rites in the Bible and in Hittite and
Mesopotamian Literature* (Atlanta, GA: Scholars Press, 1987), 140–143, who prefers
"desecrated meat."

[32] See Milgrom, *Leviticus*, 1.457–460.

and the execution of his progeny.[33] This cumulative understanding is corroborated by Hittite oath curses, such as the following which threatens "these oath gods shall thoroughly eradicate your persons, together with your wives, your sons . . . They shall also eradicate them from the dark Netherworld below."[34]

Most relevant for the present discussion is its implications for the afterlife of the *nepeš*. As a denial of a restful afterlife, this punishment constitutes the opposite of the Priestly formula of being "gathered in to one's fathers/kinsmen" as a desirable afterlife.[35] In fact, one can find a likely parallel to this punishment in the Phoenician ruler Tabnit's curse (fifth century BCE) on whoever disturbs his burial spot: "Don't, don't open it and don't disturb me, for this thing is an abomination to Astarte. And if you do indeed open it and do indeed disturb me, may you not have any seed among the living under the sun, nor a resting-place with the Rephaites."[36] In other words, P's use of *nepeš* in reference to these dietary prohibitions and the associated curse which denies the *nepeš* a restful afterlife suggests that it is precisely the individual's "spirit" that is defiled by impure foods. One may also recall in this context Katamuwa's request for "a ram for my soul, which is in this stele (*wybl.lnbšy.zy.bnṣb.zn*)," which suggests that his *nbš* still had a carnivorous appetite even after bodily death.[37]

---

[33] First, it is clearly a divine punishment which probably involves premature death, as can be seen from the association of the cutting-off formulas with parallel expressions referring to destruction (השמידו\האביד) in Leviticus 23:29–20 and Ezekiel 14:8–9 (see Walther Zimmerli, "Die Eigenart der prophetischen Rede des Ezechiel," *ZAW* 66 [1954]: 1–26; Tikva Frymer-Kensky, "Pollution, Purification and Purgation in Biblical Israel," in *The Word of the Lord Shall Go Forth: Essays in Honor of David Noel Freedman in Celebration of his Sixtieth Birthday*, eds. C. L. Meyers and M. O'Connor [Winona Lake, IN: Eisenbrauns, 1983], 404–405). Second, it implies the extirpation of the perpetrator's progeny, analogous to the "cutting off" of a tree's branches (Isa 56:3–5; Jer 11:19; Job 14:7–14). This sense fits well with the use of the verb *karet* in relation to priestly (1 Sam 2:33) and monarchal (1 Kgs 2:45) lineage (Baruch A. Levine, *Leviticus. JPS Torah Commentary* [Philadelphia, PA: Jewish Publication Society, 1989], 241–242).

[34] Translation from Gary Beckman, *Hittite Diplomatic Texts*, WAW 7 (Atlanta, GA: Scholars Press, 1999), 33 (parentheses marking secure reconstructions have been removed).

[35] E.g., Genesis 15:15; 25:8–9; 47:30; Num 20:24. For further discussion of this point, and the distinction between "good" and "bad" death more generally, see next chapter, especially n. 7.

[36] Text: *KAI* 13; translation: P. Kyle McCarter, "The Sarcophagus Inscription of Tabnit, King of Sidon," *CoS* 2.56: 181.

[37] For this text, see above, p. 136.

To summarize, the dietary laws imply a direct causal relationship between a person (*nepeš*) consuming forbidden flesh or blood and the cutting off of the *nepeš* as a consequence from this consumption. In these passages, it is ill-advised to insist on a sharp dictionary distinction between *nepeš* as "person" (i.e., the agent) and as "soul" (essential self). Moreover, one cannot deny the possibility that a more physiological sense of *nepeš* as "gullet" (i.e., the organ of swallowing) was also invoked in these contexts.[38] In other words, these instances may invoke an onto-logical connection between ingesting – taking into oneself – a forbidden food and the defilement of one's inner essence.

Perhaps some lexicographers would object to this suggestion that multiple senses of *nepeš* were activated simultaneously in these contexts, and indeed, it is not easy to demonstrate which aspects of a semantic field are activated by a given utterance. Nevertheless, unexpected confirmation for this contention can be found in a legal midrash to Lev 17:15, a verse that attributes impurity to "any person (*nepeš*), whether citizen or stranger, who eats what has died or has been torn by beasts." Though the simple reading of this passage suggests that the carrion of any animal causes the defilement, the rabbinic reading limited (for reasons which need not detain us) the application of this verse to carrion of birds. For our purposes, the interesting point is the ensuing discussion of what type of consumption entails the laundering of clothes:

Perhaps it defiles clothes when in the intestines; it is taught: "he shall launder his clothes, wash in water, and he shall be impure until the evening, and then he shall be pure." It does not defile clothes while in the intestines. Perhaps it does not defile clothes while in the intestines but defiles clothes when in the mouth; it is taught: "*nepeš*"; the *nepeš* is what defiles and not in the intestines and not in the mouth.[39]

---

[38] While generally etymology does not provide conclusive indication of meaning (usage), as rightly stressed by James Barr (*The Semantics of Biblical Language* [London: Oxford University Press, 1961], 117–119), it remains indisputable that more etymologically basic usages and additional distinct senses of a given term (in the estimation of lexicographers) can inform the semantic nuances and connotations of a particular usage (see above pp. 12ff.). In the present context, an etymological derivation from "gullet" is not only a concern for reconstructing the diachronic development of *nepeš* (so Barr), but it also serves as the basis for an ontological connection between consuming unclean foods and defiling one's soul.

[39] *Sipra Aḥarei Mot* Par. 7 12:3 (ed. Weiss 84b–85a; my translation). Hebrew text: יכול יהא מטמא בגדים בתוך המעיים תלמוד לומר יכבס בגדיו ורחץ במים וטמא עד הערב וטהר, אינו מטמא בגדים בתוך המעיים, יכול לא יטמא בגדים בתוך המעיים אבל תטמא בגדים בתוך הפה ת"ל נפש, (אביתי) [בבית] נפש היא מטמאה ולא בתוך המעיים ולא בתוך הפה.

Based on this interpretation, the rabbis derived the law that the carrion of birds defiles when in the "the place of swallowing" *(bet ha-beli'ah)*.[40] In other words, this midrash offers a precise physiological rendering of *nepeš* in this verse, determining that defilement takes place only when the forbidden meat is in the throat.

Incidentally, this same biblical verse offers an additional important insight. Just as the bodily act of ingestion can defile a person's essential self, so too an act of purification performed on the body serves to remove the defilement. In other words, a person who had consumed a defiling food does not need to regurgitate the cause of pollution, but only needs to clean the external "vessel": "Any person *(nepeš)*, whether citizen or stranger, who eats what has died or has been torn by beasts, shall wash his clothes, bathe in water, and remain impure until evening; then he shall be pure" (Lev 17:15). The implication of these observations is that the Priestly conception is analogous to the cross-cultural evidence cited above. Just like that of the Nepalese Yolmo wa, the Israelite view of pollution was based on a containment schema whereby the container, the body, can defile its content – the *nepeš*.[41]

CONCLUSION

In this chapter, we have explored how *nepeš* operates as a folk-biological concept in the HB. Recognizing its role as a Tier 2 causal force, it is not surprising to find it directly related to pollution. For example, by consuming impure meat, the *nepeš* is made susceptible to pollution. In the following chapter, which investigates the biblical notion of death pollution, it will be seen that its role can be reversed, with the *nepeš* serving as the source of defilement.

---

[40] This law pertaining to the בית הבליעה is presumed in numerous *mishnayot*, e.g., m. *Zebaḥim* 7:5–6; *Ṭohorot* 1:1, 3.

[41] It is worth stressing here that the present argument need not presuppose a strongly dualistic conception. In fact, it is most immediately compatible with the notion that the *nepeš* and the body are interdependent. Still, the basic insight that should not be over-looked is that the *nepeš* is a metaphysical concept, referring to the unseen force that is housed in the body and animates it.

8

Death and the Polluting Spirit

People stink. Rocks don't smell (or at least we don't smell them). Trees may give off smells, especially rotting ones, but they don't stink like rotting animals. There seems to be a great chain of being, whereby the more dynamic the creature (e.g., locomotion, eating, sex), the more disgust-potential is manifested in its decomposition. While biochemists may attribute this odor to emissions of sulfur and ammonia, many cultures interpret the smell of death to the spirit of the deceased at it leaves the dead body.

In the previous chapter, it was argued that the *nepeš* is susceptible to pollution by ingesting forbidden foods. This chapter will explore the possibility that in the Priestly source the human *nepeš* could also constitute the source of pollution in the context of death, when departing the body. Yet, the question of how to render *nepeš* in this context has haunted commentators. The resolution of this terminological question is part and parcel of two broader questions:

1. Was the notion of death pollution a concern in ancient Israel in the pre-exilic period, or did it emerge only later, perhaps under foreign influence?
2. What was the rationale for this pollution and what were its implications?

Doubts regarding the antiquity of this notion have been raised by those who have surveyed the literary evidence. Explicit references to death pollution appear almost exclusively in the Priestly traditions of the Pentateuch and Ezekiel. However, this topic is missing conspicuously from the place where most readers would expect it, namely the collection of purity laws contained in Leviticus 11–15. Compared with the scarce references to this pollution in Leviticus, one gets the impression that Numbers is obsessed with death. Recent critical scholarship allows a more precise characterization of this situation. Recognizing that this topic appears only in the Holiness (H) layer of Leviticus, specifically in Lev 21, and in Priestly materials in Numbers with stylistic affinities to H, Christian Frevel has recently pointed out that "the specific case of defilement by a corpse seems to be a late topic in the development of the Torah, which was accentuated especially in the Book of Numbers."[1] The immediate question raised by this evidence is whether it should be explained historically – as a Priestly "invention" from the Persian Period, or whether it should be explained on either literary or theological grounds.

The more fundamental question pertains to the rationale of death pollution; here many divergent explanations have been suggested. Comparative evidence from adjacent and more remote cultures might suggest a fear of malicious spirits (ghosts). While accepting the possibility that the ritual of Num 19 originated as an exorcistic practice, more theologically oriented scholars tend to view this pollution as representing the power of death as an abstract force, interpreting the biblical dichotomy of purity and impurity as corresponding to life and death, respectively. For example, Jacob Milgrom characterizes the aim of the Levitical laws of purity as follows: "Among all of the diachronic changes that occur in the development of Israel's impurity laws, this clearly is the most significant: the total severance of impurity from the demonic and its reinterpretation as a symbolic system reminding Israel of its imperative to cleave to life and reject death."[2] In contrast, historically oriented scholars drawing on the observations regarding the late dating of the relevant textual evidence have suggested that this notion may reflect Zoroastrian influence in the Persian Period,[3]

---

[1] "Purity Conceptions in the Book of Numbers in Context," in *Purity and the Forming of Religious Traditions in the Ancient Mediterranean and Ancient Judaism*, eds. C. Frevel and C. Nihan (Leiden: Brill, 2013), 407.

[2] *Leviticus*, AB; 3 vols. (New York, NY: Doubleday, 1991–2001), p. 1:1003. See also Thomas Hieke, "Die Unreinheit der Leiche nach der Tora," in *The Human Body in Death and Resurrection*, eds. T. Nicklas et al. (Berlin: de Gruyter, 2009), 58–63.

[3] See Thomas Kazen, "Purity and Persia," in *Current Issues in Priestly and Related Literature: The Legacy of Jacob Milgrom and Beyond*, eds. R. E. Gane and A. Taggar-Cohen (Atlanta, GA: SBL, 2015), 435–462; cf. Reinhard Achenbach, "Verunreinigung durch die Berührung Toter: Zum Ursprung einer alisraelitischen Vorstellung," in *Tod und*

or alternatively, that it was a strategic tactic to eliminate ancestral cults.[4]

In order to address these questions, the following discussion will be divided into three parts: (1) the ancient Near Eastern context for Israelite concepts of the afterlife; (2) the meaning of *nepeš* in Priestly references to death pollution; and (3) the question of the implications of this pollution. These findings will then be compared to the broader discussion of the nature of *ṭum'ah* in the Priestly source.

THE ANCIENT NEAR EASTERN CONTEXT: GOOD DEATH, BAD DEATH

A survey of literary sources and funerary inscriptions from Mesopotamia and the Northwest Semitic realm reveals remarkable consistency in their attitudes regarding death, burial and the afterlife of the spirit.[5] If modern Western culture is characterized by the pursuit of the "good life," the cultures surrounding biblical Israel were equally concerned with guaranteeing a "good death."[6] This fundamental distinction pertains to the mode of death (natural/violent), burial (or lack thereof) and subsequent care or neglect by one's descendants:

Jenseits im alten Israel in seiner Umwelt, FAT 64, eds. A. Berlejung and B. Janowski (Tübingen: Mohr Siebeck, 2009), 364–366.

[4] E.g.: Herbert Niehr, "The Changed Status of the Dead in Yehud," in *Yahwism After the Exile: Perspectives on Israelite Religion in the Persian Era*, eds. R. Albertz and B. Becking (Assen: Royal Van Gorcum, 2003), 136–155; Francesca Stavrakopoulou, *Land of Our Fathers: The Role of Ancestor Veneration in Biblical Law Claims* (New York, NY: T&T Clark, 2010), 146–148.

[5] For useful summaries, see Klaas Spronk, *Beatific Afterlife in Ancient Israel and the Ancient Near East*, AOAT 219 (Kevelear/Neukirchen: Verlag Butzon & Bercker, 1986); Theodore J. Lewis, "How Far Can Texts Take Us? Evaluating Textual Sources for Reconstructing Ancient Israelite Beliefs about the Dead," in *Sacred Time, Sacred Place: Archaeology and the Religion of Israel*, ed. B. M. Gittlen (Winona Lake, IN: Eisenbrauns, 2002), 169–217; Christopher B. Hayes, *Death in the Iron Age II and in First Isaiah*, FAT 79 (Tübingen: Mohr Siebeck, 2011), 1–201; and most recently Suriano's important synthesis of material and textual evidence: *A History of Death in the Hebrew Bible* (Oxford: Oxford University Press, 2018). In addition, one may refer to the illuminating collection of essays: Angelika Berlejung and Bernd Janowski (eds.), *Tod und Jenseits im alten Israel in seiner Umwelt*, FAT 64 (Tübingen: Mohr Siebeck, 2009), many of which will be mentioned later in this chapter.

[6] For this distinction, see Katharina Teinz, "How to Become an Ancestor – Some Thoughts," in *(Re-)Constructing Funerary Rituals in the Ancient Near East*, eds. P. Pfälzner et al. (Wiesbaden: Harrasowitz, 2012), 235–243.

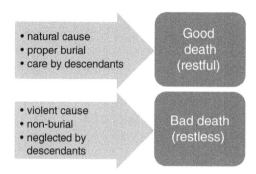

This ideal of a good death is epitomized by the report of Abraham's passing (Gen 25:8–9):

Abraham passed on and died, at a ripe old age, elderly and fulfilled, and he was gathered onto his kinsmen. His sons Isaac and Ishmael buried him in the Cave of Makhpelah in the field of Ephron, son of Zohar, the Hittite, facing Mamre.

However, a misstep at any of the stages of a "good death" endangers the soul's prospects of being "gathered into its ancestors."[7] Let us examine each of these stages more closely.

The "one slain by a sword" (2 Sam 3:29), the victim of a violent death, could not expect a restful afterlife. Rather, the spilled blood of the victim would remain in a state of turmoil (Gen 4:10; Job 16:18) until it could be avenged by one of the victim's kin, the "redeemer of blood" (*go'el ha-dam*). Regardless of the circumstances of death, there was an obligation for proper burial, preferably in the family tomb, as can be seen in curse formulas threatening transgressors with non-burial (e.g., Deuteronomy 28:26) and narratives depicting death in battle (e.g., 2 Sam 2:32; 2 Kgs 23:30).[8]

The lack of burial features prominently in curse formulas from throughout the ancient Near East. A twelfth-century BCE Babylonian

---

[7] For this ideal in the HB, see Bern Alfrink, "L'expression שכב עם אבותיו," *OTS* 2 (1943): 106–118; Bern Alfrink, "L'expression נאסף אל עמיו," *OTS* 5 (1948): 118–131; Annette Krüger, "Auf dem Weg 'zu den Vätern': Zur Tradition der alttestamentlichen Sterbenotizen," in *Tod und Jenseits im alten Israel in seiner Umwelt*, FAT 64, eds. A. Berlejung and B. Janowski (Tübingen: Mohr Siebeck, 2009), 137–150. Krüger overlooks the vast geographical span of this conception when she argues for Egyptian influence (145–149); see Nikita Artemov, "Belief in Family Reunion in the Afterlife in the Ancient Near East and Mediterranean," in *La famille dans le Proche-Orient ancien: réalités, symbolismes, et images: Proceedings of the 55th Rencontre Assyriologique Internationale at Paris 6–9 July 2009*, ed. L. Marti (Winona Lake, IN: Eisenbrauns, 2014), 27–41.

[8] See Saul M. Olyan, "Some Neglected Aspects of Israelite Interment Ideology," *JBL* 124.4 (2005): 603–605.

border stone makes this point quite succinctly: "May his corpse not be buried in the land, so that his [spirit] not join the spirits of his kin!" (*šalamtašu ina erṣeti ay iqqeber/[eṭemme]šu ana eṭem kimtīšu ay isniq).*[9] This inscription employs the term *eṭemmu* to refer to the spirit of the deceased. Notably, this term can also refer to the vital force of a living being like Hebrew *nepeš,*[10] though it is more commonly used to describe the post-mortem spirit, particularly a malicious ghost or demon that threatens the living. An Old Babylonian "forerunner" to the Neo-Assyrian Evil Demons litany reveals the circumstances that cause malicious spirits to plague the living. In this list, lack of burial appears together with untimely death:

> Whether you are the ghost coming from the Netherworld,
> Whether you are the wraith that has no resting place.
> Whether you are the man who died in the steppe
> Or whether you are the one in the steppe not covered by earth,
> Whether you are the man killed with a weapon . . .
> Whether you are the one a lion killed,
> Or whether you are the one whom a dog devoured,
> Whether you are the man who died in water . . .[11]

Calamity and especially disease were attributed to such malicious spirits.[12] While the HB does not contain unequivocal evidence for a fear of ghosts, the anxiety surrounding the possibility of non-burial raises the suspicion of a comparable conception (e.g., Deut 28:26; 1 Kgs 13:22; 14:11–13; Ezek 29:5).[13] This question will be explored below.

---

[9] Kudurru SB 26 VI 22. For background, see Nikita Artemov, "Belief in Family Reunion," 32.

[10] In Atraḫasis I, 215, this term describes the vital force animating humans as being derived from the flesh and blood of the slaughtered god: "Let there be a spirit from the god's flesh!" (*ina šīr ili eṭemmu libši*); Wilfred G. Lambert and Alan R. Millard, *Atra-Ḫasis: The Babylonian Story of the Flood* (Oxford: Clarendon Press, 1969), 58–59. For a detailed discussion of *eṭemmu*, including a comparison with *nepeš,* see Ulrike Steinert, *Aspekte des Menschseins im Alten Mesopotamien: Eine Studie zu Person und Identität im 2. und 1. Jt. v. Chr.* (Leiden: Brill, 2012), 295–384.

[11] See Markham J. Geller, *Forerunners to Udug-Hul: Sumerian Exorcistic Incantations,* FAOS 12 (Wiesbaden: Harrasowitz, 1985), 36–39, ll. 311–322; compare in the canonical series: *Evil Demons. Canonical* Utukkū Lemnūtu *Incantations* (SAACT 5; Helsinki: Neo-Assyrian Text Corpus Project, 2007), 112–116, 204–207 (4:82'–91', 131'–149').

[12] See JoAnn Scurlock, *Magico-Medical Means of Treating Ghost-Induced Disease in Ancient Mesopotamia,* Ancient Magic and Divination 3 (Leiden: Brill, 2006).

[13] Olyan, "Some Neglected Aspects," 601–616; Frances Dora Mansen, "Desecrated Covenant, Deprived Burial: Threats of Non-Burial in the Hebrew Bible" (PhD diss., Boston University, 2014).

Of course, proper burial does not itself guarantee a restful state to the dead. The sarcophagus inscription of the Phoenician ruler Tabnit (cited partially in the previous chapter) makes this point saliently:

I, Tabnit, priest of Astarte, king of Sidon, the son of Eshmunazar, priest of Astarte, king of Sidon, am lying in this sarcophagus. Whoever you are, any man that might find this sarcophagus, don't, don't open it and don't disturb me (*w'l trgzn*), for no silver is gathered with me, no gold is gathered with me, nor anything of value whatsoever, only I am lying in this sarcophagus. Don't, don't open it and don't disturb me, for this thing is an abomination to Astarte. And if you do indeed open it and do indeed disturb me, may you not have any seed among the living under the sun, nor a resting-place with the Rephaites.[14]

This inscription reveals Tabnit's dire concern regarding the disturbance of his burial place and threatens a measure-for-measure punishment, such that invaders will be deprived of their final rest. While the curse formula here makes no reference to malicious ghosts, it is the well-known terminological parallel from the HB which adds resolution to this picture. In the story of the necromancer from Endor (1 Sam 28), the ghost of Samuel does not conceal his bitterness at having been summoned from the earth (v. 15): "Why have you disturbed me (*hirgaztani*) by bringing me up?!" Taken together, these texts suggest an underlying worldview in which the disturbance (*r-g-z*) of a spirit by invading its burial place could have potentially calamitous consequences.[15] In fact, the Assyrian King Ashurbanipal (seventh century BCE) deliberately sought to cause such turmoil to the Elamite dead by the desecration of their graves:

I destroyed (and) devastated the tombs of their earlier and later kings, (men) who had not revered (the god) Aššur and the goddess Ištar, my lords, (and) who had disturbed the kings, my ancestors; I exposed (them) to the sun (lit. "the god Šamaš"). I took their bones to Assyria. I prevented their ghosts from sleeping (and) deprived them of funerary-offerings (and) libations.[16]

[14] Text: KAI 13; translation: P. Kyle McCarter, "The Sarcophagus Inscription of Tabnit, King of Sidon," CoS 2.56: 181.
[15] William H. Hallo, "Disturbing the Dead," in *Minḥah le-Naḥum: Biblical and Other Studies Presented to Nahum M. Sarna in Honour of His 70th Birthday*, JSOTS 154, eds. M. Brettler and M. Fishbane (Sheffield: JSOT Press, 1993), 183–192; also Stavrakopoulou, *Land of Our Fathers*, 82.
[16] Ashurbanipal, Rassam Cylinder (Assurbanipal 011), vi 70–80, from the RINAP 5 online corpus: http://oracc.museum.upenn.edu/rinap/rinap5/corpus (accessed 5/28/2021).

In fact, the threat of this Assyrian practice led the Babylonian king Merodach-Baladan to flee Sennacherib with the bones of his ancestors in boats.[17]

The third criterion for a peaceful afterlife was the continuous "care" for the dead by his or her descendants. This obligation is richly attested throughout Mesopotamian history and in the Levant from the third through the end of the first millennia BCE.[18] While the notion of food offerings for the dead may appear strange from a modern Western world-view, it should be understood (at least in part) as a continuation of offspring's obligation to parents in their lifetime[19] as well as reciprocation for land inheritance.[20]

Further pertinent evidence is the Katumuwa stele from Zinçirli (cited partially above) from the late eighth century BCE:

I am Katumuwa, servant of Panamuwa, who acquired for myself a stele while still alive and put it in my eternal reception room. The festal offering of this reception room is a bull for Hadad . . . a ram for Kubaba, and a ram for my soul, which is in this stele (*wybl.lnbšy.zy.bnṣb.zn*). And (from?) now, whoever from among my sons or from among the sons of anybody (else) who should come into possession of this reception room (?), let him purchase, out of the yield of this (adjoining) vineyard, a sheep every year and let him slaughter it beside my soul (*wyhrg. bnbšy*) and present me with a thigh.[21]

---

[17] Morton Cogan, "A Note on Disinterment in Jeremiah," in *Gratz College Anniversary Volume*, eds. I. D. Passow and S. T. Lachs (Philadelphia, PA: Gratz College, 1971), 31–2.

[18] The literature on this topic is vast. For convenient and insightful recent surveys, see Karel Van der Toorn, "Family Religion in Second Millennium West Asia (Mesopotamia, Emar, Nuzi)," in *Household and Family Religion in Antiquity*, eds. J. Bodel and S. M. Olyan (Malden, MA: Blackwell, 2008), 20–36; Daniel Fleming, "The Integration of Household and Family Religion," *Household and Family Religion in Antiquity*, eds. J. Bodel and S. M. Olyan (Malden, MA: Blackwell, 2008), 37–59; also the wide-ranging contributions to Peter Pfälzner et al. (eds.), *(Re-)Constructing Funerary Rituals in the Ancient Near East* (Wiesbaden: Harrasowitz, 2012).

[19] A salient depiction of how one's afterlife is dependent on the care of one's descendants comes from the Sumerian forerunner to Gilgamesh XII; see Alhena Gadotti, *Gilgamesh, Enkidu and the Netherworld and the Sumerian Gilgamesh Cycle* (Berlin: de Gruyter, 2014), 159, ll. 255–270.

[20] Regarding the latter point, see Stavrakopoulou, *Land of Our Fathers*, 1–28, passim, with pertinent references to cross-cultural analogies on p. 14, nn. 13–4; and add Emily M. Ahern, *The Cult of the Dead in a Chinese Village* (Stanford, CA: Stanford University Press, 1973), which features numerous tantalizing parallels to ancient Near Eastern practices. See also Teinz, "How to Become an Ancestor," 235–236; Suriano, *History*, 54.

[21] Text Edition: Dennis Pardee, "A New Aramaic Inscription from Zincirli," *BASOR* 356.1 (2009): 51–71. For further discussion, see Seth L. Sanders, "Naming the Dead: Funerary Writing and Historical Change in Iron Age Levant," *Maarav* 19.1–2 (2012): 11–36; Seth

In this inscription, Katumuwa charges his descendants, specifically those who inherit this burial plot, to perform yearly memorial offerings at the stele. Here it is stated explicitly that *nbš* of Katumuwa will reside in the stele.[22] A comparable concern for the care of the dead in ancient Israel is reflected in subtle references in the HB (e.g., Deut 26:14)[23] and in the archaeological record.[24]

This underlying conception, in which the soul continues to exist in the place of interment, can explain the widespread late-first-millennium-BCE practice attested throughout the Aramaic-speaking Levant of designating a mortuary structure (usually a stele or pyramid) as a *nepeš*.[25] This extrabiblical evidence corroborates the view, suggested by numerous biblical

---

L. Sanders, "The Appetites of the Dead: West Semitic Linguistic and Ritual Aspects of the KTMW Stele," *BASOR* 369.1 (2013): 35–55; Mathew J. Suriano, "Breaking Bread with the Dead: Katumuwa's Stele, Hosea 9:4, and the Early History of the Soul," *JAOS* 134.3 (2014): 385–405. The translation here is adapted from Richard C. Steiner, *Disembodied Souls: The Nefesh in Israel and Kindred Spirits in the Ancient Near East, with an Appendix on the Katumuwa Inscription* (Atlanta, GA: SBL Press, 2015), 129. As these studies point out, the vocalization of the name Katumuwa (from consonantal KTMW) is uncertain.

[22] This evidence further elaborates a conception that was already known from the Hadad statue of Panamuwa: "Whoever from among my descendants shall grasp the scepter and sit on my throne . . . and sacrifice to this Hadad . . . and mention the name of Hadad, let him then say, 'May the soul (נבש) of Panamuwa eat with you, and may the soul (נבש) of Panamuwa drink with you.' Let him keep mentioning the soul (נבש) of Panamuwa with Hadad" (KAI 214: 15–18); Josef Tropper, *Die Inschriften von Zincirli*, ALASP 6 (Münster: Ugarit-Verlag, 1993), 156 (my translation).

[23] For a balanced discussion of the textual evidence, see Christophe Nihan, "La polémique contre le culte des ancêtres dans la Bible Hébraïque: Origines et Fonctions," in *Les vivants et leur morts*, OBO 257, eds. J.-M. Durand et al. (Fribourg/Göttingen: Academic Press/ Vandenhoeck & Ruprecht, 2012), 139–173; cf. Brian B. Schmidt, *Israel's Beneficent Dead: Ancestor Cult and Necromancy in Ancient Israelite Religion and Tradition*, FAT 11 (Tübingen: Mohr Siebeck, 1996).

[24] See Elizabeth Bloch-Smith, *Judahite Burial Practices and Beliefs about the Dead*, JSOTSup 123 (Sheffield: JSOT Press, 1992); Jens Kamlah, "Grab und Begräbnis in Israel/Juda: Materielle Befunde, Jenheitsvorstellungen und die Frage des Totenkultes," in *Tod und Jenseits im alten Israel in seiner Umwelt*, FAT 64, eds. A. Berlejung and B. Janowski (Tübingen: Mohr Siebeck, 2009), 257–298; Robert Wenning, "No Cult of the Dead," in *(Re-)Constructing Funerary Rituals*, eds. P. Pfälzner et al. (Wiesbaden: Harrasowitz, 2012), 291–300; Rainer Albertz and Rüdiger Schmitt, *Family and Household Religion in Ancient Israel and the Levant* (Winona Lake, IN: Eisenbrauns, 2012), 429–473.

[25] Lothar Triebel, *Jenseitshoffnung in Wort und Stein: Nefesch und pyramidales Grabmal als Phänomene antiken jüdischen Bestattungswesens im Kontext der Nachbarkulturen* (Leiden: Brill, 2004); Dagmar Kühn, *Totengedenken bei den Nabatäern und im Alten Testament*, AOAT 311 (Münster: Ugarit-Verlag, 2005).

texts, that *nepeš* refers to the soul of the deceased which resides in the grave after death.[26]

In summary, as can be seen from a synthetic survey of ancient Near Eastern and biblical evidence, the spirit is confronted with a critical juncture at the moment of death and immediately thereafter, which will determine whether it will enjoy a restful afterlife among its ancestors or a restless state of turmoil. In the case of violent death, the spirit of the victim calls out for vengeance until the "blood redeemer" frees it from this state. A similar state of turmoil is associated with unburied remains or those that are disturbed in their place of interment. In contrast, the *nepeš* that is properly buried and commemorated by his or her offspring can rest in peace. In the following discussion, it will be shown how this background can shed light on the Priestly references to death pollution.

DEFILED BY THE *NEPEŠ*

When the Priestly source refers to the pollution caused from proximity to a corpse, it employs various permutations of the root *t-m-'* ("defile") and *nepeš,* most frequently the expression *ṭame' le-nepeš,* ("defiled by a *nepeš*"). Such expressions appear eleven times in the HB.[27] Against the more common usage of *nepeš* as referring to a vitalizing force or spirit, discussed in the previous chapter, most modern translators and commentators render *nepeš* in these expressions as "corpse."[28] This rendering has raised the question of how a single term could be used to designate opposites – vitality and death.[29] However, as will be seen, this

---

[26] See the detailed survey and discussion in Steiner, *Disembodied Souls*. For discussion of the corresponding Egyptian soul concepts *ba* and *ka*, see Jan Assmann, *Death and Salvation in Ancient Egypt*, trans. D. Lorton (Ithaca, NY: Cornell University Press, 2005), 87–102. See also Hayes, *Death in the Iron Age II*, 66–91, which discusses commonalities between Mesopotamia and Egypt.

[27] Leviticus 21:1, 11; 22:4; Numbers 5:2; 6:6; 9:6, 7, 10; 19:11, 13; Haggai 2:13.

[28] Among moderns, this translation is accepted by Jacob Licht in his commentary on Numbers, who even adds: "*nepeš* in these contexts (of impurity laws) refers to *the corpse* (המת), and one is not to derive from it anything pertaining to conceptions pertaining to the essence of the soul (נשמה) or the like" (*A Commentary on the Book of Numbers*, vol. 1 [Jerusalem: Magnes, 1985], p. 59 [in Hebrew, his emphasis]). Even Steiner, whose monograph argues cogently for the afterlife of the *nepeš*, defends this rendering (*Disembodied Souls*, 116–118). Cf. Suriano, "Breaking Bread," 389–393, 396.

[29] Admittedly, there might be an isolated instance of Akkadian *napšātu*, written logographically as ZI.MEŠ (see *CAD* N/1 301) that refers to "bodies" (cited by Steiner, *Disembodied Souls*, 117, n. 16). Though its significance should not be exaggerated for

mistaken translation obscures the rationale behind this type of pollution.[30]

For example, compare the following NJPS translation of Lev 21:11:

He shall not go in where there is *any dead body* (*kol napšot met*); he shall not defile himself even for his father or mother.

Aside from grammatical difficulties,[31] the parallelism of the verse reveals clearly that *napšot* in the first clause parallels "father and mother" in the second clause, indicating that *nepeš* corresponds not to the body but to the personality of the deceased. Furthermore, it should be noted *nepeš* never appears as the object of "touch" (*n-g-ʿ*). Instead, these passages are careful to use the expression "to come upon" (*boʾ ʿal*) in conjunction with *nepeš*, suggesting that the latter is distinct from the physical corpse (*met*).

The expression *ṭameʾ le-nepeš* is a shorthand for the fuller expression which is spelled out in Num 19:11 and 13. The first of these reads, as rendered correctly in the NJPS translation: "he who touches the corpse (*met*) of any human being (*le-kol nepeš adam*) shall be unclean for seven days." The parallel expression in v. 13 should be rendered, following Baruch Levine, as follows: "One who had contact with a corpse (*met*) belonging to any human being (*nepeš adam*) that died."[32] Accordingly, while the *nepeš* is closely related to the presence of the dead body (*met*), these terms are not interchangeable, and a delicate distinction is maintained. This semantic distinction substantiates the conclusion that *nepeš* refers to the "spirit" or "soul" of the deceased, as it does in the funerary inscriptions discussed above. Hence, there is no need to account for how the same term can refer to "vital spirit/life-force" and "corpse," seeming opposites, since the latter is simply a case of mistranslation.

understanding Hebrew *nepeš*, this would indicate the possibility of such a metonymic development.

[30] Diethelm Michel, "*Næpæš als Leichnam?*" *ZAH* 7 (1974): 81–84, followed by Seebass, "נפש nepeš," 515.

[31] מת is not an adjective but the *nomen rectum* governed by נפשות. Since the former refers unambiguously to the corpse in Numbers 19:11, 13 serving as the direct object of "touch" (נג״ע), it is clear that *nepeš* cannot mean the same, lest we end up with a tautologous "cadavers of a corpse." The JPS translation of Numbers 6:6 על נפש מת לא יבא ("He shall not go in where there is any dead body") is likewise problematic.

[32] *Numbers 1–20*, AB (New York, NY: Doubleday, 1993), 459 (my italics). He explains, "In certain contexts, Hebrew *nepeš* may designate a dead person . . . It does not necessarily do so here, because the sense of *lekol nepeš ʾādām* 'belonging to any human being' suggests that the reference may be to living persons, and because the text adds *ʾašer yāmût* 'who dies'" (465). Levine's reasoning is correct, but the conclusion should be categorical: *nepeš* never designates "corpse" in the HB.

It is now possible to seek a more precise understanding regarding how the circumstances of bodily death relate to the transfer of impurity. Focusing on the specific terminology of Num 19, we may ask: what is the relationship between the *personalized* spirit (*nepeš*) of the deceased and the state of pollution (*ṭum'ah*) caused by it? Should this *nepeš* leaving the body be characterized as a spirit of the dead (as implied by extra-biblical evidence) or merely a lost vitality, an impersonal force?

Recent studies have suggested that death in ancient Israel was conceived more as a process than as a punctuated event, involving a gradual separation of the *nepeš* from the body.[33] While numerous biblical texts (including those from the Priestly traditions) assume an afterlife for souls, resting with their kin in the Sheol,[34] it is nevertheless apparent that this post-mortem *nepeš* was relatively powerless compared to during its lifetime.[35] As such, it seems reasonable to infer that the spirit's power to animate the body was considered to gradually leave the body at the time of decomposition. According to this understanding, some of the *nepeš* was assumed to disseminate from the corpse immediately following bodily death, constituting the difference between the animating spirit activating the living person and the inactive shadow existence of the resting spirit in the grave.

This reconstructed gradual process offers a suggestive interpretation of the pervasive Judean burial practice of bench tombs. This method of burial involved a two-stage process of laying the recently dead body on a bench until it decomposed, and then later relocating the bones to a collective repository. As several scholars have pointed out, this mode of burial correlates with being "gathered into the fathers," a process where the individual spirit is absorbed into the collective of dead

---

[33] Christian Frevel, "Purity Conceptions in the Book of Numbers," in *Purity and the Forming of Religious Traditions in the Ancient Mediterranean World and Ancient Judaism*, eds. C. Frevel and C. Nihan (Leiden: Brill, 2013), 390–391; Christian Frevel, "Struggling with the Vitality of Corpses: Understanding the Rationale of the Ritual in Numbers 19," in *Les vivants et leur morts*, OBO 257, eds. J.-M. Durand et al. (Fribourg/Göttingen: Academic Press/Vandenhoeck & Ruprecht, 2012), 199–200. See also Kühn, *Totengedenken*, 130–134. Steiner relates the practice of secondary burial to distinct stages in the separation of the *nepeš* from the body (*Disembodied Souls*, 93–114).

[34] The association of these formulas (see n. 7 above) with burial are strong evidence against Steiner's suggestion that the reunion with kin takes place in heaven (*Disembodied Souls*, 93–114).

[35] See Ps 30:10; 88:10; 115:17; John W. Cooper, *Body, Soul, and Life Everlasting: Biblical Anthropology and the Monism–Dualism Debate* (Grand Rapids, MI; Eerdmans, 1989), 74–76; Steiner, *Disembodied Souls*, 119–123; also Suriano's rendering as "defunct soul" (*History of Death*, 141, with n. 30).

ancestors. Mathew Suriano writes: "Thus, through the course of action that took place inside the Judahite tomb, the liminality of the dead related directly to the biological changes that were visible in the body. In this sense, liminality represented the marginality of the dead person as they transformed from corpse to ancestor."[36]

So how does this relate to pollution? Here it is necessary to refer to the dynamics of corpse impurity discussed in Chapter 2. Num 19 makes clear that it is not only transferred by direct contact with the corpse, but also by being found together with it in an enclosure (literally a "tent"), where the pollution is disseminated like a gas. Accordingly, one may suggest that the smell of the decaying corpse was taken to be coextensive with the *nepeš* separating from the body. It was contact with the *nepeš* in this transitional phase that was considered defiling and, based on ethnographic parallels, perhaps even dangerous.[37] Yet, Num 19 situates its concern specifically as the defilement of the camp where the divine presence resides (vv. 13, 20). Accordingly, the implications of death pollution will need to be clarified below.

PRELIMINARY SUMMARY: THE TRADITIONAL BACKGROUND OF DEATH POLLUTION

While crucial issues remain to be discussed, it is worthwhile to summarize the implications of the evidence surveyed above for the antiquity of the concept of death pollution in Israel. Let us review the interpretive approaches mentioned above:

1. Symbolic: death pollution represents an abstract dichotomy between death (impurity) and life (purity)
2. Foreign influence: death pollution stems from exposure to foreign (Zoroastrian?) customs appropriated by the Israelite priesthood in the Persian Period
3. Tactical: the existence, or at least prominence, of death pollution constitutes a strategic tactic to distance the Israelite populace from ancestral cults.

Whereas the first (theological) explanation views these practices as pertaining to abstract cosmological categories divorced from practical concerns, the latter two historicize this pollution as stemming from sociohistorical factors emerging in the post-exilic period. However, by

---

[36] *History of Death*, 52.   [37] See also Ahern, *Cult of the Dead*, 163–174.

recognizing that the concept of death pollution was *organically* related to the accepted views of death and afterlife in ancient Israel, as part of its West Semitic context, it becomes clear that none of these approaches is acceptable. In fact, by invoking the standard West Semitic concept of the soul attested in funerary contexts throughout the Levant, the expression *ṭame' le-nepeš* ("defiled by the spirit") makes clear that this notion is rooted in widespread and ancient concerns related to death.

As has been seen, ancient Israelite conceptions of death and the afterlife are similar to those found in neighboring cultures. In surveying this evidence, it has been shown that the fate of the *nepeš* – or its Akkadian counterpart, *eṭemmu* – is determined by dying the "good death," characterized by the proper modes of death, burial and posthumous care. At the same time, regarding the most important point of our inquiry there is a significant disparity: whereas the Mesopotamian evidence for a fear of malicious ghosts is abundant, one finds no unequivocal evidence for such a belief in the HB.[38]

At first glance, this contrast would seem to settle the question. However, upon further consideration, it becomes clear that the biblical evidence cannot be employed uncritically as an accurate portrait of the facts on the ground in Iron Age Israel. Specifically, the existence of apotropaic objects and amulets in Judean burial contexts from the pre-exilic period and later reveals a concern that can only be vaguely inferred from biblical texts, namely the fear of the threat posed by disturbances and looting to the spirit of the dead. In particular, this can be seen in the late eighth-century "Royal Steward Inscription" from Jerusalem, which parallels the language of the Tabnit inscription (cited in the earlier section "The Ancient Near Eastern Context: Good Death, Bad Death"),[39] and especially in the Ketep Hinnom amulets, which appeal for divine protection after burial.[40] Somewhat more equivocal but worthy of note is the lack of explicit mention, particularly in the key legislative sections of the

---

[38] Theodore J. Lewis, "Dead," *DDD*: 230; Frevel, "Struggling," 219–222.

[39] "There is no silver or gold here – only [his bones] and the bones of his maidservant [who is] with him. Cursed be the man who opens this (tomb)!" (P. Kyle McCarter, "The Royal Steward Inscription (2.54)," *CoS* 2: 180.)

[40] See Jeremy D. Smoak, "May YHWH Bless You and Keep You from Evil: The Rhetorical Argument of Ketef Hinnom Amulet I and the Form of the Prayers for Deliverance in the Psalms," *JANER* 12.2 (2012): 202–236; Jeremy D. Smoak, *The Priestly Blessing in Inscription and Scripture* (Oxford: Oxford University Press, 2016); also Brian B. Schmidt, "The Social Matrix of Early Judean Magic and Divination: From 'Top Down' or 'Bottom Up,'" in *Beyond Hatti: A Tribute to Gary Beckman*, eds. B. J. Collins and P. Michalowski (Atlanta, GA: Lockwood Press, 2013), 279–294.

Pentateuch, of an ancestor cult, despite the scattered references throughout the HB to this ancient practice in Israel and the evidence of food
utensils in burial contexts.[41] In short, one suspects that the biblical texts
are not telling the whole story.

LACK OF BURIAL, CURSE AND DEFILEMENT

In pursuing these questions, it is necessary to examine the non-P biblical
evidence. Despite the paucity of explicit references to impurity, one can
find crucial hints of how the Priestly texts fit into the broader scheme of
Israelite attitudes regarding death. The first of these is from Ezekiel's
vision pertaining to the aftermath of the war against Gog in Ezek 39,
which places surprising emphasis on the need to bury Gog's fallen
soldiers:

[11]On that day I will appoint for Gog a place there, a burial plot in Israel, the valley
of the crossers, east of the sea. It will block the crossers, as there they will bury Gog
and all his multitudes. It will be called the valley of Gog's multitudes. [12]Seven
months the House of Israel will bury them, in order to purify the land.

Following the total devastation of Gog's armies, Israel will set out on
a systematic mission to bury the enemy's remains. According to the ensuing text, this process will take seven months, and it will involve combing
the battlefields, setting up markers at the find-spots of bones, and finally
transferring these bones to a massive burial mound. While this concern for
burying dead enemies may appear as simply an act of basic dignity, the
repeated focus on *purifying* the land suggests that more was at stake. In
language and context, Ezek 39 is reminiscent of a letter from Mari from
the eighteenth century BCE which discusses the interment of corpses in
a burial mound following a plague, after which "[t]he exorcists and
cantors purified (Akk. *ulilū*) the city."[42] Perhaps even more relevant, the
practice of burying one's enemies, as described in Sumerian inscriptions
from the late third millennium BCE, has been explained by scholars as
reflecting a fear of spirit vengeance: "that the victor as well as the defeated
had reason to fear the wrathful and restless spirits of the unburied
dead."[43] Such a concern is substantiated by Assyrian inscriptions that

---

[41] See nn. 23 and 24 above.
[42] ARM 26/1 263, l. 20. See also Wolfgang Heimpel, *Letters to the King of Mari* (Winona
Lake, IN: Eisenbrauns, 2003), 278–279.
[43] "Berūtum, damtum, and Old Akkadian KI. GAL: Burial of Dead Enemies in Ancient
Mesopotamia," *AfO* 23 (1970): 30. For further discussion, see Andrew C. Cohen, *Death*

glorify the desecration of graves as a means of punishing the living together with the dead, as in the Ashurbanipal inscription cited above. Once again, however, gaps in the biblical evidence have been filled with Mesopotamian parallels, leaving the real question unresolved: is there any comparable evidence from ancient Israel? Intriguing evidence comes from the law of capital punishment in Deut 21:22–23, legislating a communal obligation to bury the dead, even executed criminals:

> If a person is guilty of a capital crime, and he is executed and impaled on a stake, you must not leave his corpse overnight on the stake, but rather you shall surely bury him on that same day, *for the impaled (body) is a curse of 'elohim (ki qil^elat 'elohim talui)* so that you will not defile (*ṭ-m-'*) your land, which Yhwh is giving you as an inheritance.

This law limits the display of a criminal's impaled body to the day of execution. This requirement is followed by a motive clause which has vexed interpreters, ancient and modern: *ki qil^elat 'elohim talui*. The more conventional interpretation, taking *'elohim* as "God," is that this verse invokes a divine curse for prolonged exposure of the body. One may compare the Tabnit inscription, which designates the desecration of a tomb "an abomination of Astarte," followed by a curse.[44] A tantalizing alternative has been argued by Timo Veijola, taking *'elohim* as referring to the offended spirit of the dead (as in 1 Sam 28:13).[45] According to this interpretation, the spirit of the impaled criminal threatens the community until it is given a proper burial.[46] For our purposes, the key point is that

---

Rituals, Ideology, and the Development of Early Mesopotamian Kingship (Leiden: Brill, 2005), 67–69; Seth Richardson, "Death and Dismemberment in Mesopotamia: Discorporation Between the Body and the Body Politic," in *Performing Death: Social Analyses of Funerary Traditions in the Ancient Near East and Mediterranean*, OIS 3, ed. N. Laneri (Chicago, IL: Oriental Institute, 2007), 189–208.

[44] Text: KAI 13; translation: McCarter, "The Sarcophagus Inscription," CoS 2.56: 181. See above, n. 14.

[45] "'Fluch des Totengeistes ist der Aufgehängte' (Dtn 21, 23)," UF 32 (2000): 643–653. See also Jeffrey H. Tigay, *Deuteronomy*, JPS Torah Commentary (Philadelphia, PA: JPS, 1996), 198; Jeffrey H. Tigay, *Deuteronomy: Introduction and Commentary*, vol. 2, Mikra Leyisra'el (Tel Aviv/Jerusalem: Magnes, 2016), 541 (in Hebrew), who cites a similar view expressed by the early-sixteenth-century rabbinic commentator Sforno. As Veijola points out ("Fluch des Totengeistes," 551–552), the use of *'elohim* in reference to Yhwh is rare in Deuteronomy, and usually refers to "other gods," aside from specific cases when it is citing previous texts.

[46] Veijola (ibid., 547) cites the earlier elucidation of Bertholet: "Der Geist des Unbegrabenen treibt allerhand Spuk; man ist vor ihm nicht sicher. Und erst recht gilt dies vom Gehängten, werden doch nur die schlimmsten Bösewichter gehängt . . . So lange einer

the failure to carry out a prompt burial – even in this extreme case – entailed an immediate threat of curse to the community. This danger serves as the basis for the following exhortation in which the idiom of contaminating the land serves to concretize the collective threat posed by the unburied corpse.

An additional source which shows a close relationship between defilement and malediction is David's curse of Joab (2 Sam 3:29): "May there never cease to be in the house of Joab a gonorrheic (*zab*), leper (*mᵉṣora*), a holder of the spindle, one fallen by the sword or a person lacking bread." In an article devoted to elucidating this passage, Meir Malul finds a common denominator of these various conditions: "Whether the person is gonorrheal, leprous, poor or has fallen by the sword (and his corpse is assumed to have been left without burial), in all cases he or his spirit is relegated to the status of an outcast from society, having to roam the sphere of outlawry outside society."[47] It is significant that two elements of this curse, leprosy and gonorrhea, are two of the most serious types of pollution according to Lev 13–14 and 15, respectively, both requiring a seven-day period of purification followed by expiatory rituals. The "one fallen by a sword" refers to the victim of a violent death, most likely in battle, especially one whose remains have not been properly buried. Malul observes that this expression "must then be interpreted in the light of this common custom of denying burial to soldiers fallen in war which then affected the dead person's spirit."[48]

Strikingly, one finds a correspondence between these three elements of David's curse and the three severe types of impurity-bearers that are banished from the camp in Num 5:2: "Command the Israelites to remove from the camp anyone with leprosy or gonorrhea and anyone defiled by a *nepeš*." These correspondences, though surely serendipitous, have important implications for understanding the prehistory of the Priestly concept of purity. The reason for banishment given by Num 5:3 is the following: "Put them outside the camp so that they will not defile the camp where I reside in their midst." Like the rationale given for the purity laws of Lev 11–15 in Lev 15:31 and that given for purification for death pollution in Num 19:13 and 20, the emphasis is placed on the fear of

---

hangen bleibt, geht sein böser Geist herum" (*Deuteronomium*, KHC 5 [Freiburg: JCB Mohr, 1899], 67).

[47] "David's Curse of Joab and the Social Significance of *mḥzyq bplk*," *Aula Orientalis* 10 (1992): 62.

[48] Ibid., 58.

defiling the Tabernacle, site of the divine presence.[49] The fact that these statements appear in similar language, apparently reflecting a common redactional layer of the Priestly materials, suggests that this rationale is probably not the original one.[50] David's curse confirms this suspicion, showing that these conditions elicited fear irrespective of cultic concerns. Specifically regarding death pollution, one suspects that this fear involved the threat of malicious spirits or at least some kind of negative influence caused by contact with the departing *nepeš*, as implied by the association of non-burial and curse in other biblical sources.

From Restless Dead to Depersonalized Bloodguilt: A Greek Analogy

In trying to reconstruct the early background for biblical death pollution, it is necessary to confront an additional problem, daunting in its own right: the near absence of explicit references to ghosts in the HB. In this context, the narrative of 1 Sam 28 is the exception that proves the rule. If Israelites believed in ghosts (as this story implies), why don't they appear in other narratives? Similarly, there is no unequivocal evidence in the HB for a danger posed by dead spirits. Yet, there is a context where such a concern does find expression – namely that of bloodguilt.

The biblical texts employ several different idioms to depict the guilt incurred by the murderer. A key image is that of the blood of the victim crying out for vengeance (Gen 4:10; Ezek 24:7–8; Job 16:18). It is this idiom which underlies the notion of the "blood redeemer" (*go'el ha-dam*), the kinsman of the victim who is charged with taking vengeance and thereby releasing the "blood" (= spirit) of the deceased from its turmoil (Num 35; Deut 19; Josh 20). A far more common image is that of an invisible stain (literally "blood": *damim*) that marks the perpetrator for

[49] See Yitzhaq Feder, "The Wilderness Camp Paradigm in the Holiness Source and the Temple Scroll: From Purity Laws to Cult Politics," *JAJ* 5.3 (2014): 290–295; Feder, "Behind the Scenes of a Priestly Polemic: Leviticus 14 and Its Extra-Biblical Parallels," *JHS* 15.4 (2015): 1–26 (https://doi.org/10.5508/jhs.2015.v15.a4). As was shown in Chapters 4 and 5 above, these statements should be viewed as a secondary tendency.

[50] Regarding the lateness of these verses, see Israel Knohl, *Sanctuary of Silence: The Priestly Torah and the Holiness School* (Winona Lake, IN: Eisenbrauns, 2007 [1995]), 86; Jacob Milgrom, *Leviticus*, AB, 3 vols. (New York, NY: Doubleday, 1991–2000), 2.1337, 1344; Christophe Nihan, *From Priestly Torah to Pentateuch*, FAT 2/25 (Tübingen: Mohr Siebeck, 2007), 283; Frevel, "Purity Conceptions," 400–405.

cosmic retribution.[51] The imagery of the stain is often associated with the belief that the community will be held responsible until this blood debt is expiated (i.e., paid off, Heb. *k-p-r*) by the death of the perpetrator (Deut 19:10; 21:1–9; 2 Sam 21). Despite the widespread practice in Near Eastern and Mediterranean societies of accepting substitutionary payments in lieu of revenge, biblical law is unanimous and uncompromising in rejecting such settlements, based on the fundamental belief that the spilled blood cannot be appeased except by payment in kind (Gen 9:6; Num 35:31–34; cf. Ex 21:28–30).

Though little attention is given to spirits of the dead in most contexts, it is striking that the term *nepeš* is repeatedly invoked in the context of homicide in the Priestly account of God's blessing to Noah following the flood (Gen 9:4–6):

[4]However, you may not eat flesh with its spirit (*nepeš*), that is, its blood. [5]But for the blood of your lives (*dimkem le-napšotekem*) I will demand a reckoning; I will demand a reckoning from the hand of every creature, and from the hand of humans. For (killing) one another, I will demand the life (*nepeš*) of the human. [6]The one who spills the blood of a human, by a human his blood will be spilled, for humanity was made in the image of God.

This text juxtaposes two ostensibly different topics – the prohibitions against consuming animal blood and against spilling human blood. While one might understand this juxtaposition as a superficial associative connection related to the word "blood," the connection proves to be more substantial. The rationale for the dietary prohibition in v. 4 (and its parallels) is the presence of the *nepeš* in the blood; it is forbidden for a human to ingest the spirit of the animal together with its meat. In comparison, the homicide injunctions in vv. 5–6 are based on the reckoning for spilled blood. Though the association of the *nepeš* with the spilled blood of the victim is stressed, there is no indication that the spirit of the dead can avenge itself. Rather, this text appears to presume the traditional kin-vengeance system, with the administration of justice overseen by God.

[51] E.g., Exodus 22:1–2; 2 Samuel 3:28–9; 1 Kings. 2:5, 33. One may also include expressions such as "your blood is on your head" (דמך על ראשך 2 Sam. 1:16) and the expression "his blood is with him" (דמיו בו) in reference to a person who has committed a crime which incurs capital punishment (Lev 20:9–16, 27), signifying that his executioner incurs no guilt. For recent discussion, see Jan Dietrich, *Kollektive Schuld und Haftung: Religions- und rechtsgeschichtliche Studien zum Sündenkultritus des Deuteronomiums und zu verwandten Texten* (Tübingen: Mohr Siebeck, 2010); Yitzhaq Feder, *Blood Expiation in Hittite and Biblical Ritual: Origins, Context and Meaning* (Atlanta, GA: SBL, 2011), 173–196.

Subtly, emphasis is moved from *appeasing* the dead spirit to *expiating* the objective bloodguilt.

Accordingly, the depiction of bloodguilt in this Priestly text is similar to that found in the homicide laws of Deuteronomy, which refer repeatedly to the danger of "blood" staining the community, resulting in collective retribution (19:10; 21:1–9; 22:8). Despite the impersonal depiction of the bloodguilt in these sources, it is noteworthy that they do not employ the idiom of pollution. Exceptional in this regard is the late Priestly law of homicide in Num 35, which states its emphatic rejection of a substitution payment in the following terms:

[33]You shall not incriminate (*ḥ-n-p*) the land in which you live, for blood incriminates the land and no expiation can be made for the land for the blood that was shed on it except by means of the blood of him who shed it. [34]You shall not pollute (*t-m-'*) the land in which you live, in which I myself dwell, for I, Yhwh, dwell among the Israelites.

This isolated use of pollution terminology, instead of the ubiquitous references to "blood," is a clear indication that this usage is innovative and even metaphorical. As such, it is an extreme expression of a tendency found throughout the HB to replace the traditional image of a vengeful spirit with the impersonal terminology of a bloodstain or (in this case) defilement. Importantly, the reference to polluting (*t-m-'*) the land in v. 34 parallels the language of "incriminating" (*ḥ-n-p*) the land in v. 33 – the latter verb bearing associations with curse.[52] Once again, the threat of collective retribution in the form of a curse on the land is described in the language of defilement.

It is interesting to note that ancient Greek sources reveal striking parallels to these biblical conceptions and the institutions related to them. In his 1897 monograph on the Greek conception of the "soul" (*psyche*), Erwin Rohde argued that the rationale for the adjuration of homicide can only be properly understood in reference to the ancient belief in the need to appease the spirit of the victim:

At Athens even in the fourth and fifth centuries the belief still survived in undiminished vigour that the soul of one violently done to death, until the wrong done to him was avenged by the doer of it, would wander about finding no rest, full of rage at the violent act, and wrathful, too, against the relatives who should have avenged him, if they did not fulfil their duty. He would himself

---

[52] See K. Seybold, "חנף," TDOT 5: 42–43; J. Licht, A Commentary on the Book of Numbers, vol. 3 (Jerusalem: Magnes, 1995), *ad loc.* (Hebrew).

become an "avenging spirit"; and the force of his anger might be felt throughout whole generations.[53]

As in ancient Israel, this belief led to a categorical rejection of the notion of monetary compensation. Importantly, the Greek sources also depict this bloodstain in terms of an impersonal pollution (*miasma*). In cases of intentional murder, this miasma could evoke retribution from the vengeful spirits themselves (*biaiothanatoi*) or by the Erinyes (chthonic curse-deities), but even in cases of unintentional homicide, the perpetrator was banished (paralleling the biblical asylum cities) and required to perform purification upon return.[54] Elaborating on this fluidity of idiom, Sarah Ilyes Johnston points out that "*miasma* could be understood as an impersonalized way of representing the danger lurking around the murderer, a danger that, in personalized form, was represented instead by the dead or his agents."[55] Distinguishing these two modes of depiction is complicated by the fact "that rites described as 'purificatory' sometimes include elements that look far more like efforts to appease the dead or chthonic powers who championed them."[56]

   In the biblical and Greek sources, one finds a tendency to move away from the notion of appeasing the spirit of the victim in favor of more mechanistic terms such as curse or pollution. It bears stressing that Rohde's pertinent discussion appeared in a monograph devoted to the Greek concept of the "soul" (*psyche*), which bears considerable similarity to the biblical *nepeš* (with its West Semitic cognates), both terms referring to the "soul" (root of individual identity) and the spirit of the deceased.[57] Like the Greek sources, the Priestly references to bloodguilt in Gen 9:5–6 and Num 35 seem to deliberately avoid the notion of appeasing the *nepeš* of the victim; the latter source instead employs the seemingly interchangeable terminology of curse and pollution. Yet, as indicated by evidence from elsewhere in the HB and in Greek literature, this transition should

---

[53] *Psyche: The Cult of Souls and Belief in Immortality Among the Greeks*, trans. W. B. Hillis (New York, NY: Harcourt Brace, 1925), 176–177. For a similar comparison, see Moses Buttenwieser, "Blood Revenge and Burial Rites in Ancient Israel," *JAOS* 39 (1919): 303–321.

[54] See Rohde, *Psyche*, 177–180; Robert Parker, *Miasma: Pollution and Purification in Early Greek Religion* (Oxford: Clarendon Press, 1983), 104–143; Sarah I. Johnston, *Restless Dead: Encounters Between the Living and the Dead in Ancient Greece* (Berkeley, CA: University of California Press, 2013), 69–82.

[55] *Restless Dead*, 70.   [56] Ibid.; Parker, *Miasma*, 104–143.

[57] The idea of a disembodied *nepeš* in the HB has often been denied, but this view has been cogently defended by James Barr, "Scope and Problems in the Semantics of Classical Hebrew," *ZAH* 6.2 (1993): 6–8, and at length in Steiner, *Disembodied Souls*.

TABLE 8.1 *"Bad death" and land pollution*

Situation	Pollution	Alternative terminology	Underlying concern
Lack of Burial	Defilement of land	Curse (*q^elala*)	Restless spirit
Murder	Defilement of land	Blood (*damim*)	Spirit calling for vengeance

probably not be interpreted as reflecting a specifically Priestly ideology, but rather as representing a general tendency in ancient Israel to deemphasize the agency of spirits of the dead.

Was Death Really That "Bad"?

The previous two sections focused on two factors contributing to a "bad death," lack of burial and homicide, showing a fluidity of terminology that can be represented as shown in Table 8.1. These sources demonstrate that the idiom of defiling the land could be used interchangeably with the terminology of curse and bloodguilt. Despite the variation of expression, there are grounds for assuming that both idioms are based on an original concern with the restless spirit of the dead.

But can such evidence of "bad death" really serve as the model for death in general in order to explain this pollution? More to the point, did the ancient Israelites assume that their loved ones turned into malicious spirits at the moment of death? Such inferences might seem illogical.

As a first step in addressing this problem, it should be recognized that association of death with pollution is not confined to cases of "bad death." While the biblical text generally avoids discussing the existence of ghosts, the practice of necromancy is widely attested, albeit in contexts of condemnation and prohibition (e.g., Lev 19:31; 20:6, 27; Deut 18:11).[58] These texts divulge the basic fact that some Israelites would

---

[58] See Hayes, *Death in the Iron Age II*, 168–174. Regarding the etymology of אוב, the derivation from *api-* "ritual pits" (attested in Mesopotamian, Hurrian and Hittite texts) still warrants serious consideration. See Harry A. Hoffner, "Second Millennium Antecedents to the Hebrew 'Ôb," *JBL* 86 (1967): 385–401; Billie Jean Collins, "Necromancy, Fertility and the Dark Earth: The Use of Ritual Pits in Hittite Cult," in *Magic and Ritual in the Ancient World*, eds. P. Mirecki and M. Meyer (Leiden: Brill, 2002), 224–241, though admittedly the term acquired multiple senses in the HB.

turn to dead spirits in order to attain privileged knowledge. Here the prohibition of necromancy in Lev 19:31 is of special interest. Of the numerous prohibitions listed in Lev 19, it is significant that only the act of evoking spirits of the dead is followed by the motive clause "to be defiled by them." While Milgrom is probably correct to interpret the language of impurity here as metaphorical (i.e., for rhetorical emphasis),[59] it should be recognized nonetheless that the association of pollution with spirits of the dead is not coincidental. This point is reinforced by consideration of the key Priestly idiom for death pollution *ṭame' le-nepeš*: "defiled by a spirit."

A second point pertains to possible hidden implications of ancient Israelite (together with ancient Near Eastern and Mediterranean) mourning practices. There is considerable overlap in the biblical sources between mourning practices and corpse impurity (together with offerings to the dead), as reflected in texts such as Deut 26:14 and Hosea 9:4, as Table 8.2 shows.

Despite differences in genre and emphasis, these two sources are strikingly similar in content.[60] The tithing declaration of Deut 26:14 lists the following conditions as potentially disqualifying the tithe: consumption when in mourning or in a state of impurity, or having been offered to the dead. Hosea 9:4 disqualifies the offerings of the Ephraimites, equating them with the food of mourning that defiles whoever consumes it. The following expression *ki laḥmam le-napšam* permits two possible readings and may be based on a play on words: (1) "their food is for themselves/their appetite" (not for God); (2) "their

TABLE 8.2 *Mourning and defilement*

Deut 26:14	Hosea 9:4
I have not eaten of it while mourning (*be-'oni*), nor have I separated it while impure, nor have I given from it to the dead.	[Their offerings] will be like the food of mourning (*ke-leḥem 'onim*) to them – whoever eats it will be defiled. Because their food is for their *nepeš*, it will not enter the house of Yhwh.

[59] *Leviticus*, 2.1702.
[60] For further analysis of this parallel, see the lucid discussion of Suriano, "Breaking Bread," 96–101.

food is for their *nepeš*" (i.e., the spirit of their deceased relative) and hence unacceptable in the "House of Yhwh." For our purposes, the key point is that these sources treat the situations of mourning and impurity as inextricably connected. It would seem that pollution was an unavoidable aspect of the experience of death for relatives of the deceased. This point is supported by the correspondence between the seven days of mourning and the seven days of purification for death pollution,[61] inviting comparison with other cultures where "death-pollution is spread by relationship as well as contact."[62]

Further evidence for fear of the dead may be adduced from mourning practices. In particular, it is possible that such practices, not only "legitimate" ones such as lamentation and wearing sackcloth but also, and especially, "illegitimate" ones such as self-laceration and shaving (Lev 19:27–28; Deut 14:1), were intended as public displays of grief for the benefit of the deceased. In other words, these acts of disheveling oneself and of self-mutilation served not only as an emotional outlet to express grief, but also – perhaps more importantly – served to placate the spirit of the deceased, who was assumed to be still present.[63]

From a cross-cultural perspective, a fear of antagonism from deceased relatives is probably the rule rather than the exception.[64] Ancient Egyptian "Letters to the Dead" articulate this concern unequivocally. In these texts, petitioners appeal to their loved ones to cease afflicting them.[65] For example, a man pleads with his dead wife as follows: "What evil have I done to you that I should be in the bad state which I am in? What have I done to you? This (is what) you have done: you have put (your)

---

[61] Saul M. Olyan, *Biblical Mourning: Ritual and Social Dimensions* (Oxford: Oxford University Press, 2004), 39; Albertz and Schmitt, *Family and Household Religion*, 435.

[62] Parker, *Miasma*, 39.

[63] Schmidt suggests that "self-mutilation might be more appropriately viewed as an attempt to assuage the envy which the dead possesses for the living by inflicting suffering on oneself" (*Israel's Beneficent Dead*, 297); see also Cohen, *Death Rituals*, 47–51; Dina Katz, "The Naked Soul: Deliberations on a Popular Theme," in *Gazing on the Deep, Studies in Honor of Tzvi Abusch*, eds. J. Stackert, B. Nevling Porter and D. P. Wright, 107–120 (Winona Lake: IN, 2010) 119–120. Cf. Olyan, *Biblical Mourning*, 111–123. It should be mentioned that a similar view was fairly common at the turn of the twentieth century as part of "animistic" reconstructions of early Israelite religion (see Spronk, *Beatific Afterlife*, 33–34).

[64] E. Bendann, *Death Customs: An Analytical Study of Burial Rites* (London: K. Paul, 1930), 57–81.

[65] Hayes, *Death in the Iron Age II*, 80–81.

hand on me. I have not done evil to you, since I have held (fast) together with you as husband (even) down to this day."[66] Here Frazer's wry generalization may also apply to ancient Israel: "the attentions bestowed on the dead sprang not so much from the affections as from the fears of the survivors."[67] Hence, numerous concerns pertaining to the unstable situation of the *nepeš* as well as fears of retaliation may have added a sense of danger even in cases of "good death."[68]

However, these human anxieties find no place in the theocentric framework advanced by the Priestly editors. The late editorial layers of Leviticus and Numbers depict sources of severe bodily impurity, including corpses, as merely affecting participation in the cult (Lev 15:31; Num 5:1–4; 19:13, 20), implying that laypeople need not be concerned with pollution in their everyday activities. This impression is reinforced by the restrictions on priests (Lev 21) and Nazirites (Num 6) from approaching corpses, which indicates that this pollution concerns only those of elite cultic status. In comparison, as has been shown, inscriptional and archaeological evidence, taken together with subtle references to curses associated with "bad death" in the HB, suggest that interactions with the dead were accompanied by apprehension.

Interestingly, even the final form of Num 19 is suggestive of an exorcistic ritual. Anticipating the widely accepted view in modern scholarship, the following apocryphal anecdote attributed to Rabban Yohanan ben Zakkai is illuminating:[69]

A gentile asked Rabban Yohanan ben Zakkai, saying to him, "These rites that you carry out look like witchcraft. You bring a cow and slaughter it, burn it, crush the remains, take the dust, and if one of you contracts corpse uncleanness, you sprinkle on him two or three times and say to him, 'You are pure.'"

---

[66] Sharon Ruth Keller, "Egyptian Letters to the Dead in Relation to the Old Testament and Other Near Eastern Sources" (PhD diss., New York University, 1989), 108–109.

[67] James G. Frazer, "On Certain Burial Customs as Illustrative of the Primitive Theory of the Soul," *Journal of the Anthropological Institute of Great Britain and Ireland* 15 (1886), 63–104 (64). Dina Katz echoes these sentiments in a Mesopotamian context: "Thus, a spirit could escape the body, but without the ritual it could not enter the netherworld. The spirit roams the world as a liminal, terrifying entity, but is dangerous mostly to its own neglectful family members" ("The Naked Soul," 117).

[68] b. *Shab.* 105b–106a cites another potential concern not mentioned in the HB, collective familial punishment: "One of the brothers has died, all of the brothers will worry" (אחד מן האחין שמת ידאגו כל האחין).

[69] *Pesiq. Rab Kah* 4:7; translation: Jacob Neusner, *Pesiqta deRab Kahana: An Analytical Translation*, vol. 1 (Atlanta, GA: Scholars Press, 1987), 65 (adapted); see also Milgrom, *Leviticus*, 1.270–271.

... He said to him: "And have you ever seen someone into whom a wandering spirit entered?"

He said to him: "Yes."

"And what do you do?"

"People bring roots and smoke them under him and sprinkle water on the spirit and it flees."

He said to him: "And should your ears not hear what your mouth speaks? So this spirit is the spirit of impurity . . . "

After the man had gone his way, his disciples said to him, "My lord, this one you have pushed off with a mere reed. To us what will you reply?"

He said to them, "By your lives! It is not the corpse that imparts uncleanness nor the water that effects cleanness. But it is a decree of the Holy One, blessed be He."

This story acknowledges the formal similarity of the red cow ritual to an exorcism but proceeds to reinterpret it to fit the monotheistic sensibilities of the interlocutors. This passage offers a cogent model for how the Priestly source did in fact reinterpret traditional beliefs and practices pertaining to corpses. By limiting the concern of death pollution to the holy precincts (Num 19:13, 20), similar to the corresponding rationales in Lev 15:31 and Num 5:3, the popular belief in the threatening nature of pollution, associated with vengeful spirits, was marginalized. These efforts to minimize the fear of death pollution and thereby reconstrue a ritual that was intended initially to drive out spirits should not surprise us. A similar tendency was identified in previous chapters, namely, to diminish the fear of contagious disease due to its association with exorcistic rites.

The biblical text, like death itself, is characterized by ambivalence. Textual and archaeological evidence suggests a need to maintain a delicate balance in relation to the dead. This tension is built into the special defilement limitations imposed on priests (Lev 21) and Nazirites (Num 6), which imply that in normal cases relatives were expected to defile themselves in caring for the deceased. While the archaeological evidence has received various interpretations,[70] the dominant Iron Age tendency to bury directly outside settlements can be best explained by this ambivalence between the need to care for the deceased and the desire to separate from their "pollution." Similarly, the halakhic literature of the Second Temple Period recognizes an imperative to distance corpse impurity from the settlement, while at the same time resisting stringency in favor of maintaining a "safe" proximity to graves.[71]

---

[70] See Stavrakopoulou, *Land of Our Fathers*, 18, n. 68.
[71] A full discussion of this topic is beyond the purview of this article, but the Temple Scroll offers a salient example, admonishing its audience: "You shall not defile your land. And

CONCLUSION

In this chapter, it was seen that the Priestly conception of death pollution, designated *tame' le-nepeš*, builds on widespread West Semitic attitudes regarding the soul, involving exposure to the *nepeš* as it leaves the body. Though the present form of Num 19 emphasizes the cultic ramifications of this pollution, there are reasons to suspect that exposure to the *nepeš* in this transitional phase was perceived to be dangerous, particularly under conditions of "bad death." Admittedly, the interpretation of the textual evidence is complicated by the likelihood that the biblical authors – Priestly and non-Priestly alike – sought to deny the agency of ghosts. A further complication is the fluidity of terms that appear in the contexts of bad death. In the context of violent death, the texts generally refer to a depersonalized metaphysical bloodstain (*damim*) rather than spirit vengeance. In connection with lack of burial, the preferred idiom is curse. Nevertheless, both of these situations are described as *defiling* the land, and in the case of Ezek 39, burial is described as *purifying* the land. This fluidity is highly significant for the present investigation, showing how the biblical authors used the terminology of pollution in a flexible – nonscientific – manner to describe circumstances of negative contagion. This finding reinforces the conclusions of Chapter 2. Serving as a generic category that encompasses diverse experiential schemas, the systematicity of *tum'ah* should not be exaggerated.

In conclusion, these past two chapters have explored how Priestly rules of pollution relate to the partially dualistic concept of self reflected in these sources. It has been shown that the *nepeš* can play different roles and be both defiled and defiling. By consumption of impure animal flesh and blood – involving a merging of a person's *nepeš* with that of the animal, the person's spirit is defiled. In the case of a dead body, contact with the *nepeš* of the deceased in this transitional phase constitutes a severe pollution. Though some exegetical points are disputable, the broader theoretical point that pollution beliefs are rooted in culture-specific ontological

you shall not do as the nations do: they bury their dead in every place and they even bury inside their houses" (48:10–12). The solution offered by the scroll, to bury the dead at the juncture point of four cities, reduces the number of cemeteries and locates them outside the settlements, while nevertheless maintaining proximity to them. Note also the following section that banishes severe impurity bearers from all cities (in a strict interpretation of Num 5:1–4), while making a lenient exception for corpse impurity (48:14–17). For the text, see Elisha Qimron, *The Temple Scroll: A Critical Edition with Extensive Reconstructions* (Jerusalem: Beer Sheva, 1996), 70. Note also that Josephus omits death pollution in his account that parallels Numbers 5:1–4 (*Antiquities* 3: 261–264).

presumptions is not. Nevertheless, the basis of these cultural theories in universal human experience can explain the large degree of cross-cultural similarity characterizing both these conceptions of the soul (e.g., the shared terminology of "breath"/"wind") and their implications for pollution.

In the preceding chapters, our primary concern has been with understanding pollution in Priestly ritual texts as an expression of implicit ontology. It will now be possible to address a further potentiality of pollution discourse as applied to the moral domain. In addressing sexual pollution, we will examine, in the words of Louis Dumont: "the irruption of the biological into social life,"[72] specifically how impurity becomes a key idiom in moral discourse.

---

[72] *Homo Hierarchicus: The Caste System and Its Implications*, trans. M. Sainsbury, L. Dumont and B. Gulati (Chicago, IL: University of Chicago Press, 1970), 139; cited by Nihan, *From Priestly Torah*, 317.

Mating

9

Sexual Pollutions: The Moralized Body

In biblical Israel, sex was not considered sinful, but it was messy. Yet, commerce in bodily fluids by itself is insufficient to account for the attention sex receives as a source of pollution, throughout the HB and cross-culturally. In terms of sheer messiness, one could think of numerous activities that far exceed intercourse, for example frolicking in a dung heap, which for some reason did not merit the attention of purity regulations.

In surveying the numerous passages related to pollution in the Hebrew Bible, one finds a seemingly disproportionate amount of attention given to sexual pollution. The types are numerous. Physiological causes of sexual pollution include ordinary genital emissions (semen, menstruation) and irregular, pathological emissions. Alongside these sources of "ritual" impurity, which fit into the system of purifications described in Leviticus 11–15, one finds various causes of "moral" impurity, caused by violation of sexual norms.[1] This category is itself diverse, including intercourse during menstruation; adultery; incest; male homosexuality; and bestiality.

---

[1] The use of the term "moral" is potentially anachronistic since there is no equivalent in biblical Hebrew. Nonetheless, as will be seen, the biblical texts do seem to recognize a fundamental distinction between physiological (ritual) and moral impurity. The use of "moral" should be equated with normative behavior, understood in the widest sense, hence not restricted to concerns of harm and care. See Roger Giner-Sorolla, *Judging Passions: Moral Emotions in Persons and Groups* (London: Psychology Press, 2013), 10–18 for the distinction between "single-concern" and "multiple-concern" morality. For pluralism in moral psychology, see Jonathan Haidt, *The Righteous Mind* (New York, NY: Pantheon Books, 2012); Jesse Graham et al., "Moral Foundations Theory: On the Advantages of Moral Pluralism over Moral Monism," in *Atlas of Moral Psychology*, eds. K. Gray and J. Graham (New York, NY: Guilford Press, 2018), 211–222.

Some sources extend this defilement to sex with non-Israelites. Accordingly, the biblical data raise several questions: Why is sexuality so frequently associated with pollution? Why is *sexual* pollution – more than any other domain – moralized?

In order to make sense of the biblical evidence, it will be necessary to provide a theoretical framework which can account for the relationship between embodied experience, social norms and discourse. This framework will be introduced in several stages. The first section of this chapter will return to the distinction between abstract and embodied approaches to pollution discussed in Chapter 2, using biblical and ancient Near Eastern evidence to provide a tentative phenomenology of sexuality as reflected in these texts. The following section will introduce some theoretical principles in the evolutionary study of emotions, namely the role of emotions in mediating social interaction. Relevant research bearing on the social implications of disgust and contagion will set the stage for the following section, which will examine the biblical evidence pertaining to physiological and moral pollution. The final section of this chapter will draw some broader theoretical conclusions based on the distinction between images, codes and discourse introduced in Chapter 1. Specifically, it will show that the interaction between embodiment and cultural discourse is a two-way street. Through "bottom-up" processes, embodied experience provides the materials for social codes and cultural discourse, just as, through "top-down" processes, culture shapes attitudes regarding the body.

ARE YOU EXPERIENCED? INTIMACY, ATTRACTION AND REPULSION

As noted above,[2] scholars have sought to understand sexual pollution as part of broader symbolic schemes, seeking a common rationale for all of the Priestly laws of *ṭum'ah*. For example, commentators have discerned a life–death dichotomy in interpreting physiological causes of pollution in Lev 12 and 15, ascribing impurity to the loss of seed in intercourse and blood in menstruation.[3] Representative of this tendency, Jacob Milgrom

---

[2] See Chapter 2.

[3] Gordan Wenham, "Why Does Sexual Intercourse Defile (Lev 15, 18)?" *ZAW* 95.3 (1983): 432–434; Edward L. Greenstein, "Biblical Law," in *Back to the Sources: Reading the Classic Jewish Texts*, ed. B. W. Holz (New York, NY: Summit, 1984), 95, who coins the expression "life-leaks." See also Richard Whitekettle, "Levitical Thought and the Female Reproductive Cycle: Wombs, Wellsprings, and the Primeval World," *VT* 46.3 (1996):

writes: "The loss of vaginal blood and semen, both containing seed, meant the diminution of life and, if unchecked, destruction and death. And it was a process unalterably opposed by Israel's God, the source of its life: 'you shall keep my laws and my norms, by the pursuit of which men shall live: I am the Lord' (Lev 18:5)."[4] However, this focus on procreation, the biological function of sex, is misleading, since Lev 15 does not distinguish potentially reproductive sexual relations from nocturnal emissions. This difficulty is symptomatic of a more general weakness of such attempts, which tend to intellectualize the biblical purity laws from a disembodied, abstract perspective. These arguments have already been evaluated above. Here our interest will be in showing how such an embodied approach can provide a more satisfying account for the social ramifications of pollution.

Ancient Near Eastern texts do not treat sex as just another bodily function like eating and sleeping. Sexual experience is treated as a life-transforming event that pertains to males and females alike. In the Mesopotamian Epic of Gilgamesh, the Tarzan-like Enkidu, who suckles milk from wild animals, is domesticated by his seven-day-and-night sexual romp with a harlot, after which he joins human civilization.[5] The idiom of sexual knowledge, as represented in the biblical expression "and Adam *knew* Eve, his wife" (Genesis 4:1), is pregnant with these implications.[6]

Assuming the reader is of flesh and blood, these points need not be belabored. In relation to contagion, it is worth stressing that sexuality is characterized not only by attraction but also repulsion. In general, sexual attraction and disgust are inversely related, as has been demonstrated by several recent experimental studies where it has been shown that disgust and fear of contamination tend to inhibit sexual excitement. However, the converse effect is also evident: sexual arousal can inhibit disgust, stimulating approach behavior despite the presence of otherwise

---

376–391. However, as Hyyam Maccoby points out, these approaches are undermined by the fact that the life-threatening loss of blood from an open wound is not defiling (*Ritual and Morality: The Ritual Purity System and Its Place in Ancient Judaism* [Cambridge: Cambridge University Press, 1999], 49).

[4] Jacob Milgrom, *Leviticus*, AB, 3 vols (New York, NY: Doubleday, 1991–2000), 1:767.
[5] See Andrew George, *The Babylonian Gilgamesh Epic: Introduction, Critical Edition and Cuneiform Texts*, vol. 1 (Oxford: Oxford University Press, 2003), 174–175.
[6] See Meir Malul, *Knowledge, Control and Sex. Studies in Biblical Thought, Culture and Worldview* (Tel-Aviv/Jaffa: Archaeological Center Publication, 2002).

disgusting stimuli.[7] This antithetical relationship can help explain the radical polarization of language pertaining to sex, spanning from the erotic imagery of the Song of Songs to the texts that thematize shame and degradation such as the overtly vulgar descriptions of promiscuity in Ezekiel 16 and 23,[8] which, for example, describe Jerusalem as satisfying her lusts with Egyptians "whose members were like those of asses and whose outpourings were like those of horses" (Ezek 23:20). These gratuitously obscene idioms are guided by a programmatic aim to transform any possible eroticism associated with the sexual domain into repulsion. Likewise, the sexual taboos of Lev 18 and 20 are deliberately formulated to evoke shame and outrage. In particular, the use of the euphemism "reveal nakedness" to describe these behaviors eliminates the possibility that mention of these "perverse" behaviors might arouse the kinky curiosity of the audience.[9] By extension, there is nothing particularly erotic in a chapter about sexual pollution.

In short, the biblical treatment of sexual pollution reflects, in its evocation of disgust and shame, a polarity rooted in the psychology of sex. It manifests the tension between attraction and revulsion and seeks to enlist the latter to safeguard against norm violations. The recognition of this high level of emotional involvement is key to understanding the pervasiveness of moral pollution within the sexual domain.

SOCIAL IMPLICATIONS OF DISGUST AND CONTAGION: THEORETICAL FOUNDATIONS

In tracing the role of sexuality from embodied experience to socio-moral discourse, it is necessary to address the role of emotional expression in

---

[7] Peter J. de Jong, Mark van Overveld and Charmaine Borg, "Giving in to Arousal or Staying Stuck in Disgust? Disgust-Based Mechanisms in Sex and Sexual Dysfunction," *Journal of Sex Research*, 50.3–4 (2013): 247–262; Diana S. Fleischman, Lisa D. Hamilton, Daniel M. T. Fessler and Cindy M. Meston, "Disgust Versus Lust: Exploring the Interactions of Disgust and Fear with Sexual Arousal in Women," *PLOS ONE* 10 (2015)// e0118151. doi:10.1371/journal.pone.0118151; Kelly Knowles, Charmaine Borg and Bunmi O. Olatunji, "Disgust, Disease, and Disorder: Impurity as a Mechanism for Psychopathology," in *Purity and Danger Now: New Perspectives*, eds. R. Duschinsky, S. Schnall and D. Weiss (New York, NY: Routledge, 2017), 103–120.

[8] Athalya Brenner, "Pornoprophetics Revisited: Some Additional Reflections," *JSOT* 70 (1996): 63–86 (reprinted as *The Intercourse of Knowledge: On Gendering Desire and "Sexuality" in the Hebrew Bible* [Leiden: Brill, 1997], 153–174); Aaron Koller, "Pornography or Theology? The Legal Background, Psychological Realism, and Theological Import of Ezekiel 16," *CBQ* 79.3 (2017): 402–421.

[9] For this idiom, see also Isa 47:3; Ezek 16:36–37; 23:10, 18, 29.

mediating social interaction. As early as 1872, Charles Darwin set forth a theoretical principle that has guided evolutionary studies ever since in his work *The Expression of Emotion in Man and Animals*. There he observed that functional behaviors can also serve as communicative signals. For example, he suggested that the baring of teeth as an expression of anger in humans can be traced back to its role in other animals as a preparation for actual biting.[10] Originating as "intention movements" as the animal prepared for its action, these responses could be interpreted by other animals as communicative expressions.[11] Of course, behavior need not be classified as *either* functional *or* communicative. It does not take an expert in animal behavior to recognize that instinctual affective behaviors (e.g., erect ears, wagging tails) can serve as communicative signals guiding responses for other animals.[12]

This general Darwinian framework has served as a springboard for the psychology of the emotions more generally. Building on the notion of "basic emotions," Keith Oatley and Philip Johnson-Laird argued that these emotions serve as the developmental basis for social emotions in infants and adults.[13] Similarly minded evolutionary studies have sought to identify the immediate biological functions of emotions in promoting survival and reproductive success, which can then serve significant social functions in facilitating cooperation.[14]

These theoretical principles have already been applied profitably to disgust. Though the original function of disgust was apparently avoidance of toxins (by ingestion) and pathogens (by contact), its external manifestations could also serve as warning signals to other members of

---

[10] *The Expression of the Emotions in Man and Animals* (Chicago, IL: University of Chicago Press, 1965 [1872]).

[11] See Paul E. Griffiths, *What Emotions Really Are* (Chicago, IL: University of Chicago Press, 1997).

[12] See Michele Merritt, "Dismantling Standard Cognitive Science: It's Time the Dog Has Its Day," *Biological Philosophy* 30.6 (2015): 811–829. While these responses may be instinctual and involuntary, they can also be learned and ritualized. See Michael Tomasello, "Two Hypotheses about Primate Cognition," in *The Evolution of Cognition*, eds. C. Heyes and L. Huber (Cambridge, MA: MIT Press, 2000), 165–183; Marta Halina, Federico Rossano and Michael Tomasello, "The Ontogenetic Ritualization of Bonobo Gestures." *Animal Cognition* 16.4 (2013): 653–666.

[13] Keith Oatley and Philip Johnson-Laird, "Towards a Cognitive Theory of Emotions," *Cognition and Emotion* 1.1 (1987): 40–41.

[14] Dacher Keltner, Jonathan Haidt and Michelle N. Shiota, "Social Functionalism and the Evolution of Emotions," in *Evolution and Social Psychology*, eds. M. Schaller, J. A. Simpson and D. T. Kenrick (New York, NY: Psychology Press, 2006), 115–142.

the species.[15] In humans, disgust also plays a fundamental role in the formation of social norms and manners.[16] More generally, the repertoire of disgust terminology is available for use in social contexts which relate weakly – if at all – to sources of physiological disgust. Young children quite regularly and naturally employ exclamations such as "yuck" as all-purpose expressions of disapproval and rejection. Indeed, older children will go to great lengths to avoid the "cooties" (imaginary lice/germs) of their classmates.[17]

This principle has even been observed in relation to contagion among chimpanzees. In her early years working at Gombe when a polio outbreak struck the chimpanzees, Jane Goodall and her assistants observed how the chimpanzees fearfully quarantined their peers who showed signs of debilitation:

Pepe, for instance, shuffled up the slope to the feeding area, squatting on his haunches with his useless arm trailing behind him, the group of chimps already in camp stared for a moment, and then, with wide grins of fear, rushed for reassurance to embrace and pat each other while staring at the unfortunate cripple. Pepe, who obviously had no idea that he himself was the object of their fear, showed an even wider grin of fright as he repeatedly turned to look over his shoulder along the path behind him … Eventually the others calmed down; but, though they continued to stare at him from time to time, none of them went near him …[18]

Yet an even more fascinating example derives from her later discussion of territorial behavior, specifically the systematic annihilation of rival groups. The following description pertains to one of these attacks on a rival female:

Thirty minutes after she was first attacked, she again approached one of the males, Satan, and presented, twice reaching to touch him. Satan actively rejected these

---

[15] Daniel R. Kelly, *Yuck! The Nature and Moral Significance of Disgust* (Cambridge, MA: MIT Press, 2013), 61–100.

[16] Valerie Curtis, *Don't Look, Don't Touch, Don't Eat: The Science Behind Repulsion* (Oxford University Press: Oxford, 2013), 53–66; Shaun Nichols, "On the Genealogy of Norms: A Case for the Role of Emotion in Cultural Evolution," *Philosophy of Science* 69 (2002): 234–255, to be discussed in the section "From Embodiment to Discourse – and Back."

[17] Sue Samuelson, "The Cooties Complex," *Western Folklore* 39.3 (1980): 198–210; Giner-Sorolla, *Judging Passions*, 74–77.

[18] *In the Shadow of Man* (Boston, MA: Houghton Mifflin Co, 1971), 221; Jane Goodall, "Social Rejection, Exclusion, and Shunning Among the Gombe Chimpanzees," *Ethology and Sociobiology* 7.3–4 (1986): 232–233; Megan Oaten, Richard J. Stevenson and Trevor I. Case, "Disease Avoidance as a Functional Basis for Stigmatization," *Philosophical Transactions of the Royal Society B* 366 (2011): 3441–3442.

contacts – the second time he picked a large handful of leaves and scrubbed his leg where her hand had rested. Immediately after this she was attacked again.[19]

When this female attempted to make a submissive touching gesture, the male's response was to wipe off the place of contact, employing a regular grooming practice, before attacking her. These anecdotes demonstrate the versatility of contagion responses. In these examples, contagion is associated with fear of infection (in the first case) and anger/aggressiveness (in the second case), showing that contamination is not limited to disgust, contrary to a widespread view in psychological literature.[20]

Along these lines, Walter Burkert made the following apt remarks regarding pollution in ancient Greek literature:

It is clear that the alertness concerning pollution and purification, universal as it appears to be, has biological roots. To keep oneself clean is a basic necessity for all higher animals ... What is functional in even humans – to wipe and wash one's body, to fumigate with sulphur to destroy pests – long ago became ritual ...[21]

These remarks can go a long way in explaining the ubiquitous role of washing in relation to moral cleansing, attested in ancient rituals and rediscovered by modern psychological research. The metaphoric projection of hygiene onto the moral domain finds salient expression in Proverbs 31:11–12: "There is a generation that brings curse upon its fathers ... a generation that is pure (*ṭahor*) in its own eyes but has not washed itself from its excrement."

Here it is necessary to call attention to a relevant debate taking place in the intersection of emotion research and moral psychology, namely the status of "moral disgust." One line of research has focused on the question: are moral judgments shaped by disgust?[22] One of the pioneers of this line of research, Jonathan Haidt, sought to demonstrate the role of emotion – and disgust in particular – in shaping moral intuitions through cases of "moral dumbfounding" in which respondents were unable to justify their disapproving responses to scenarios in which no harm was

[19] Jane Goodall, *The Chimpanzees of Gombe: Patterns of Behavior* (Cambridge, MA: Belknap Press of Harvard University Press, 1986), 502.
[20] See Chapter 1.
[21] *Creation of the Sacred: Tracks of Biology in Early Religions* (Cambridge, MA: Harvard University Press, 1996), 123.
[22] Hanah A. Chapman and Adam K. Anderson, "Things Rank and Gross in Nature: A Review and Synthesis of Moral Disgust," *Psychological Bulletin* 139.2 (2013): 300–327; Hanah A. Chapman and Adam K. Anderson, "Trait Physical Disgust Is Related to Moral Judgments Outside of the Purity Domain," *Emotion* 14.2 (2014): 341–348.

involved.[23] An additional body of research involved inducing disgust by various modalities (hypnosis, word associations, taste, odor, video clips) and examining its effect on moral evaluations.[24] The key issue in these studies is to examine the effect of these manipulations on moral assessments of harm/fairness scenarios (e.g., stealing, corruption) which are unrelated to concrete bodily elicitors of disgust (e.g., gore, excrement, sex). These studies appear to indicate an "amplification effect" of disgust which influences moral judgment in the harm/fairness domain.[25] Research has even shown that participants feel compulsion to physically wash (aptly labeled the "Macbeth effect") when feelings of guilt are aroused, reflecting a natural transition from functional to symbolic washing.[26]

While many of these studies have focused on the possibility of an unconscious role of disgust in shaping moral judgments, other studies have addressed the explicit use of disgust terminology and even of associated facial expressions to express disapproval. Regarding this topic, a fundamental disagreement can be found between scholars who recognize the existence of "moral disgust" and those who remain skeptical and are inclined to assume that these expressions are metaphorical.[27] More specifically, there is growing experimental evidence that the use of disgust terminology in response to moral scenarios reflects anger.[28]

Between these two extremes, a nuanced position has been proposed by Pascale Sophia Russel and Roger Giner-Sorolla suggesting that expressions of disgust in relation to harm/fairness violations are metaphorical

---

[23] "The Emotional Dog and Its Rational Tail: A Social Intuitionist Approach to Moral Judgment," *Psychological Review* 108.4 (2001): 814–834.

[24] Simone Schnall, Jonathan Haidt, Gerald L. Clore and Alexander H. Jordan, "Disgust as Embodied Moral Judgment," *Personality and Social Psychology Bulletin* 34.8 (2008): 1096–1109.

[25] For a critique of this claim, see Justin F. Landy and Geoffrey P. Goodwin, "Does Incidental Disgust Amplify Moral Disgust? A Meta-Analytic Review of Experimental Evidence," *Perspectives on Psychological Science* 10.4 (2015): 518–536.

[26] See Chen-Bo Zhong and Katie Liljenquist, "Washing Away Your Sins: Threatened Morality and Physical Cleansing," *Science* 313 (2006): 1451–1452; Colin West and Chen-Bo Zhong, "Moral Cleansing," *Current Opinion in Psychology* 6 (2015): 211–215.

[27] Robin L. Nabi, "The Theoretical Versus the Lay Meaning of Disgust: Implications for Emotion Research," *Cognition and Emotion* 16.5 (2002): 695–703; Edward B. Royzman and John Sabini, "Something It Takes to Be an Emotion: The Interesting Case of Disgust," *Journal for the Theory of Social Behaviour* 31.1 (2001): 29–59; Paul Bloom, *Descartes' Baby* (New York, NY: Basic Books, 2004).

[28] Edward Royzman et al., "CAD or MAD? Anger (Not Disgust) as the Predominant Response to Pathogen-Free Violations of the Divinity Code," *Emotion* 14.5 (2014): 892–907.

expressions of disapproval, but that those elicited in cases of transgressions involving bodily elicitors of disgust are genuinely based on a physiological/emotional disgust response.[29] In several experiments comparing anger and disgust as they relate to bodily norms and non-bodily norms, the researchers found that self-reported disgust in relation to bodily norm violations (e.g., pedophilia, prostitution) exhibited more of the characteristics of disgust than non-bodily norm violations (e.g., corrupt politicians). For example, participants found their self-reported anger and disgust easier to justify in cases of non-bodily norm violations, whereas bodily norm violations were often justified using tautologies ("Pedophiles are disgusting because they are gross").

As will be seen, the biblical evidence seems to support this distinction. If "moral pollution" was purely metaphorical, it could be expected to be employed indiscriminately for various types of transgression, including those that are unrelated to physiological pollution. However, the fact that the preponderance of evidence bearing on moral pollution pertains specifically to the sexual domain suggests that there was a deeper psychological motivation for using such language.

THE BIBLICAL EVIDENCE

It is now possible to engage the biblical evidence. Building on an earlier distinction by Adolph Büchler, Jonathan Klawans argued compellingly that the Priestly source distinguishes between "ritual" and "moral" impurities.[30] Although the texts refer to both of these types using the same terminology, namely the root *ṭ-m-'*, they are distinguished from one another regarding their implications: ritual pollution defiles the person and must be purified by a ritual procedure, whereas moral pollution defiles the land and lacks a ritual remedy. Importantly, this distinction corresponds to a source-critical distinction in the editing of the Priestly source: ritual pollution appears primarily in P, especially Lev 11–15, whereas moral pollution is peculiar to H (Lev 17–27, especially 18 and

---

[29] Pascale S. Russell and Roger Giner-Sorolla, "Bodily Moral Disgust: What It Is, How It Is Different from Anger, and Why It Is an Unreasoned Emotion," *Psychological Bulletin* 139.2 (2013): 328–351.

[30] Adolph Büchler, *Studies in Sin and Atonement in the Rabbinic Literature of the First Century* (New York, NY: Ktav, 1967), 212–269; Jonathan Klawans, *Impurity and Sin in Ancient Judaism* (New York, NY: Oxford University Press, 2000), 21–42. Cf. Tracy Lemos, "Where There Is Dirt, Is There System? Revisiting Biblical Purity Constructions," *JSOT* 37.3 (2013), 265–294.

20) and sources stylistically similar to H (Numbers 35:33–34). The fact that H emphasizes moral pollution is not coincidental and will be examined in more depth below.[31]

Klawans' discussion cites the following causes of moral impurity: idolatry, child sacrifice, murder and sexual sins. Subsequent scholars have tended to follow his lead in viewing sexual pollution as one type within this broader category. However, a quantitative survey of the relevant biblical evidence which applies the terminology of pollution (*ṭ-m-*') to norm violations reveals that this picture is skewed. Once disputable (child sacrifice) and one-time (bloodshed) examples are set aside,[32] the main evidence for moral impurity pertains to idolatry and sexual pollution. The defilement of idolatry does not appear in Priestly writings,[33] and in non-P texts is often mediated by a metaphor of sexual promiscuity (see below).

Viewed from this perspective, an overlooked and highly significant point becomes evident: *nearly all of the evidence for moral pollution pertains to sex*. Paul Ricoeur noticed this imbalance also in ancient Greek literature, commenting:

Thus one is struck by the importance and gravity attached to the violation of interdictions of a sexual character in the economy of defilement. The prohibitions against incest, sodomy, abortion, relations at forbidden times – and sometimes places – are so fundamental that the inflation of the sexual is characteristic of the whole system of defilement, so that an indissoluble complicity between sexuality and defilement seems to have been formed from time immemorial.[34]

---

[31] This topic is further developed in Chapter 12.

[32] The reference to child sacrifice polluting the temple in Lev. 20:3–4 is quite similar to that found in Ezek 23:38–39 (see also Ezek 20:31; Jer 7:30–31), which seems to emphasize the desecration of Yhwh's cult, so can hardly provide strong evidence for moral pollution. Ezek 23:38–39 reads: "At the same time they also did this to me: they defiled (טמא) my sanctuary and profaned my sabbaths. On the very day that they slaughtered their children to their fetishes, they entered my sanctuary to desecrate it. That is what they did in my house" (NJPS translation). For further discussion, see Milgrom, *Leviticus*, 2.1734–1735; Roy Gane, *Cult and Character: Purification Offerings, Day of Atonement, and Theodicy* (Winona Lake, IN: Eisenbrauns, 2005), 144–162.

[33] David P. Wright, *The Disposal of Impurity: Elimination Rites in the Bible and in Hittite and Mesopotamian Literature* (Atlanta, GA: Scholars Press, 1987), 283.

[34] *The Symbolism of Evil*, trans. E. Buchanan (Boston, MA: Beacon Press, 1967), 28. For the Greek evidence, see Robert Parker, *Miasma: Pollution and Purification in Early Greek Literature* (Oxford: Clarendon Press, 1983), 74–103; Moshe Blidstein, *Purity, Community, and Ritual in Early Christian Literature* (Oxford: Oxford University Press, 2017), 20–26.

Scholars in recent years have identified several key metaphors for sin in the HB, depicting it as a burden, debt or a stain.[35] It is striking that among these numerous expressive possibilities, one finds such a consistent use of pollution terminology in relation to sexual prohibitions. How can this association be explained?

Considering an example from modern society, the stark reality of sexual assault suggests that this association is anything but coincidental. Specifically, modern clinical evidence pertaining to sexual assault confirms what might have otherwise been expected, that women who have fallen victim to sexual assault suffer from "mental pollution."[36] This sense of being defiled persists in the absence of actual dirt and is not responsive to washing. Furthermore, it can be produced by mental images and memories in the absence of physical contact.

There are several psychological factors that contribute to this sense of defilement. The violent act is felt to be an intrusion into the victim's body image: "When a victim is raped, there is a massive, physical intrusion into her internal, private body space. Her body space and body boundaries are violated."[37] The feeling is magnified by the violation of the victim's moral code, especially within social contexts which stress the need for women to guard their sexuality, often described in terms of her "purity": "The idea that women's sexuality is spoiled or disgraced by forced sexual intercourse stems in part from the historical importance of women's virginity, purity, or 'saving' themselves until marriage."[38] Needless to say, these psychological aspects of the response to sexual assault are attuned to the realities of its possible concrete ramifications, namely the dangers of unwanted pregnancy and sexually transmitted diseases. This clinical evidence reveals that there is nothing particularly metaphysical about attributing impurity to unwanted sexual contact.

---

[35] See Gary Anderson, *Sin: A History* (New Haven, CT; Yale University Press, 2009); Joseph Lam, *Patterns of Sin in the Hebrew Bible* (Oxford: Oxford University Press, 2016).

[36] Nicole Fairbrother and Stanley Rachman, "Feelings of Mental Pollution Subsequent to Sexual Assault," *Behaviour Research and Therapy* 42.2 (2004): 173–189; Christal L. Badour et al., "Disgust, Mental Contamination, and Posttraumatic Stress: Unique Relations Following Sexual versus Non-Sexual Assault," *Journal of Anxiety Disorder* 27.1 (2013): 155–162; Ryotara Ishikawa, Eiji Shimizu and Osamu Kobori, "Unwanted Sexual Experiences and Cognitive Appraisals That Evoke Mental Contamination," *Behavioural and Cognitive Psychotherapy* 43.1 (2015): 74–88.

[37] Moshe Isac and Stanley Schneider, "Some Psychological Reactions of Rape Victims," *Medicine and Law* 11.3–4 (1992): 306.

[38] Karen G. Weiss, "Too Ashamed to Report: Deconstructing the Shame of Sexual Victimization," *Feminist Criminology* 5.3 (2010): 289.

TABLE 9.1 *Sexual impurities: Physiological and moral*

Pollution type	Schema	Causes	Ramifications
Physiological	Uncleanness	Ordinary genital emissions	Exclusion from the holy domain[1]
	Infection	Pathological genital emissions	Extended purification rituals, including expiatory sacrifices
Moral	Stain of transgression	Adultery, illicit sex acts	Defilement of land, divine retribution

[1] For the prohibition of sex with a menstruant (Lev 18:19; 20:18), see next chapter.

In short, the fact that defilement is closely related to sexuality should not surprise us. Yet, the biblical evidence does not focus on sexual assault; rather it presents a wide spectrum of causes. Table 9.1 summarizes the different schemas identified in Chapter 2 as they apply specifically to sexual pollution.

These various categories will be analyzed below, with an emphasis on moral pollution. Based on the theoretical principles outlined earlier in the chapter, the following hypothesis regarding the biblical data will be evaluated: *the notions of pollution which are immediately concerned with physiological danger are historically primary, whereas notions of pollution focusing on social and religious boundaries are secondary derivatives.* If correct, the historical evidence of the HB would demonstrate the process of scaffolding (see Chapter 1), whereby bodily experience provides the raw materials for more sophisticated social discourse. Moreover, as will be seen below, an appreciation for the embodied origins of these images provides the logic for understanding the various permutations of pollution. The following analysis will test this theory by surveying the various types of sexual pollution in the HB and attempting to place them in a historical sequence.

The aim of tracing historical developments in the usage of pollution language in the biblical corpus appears simple enough in theory, but in practice it must confront a formidable methodological obstacle – the notorious difficulty of dating specific biblical texts, mentioned briefly in the introduction to this book. The texts comprising the Pentateuch, for example, can only be dated by a very contentious process of delineating and dating individual layers or sources. A further problem which cannot be underestimated is the reliance of literary compositions on earlier oral or written traditions. For example, even if one assumes that the Priestly source received its definitive form in the sixth century BCE or later, it remains nevertheless possible and even probable that the various ritual and cultic institutions presumed by it were in existence much earlier. Indeed, even many biblical critics that date P to the exilic or postexilic period have acknowledged openly that the ritual traditions originated in a much earlier period.

To overcome these challenges, the present analysis will pay special attention to the rhetorical aims of each text in order to discern the implications of pollution language. Implicit in this method is the assumption that it is possible to distinguish primary and secondary notions of pollution by careful consideration of the rhetorical functions of the texts in their literary context.

RITUAL POLLUTION

One category of pollution which is relatively uncontroversial is "ritual." Minimally, this label means that these types of pollution are purified by ritual means. Some scholars would take a step further and view these types of pollution as relatively minor because they are *only* related to the cult (i.e., the sanctuary, offerings and officiating priests). According to this view, the label "ritual impurities" serves to limit their scope.[39]

This minimal characterization of ritual pollution should be modified by the recognition that many of these sources were originally believed to be inherently dangerous, particularly in sources related to disease or death. Although the text as it stands focuses on the antithetical relationship between pollution and the divine presence (Lev 15:31; Num 5:1–4; 19:13, 20), this emphasis reflects the ideological slant of the late editor(s) of these texts, as seen in previous chapters.

Though many scholars would date P in its present form to the Persian period (sixth–fifth centuries BCE), it seems clear that these sources of pollution were well known beforehand. Without getting sidetracked with detailed arguments for dating individual texts, the following forms of pollution are mentioned outside of P in sources which are datable to the

---

[39] Their innocuous nature is also reflected in Wright's alternative designation: "tolerated" impurities. See David P. Wright, "The Spectrum of Priestly Impurity," in *Priesthood and Cult in Ancient Israel*, JSOTSup 125, eds. G. A. Anderson and S. M. Olyan (Sheffield: JSOT Press, 1991), 150–158.

pre-exilic or early exilic period: seminal emissions (1 Sam 20:26; 21:5–6); menstruation (2 Sam 11:4; Isaiah 30:22; Lamentations 1:9); and dietary restrictions (Deuteronomy 14; Hosea 9:3–4).[40] In general, these passing references to impurities substantiate what most scholars would take for granted, namely that P did not invent these ritual impurities. This presumption finds further support in the fact that these types of pollution are amply attested in the texts from Israel's Near Eastern neighbors, as well as other more remote ancient and traditional cultures.

MORAL POLLUTION

Before examining the evidence pertaining to sexual pollution, it is worth recalling the discussion of bloodguilt from the previous chapter. As was noted, the reference to the defilement of the land in Num 35:33–34 substitutes the terminology of pollution for the traditional image of a bloodstain (*damim*), offering a salient example of the "stain-of-transgression" model described in Chapter 2. The underlying conception is that if this blood-debt were not properly repaid – by execution of the perpetrator at the hands of the victim's kin ("the redeemer of blood") – the entire community would face divine retribution (Deut 21:1–9; 2 Sam 21). As noted, there is a seemingly redundant parallel in this passage between the two verses:

> V. 33: You shall not incriminate (*ḥ-n-p*) the land in which you live . . .
> V. 34: You shall not pollute (*ṭ-m-'*) the land in which you live . . .

Through this juxtaposition, one sees that the curse (*ḥ-n-p*) of the land left by homicide is conceptualized as a stain. This blend can be represented as seen in Table 9.2.

In light of the schematic similarity between bloodguilt and pollution, it is not surprising that the former can be described in the language of the latter. This shared schematic structure – an invisible essence entailing threatening implications – explains why bloodguilt can be effectively described as pollution. This isolated instance of pollution terminology, alongside the ubiquitous references to "blood," is a clear indication that this usage is metaphorical. Without denying that the threat of divine retribution was taken to be real, the fundamental point in labeling this

---

[40] See Thomas Kazen, "Purity and Persia," in *Current Issues in Priestly and Related Literature: The Legacy of Jacob Milgrom and Beyond*, eds. R. E. Gane and A. Taggar-Cohen (Atlanta, GA: SBL, 2015), 435–462.

TABLE 9.2 *Bloodguilt as a conceptual blend*

Experiential subscenes	Metaphysical concept (synthesis)
Physical bloodstain	bloodguilt as an invisible stain
Culpability (causing retribution)	

usage as "metaphorical" is that it recognizes that the depiction of blood-guilt (previously described as an invisible bloodstain) as *tum'ah* was innovative.[41]

ADULTERY AND PROMISCUITY

Now we turn to the evidence for sexual pollution, which is based on similar imagery of an invisible stain. Compared with its limited use in reference to bloodguilt, the association of the root *ṭ-m-'* with sexual violations is much more pervasive. It appears in several genres (including law, narrative and prophecy) and pertains to a wide range of causes, with the sense of *ṭ-m-'* varying according to these differences in context.

Many biblical examples refer to adultery and promiscuity. In her comprehensive study of sexual pollution, Eve Levavi Feinstein observes that intercourse serves a territorial marking function in the Hebrew Bible, within the social context that the wife was viewed as the sexual property of her husband. Accordingly, sexual relations with another man were viewed as contaminating her.[42] This point is confirmed by Deut 24:1–4, a legal text which prohibits a husband from taking back his divorced wife

---

[41] *Pace* Klawans (ibid.) who denies that the defilement of the land in Lev. 18:24–25 is metaphorical since it presumes a *real* threat of the land vomiting out its inhabitants (ibid.). See also Eve Levavi Feinstein, *Sexual Pollution in the Hebrew Bible* (Oxford: Oxford University Press, 2014), 5–6. For our purposes, the key question is not whether the pollution is real, but whether it is "pollution" (*ṭum'ah*) in the strict sense. In light of the explicitly emotive character of these writings, it does not seem far-fetched to claim that the authors were deliberately extending the traditional notion of pollution to maximize rhetorical effect. This point is particularly evident in Ezekiel, whose use of pollution terminology is freer than that of H, and considering its concern with justifying the divine judgment against Jerusalem. Cf. Tova Ganzel, "The Transformation of Pentateuchal Descriptions of Idolatry," in *Transforming Visions: Transformations of Text, Tradition, and Theology in Ezekiel*, eds. W. A. Tooman and M. A. Lyons (Eugene, OR: Pickwick, 2009), 33–49.
[42] *Sexual Pollution*, 43.

after she has been married to another man: "Then the first husband who divorced her shall not take her back as his wife, after she has been defiled – for that would be abhorrent to Yhwh. You must not bring sin upon the land that Yhwh, your God, is giving you as a heritage" (4). As Feinstein points out, this case is analogous to adultery: "Just as a woman who commits adultery is contaminated and ruined for her husband, so is a woman who has sex within a legal second marriage ruined for her former husband."[43] Still, it bears stressing that the woman's "defilement" is relational, existing only for her first husband, unlike ritual pollution, which is viewed as an objective metaphysical state.

In the ordeal for the suspected adulteress (Num 5:11–31), the "straying" (*śoṭah*) woman is forced to drink a potion containing the following conditional curse (vv. 19–20, 22):[44]

The priest shall make her swear, saying to the woman: "If a man did not lie with you and you did not stray impurely from your husband, you shall be absolved by these cursing waters. [But] if you did stray from your husband and have been polluted, and a man aside from your husband put his *laying* inside you,[45] these cursing waters will enter your abdomen, causing your belly to swell and your hip to fall." And the woman shall answer, "Amen, amen."

Here the dichotomy "defiled"/"not defiled," refers to whether or not she is guilty of her husband's accusations. Though these references to her culpability should not be confused with the physiological impurities of Lev 15, which operate according to physical rather than moral criteria,[46]

---

[43] Ibid., 63. For similar attitudes in the Qumran sect bearing even on premarital sex, see Aharon Shemesh, "4Q271.3: A Key to Sectarian Matrimonial Law," *JJS* 49 (1998): 244–263.

[44] I have omitted v. 21, as it is not immediately relevant to the discussion. Some scholars suspect, in fact, that this verse is a later addition, see Jaeyoung Jeon, "Two Laws in the Sotah Passage (Num. v 11–31)," *VT* 57.2 (2007): 189.

[45] For the sense of this expression (also in Lev 18:20, 23; 20:15) and its relation to the common idiom שכבת זרע (Lev 15:16, 17, 18, 32; 19:20; 22:4; Num 5:13), see D. Hoffmann, *Das Buch Leviticus*, vol. 2 (Berlin: Poppelauer, 1906), 21–22. Cf. Harry M. Orlinsky, "The Hebrew Root škb," *JBL* 63.1 (1944): 37–40. Unlike Orlinsky who takes שְׁכְבָת* as an expression for "penis," I view it as metonymically referring to the man's semen (so explicitly in Lev 18:20).

[46] Several scholars have correctly recognized that Num 5:11–31 does not refer to "ritual" impurity, e.g.: Baruch A. Levine, *Numbers 1–20*, AB (New York, NY: Doubleday, 1993), 207; Wright, "Unclean and Clean," 734. See also Yitzhaq Feder, "The Semantics of Purity in the Ancient Near East: Lexical Meaning as a Projection of Embodied Experience," *JANER* 14.1 (2014):100–104; *pace* Ellen van Wolde, *Reframing Biblical Studies: When Language and Text Meet Culture, Cognition and Context* (Winona Lake, IN: Eisenbrauns, 2009): 260. Lev 18:20 warns against adultery by threatening the man with being defiled: "Do not lay with your fellow's wife and be defiled by her."

they nevertheless referred to a metaphysical reality. If, as is suspected, the seed of another man has penetrated her, the waters of cursing will discern the traces of the pollution within her and carry out her punishment.[47]

Lest this use of defilement language appear idiosyncratic, Mesopotamian and Hittite ordeals (not only those dealing with adultery)[48] use the terminology of impurity in reference to *culpability*. For example, in the Hittite Instructions for Temple Officials (CTH 264), a person who brings inappropriate first-fruit offerings must undergo the following ordeal: "Then you (pl.) shall drink from the rhyton of the will of god. If you are pure (*parkuwaeš*), it is your protective deity. But if you are defiled (*paprantes̆*), you shall perish together with your wives and children" (IV, 52–55).[49] Likewise, Section 2 of the Laws of Hammurabi employs the verb *ebēbu* ("be pure") to describe a person cleared of guilt by means of a river ordeal in a suspected case of witchcraft: "If the River clears (*ūtebbib*) that man and he survives, the man who accused him of witchcraft shall be killed."[50] In these contexts, one might say that the designation "impure" refers to a metaphysical state, an invisible stain, that could be discerned only by means of the ordeal.

A variation of this usage is found in prophetic indictments, which employ the language of defilement in their depiction of worship of foreign gods as sexual promiscuity and harlotry. For example, Hos 5:3 reads "Ephraim, you have prostituted yourself, Israel has been defiled" (also 6:10; Jeremiah 2; Ezek 16; 23). These texts offer further evidence that disgraceful sexual acts were viewed as "staining" the woman.[51]

---

[47] Specifically, the waters are described as infiltrating her "innards" (מעים) in v. 22. This term is general and can refer to the digestive tract (Ezek 7:19) as well as the womb (Isa 49:1; Ps 71:6). Hence, it seems likely that the rite envisions the waters as seeking out the "defiling" seed inside the woman and taking retribution on her.

[48] Feder, "Semantics of Purity," 100–104.

[49] Text: Ada Taggar-Cohen, *Hittite Priesthood*, THeth 26 (Heidelberg: Winter, 2006), 67–68 (my translation). For similar passages, see IV, 32–33 and 69–77.

[50] Text: M. Roth, *Law Collections from Mesopotamia and Asia Minor*, 2nd ed. Atlanta, GA: SBL, 1997), 81 (with slight adaptation). For a comparable use of *zakû*, see CAD Z 26. Note also that the Laws of Ur-Namma §§13–14 use Sumerian dadag to denote "clearing" of guilt through a river ordeal. Roth, ibid., 18. See also Tikva Frymer-Kensky, *The Judicial Ordeal in the Ancient Near East* (diss., Yale University, 1977), 493.

[51] As far as I can see, there is no clear biblical evidence for the association found in many other cultures between promiscuous women and the stench of the sexual fluids they absorb. For example, the derogatory terms for prostitutes in European languages (e.g., *putain* from *puer*, "stink") reflect this association. See Alain Corbin, *The Foul and the Fragrant: Odor and French Social Imagination* (Cambridge, MA: Harvard University Press, 1986), 43–46, 143; Constance Classen, "The Odor of the Other: Olfactory Symbolism and Cultural Categories," *Ethos* 20 (1992): 142–143; Curtis, *Don't Look*, 89.

Compared to the use of pollution terminology in relation to adultery, where it refers to a bona fide norm violation (punishable by death), its metaphorical use in relation to promiscuity implies a severe social stigma, emphasizing the shameful character of Israel, the whore. Eve Levavi Feinstein captures the message of this rhetoric, particularly for a male audience: "It evokes the repulsion that men would feel at the idea of their own wives committing adultery and suggests that God feels the same way about them."[52] As will be discussed below, this application of sexual imagery to foreign cults is clearly a secondary development of pollution discourse.

TABOOED BEHAVIORS

The codification of sexual violations in Lev 18 and 20 has a different focus. The bulk of these two chapters consists of detailed lists of the various blood relations for whom sexual relations are considered incestuous. These are supplemented by further sexual violations: sex with a menstruant, bestiality and a man who lies with another male "the laying of a woman." These prohibitions are accompanied by emphatic expressions of condemnation but no rationale. For example, in justifying the prohibition of sexual relations with a half-sister, Lev 18:11 states: "The nakedness of your father's wife's daughter, who was born into your father's household – *she is your sister*; do not uncover her nakedness." There is no attempt to explain why sex with a sister is beyond the pale. Accordingly, these chapters appear to support the moral intuitive view by David Hume and developed by modern moral psychologists and philosophers, that moral justifications are secondary to intuitions rooted in the "passions."[53] According to this view, moral judgments are based primarily in feelings of approval or disapproval. Along these lines, the presentation of illicit sex acts in Lev 18 and 20 presumes that they elicit disgust and shame. In fact, these behaviors are so abhorrent that they cause the land to vomit out its inhabitants (Lev 18: 25, 28).

[52] *Sexual Pollution*, 53.
[53] David Hume, *A Treatise of Human Nature*, ed. Peter H. Niditch (Oxford: Oxford University Press, 1978 [1739]); David Hume. *An Enquiry Concerning the Principles of Morals*, ed. Tom. L. Beauchamp (Oxford: Oxford University Press, 1998 [1751]). In psychology: e.g., Haidt, *Righteous Mind*; in philosophy: e.g., Oliver S. Curry, "Who's Afraid of the Naturalistic Fallacy?" *Evolutionary Psychology* 4.1 (2006): 234–247; Jesse Prinz, *The Emotional Construction of Morals* (Oxford: Oxford University Press, 2007).

While this highly emotive language makes clear that these behaviors are expected to elicit repulsion, it is the inevitability of divine sanctions that bestow upon them objective reality. Hence, they are depicted as sexual "taboos" in the technical sense of forbidden acts that incur automatic punishment.[54] Specifically, Lev 18 and 20 associate these sexual violations with a collective punishment, exile (expressed in the idiom of the land "vomiting out"), as well as the "cutting off" (*karet*) of the individual and his/her lineage (Lev 18:29; 20:17–18).[55]

Here it is worthwhile returning to attempts to apply symbolic interpretations to these tabooed sex acts. Some scholars have inferred that a concern with wasting the male seed underlies these prohibitions. For example, Jacob Milgrom writes: "The common denominator of all the prohibitions, I submit, is that they involve the emission of semen for the purpose of copulation, resulting in either incest and illicit progeny or, as in this case [male homosexuality], lack of progeny (or its destruction in the case of Molek worship, v. 21). In a word, the theme . . . is procreation."[56] Nicole Ruane has elaborated on this rationale: "The logic of Lev 18 and 20 is centered around a concern to preserve the 'seed' of men. Seed may not go into unproductive places, such as a man or an animal. By this logic, a menstruant is also an unproductive place."[57] According to these accounts, one is led to believe that nonreproductive sex, that is – sex for the sake of pleasure, was considered illicit. Yet, as Milgrom himself notes, the biblical law in no place forbids masturbation or birth control.[58] Furthermore, this rationale would not apply to the type of sexual prohibition that receives the most attention in these chapters, namely incest, which could be expected to yield offspring.[59]

More fundamentally, there is no reason to assume that the biblical authors (priests included) looked disdainfully on sex for its own sake. On

---

[54] Roy Wagner, "Taboo," in *Encyclopedia of Religion*, vol. 14; ed. M. Eliade (New York, NY: Macmillan, 1987), 233–236. For discussion of "taboo" as an analytic concept, see Valerio Valeri, *The Forest of Taboos: Morality, Hunting, and Identity among the Huaulu of the Moluccas* (Madison, WI: University of Wisconsin, 2000).

[55] For this punishment, see above p. 170.

[56] *Leviticus*, AB, 3 vols. (New York, NY: Doubleday, 1991–2000), 2.1567.

[57] *Sacrifice and Gender in Biblical Law* (New York, NY: Cambridge University Press, 2013), 182.

[58] *Leviticus*, 2.1567–1568 (with a cogent discussion of Gen 38:9–10).

[59] A question which warrants further study pertains to what extent, if at all, ancient civilizations were aware of the significantly higher probability of birth defects resulting from incestuous couplings. For an exploration of this question as it pertains to ancient Egypt, see Joanne-Marie Robinson, *"Blood Is Thicker Than Water": Non-Royal Consanguineous Marriage in Ancient Egypt* (Oxford: Archaeopress, 2020).

the contrary, the HB appears to celebrate the pleasure of sex, raising it to the level of an existential requirement of life itself. In this regard, the biblical view is consistent with ancient Near Eastern literature in general, in which life without sex was hardly worth living. This theme finds expression in a Sumerian forerunner to Gilgamesh, in which Enkidu relates his observations from a dream visit to the netherworld. There he observed miserable spirits lamenting the unfulfilled opportunities of their previous bodily existence, including "the young man who never removed the cloth from the lap of his spouse" and "the young maiden who never removed the cloth from the lap of her spouse" weeping bitterly.[60] These sentiments are echoed in biblical narrative and law. For example, the war legislation of the Book of Deuteronomy releases a soldier who has betrothed a woman lest he die in battle and never get the chance to consummate his marriage (20:7). Elsewhere Deut exempts bridegrooms from military service for the first year of marriage "to please (*ś-m-ḥ*) the woman that he has married" (24:5). When Jephthah impetuously swears an oath forcing him to sacrifice his daughter, she spends her last two months "bewailing her maidenhood among the hills . . . for she had not known a man" (Judges 11:38–39). Most strikingly, the Song of Songs presents an extended celebration of premarital sex.

Once again, we may suspect that these scholars have gone astray in their search for a rational common denominator (nonprocreation) for the tabooed sex acts. Ricoeur attended to the peculiarities of sexual pollution when he observed that "the defilement of sexuality as such is a theme foreign to the ethics that proceeds from the confession of divine holiness as well as to the ethics that is organized around the theme of justice or the integrity of the moral person," leading up to the assertion: "The defilement of sexuality is a belief that is pre-ethical in character."[61] This point is based, *inter alia*, on the recognition that the illicitness of these sexual transgressions was not dependent on the intentions of the transgressor: the transgression was viewed as a norm violation in objective terms.[62] These comments regarding the irrelevance of intention in relation to sexual violations correlates with the observation in modern research that disgust (as opposed to anger) is an "object-related" emotion, meaning that it can be elicited irrespective of a particular situational context and in

---

[60] Alhena Gadotti, *Gilgamesh, Enkidu and the Netherworld and the Sumerian Gilgamesh Cycle* (Berlin: de Gruyter, 2014), 159, ll. 275–278.
[61] *Symbolism of Evil*, 28.   [62] Ibid., 26–27.

the absence of malicious intent.[63] Therefore, these taboos are best interpreted within an enactivist appreciation for the role of emotions in cognition (and in line with Hume's "sentimentalist" view of moral judgment), rather than in reference to a disembodied logic.[64]

INTERMARRIAGE

An additional domain of illicit sexual behaviors where pollution terminology manifests itself pertains to intermarriage. These references appear in narratives and are absent from legal sources, reflecting a clearly rhetorical, even polemical, basis. Importantly, the period in which this linguistic usage emerged can be confidently identified as the postexilic (Persian) period (fifth–fourth centuries BCE).

The first explicit attacks on mixed marriages in general can be found in the books of Ezra and Nehemiah. Whereas Deut 7:1–7 proscribes intermarriage with the Canaanite peoples on the grounds that they will seduce the Israelites into worshipping their gods,[65] Nehemiah reinterprets this text to formulate a general prohibition of mixed marriages (Neh 13:1–3; also 9:1–2; 10:29–31). Similarly, facing a crisis of intermarriage between the returnees and the "peoples of the land," Ezra demands that all such marriages be dissolved. This outrage is described as a "desecration" (*ma'al*) caused by "intermingling the holy seed with the peoples of the land" (9:2).

Similarly, the narrative in Gen 34, describing the coerced sexual relations of Dina with the Hivite prince Shechem, is based on an implicit polemic against mixed marriages.[66] The case of Dina can be differentiated from civil violations such as seduction or rape that can be resolved by monetary sanctions and forced marriage (Exodus 22:15–16; Deut 22:28–29). In comparison, Gen 34 refers repeatedly to the fact that Shechem has "defiled" (*ṭimme'*) Dina (vv. 5, 13, 27), reflecting the conviction that sex with the Hivite precluded any type of conventional legal resolution. This use of pollution terminology coincides with other

---

[63] Russell and Giner-Sorolla, "Bodily Moral Disgust," 340.   [64] See above, p. 21.

[65] For other polemics against intermarriage in the Torah, see Benedikt J. Conczorowski, "All the Same as Ezra? Conceptual Differences Between the Texts of Intermarriage in Genesis, Deuteronomy 7 and Ezra," in *Mixed Marriages: Intermarriage and Group Identity in the Second Temple Period*, ed. C. Frevel (New York, NY: T&T Clark, 2011), 90–98.

[66] See Yitzhaq Feder, "The Defilement of Dina: Uncontrolled Passions, Textual Violence and the Search for Moral Foundations," *Biblical Interpretation* 24.3 (2016): 281–309.

indications, such as the ploy involving circumcision, that the story is primarily concerned with the violation of ethnic boundaries. This opposition to intermarriage is analogous to that represented in the "holy seed" rhetoric of Ezra and paves the way for the references to impurity in the even more fervent rhetoric against intermarriage in Second Temple period works such as the Book of Jubilees.[67]

The historical background for the emergence of this new emphasis on intermarriage as defiling is easily reconstructed. Throughout the preexilic period, the social boundaries of "Israel" remained fluid, such that an outsider (*ger*) could live together with the Israelite community and ultimately assimilate.[68] Geographic boundaries played the key role in determining affiliation. However, once transplanted to Babylonia, some factions of the Judean diaspora – led by the figures Ezra and Nehemiah – were led to a redefinition of "Jewish" identity that placed much more emphasis on genealogy.[69] In this respect, the use of the purity/defilement dichotomy in Ezra, Neh and Gen 34 signals a significant transformation in Israel's self-definition.[70] This notion of "genealogical purity" represents an essentialist conception of ethnicity which is distinguishable from the view of Israel as a mere sociopolitical grouping.[71] On this point, Mary Douglas has duly stressed the role of pollution in policing social boundaries –

---

[67] The Book of Jubilees (second century BCE) is a Jewish work from the late biblical period which was excluded from the rabbinic canon. Other writings of this sort (classified as Apocrypha and Pseudepigrapha) include the books of Judith and Tobit and the Wisdom of Solomon. See Christian Frevel, "'Separate Yourself from the Gentiles' (Jubilees 22:16); Intermarriage in the Book of *Jubilees*," in *Mixed Marriages: Intermarriage and Group Identity in the Second Temple Period*, ed. C. Frevel (New York, NY: T&T Clark, 2011), 220–250.

[68] Shai J. D. Cohen, *The Beginnings of Jewishness: Boundaries, Varieties, Uncertainties* (Berkeley, CA: University of California Press, 1999), 264–266.

[69] Katherine E. Southwood, *Ethnicity and the Intermarriage Crisis in Ezra 9–10* (Oxford: Oxford University, 2012). This exclusionist position was hardly unanimous, as the narrative in Ezra 9-10 makes clear. Furthermore, an opposing, inclusionist position is represented by the exilic prophecy in Isa 56:3–7.

[70] For discussion regarding the composition of Gen 34 and the provenance of the intermarriage polemic, see Feder, "Defilement of Dina," 301–307.

[71] Christina Hayes, *Gentile Impurities and Jewish Identities: Intermarriage and Conversation from the Bible to the Talmud* (New York, NY: Oxford University Press, 2002), 27–34. For essentialist views of race, see Lawrence A. Hirschfeld, *Race in the Making* (Cambridge: MIT Press, 1996); Gil Diesendruck and Lital Haber, "God's Categories: The Effect of Religiosity on Children's Teleological and Essentialist Beliefs about Categories," *Cognition* 110.1 (2009): 100–114. For essentialism as analytic concept, see the next chapter.

especially when they are otherwise compromised due to their ambiguity.[72] However, Douglas has left us with little direction regarding *how* pollution takes on these social implications; it is on this question that an embodied approach can make an important contribution.

FROM EMBODIMENT TO DISCOURSE: AND BACK

Despite eloquent arguments for "symbolic patterns" in which the human body represents the body politic of the society,[73] Douglas failed to offer any explanation for how such a sophisticated metaphoric mapping could unconsciously emerge. Even more fundamentally, recent scholars have criticized the implicit dualism of Douglas' account, which privileges intellectual "meanings" as represented by the vehicle of the body. As Tracy Lemos has pointed out, "[T]he type of analysis that seeks ever to schematize almost always sees ritual as secondary to belief and the body as secondary to the mind."[74]Against this tendency to explain purity practices in terms of a disembodied rationality, the task of this section will be to identify the mechanisms by which the socio-moral implications of purity emerge as part of a bottom-up process grounded in bodily experience.[75]

Embracing this challenge, two mechanisms can be identified by which purity concerns are translated into social boundaries and hierarchies. Though a sharp distinction is not always possible, it is helpful to differentiate between

1. Purity praxis: social ramifications and distinctions emerging as natural outgrowths of fear and repulsion from pollution;
2. Purity language: deliberate and novel appropriation of purity terminology for rhetorical purposes.

In the first mechanism, purity for its own sake becomes a tool for advancing one's interests (or those of one's group) in situations of competition. Alternatively, purity considerations may serve as a boundary marker in

---

[72] *Purity and Danger: An Analysis of the Concepts of Pollution and Taboo* (London: Routledge, 1966), 131–133.
[73] Ibid., 116, 124, discussed above, Chapter 2.   [74] "Where There Is Dirt," 294.
[75] Andreas de Block and Stefaan E. Cuypers, "Why Darwinians Should Not Be Afraid of Mary Douglas – and Vice Versa: The Case of Disgust," *Philosophy of the Social Sciences* 42 (2012): 459–488, attempt a synthesis of modern disgust research and Douglas' pollution theory, but they fail to recognize the explanatory weaknesses of Douglas' approach and instead build a case for evolutionary adaptation upon her vague notion of disorder.

policing group boundaries. For example, H's prohibition of priests from consuming dead or torn animals (Lev 22:8; also Ezek 44:31) serves to differentiate priests from the laity, who may consume such animals but must then undergo purification (Lev 11:40; 17:15). These gradated purity requirements help solidify the distinction between the priesthood and the laity. Whereas these sources, representing established priestly traditions, indicate that the complete avoidance of non-slaughtered meat was a priestly stringency, other sources (apparently later) extend this distinction to all of Israel, supplying the rationale: "for you are a holy nation to Yhwh, your God" (Deut 14:21; also Ex 22:30).[76] Some passages attach a similar significance to the distinction between pure and impure animals, framing the dietary laws as a means of transforming Israel into a holy nation (Lev 11:44–45 and Deut 14:2, 21). In other words, while in an earlier tradition (represented in H), the avoidance of non-slaughtered meat served as a basis for establishing an intragroup hierarchy between Israelites priests and the laity, later iterations of this avoidance could be transformed into a point of distinctiveness of the Israelite people in relation to other nations, defining them as a "kingdom of priests" (Ex 19:6).[77] Yet, it should be remembered that non-slaughtered meat was considered inherently impure, only secondarily serving as an index for hierarchal social relations. In a context of intragroup and intergroup competition,

[76] According to traditional source criticism, the Priestly texts were assumed to be later than the Covenant Code (Ex 22:30) and Deut. More recent research, however, has tended to identify the verses in question as late redactional statements in their present literary contexts, making the dating of these specific verses problematic. See David P. Wright, *Creating God's Law: How the Covenant Code of the Bible Used and Revised the Laws of Hammurabi* (Oxford, UK: Oxford University Press, 2009), 496–497, n. 15; Christophe Nihan, "The Laws About Clean and Unclean Animals in Leviticus and Deuteronomy and Their Place in the Formation of the Pentateuch," in *The Pentateuch: International Perspectives on Current Research*, eds. T. B. Dozeman, K. Schmid and B. J. Schwartz (Tübingen: Mohr Siebeck, 2011), 401–432 (421–422, n. 42). Without engaging in a detailed diachronic text analysis, there are essentially two possibilities which need to be considered: (1) a priestly stringency was extended to the whole nation to establish Israel's unique holiness in relation to other peoples (my view); or (2) a stringency bearing on lay Israelites was restricted to priests, perhaps as a means of emphasizing the priests' elevated status vis-à-vis the rest of the nation (Nihan's view). Whereas the rhetoric of Ex 22:30 and Deut. 14:21 fits the first possibility, no comparable rhetoric can be identified in the relevant Priestly texts supporting the second hypothesis. Therefore, regardless of the date of composition of these Priestly texts, it is clear that the law as reflected in the Priestly sources is earlier than the statements in Ex 22:30 and Deut. 14:21. In any case, either of these views is consistent with the theoretical point being made here.

[77] The similar emphases of this verse and Ex 22:30 may suggest that they pertain to the same supplementary layer. See Wright, ibid. for discussion.

this particular purity practice was exploited as a means of elevating social and religious status.[78]

This approach is fully consistent with a rapidly growing body of psychological research. As already recognized in the research of Nemeroff and Rozin, contagion is highly sensitive to social attitudes.[79] To take a mundane example, it is a common experience that the prospect of drinking from a stranger's glass of water is more disgusting than drinking from that of a close family member. Needless to say, this type of xenophobia fits well with evolutionary accounts focusing on the pathogen-avoidance function of disgust. More pertinent to this discussion, however, is the recognition that avoidance behavior is shaped by positions in the social hierarchy.[80] As Louis Dumont noted in the context of the Hindu caste system, purity rules serve to produce social divisions when these values are manipulated by competing factions for the sake of aggrandizement. He writes:

In general a caste will be recognized as inferior to some and superior to others. To settle its rank, a certain number of criteria will be used . . . For example one can imagine the members of a caste saying: "We are vegetarians, which places us above X, Y, Z, who eat meat; but we allow the remarriage of widows, which places us below A, B, C, who forbid it."[81]

The result of this system is that "superiority and superior purity are identical; it is in this sense that, ideologically, that distinction of purity is the foundation of status."[82] These considerations find unfortunate expression in attitudes toward sexual assault in India, where the chastity of upper-caste women is vigilantly protected against defilement by lower-caste men but rape of lower-caste women is often disregarded: "The body of a lower caste, lower class woman is already polluted and further pollution through rape is normalized, not capturing much attention of the nation."[83]

---

[78] See Saul Olyan, *Rites and Rank: Hierarchy in Biblical Representations of Cult* (Princeton, NJ: Princeton University Press, 2000), 38–62.

[79] Carol Nemeroff and Paul Rozin, "The Contagion Concept in Adult Thinking in the United States: Transmission of Germs and Interpersonal Influence," *Ethos* 22.2 (1994): 158–186; "The Makings of the Magical Mind: The Nature and Function of Sympathetic Magical Thinking," in *Imagining the Impossible: Magical, Scientific and Religious Thinking in Children*, ed. K. S. Rosengren, et al. (Cambridge: Cambridge University Press, 2000), 1–34.

[80] Giner-Sorolla, *Judging Passions*, 76–77.

[81] *Homo Hierarchicus: The Caste System and Its Implications*, trans. M. Sainsbury, L. Dumont and B. Gulati (Chicago, IL: University of Chicago Press, 1970), 56–57.

[82] Ibid.

[83] Piyali Sur, "Women, Bodies and Discourse on Rape," *Indian Journal of Social and Natural Sciences* 4 (2015): 40–48 (44).

Turning to the second mechanism, purity language, a salient example is the depiction of intermarriage as pollution, discussed in the above section "Intermarriage." An even more pervasive example is the extension of defilement discourse to idolatry.[84] Whereas other sources of impurity relate in one way or another to the body, this category appears exceptional in its theological focus, relating specifically to cultic devotion to gods other than Yhwh. However, closer examination reveals that the pollution of idolatry is expressed in the language of bodily sources of disgust and pollution, specifically: (1) feces; (2) death; (3) sickness and (4) promiscuity.

While excrement is not regarded as defiling in P, it certainly constitutes an elicitor of disgust and appears in several sources as closely related to impurity (Deut 23:10–15; Ezek 4:12–14).[85] This image seems to underlie the term *gilulim* that is used throughout the book of Ezekiel and Deuteronomistic literature to refer to idols. Though its meaning is not beyond dispute, the most likely derivation comes from the word *galal* ("dung/dung balls"). Accordingly, this term for idols has been rendered "shit-things."[86]

The association of idolatry with death is subtler. Several biblical passages refer to foreign lands as being defiling (Joshua 22:19; Amos 7:17; Ezek 4:12), but these sources do not provide a rationale for this idea. Apparently, these texts presume that the Israelites will be unable to worship Yhwh in the foreign land and that their feasts will be part of idolatrous cults. Hos 9:3–4 is the most explicit in explaining the association of impurity with foreign lands. Though this passage was mentioned in the previous chapter, it deserves to be quoted here in its entirety:

---

[84] Although the term "idolatry" is problematic in its pejorative connotations, it is helpful to retain it for this discussion since it accurately captures both the underlying assumption that gods aside from Yhwh were worshipped in the form of cult images and the condemnation of this practice. For the authors, the worship of idols was by necessity devotion to other gods; see Yitzhaq Feder, "The Aniconic Tradition, Deuteronomy 4 and the Politics of Israelite Identity," *JBL* 132.2 (2013): 251–274.

[85] Eve Levavi Feinstein (*Sexual Pollution*, 163–166) treats feces as a "borderline pollutant." See also the beginning of next chapter. See Thomas Staubli, "Feces: The Primary Disgust Elicitor in the Hebrew Bible and in the Ancient Near East," in *Sounding Sensory Profiles in the Ancient Near East*, eds. A. Schellenberg and T. Krüger (Atlanta, GA: SBL Press, 2019), 119–144.

[86] Following Thomas Staubli, "Disgusting Deeds and Disgusting Gods: Ethnic and Ethical Constructions of Disgust in the Hebrew Bible," *HeBAI* 6 (2017): 472–473. The Masoretic vocalization seems to be patterned after *šiqquṣim*; hence, its actual pronunciation is uncertain. See also Milgrom, *Leviticus*, 3.2319–2320.

They shall not remain in the land of Yhwh. Ephraim shall return to Egypt; in Assyria, he shall eat impure food. They will not libate to Yhwh, nor will their offerings be favorable to him. They will be like the food of mourning to them – whoever eats it will be defiled. Because their food is for their *nepeš* (selves/dead spirit), it will not enter the house of Yhwh.

This passage portrays the meals of Israelites in exile as funerary offerings, apparently suggesting that these other gods are dead.[87] According to this understanding, the impurity of foreign lands – at least in this passage – is based on the notion of sharing a meal with dead gods, hence drawing an analogy to death pollution. A terser expression of these themes is found in Am 7:17: "And you yourself shall die on impure soil," which likewise plays on the intersection of these themes: foreign land (= alienation from Yhwh), impurity and death.

The third image for depicting illicit worship, sickness, is likewise subtle in its presentation and is found only in Zechariah 13:2, which associates idolatrous influence with pollution:

In that day . . . I will erase the very names of the idols from the land; they shall not be uttered any more. And I will also make the "prophets" and the spirit of impurity (*ruaḥ ha-ṭum'ah*) vanish from the land.

The depiction of the tendency to worship idols as a "spirit of impurity," associated also with false prophecy, suggests a wayward disposition which has taken hold of the minds of the Judeans. One is reminded of the "evil spirit" (*ruaḥ ra'a*) – a form of madness – which took hold of Saul and led him to his homicidal jealousy of David (e.g., 1 Samuel 16:14–15). The depiction of foreign cults in this manner implies that this behavior is both an external influence (i.e., un-Israelite) and deluded.[88] One may compare the statement in the Assyrian King Esarhaddon's vassal treaty (seventh century BCE) that warns its audience against disloyalty and failure to inculcate loyalty to their progeny, transgressions that are

---

[87] Compare Ps 106:28: "They attached themselves to Baal Peor, ate sacrifices of the dead (*zibḥê metim*)."

[88] This idiom is developed in the "Plea for Deliverance" from Qumran (second century BCE), which juxtaposes the "spirit of impurity" (*ruaḥ ha-ṭum'ah*) with a "spirit of faithfulness" (*ruaḥ 'emunah*) in a prayer to God to rescue the petitioner from evil influences, both internal and external: "Let not a satan rule over me, nor a spirit of impurity" (11Q5 19:14–16); translation: Miriam T. Brand, *Evil Within and Without: The Source of Sin and Its Nature as Portrayed in Second Temple Literature* (Göttingen: Vandenhoeck & Ruprecht, 2013), 208.

described as placing an "impure illness" on themselves.[89] These texts seem to evoke a web of associations related to contagion, sickness and even madness, drawing on everyday experience to depict the threat of subversive influences.

As discussed above, the fourth image, promiscuity, is widespread in the prophetic books of the HB, which focus on sexuality from the perspective of shame and defilement. To sum up this point, although idolatry might appear to be a theological source of pollution with no connection whatsoever to the standard physiological types of impurity, the biblical rhetoric draws on bodily experience through its allusions to excrement, death, sickness and sex.

Having identified these two mechanisms by which pollution informs socio-moral discourse, we can look more generally at the role of the emotions in shaping social norms. In the context of disgust research, numerous scholars have attempted to trace the process by which rules of etiquette and behavioral norms can emerge in reaction to disgust. For example, the philosopher Shaun Nichols, building on the observations of Norbert Elias' *The Civilizing Process,* suggested that disgust-based manners are more likely to be preserved and perpetuated than completely arbitrary rules.[90] To test this hypothesis, he instructed independent coders to evaluate selections from Erasmus' sixteenth-century treatise *On Good Manners for Boys.* The coders evaluated passages in relation to two parameters: (1) whether they involve disgust; and (2) whether they are still accepted as proper manners in modern Western society. For illustration, let us cite some instances of manners unrelated to disgust:

(281) When sitting down [at a banquet] have both hands on the table, not clasped together, nor on the plate . . .
If given a napkin, put it over either the left shoulder or left fore-arm.

In comparison, many examples related to disgust seem to us too obvious to bear mention:

(274) It is boorish to wipe one's nose on one's cap or clothing, and it is not much better to wipe it with one's hand, if you then smear the discharge on your clothing.
(276) Withdraw when you are going to vomit.

---

[89] This verse is preserved on the version from Tel Tayinat: *marṣu* (GIG) *lā ellu* (SIKIL) *ina muḫḫi* (UGU) *ramānīkunu tašakkanāni* (v 55); see Jacob Lauinger, "Esarhaddon's Succession Treaty at Tel Tayinat: Edition and Commentary," *JCS* 64 (2012): 98, with discussion of other copies (116).
[90] *The Civilizing Process,* trans. E. Jephcott (Malden, MA: Blackwell, 2000 [1939]). Nichols, "On the Genealogy."

(277) To repress the need to urinate is injurious to health but propriety requires it to be done in private.

Codifiers of the study identified thirteen behaviors from Erasmus' list as related to disgust, as compared with thirty-two behaviors that were unrelated to disgust. They were then asked to determine which of these behaviors were also unacceptable from the point of view of contemporary manners. The results of this study were as follows: twelve out of thirteen (92.3 percent) disgust-related behaviors were considered relevant to contemporary manners, compared with only twelve out of thirty-two (37.5 percent) of behaviors not related to disgust. Based on these findings, Nichols concludes that "the emotions played a significant historical role in determining which norms survived into the present, and this evidence also suggests that an adequate naturalistic account of cultural evolution must begin to accommodate the role of affect in cultural transmission."[91] To the extent that these behaviors can be viewed as inherent extensions of disgust, this mechanism can be viewed as "bottom-up."

At the same time, it is also possible to observe a reversed line of causation – to identify cases where cultural discourse expands the purview of disgust. This was, in fact, Elias' initial claim: that social pressures lower the threshold of disgust. In the biblical evidence surveyed above, we have observed how the rhetoric of pollution could achieve this effect when applied to idolatry and intermarriage. In both of these cases, we may safely assume that they were not perceived as disgusting by those who engaged in them. In fact, it appears that more forceful and explicit rhetoric (e.g., Ezek 16; 23; Ezra 9–10) is indicative of greater effort being needed to evoke disgust in the audience. In general, this capability for cultural discourse to shape the physiological response of individuals can be viewed as a "top-down" process.[92]

Placing the survey of the biblical evidence within an evolutionary framework, it appears that biblical notions of pollution originated in response to physiological concerns, related both to disgust-based discomfort with uncleanness (e.g., seminal discharge) and fear of infection. These notions of pollution, rooted in embodied experiential schemas, were also

---

[91] Nichols, ibid., 253. See also Kelly, *Yuck*, 61–152; Curtis. *Don't Look*, 53–66.

[92] See Michael Kimmel, "The Arc from the Body to Culture: How Affect, Proprioception, Kinesthesia, and Perceptual Imagery Shape Cultural Knowledge (and vice versa)," *Integral Review* 9.2 (2013): 300–348; Ezequiel A. di Paolo, Elana C.Cuffari and Hanna de Jaegher, *Linguistic Bodies: The Continuity Between Life and Language* (Cambridge, MA: MIT Press, 2018), 105–212.

the basis for conceptualizing norm violations (e.g., bloodshed, incest, illicit sexual behavior) that were schematically similar to the core pollutions and could themselves evoke disgust or fear. The third tier of this model refers to modes of pollution that are more dependent on cultural discourse, namely idolatry and intermarriage. Interestingly, the portrayal of the "Other's" religious practices as defiling (e.g., Hos 5:3, 6:10) seems to have emerged several centuries before the association of pollution with intermarriage.[93] This point would suggest that religious affiliation was a more central determinant of Israelite identity in the preexilic period than genealogy.

The diagram in Figure 9.1 attempts to summarize this evidence while taking into consideration the complementary role of "bottom-up" (originating in embodied experience) and "top-down" (originating in cultural norms and discourse) processes in the formation of pollution beliefs.

In this diagram, the columns represent experiential domains (e.g., sex, food) and the bubbles represent the various types of pollution and how they fit into these domains. The aim of this diagram is to illustrate that pollution concepts can be viewed both in terms of their conceptual form and their meaning (implications). The *form* comes from experiential images (i.e., image schemas, represented by the black and white dashed circles), and to a lesser extent, social relations (e.g., adultery). Their *implications* may derive from either the level of embodiment itself (Tier 1), from folk beliefs/social norms involving fear of divine punishment (Tier 2) or from cultural discourse (Tier 3).

By means of this diachronic analysis, it is possible to trace the trajectories of various pollution images as they unfold in later biblical and post-biblical traditions. This appreciation can help us avoid the pitfalls of a synchronic approach to pollution which focuses on ancient Israelite notions of purity as a static system. The latter approach has often opened the door to claims that the purity laws are arbitrary: Once a scholar can identity an example or two (e.g., the impurity of shellfish) whose motivation is not obvious, the whole scheme of purity can be portrayed as a wholly "symbolic" system, divorced from real-world implications.[94] Furthermore, the diachronic approach enables us to fill in a troubling gap in Mary Douglas' account by suggesting the mechanisms by which embodied pollution concepts can take on social implications. Finally, it

---

[93] See further Yitzhaq Feder, "Defilement and Moral Discourse in the Hebrew Bible: An Evolutionary Framework," *Journal of Cognitive Historiography* 3 (2016): 170–172.

[94] Cf. de Block and Cuypers, "Why Darwinians," 469.

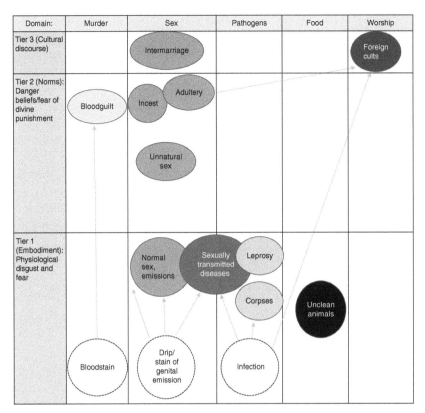

FIGURE 9.1 Pollution as the synthesis of embodied form (images) and cultural norms (discourse)

allows us to identify two complementary tendencies manifested in the biblical evidence: **the decreasing concern with physiological defilement resulting from its limitation to the cultic domain and the increasing emphasis on moral pollution.** These developments, manifested in H, represent an attempt to expand the relevance of Priestly concepts to Israelite laypeople, as is also evident in H's conception of holiness (see Chapter 12). In sum, historical analysis enables us to recognize that pollution is a dynamic concept.

CONCLUSION

The fact that the sexual domain features so prominently in both the rules and rhetoric of pollution in the HB is not accidental. The multifarious extensions of sexual pollution into the moral domain are tied closely to the materiality and significance of sex in experience. Recognizing the similar imagery pertaining to the "stain-of-transgression" model discussed above in Greek and biblical sources, Paul Ricoeur observed: "The comparison between sexuality and murder is supported by the same play of images: in both cases, impurity is connected with the presence of a material 'something' that transmits itself by contact and contagion."[95]

These observations reveal the fallacy of over-intellectualizing pollution in general, and sexual pollution in particular. The *experience* of sex – distinct from its reproductive function and abstract associations with the categories of life and death – was perceived as effecting an epistemological transformation in the partners. To properly understand the dynamics of sexual pollution, no amount of analytic exposition can compensate for a deficit in carnal knowledge.

[95] *Symbolism of Evil*, 28.

10

Gender Fluidity and the Danger of Leaky Manhood

The intensity of attention to the sexual domain within the defilement discourse of the HB raises important questions that have yet to be addressed. It is straightforward to understand, on the one hand, how sexually transmitted diseases (STDs) were perceived as contagious and threatening, and on the other hand to understand why sexual transgressions were believed to produce a stain of culpability that carried the threat of divine retribution. What remains to be explained is the following: why were ordinary sexual emissions, specifically semen, menstruation and birth lochia, regarded as defiling when other bodily emissions were not? In particular, according to the largely compelling view that pollution relates to disgust, one would expect excrement to be defiling, yet surprisingly one finds that P does not mention it as a source of impurity. Intriguingly, even the law of the war camp in Deuteronomy 23:10–15 (discussed below), which explicitly requires the distancing of impurity (specifically seminal emission) and excrement, treats these topics independently and does not ascribe pollution to the latter.[1]

In order to address this problem, it is necessary to probe the nature of sexuality itself – specifically, the metaphysics of gender as understood in

[1] Eve Levavi Feinstein comments regarding Deut 23:10–15: "The juxtaposition of the laws underscores their similarity and common rationale – both seminal emissions and excrement are loathsome to God – but one law deals with pollution while the other does not" (*Sexual Pollution in the Hebrew Bible* [Oxford: Oxford University Press, 2014], 163), though "loathsome" is probably too strong a word. The only exception is Ezekiel 4:12–15, in which the command to eat barley cake baked on human excrement is associated with pollution. Ezekiel's intuitive association of excrement with impurity further highlights the remarkable absence of this connection in P's purity legislation.

ancient Israel and surrounding cultures. In particular, it will be argued that these cultures perceived the difference between masculinity and femininity in *essentialist* terms. Not only does this entail that gender distinctions were attributed to inherent forces characterizing men and women, respectively, but there are indications that these forces could be transferred via contagion. It is in the latter contexts that we find some fleeting hints that femininity itself could be viewed as defiling.

This chapter will introduce the concept of essentialism as understood in psychology, which will then be used as an analytic tool for understanding ancient Near Eastern views of gender difference. It will then examine some ancient Near Eastern and ethnographic evidence of the possibility of transferring gender. This discussion will provide the background for reassessing the relation between sexuality and pollution. In particular, the threat of losing masculinity will be examined in relation to the loss of semen, sexual intercourse in general and the defiling influence of menstrual blood.

THE ESSENCE OF THE MATTER

In current psychological research, essentialism refers to an intuitive belief that assumes that "there is some unobservable property (be it a part, substance, or ineffable quality) – the essence – that causes things to be the way they are."[2] Following its role in Western philosophy, "essentialism" is often related to the underlying basis for linguistic categories: "a naive ontology positing that categories have a deep and unobservable reality, that this reality or 'essence' gives rise to the surface features of category members."[3] Over decades of research, developmental psychologist Susan Gelman amassed evidence for the existence of essentialist tendencies already in preschoolers. Based on this research, one would be inclined to view the predisposition for essentialism to be universal capacity for drawing causal inferences. In contrast with this neutral view of essentialism, critical theory tends to emphasize the role of social construction, often resulting with "essentialism" being treated as a pejorative term, due to its association with discriminatory attitudes regarding race and

---

[2] Susan Gelman, *The Essential Child: Origins of Essentialism in Everyday Thought* (Oxford: Oxford University Press, 2003), 7.
[3] Nick Haslam, Brock Bastian, Paul Bain and Yoshihisa Kashima, "Psychological Essentialism, Implicit Theories, and Intergroup Relations," *Group Processes and Intergroup Relations* 9.1 (2006): 64.

gender. This opposition has given rise to "anti-essentialism," which asserts the social and even political construction of categories.[4] From the perspective of the current study, many of the controversial aspects of essentialist thinking and its political ramifications can safely be set aside. Following the lead of current psychological research, essentialism will be treated from a descriptive rather than normative perspective, taking the human tendency to essentialist thinking as a given.

The aim of this discussion will to be to examine how essentialist thinking informs biblical notions of sexual pollution. Since the term "essentialism" is used in various ways in philosophy and psychology,[5] it is necessary to specify that it will be used here in reference to an invisible essence that can be transferred by contagion.[6] In particular, cognitive responses to elicitors such as toilets, insects and rotting meat, which have been designated "contamination appraisals," are based on an implicit understanding of a contaminating *essence* in these objects, and as such, offer prime examples of the type of essentialism that is relevant to biblical notions of pollution. While essentialism as an analytic concept is applicable to the idea of pollution in general, it is particularly helpful to elucidate the way gender can be attributed to an invisible causal essence.

GENDER AS ESSENCE

The debate between essentialists and anti-essentialists may seem arcane to many modern readers, especially regarding a notion such as pollution that is ostensibly discredited by Western science. To illustrate what is at stake, it may be helpful to briefly examine essentialist attitudes regarding gender. Even today, one finds proponents of the view that "men are from Mars and women from Venus," including those that distinguish between men's and women's brains with postulated neurological differences serving as the modern substitute for invisible essences. This essentialist view faces off against those who view these differences as results of differential upbringing and societal pressures on males and females.

---

[4] For an example relevant to the topic of this chapter: David S. Cohen, "Keeping Men Men and Women Down: Sex Segregation, Anti-Essentialism, and Masculinity," *Harvard Journal of Law and Gender* 30 (2010): 509–553.

[5] For example, considerable attention and experimental research has been devoted to questions of natural kinds, for example how children perceive the underlying basis for linguistic categories such as "horses" and the like. These discussions tend to focus on the role of language in shaping essentialist concepts.

[6] See Gelman, *Essential Child*, 306–325.

Along these lines, ancient Near Eastern (including Israelite) conceptions of gender can offer a helpful point of entry into essentialism, which will later emerge as relevant in the context of purity.

The modern analytical distinction between (biological) sex and (socially constructed) gender offers a helpful antithesis to ancient Near Eastern conceptions, whereby gender was understood in essentialist terms. This attitude is implicit in the etymology of words and in ritual behavior. For example, the Hebrew term for "compassion" *raḥamim* is a pluralized form of the word for "womb," *reḥem*.[7] This etymology reflects the belief that a woman's propensity to be compassionate is rooted in her physiology. It is important to add that similar conceptions inform the etymology of compassion not only in the cognate language of Akkadian (*râmu*), but also the Indo-European Hittite term *genzu*, which also means both "compassion" and "womb." This association is even represented visually in Sumerian, the earliest written language, where the pictographic sign for *arḫuš* ("compassion") is a schematic depiction of a womb.[8]

Not surprisingly, a similar attitude informs the Hebrew term for strength, virility and heroic behavior, *gebura*, which is etymologically derived from the same root as "man," *geber*.[9] Similar observations can be made regarding Akkadian and Hittite terminology and seem to be universal in traditional societies.[10] Conceptions of manliness are vividly reflected in the Hittite ritual of Paskuwatti for sexual dysfunction. This text states its aims as rectifying the following situation: "If some man has no reproductive power (*ḫaššatar*) or is not a man vis-à-vis a woman."[11] In order to address this problem, the text outlines a multistage process that must be followed to restore the patient's manliness. In the first stage,

---

[7] See also Phyllis Trible, *God and the Rhetoric of Sexuality*, OBT (Philadelphia, PA: Fortress, 1978), 33.

[8] This sign is composite, rendered ĜÁxMUNUS in modern transcriptions. See further Margaret Jaques, *Le vocabulaire des sentiments dans les textes sumériens*, AOAT 332 (Münster: Ugarit Verlag, 2006), 495–496.

[9] Relatedly, the root *b-ʿ-l*, serves as the basis for the word *baʿal* which designates both "master" and "husband," and whose verbal forms pertain to control, including sexual mastery. See Meir Malul, *Knowledge, Control and Sex: Studies in Biblical Thought, Culture and Worldview* (Tel Aviv–Jaffa: Archaeological Center Publication, 2002), 239–240.

[10] For an illuminating collection of essays bearing on the ancient Greek terminology of manhood, see Ralph M. Rosen and Ineke Sluiter (eds.), *Andreia: Studies in Manliness and Courage in Classical Antiquity* (Leiden: Brill, 2003).

[11] Text edition and translation: Harry A. Hoffner, "Paskuwatti's Ritual Against Sexual Impotence (CTH 406)," *Aula Orientalis* 5 (1987): 271–287.

before passing through a gateway made out of reeds, the patient gives up symbols of femininity, namely weaving utensils.[12] It is worth adding that the idiom "holder of the spindle" to refer to a man with feminine, probably homosexual, proclivities, is known from the HB (2 Samuel 3:29) and Mesopotamian literature.[13] Upon passing through the gate, the patient receives a bow and arrow, symbols of masculinity. The Hittitologist Harry Hoffner explains the associations underlying these symbols as follows:

> The masculinity of the ancient was measured by two criteria: (1) his prowess in battle, and (2) his ability to sire children. Because these two aspects of masculinity were frequently associated with each other in the mind of the early Near Easterner, the symbols which represented his masculinity to himself and his society often possessed a double reference. In particular, those symbols which primarily referred to his military exploits often served to remind him of his sexual ability as well. So too with symbols associated with femininity: objects which recall her domestic duties frequently carry overtones of her fertility and sexual drives.[14]

In the following phase of the ritual, the patient is supposed to have sexual relations with a virgin. This section is reminiscent of the narrative in 1 Kings 1, where the attendants of the dying King David bring the beautiful virgin Abishag to sleep with him with the hopes that she will "warm" him. Implicitly, this latter text conceptualizes the health of David in terms of "cold" versus "hot," with the latter closely associated with his virility and vitality – in a word, his *gebura*.[15] In the Paskuwatti ritual (like in 1 Kgs 1), the virgin therapy fails, and more drastic measures are required, specifically a higher degree of direct divine intervention. The final stage of the ritual involves an incubation ritual in a hut, where the patient hopes to have an intimate dream encounter with the goddess. It is worthy of note that this escalation of measures to cure the patient, first by ritual and then, when this fails, by direct appeal to the goddess, corroborates the distinction between causal Tiers 2 and 3 in the model discussed in Chapter 6,

---

[12] For use of similar symbols in Mesopotamian birth rituals, see Graham Cunningham, *Deliver Me From Evil: Mesopotamian Incantations 2500–1500 B.C.* (Rome: Editrice Pontificio Instituto Biblico, 1997), 68–75; Barbara Böck, "Gilgamesh's Dreams of Enkidu," *Bibliotheca Orientalis* 71.5–6 (2014): 667–668.

[13] See Meir Malul, "David's Curse of Joab and the Social Significance of *mḥzyq bplk*," *Aula Orientalis* 10 (1992): 49–67.

[14] Harry A. Hoffner, "Symbols for Masculinity and Femininity," *JBL* 85.3 (1966): 327.

[15] This incident is an ironic reversal of David's previously uncontrollable virility, as represented in his forceful seizure of Bathsheba (2 Samuel 11).

whereby the gods represent the ultimate level of agency and oversee the mechanics of the metaphysical world.

What does this text imply regarding the Hittite view of masculinity? Clearly, they didn't think it was a mere social construct. It is worth mentioning that scholars have been in disagreement regarding the specific circumstances addressed by this ritual. Some have defined it as erectile disfunction, while others have interpreted it as referring to homosexual inclinations.[16] In fact, the incipit of the text appears to encompass both "symptoms" with its either/or formulation: lack of reproductive power (*ḫaššatar*) and inability to behave as a man vis-à-vis a woman. It would appear that these scholarly distinctions were foreign to the Hittite conception, which attributed both symptoms to a single cause: a lack of masculinity.

GENDER AND POLLUTION: GO WITH THE FLOW

This essentialist understanding of gender, in which the external manifestations of masculinity and femininity are attributed to unseen causal forces, has important implications for sexual pollution. While anthropological discussions may sometimes describe traditional attitudes of gender difference in reference to "mysterious" forces, it is worth stressing that these folk conceptions can easily be translated into modern biological terms in the distinction between phenotype (manifested characteristics) and genotype (microscopic genetic cause). This point can be made in the opposite direction: the existence of a scientific terminology need not diminish appreciation for the miraculous nature of reproduction, especially as manifested in a woman's ability to conceive.

An immediate practical implication of the metaphysical understanding of sexual difference is the possibility to transfer gender through ritual acts, as evident in Paskuwatti's ritual. This contagious aspect of gender can have unexpected implications in relation to pollution. An interesting example comes from the Kikuyu of East Africa, for whom sex serves as an important means of *removing* pollution. Though these practices might

[16] See Jared L. Miller, "Paskuwatti's Ritual: Remedy for Impotence or Antidote to Homosexuality?" *JANER* 10.1 (2010): 83–89; Ilan Peled, "Expelling the Demon of Effeminacy: Anniwiyani's Ritual and the Question of Homosexuality in Hittite Thought," *JANER* 10.1 (2010): 69–81; Zsolt Simon, "Why Did Paškuwatti's Patient Fail in the Marital Bed?" in *Fortune and Misfortune in the Ancient Near East: Proceedings of the 60th Rencontre Assyriologique Internationale at Warsaw 21–25 July 2014*, eds. O. Drewnowska and M. Sandowicz (Winona Lake, IN: Eisenbrauns, 2016), 97–103.

seem strange compared to the biblical emphasis on the impurity caused by sex, the rationale is straightforward as elucidated by Louis Leakey:

> The chief idea underlying purification by sexual intercourse was that by sexual contact two people become more closely unified than by any other means, and the contagion which was inherent in all forms of uncleanness was completely transferred from the affected person to the other party. Since certain forms of uncleanness could affect only certain individuals, it was obvious that sexual intercourse with someone who was not subject to that uncleanness would remove it and render it ineffectual.[17]

From this perspective, the unrivaled intimacy involved in the sexual act served not only as a conduit to transmit pollution to contaminate the other but also as a means of transferring it from a contaminated person to the sexual partner who could neutralize its effects. As can be seen, the uniqueness of this experience of intimacy – as a physiological sharing of bodily fluids within a liminal act of mutual disclosure – could have unexpected consequences for purity practices.

This perspective can perhaps explain the initially perplexing fact that intercourse in the biblical rules exhibits a certain gender-bending effect. As will be discussed in the following chapter, Lev 15 does not explicitly require female impurity bearers to wash following their genital emissions. The exceptional case where it is stated pertains to sexual intercourse, where the man is the source of pollution: "And a woman, if a man has sexual relations [lit. a laying of seed] with her, they shall bathe in water and remain impure until evening" (18). Conversely, a man who sleeps with a menstruating woman contracts her seven-day impurity and, like her, conveys pollution to his place of laying, such as his bed (24). Notably, like the females, no washing is mentioned in this context for the male. On this point, Nicole Ruane comments, "The sexual partner contracts the same impurity as the source and has the same ritual treatment. Thus, ritually speaking, intercourse has the power to change a sexual partner into a person of the opposite gender."[18]

This may be overstating the case, however, especially since the laws of purification contain numerous ambiguities (to be discussed in the following chapter). A more modest formulation might assert that the contagion associated with the exchange of bodily fluids effects

---

[17] *The Southern Kikuyu Before 1903*, vol. 3 (London: Academic Press, 1977), 1275.
[18] "Bathing, Status and Gender in Priestly Ritual," in *A Question of Sex: Gender and Difference in the Hebrew Bible and Beyond*, ed. D. W. Rooke (Sheffield: Sheffield Phoenix Press, 2007), 79.

a blurring of selfhood. Note the following comment by Paul Rozin and April Fallon on the relationship between disgust and self–other boundaries:

> With respect to disgust, the borders of the self can extend beyond the bodily self, depending on the context . . . Normally disgusting substances or objects that are associated with admired or beloved persons cease to be disgusting and may become pleasant. Body substances including saliva and vaginal secretions or semen can achieve positive value among lovers, and some parents do not find their young children's body products disgusting. In the case of both lovers and children, the source of the object can be considered a social extension of the biological self.[19]

On this background, one can better understand how the synthesis of two bodies in becoming "a single flesh" (Genesis 2:24) can blur the otherwise distinct purity requirements of the sexes. Here it may be recalled that within the structure of Lev 15, the verse dealing with the defilement from sexual relations (v. 18) serves as the hinge between the laws of male (2–17) and female (19–30) impurities.[20] One might say that intercourse constitutes a liminal situation where the otherwise sharp distinction between the sexes dissolves.

THE WAR CAMP AND THE THREAT OF FEMININITY

As mentioned above, the *uncleanness* caused by ordinary sexual relations and its immediate implication – banishment from sites of divine presence and from cultic participation – is amply attested in the HB and in ANE documents.[21] A similar attitude would seem to pertain to the law of the war camp in Deut 23:10–15, mentioned at the outset of this chapter:

> [10]When your camp goes forth against your enemies, be on your guard against anything improper. [11]If anyone among you is not pure (*lo'* . . . *ṭahor*) by a happening of the night (i.e., a nocturnal emission), he must leave the camp. He shall not reenter the camp. [12]Toward evening he shall bathe in water, and at sundown he may reenter the camp. [13]Further, there shall be an area for you outside the camp, where you may go out (to relieve yourself). [14]With your gear you shall have a spike, and when you have squatted you shall dig a hole with it and cover up your excrement. [15]Since Yhwh, your God, moves about in your camp to protect

---

[19] Paul Rozin and April E. Fallon, "A Perspective on Disgust," *Psychological Review* 94.1 (1987): 26–27.

[20] See above, p. 123.

[21] The reference to "uncleanness" here refers specifically to the schema described in Chapter 2.

you and to deliver your enemies to you, let your camp be holy; let him not find anything unseemly among you and turn away from you. (adapted from NJPS)

According to this law, a man who has a nocturnal emission is required to leave the camp and purify himself, due to the divine presence in the camp, which is perhaps localized in the Ark of the Covenant (Num 10:35). Ostensibly, the law's rationale is comparable to that of the sanctuary, where the highest level of etiquette is expected when approaching the divine residence.

Less straightforward is the story of David and his band of outcasts seeking refuge from King Saul (1 Sam 21). When the fugitive David and his men seek lodging and sustenance among the priests at Nob, the priest Ahimelech replies, "I have no ordinary bread on hand; there is only consecrated bread – provided the young men have kept away from women" (1 Sam 21:5; NJPS), and David reassures him in v. 6 that the men have been kept away from women and their vessels consecrated: "Of a truth, women have been kept from us always when I go on an expedition; the vessels of the young men are holy, even when it is a common journey; how much more today will their vessels be holy?"[22] Admittedly, the language of this verse is obscure,[23] but its overall intent seems clear and suggests that the avoidance of women was deliberate. Since there is no reason to assume that the Ark of the Covenant was accompanying David on his flight from Saul, one must seek an alternative reason for the men's sexual abstinence.

In many cultures, sexual intercourse is associated with a loss of virility, such that men would avoid sex before any dangerous endeavor. For example, Harriet Ngubane relates regarding the Zulu of southern Africa that men abstained from sex before undertaking enterprises such as hunting, sacrifice, forging spears and participating in war campaigns.[24] The potential detriments of sex are twofold: the loss of male seed, along with its vigor, and the exposure to feminine contamination. As an expression of the former attitude, Jacob refers to his firstborn son, Reuben, as "my might and the first fruit of my vigor" (Gen 49:3), and this sentiment is echoed in the law of the firstborn in Deut 21:17. One may compare the Hua tribe of Papua New Guinea, where "[t]he firstborn is habitually

---

[22] RSV translation (v. 5).
[23] Jan P. Fokkelman comments that "this passage is possibly the most obscure of I Sam" (*Narrative Art and Poetry in the Books of Samuel. Volume 2: The Crossing Fates* [Assen/ Maastricht: Van Gorcum, 1986], 731).
[24] *Body and Mind in Zulu Medicine* (London: Academic Press, 1977), 79.

described as the child on which the parents waste their strength. His or her body is one into which large amounts of their *nu* [vital essence] is drained."[25]

Numerous ANE war rituals involve manipulation of gender, seeking to eliminate femininity from one's army and convey it to the enemy. For example, in the Hittite ritual known as "The First Soldiers' Oath," which is highly reminiscent of the Paskuwatti ritual, the soldiers are forced to take an oath of loyalty. The soldiers are presented with feminine symbols and warned that any disloyalty will result in them and any enemy of the king turning into "women":

They bring a woman's garment, a distaff and a spindle and they break an arrow [lit., reed].
You say to them as follows: "What are these? Are they not the dresses of a woman? We are holding them for the oath-taking. He who transgresses these oaths and takes part in evil against the king, queen and princes may these oath deities make (that) man (into) a woman.
May they make his troops women. Let them dress them as women. Let them put a scarf on them. Let them break the bows, arrows, and weapons in their hands and let them place the distaff and spindle in their hands (instead)."[26]

A different dynamic is exhibited in a ritual of the Maori of New Zealand to remove fear of battle from a warrior. In this ritual, the affected warrior passes between the legs of a high-status woman, who apparently absorbs the femininity from him.[27] Although the ritual process varied, these war rituals share a common theme of associating cowardice with femininity, which is understood as a force that could be ritually manipulated. The ubiquity of these rites throughout the ANE is ample testament of the high level of anxiety which accompanied warfare – justifiably so. On

---

[25] Anna S. Meigs, *Food, Sex and Pollution: A New Guinea Religion* (New Brunswick, NJ: Rutgers University Press, 1988), 104. Meigs renders *nu* "vital essence" (18); it can be transferred and has various implications dependent on context (diet, sex, etc.). For the Sambia of New Guinea, the initiation rites to prepare a new generation of warriors involved semen consumption, assumed to convey vigor to the initiates. See Gilbert Herdt, *The Sambia: Ritual and Gender in New Guinea* (Fort Worth, TX: Harcourt Brace Jovanovich College Publishers, 1987), 101–170 (passim). Considering the context, Herdt's designation "ritualized homosexuality" is misleading.

[26] Translation: Billie Jean Collins, "The First Soldiers' Oath (1.66)," *CoS* 2: 165–166.

[27] Reported by Elsdon Best, "Notes on the Art of War: Part II," *Journal of the Polynesian Society* 11 (1902): 51; see also Adele Fletcher, "Sanctity, Power, and the 'Impure Sacred': Analyzing Maori Comments of *Tapu* and *Noa* in Early Documentary Sources," *History of Religions* 47.1 (2007/2008): 64–65. In his report, Best refers to the patient as being "unclean," qualified in a note that "he has infringed a law of *tapu*," but he then cites a related tradition which refers to *pahunu*, defined as an anxiety of battle.

this background, one can appreciate the Sumerian designation of the battlefield as "the place of masculinity" (ki-nam-nita-ka), meaning the place where masculinity was performed.[28] In light of these sources, it seems likely that the abstinence of David's warriors stems not from considerations of sanctity but rather from concerns of contagious femininity. It is worth adding that the law of the war camp in Deut 23 mentions only nocturnal emissions, taking for granted that the soldiers would not be engaging in sexual intercourse.

In this context, it is worth mentioning an enigmatic passage in the Gilgamesh epic, which uses the language of defilement to describe the debilitating effects of sex. After his marathon sex romp with a prostitute,[29] the wild-man Enkidu suddenly discovers his initial vigor has left him:

> For six days and seven nights Enkidu, erect, did couple with Šamḫat,
> After he was sated with her delights,
> He turned his face toward his herd,
> The gazelles saw Enkidu and they started running,
> The animals of the wild moved away from his person.
> Enkidu had defiled his body so pure (*ultaḫḫi Enkidu ullula pagaršu*)
> His legs stood still, though his herd was on the move.[30]

Enkidu's copulation with Šamḫat severs his once intimate association with the wild animals. This transformation is described as "defiling" (*šuḫḫû*) his once "pure" (*ullulu*) state, which may suggest virginity.[31] In his later recollection, the former term is replaced with "weakness" (*šumṭû*).[32] Andrew George elucidates:

The animals take him for a human and shy away. The encounter with Šamḫat has brought "defilement" and loss of strength, so that Enkidu repels his former playmates and cannot keep up with them (197–200). At the same time he has gained in intelligence and is able now to understand what Šamḫat tells him (201–6). The concept of defilement through sexual experience is one that tallies

[28] Joan Goodnick Westenholz and Ilona Zsolnay, "Categorizing Men and Masculinity in Sumer," in *Being a Man: Negotiating Ancient Constructs of Masculinity* (London: Routledge, 2017), 31.
[29] See above, p. 177.
[30] SB I 194–200; see Andrew George, *The Babylonian Gilgamesh Epic: Introduction, Critical Edition and Cuneiform Texts*, 2 vols. (Oxford: Oxford University Press, 2003), 1.548–551, with philological notes (2.798).
[31] Also MB Ur 38–40 (George, *Gilgamesh*, 1.298–299). For discussion of *šuḫḫû*, see also Werner R. Mayer, "Ein neues Königsritual gegen feindliche Bedrohung," *Orientalia New Series* 57 (1988): 155–158.
[32] SB VII 129–131 (George, *Gilgamesh*, 1.640–641)

with a widespread human belief that sexual knowledge brings the end of inno-cence. The idea that ejaculation engenders weakness is also common.[33]

In summary, among the numerous themes manifested in this short pas-sage, it appears that the debilitating effect of sexual intercourse with a woman is central. The fact that this effect is described in the terminology of defilement is further testament to the flexibility of pollution termin-ology and its prominence in discourse on sexuality.[34]

MENSTRUATION AND MISOGYNY

Having suggested that sexual intercourse may have been considered detri-mental to virility, particularly in the context of warfare, it is necessary to examine the even more severe pollution associated with menstruation. Was it considered dangerous, or was it merely a cultic concern? The Holiness Code warns of the severe penalty of "cutting-off" (*karet*) for sexual relations with a menstruant (Lev 20:18),[35] but the fact that this transgression is not mentioned in P has led some scholars to conclude that H has innovated this prohibition (see next chapter). Nevertheless, as suggested by cross-cultural evidence and by some explicit statements in rabbinic literature, it seems more probable that menstrual pollution was a taboo that existed long before the codification of H.[36]

Here the designation *niddah* may play a key role in determining the implications of menstrual impurity. At first glance, Lev 15 might suggest that the exclusion of the menstruant was solely a cultic concern. For example, Dorothea Erbele-Küster offers a neutral characterization: "*Niddah* was coined in Leviticus 12 and 15 as a technical cultic term for the description of a woman's state due to menstruation that obliged her to stay away from the sanctuary."[37] However, consideration of the use of the term outside of the Priestly source provides a different perspective. In an article dedicated to the etymology of this term, Moshe Greenberg

---

[33] *Gilgamesh*, 1.451. See also Aage Westenholz and Ulla Koch-Westenholz, "Enkidu – The Noble Savage?" in *Wisdom, Gods and Literature: Studies in Assyriology in Honour of W. G. Lambert*, eds. A. R. George and I. L. Finkel (Winona Lake, IN: Eisenbrauns, 2000), who write: "It is hardly the sexual experience alone that robs Enkidu of his pristine purity . . . Rather, the defiling aspects of sex, as conveyed by the word *šuḫḫu*, serve in a partly metaphorical way to say that he had become 'impure' to the animals from his (sexual) contact with a (civilized) human" (437–451 [442, n. 13]).

[34] See previous chapter. [35] See also Lev 18:19; Ezek 22:10.

[36] See Jacob Milgrom, *Leviticus*, AB, 3 vols. (New York, NY: Doubleday, 1991–2000), 1.948–953; for rabbinic writings, see m. *Shabbat* 2:6 and Nahmanides on Gen 31:35.

[37] *Body, Gender and Purity in Leviticus 12 and 15* (London: T&T Clark, 2017), 125.

explicates the widely accepted derivation of this term from the root *n-d-d*; "The semantic fields of Hebrew and Syriac *ndd* indicate a basic meaning of 'distance oneself' with negative connotation, as in flight from disgust or abhorrence."[38] The pejorative connotations of this term are represented in its metaphoric usages, such as Lamentations 1:8–9: "Jerusalem has greatly sinned, therefore she has become a *niddah*. All who admired her despise her, for they have seen her disgraced . . . Her uncleanness clings to her skirts" (adapted from NJPS).[39] The negative associations represented by this text (and others) suggest that the avoidance of menstruating women was not limited to the cultic sphere.[40] Some scholars have even suggested that menstruating women were segregated from the community or at least within the home.[41] Possible support for this assumption has been adduced from archaeology, but ultimately the evidence remains inconclusive.[42]

The extent of the concerns in ancient Israel regarding contact with menstruating women is difficult to determine. Ethnographic evidence attests to various stringencies that are common in traditional cultures, but also to a high level of variability.[43] Often fear of menstruants

[38] "The Etymology of נדה 'Menstrual Impurity,'" in *Solving Riddles and Untying Knots: Biblical, Epigraphic, and Semitic Studies in Honor of Jonas C. Greenfield*, eds. Z. Zevit, S. Gitin and M. Sokoloff (Winona Lake, IN: Eisenbrauns, 1995), 76. Cf. Baruch Levine's more strictly physiological interpretation based on Akkadian *nadû* ("emit, discharge"): "one who is spilling (blood)" (*Numbers 1–20* [New York, NY: Doubleday, 1993], 463–464), followed by Erbele-Küster, *Body, Gender and Purity*, 120. This etymology is poorly equipped to account for the pejorative usage of this term. Nor can insight be derived from the expression מי נידה referring to an agent of purification in Numbers 19, since this expression is probably a homophone derived from the cognate root נז׳׳י "sprinkle" > "water of sprinkling"; see Zev Ben-Hayyim, "Word-Studies IV," *Tarbiẓ* 50 (1980): 199–200 (Heb).

[39] For recent analyses of the semantic field of this term, see Goldstein, *Impurity and Gender*, 51–61, Levavi Feinstein, *Sexual Pollution*, 181–183.

[40] In Gen 31:35, Rachel is unable to stand up for her father (or so she claims) because the "way of women is upon her," suggesting both shame and incapacitation.

[41] Some rabbinic and Karaite commentators found support for this idea in the verb *tešeb* "she shall sit/remain be in abstinence" in Lev 12:4–5; see Milgrom, *Leviticus*, 750 and Hosea 3:3 for the last sense.

[42] See Avraham Faust and Haya Katz, "The Archaeology of Purity and Impurity: A Case-Study from Tel 'Eton, Israel," *Cambridge Archaeological Journal* 27.1 (2017): 1–27. A related question pertains to the seclusion of impure women in Second Temple period literature.

[43] Gilbert H. Herdt and Fitz J. P. Poole, "'Sexual Antagonism': The Intellectual History of a Concept in New Guinea Anthropology," *Social Analysis: The International Journal of Anthropology* 12 (1982): 3–28; Lewis L. Langness, "Discussion," *Social Analysis: The International Journal of Anthropology* 12 (1982): 79–82.

correlates with the degree of antagonism between men and women in general.[44] For cultures which exhibit strong sexual antagonism, to separate misogyny from menstruation is like asking: which came first, the chicken or the (aborted) egg? In particular, continuing the observations of the previous section, tribes that stress the need to prepare their adolescent boys for warfare tend to place a greater emphasis on the danger of contact with women, whose most extreme expression is the pollution associated with menstruation.

These considerations call attention to the law of birth impurity in Lev 12, in which the specification of the mother's seven-day pollution upon the birth of a male (v. 2) is immediately followed by the command to circumcise the baby on the eighth day (3). Is there a causal relation between these two rules, or is Lev 12 merely outlining the chronology of ritual acts following birth? Admittedly, there is no indication that the woman's impurity is conveyed to the child. Nevertheless, some Second Temple period literature, most explicitly Luke 2:22–24, infers that the child was expected to undergo purification along with his mother. Matthew Thiessen has taken this point a step further, claiming: "In light of both the Ancient Near Eastern context and the logic driving the legislation of the Book of Leviticus, the reader cannot take the silence surrounding the question of the purity of a newborn in Lev 12:1–8 as evidence that the newborn existed outside the purity system."[45] In other words, these interpreters infer that the child must also need to undergo purification.

If so, is it possible that circumcision served as part of this process? Jacob Milgrom responds in the negative: "Nor can it be claimed that the circumcision is a purificatory rite for the boy and thus comparable to the purificatory rites enjoined upon his mother, for there is no equivalent rite for a newly born girl."[46] Yet, this rationale is not conclusive when one considers cross-cultural evidence, where it is specifically the male offspring that is polluted by feminine contamination.[47] In some such contexts, penile bloodletting serves to remove this influence.[48] According

[44] M. J. Meggitt, "Male–Female Relationships in the Highlands of Australian New Guinea," *American Anthropologist* 66.4 (1964): 204–224.
[45] Matthew Thiessen, "Luke 2:22, Leviticus 12, and Parturient Impurity," *Novum Testamentum* 54.1 (2012): 23.
[46] *Leviticus* 1.746–747.   [47] See, e.g., Meggitt, "Male–Female Relationships," 208.
[48] Melissa Meyer writes: "Nose bleeding, penile incising, scarification, and tongue incising all drained away their mothers' debilitating blood potency experienced in utero, while breast-feeding, and during childhood" (*Thicker Than Water: The Origins of Blood as Symbol and Ritual* [New York, NY: Routledge: 2005], 114).

to this suggestion, circumcision on the eighth day would serve to purge the feminine defilement of the mother. Still, this interpretation depends on a series of assumptions, first that the child is defiled by birth and second that the circumcision removes this pollution, so it remains speculative.

In addressing the severity of menstrual pollution in ancient Israel and elsewhere as compared to other forms of blood loss (e.g., injuries, nosebleeds) that are not defiling, it is necessary to mention a factor that scholars usually shy away from mentioning: the odor of menstrual blood.[49] Particularly in developing societies where hygienic supplies and facilities are less accessible, the foul smell of menstruation is widely recognized.[50] Many of these cultures explicitly associate danger with the odor of menstrual blood.[51] Though the HB does not refer specifically to the smell of menstruation, the book of Job's repeated expression of the lowliness of humans as "one born of woman" (*y^{e}lud 'isha*) implies repugnance to birth via the female womb (14:1; 15:14; 25:4), reflecting a common view of the female genitalia as disgusting due to associations with foul odors. Further support comes from the Mesopotamian term for an impure woman *musukkatu*, which is semantically parallel to *niddah* and can be rendered "disgusting one/outcast." It is derived from the root *m-s-k* ("bad, ugly, rotten"), whose lexical evidence attests to both physiologically repugnant (e.g., rotten fish, cadavers) and morally despicable referents.[52]

---

[49] This point was brought to my attention by Valerie Curtis (personal communication), drawing on her extensive public health work in developing societies.

[50] E.g., Shivaleela P. Upashe, Tesfalidet Tekelab and Jalane Mekonnen, "Assessment of Knowledge and Practice of Menstrual Hygiene Among High School Girls in Western Ethiopia," *BMC Women's Health* 15.1, 84 (2015); (https://doi.org/10.1186/s12905-015-0245-7; accessed 4/9/2020), in which 63.6 percent of respondents affirmed that they "knew that there is foul smelling during menstruation"; Fiona Scorgie, Jennifer Foster and Jonathan Stadler, "'Bitten By Shyness': Menstrual Hygiene Management, Sanitation, and the Quest for Privacy in South Africa," *Medical Anthropology* 35.2 (2016): 161–176.

[51] See Constance Classen, "The Odor of the Other: Olfactory Symbolism and Cultural Categories," *Ethos* 20.2 (1992): 133–66 (141–142); Meyer, *Thicker Than Water*, 136–142.

[52] *CAD* M/1 324 (*masku*); see also the verb *masāku* (*CAD* M/1 322); Yitzhaq Feder, "Defilement, Disgust and Disease: The Experiential Basis for Akkadian and Hittite Terms for Pollution," *JAOS* 136.1 (2016): 106, 112–116. Note also the term *urruštu*, from *(w)aršu* ("dirty") as a designation for menstruants and parturients (ibid., 104). Erica Couto-Ferreira and Agnès Garcia-Ventura have recently challenged some accepted views regarding the segregation of these women, but their reservations fail to address the considerable evidence for the general disdain insinuated by these terms: see their "Engendering Purity and Impurity in Assyriological Studies: A Historiographical Overview," *Gender & History* 25.3 (2013): 513–528.

In summary, despite the rather frequent references to menstrual impurity, the biblical text is somewhat ambiguous regarding its practical implications. Within Priestly literature, there is no explicit requirement to segregate menstruating women; the only restriction, albeit one bearing severe sanctions, pertains to sexual relations. The main evidence for the stigmatization of menstruating women comes from the word *niddah*, especially outside P, where the term is often accompanied with descriptions of shame, repugnance and isolation. It seems futile to try to disentangle these emotional responses from the belief in the danger posed by menstruation, at least in the context of intercourse. Following the enactivist view of cognition discussed in Chapter 1,[53] emotion and judgment are mutually reinforcing and are inextricably tied to one another. Apparently, it is within the context of this more primal response that the mixing of the male seed with menstrual blood was viewed as an inviolable taboo. Hence, scholarly interpretations that speak of the tensions between the forces of life and death may be partially correct, though they translate an intuitive, emotional response into abstract concepts.

CONCLUSION

This chapter has attempted to address the question of why P deems ordinary sexual intercourse and its associated bodily emissions defiling, compared with numerous other such emissions that do not defile. While any answer to this question will be speculative, two possible directions, which should be viewed as complementary, have been suggested here. The first of these is the concern, widely attested cross-culturally, of the negative effects of semen loss. It is fascinating to note that even within Western medical discourse up to the turn of the twentieth century, physicians (including, not surprisingly, Sigmund Freud) attributed numerous debilitating conditions to loss of semen, whether pathologically or as a side-effect of masturbation or sexual excess. Significantly, one finds frequent reference in these writings to "pollution," usually in reference to uncontrolled ejaculations.[54] In a survey seeking to demonstrate the wide distribution of these ideas, the anthropologist Alain Bottéro writes:

---

[53] See above, p. 21.

[54] Note the following observation from a medical journal, which explicitly relates "pollution" to involuntary emission: "The parts concerned in ejaculation are morbidly irritable; the vesiculae seminales contract upon the smallest quantity of semen, and are induced to the discharge of it upon the slightest irritation; and thus follows, in the first instance, precipitate ejaculation in coitus, and eventually pollutions, with their invariable

Our survey made it clear – yet is it so surprising when we think about its obvious importance in man's life? – that semen is regarded as a primordial vital or energetic principle by very different and distant cultures, each of which, consistent with such a conception, fears the dangers resulting from its destruction or its misuse, going against the natural order. Starting from similar premises, and drawing on the human need for explanations of the mysteries of illness, these cultures converge in their placing primary pathogenic value on the loss of such an essential substance.[55]

It seems to be the hidden power of the male seed that underlies its association with defilement, which distinguishes it from other bodily emissions like sweat, mucus and feces. Along similar lines, Eve Levavi Feinstein suggests that "feces may not have been as strongly associated with a person's 'essence' as his or her genital fluids or dead body and were therefore not thought highly contaminating, even if they were thought highly disgusting."[56]

As a second line of explanation, there are indications that sexual intercourse had a weakening effect due to the contagious influence of femininity. While the biblical evidence suggests that this concern was less pronounced in ancient Israel than some other cultures that are more thoroughly permeated by sexual antagonism, the references to impurity in the context of the war camp in Deut 23 and the story of David's warriors suggest that feminine influence was viewed as threatening in the context of warfare.

While much of this discussion has been speculative, what seems clear is that masculinity and femininity were not viewed by ancient Israelites as products of social construction. Though the biblical authors did take note of exceptional women who could assume leadership roles even in warfare (Judges 4:6–9) and acknowledged that men could express compassion (*raḥamim*; Gen 43:30), this observation should not obscure the more general point that gender was understood in terms of an essentialist folk biology. Within this context, manliness needed to be carefully preserved, particularly in the context of warfare, where it was most needed.

Regarding biblical attitudes toward menstruation, we have examined whether avoidance practices and negative rhetoric are indications of

---

concomitant, a greater or less degree of impotence" (W. H. Ranking, "Observations on Spermatorrhœa; or the Involuntary Discharge of the Seminal Fluid," *Provincial Medical Journal and Retrospect of the Medical Sciences* 7.159 [1843]: 26–29 [27]); also the influential *De Pollutione Diurna* by J. E. Wichman, published in 1791.

[55] "Consumption by Semen Loss in India and Elsewhere," *Culture, Medicine and Psychiatry* 15 (1991): 316.

[56] *Sexual Pollution*, 164.

misogynistic attitudes with regard to women in ancient Israel. While the evidence is far from conclusive, ancient Israelite society does not seem to have been characterized by pervasive sexual antagonism.[57] More likely, these attitudes seem to reflect a repugnance toward the emissions themselves, which may have led to more general attitudes regarding the uncleanness of women's bodies. Even here, the polluting aspect of the *niddah* suggests that this impurity was not merely a cultic status but a dangerous force that could be transferred to the man in sexual intercourse.

---

[57] For the question of misogyny in the HB, see Yael Shemesh, "'I Find Woman More Bitter Than Death' (Ecclesiastes 7:26): Is There Misogyny in the Bible?" *Shnaton* 19 (2009): 77–104 (Heb.).

Did Women Need to Wash?

In Chapter 9, it was argued that a primary mechanism by which pollution irrupts into the social sphere is through purity *praxis*. In this chapter, we will examine how biblical purity rites and regulations manifest subtle aspects of gender relations in ancient Israel. At first glance, P's dry instructions, lacking rhetorical embellishments, appear to provide a direct window into praxis. Yet, as scholars have pointed out, the text is hardly equivalent to a firsthand observation of ritual performance. Fortunately, in the present case, this drawback turns to our advantage, since subtle indications in the textualization of rituals – what is said, and even more importantly, what is *not* said – can divulge key insights into the gender concerns that have shaped these texts.

The emergence of the methodologically reflective field of ritual studies and its application to the HB has called into question the naïve assumption that a ritual as represented in the text is comparable to an ethnological study *in situ*.[1] Further analytic and historical assumptions compound the problem. According to the view that P constitutes an ideal cult that was never practiced, James W. Watts opens his Leviticus commentary with the provocative question: "What is the significance of an unperformed ritual?"[2] Some scholars even suggest that P's prescriptions were never intended to be implemented, but were meant to remain as an idealized

---

[1] Or to paraphrase the name of the famous painting by René Magritte: "Ceci n'est pas un rituel." See Frank H. Gorman, *The Ideology of Ritual: Space, Time and Status in the Priestly Theology*, JSOTSupp 91 (1991), 30–31; William K. Gilders, *Blood Ritual in the Hebrew Bible: Meaning and Power* (Baltimore, MD: Johns Hopkins University, 2004), 8–9.

[2] *Leviticus 1–10, Historical Commentary of the Old Testament* (Leuven: Peeters, 2013), 1.

"reading space."[3] Clearly, our interpretive assumptions will have implications for understanding P's conception of purity, and these issues come to a head when addressing the issue of sexual pollution.

Some helpful methodological guidelines have been offered by William K. Gilders in his study of biblical blood rituals. In particular, he draws on reader-response criticism in focusing attention on the necessity for gap-filling when reading biblical rituals and the role of interpretive communities in forming plausible interpretations.[4] In general, these observations have provided a much-needed call for interpretive caution. Yet, once the laconic aspect of ritual texts is recognized, that is, that they are not self-explanatory and presuppose a competent reader,[5] it becomes clear that readers cannot shirk their duty in filling these gaps.

The following discussion will address three legal details pertaining to women and impurity. Aside from exemplifying the methodological considerations alluded to above, they offer dramatic illustrations of how seemingly technical points can have wide-reaching implications in understanding the network of ritual practices represented in P. The following topics will be addressed:

1. Sexual relations with menstruants
2. Whether women needed to wash following their sexual impurities
3. Whether women were permitted in the temple city according to the Temple Scroll from Qumran.

While the third topic is distinct from the other two in its subject matter and its provenance (the Dead Sea Scroll corpus), the interpretive process involved turns out to be highly relevant and illuminating for framing the prior two issues.

CASE STUDY #1: SEXUAL RELATIONS DURING MENSTRUATION

Let us begin with a well-known contradiction. The laws in Lev 15:19–24 outline in detail the impurity imparted by various forms of contact with a menstruant. Verse 24 specifically states that "if a man lies with her, her menstrual impurity (*niddatah*) is communicated to him; he shall be impure

---

[3] Dorothea Erbele-Küster, *Body, Gender and Purity in Leviticus 12 and 15* (London: T&T Clark, 2017), 159–163.
[4] *Blood Ritual*, 9–12.
[5] This point is characteristic of ritual texts from the ancient Near East in general.

seven days, and any bedding on which he lies shall become impure."
Despite the lengthy period of defilement, no prohibition of sexual intercourse is mentioned. In contrast, Lev 18:19 sets forth explicitly: "Do not
come near a woman during her menstrual impurity to uncover her nakedness," and 20:18 elaborates: "If a man lies with a woman in her infirmity
and uncovers her nakedness, he has laid bare her flow and she has exposed
her blood flow; both of them shall be cut off (*k-r-t*) from among their
people." According to this last verse, these relations are not only prohibited but incur the severe penalty of "cutting off."[6] How are we to adjudi-
cate this discrepancy between seemingly tacit permission (15:24) and
stringent prohibition, carrying the threat of automatic divine punishment
(18:19; 20:18)?[7]

Many scholars are resistant to a harmonistic reading of these contradictory verses and take the permissive view of Lev 15 at face value. This
position is significantly strengthened by the distinction between sources,
attributing the permissive view in Lev 15 to the earlier P layer and the
more stringent view in Lev 18 and 20 to H.[8] In other words, this difference
of legal opinion maps onto the distinction between these compositional
layers.[9] Ostensibly, further evidence for this view could be adduced from
the dietary laws in Lev 11, a text where the oppositions of prohibited/
permitted and pure/impure are explicit and intersect in multifarious
combinations. Regarding these laws, Naphtali Meshel points out that
"the priestly legislators tend to offer instructions for purification only
where defilement was not prohibited in the first place."[10] By analogy,
the description of the man's seven-day impurity might be construed as
presuming that these sexual relations were permitted.[11] On the other
hand, unlike the example in Lev 11, the text does not explicitly permit

[6] Regarding the *karet* punishment, see above, pp. 141f.
[7] A severe prohibition is also implied by Ezekiel 22:10, though this text probably depends on Lev 18; 20.
[8] For the relationship between P and H, see Chapter 1.
[9] See Jacob Milgrom, *Leviticus*, AB, 3 vols. (New York, NY: Doubleday, 1991–2000), 2.152–155 for a list of topics where H breaks with P, including a change in his own view regarding sex with a menstruant (ibid., 1.940).
[10] See Lev 11:24–8, 39–40; Naphtali S. Meshel, "Pure, Impure, Permitted, Prohibited: A Study of Classification Systems in P," in *Perspectives on Purity and Purification in the Bible*, eds. Naphtali S. Meshel, Jeffrey Stackert, David P. Wright and Baruch J. Schwartz. (New York, NY: T&T Clark, 2008), 38.
[11] Contrast the Ibn Ezra *ad loc.*, who suggest that this verse deals with a case where the "transgression" was unintentional, in which the woman's menstruation was discovered only afterwards.

these relations, nor does it even describe the subsequent purification, merely specifying the length and transmissibility of the man's defilement.

This non-harmonistic view is predicated on a particular understanding of the relationship between P and H as distinct sources. However, this ostensibly compelling argument has been called into question in light of the contention that this case is the most blatant contradiction between these two layers.[12] A more comprehensive examination of the relationship between these two layers might take H as complementing P.[13] Moreover, if it is presumed that H is responsible for the present form of the Book of Leviticus, one may ask whether the later author holding a stringent view would preserve an earlier P law that was in contradiction to it. Assuming H's authority over the final form of Leviticus, the issue of forbidden sexual relations could be deferred to its more appropriate context. Specifically, Lev 18 and 20 thematize the topic of sexual prohibitions, leaving Lev 15 to focus on the issue of the transmission of impurity. For the sake of comparison, the law of the woman who has just given birth in Lev 12:2 has no qualms with comparing her status with that of the menstruant, stating "she shall be impure seven days; she shall be impure as at the time of her menstrual infirmity," even though the topic of the menstruant has not yet sequentially appeared in Leviticus, being deferred until Lev 15.[14] That is to say, the editor had no anxiety over the fact that the reader of Lev 12 would not make it to Lev 15. Alternatively, the author of Lev 12 may be appealing to the reader's prior knowledge of the laws of *niddah*; if so, then this point would even more strongly support reading the text as deliberately laconic and dependent on prior knowledge.

To summarize, several different reading strategies are possible. The reading of Lev 15 as an isolated text suggests that sexual relations with a menstruant were not prohibited by P. On the other hand, a harmonistic

---

[12] Baruch J. Schwartz, *The Holiness Legislation: Studies in the Priestly Code* (Jerusalem: Magnes, 1999), 26–27 (Heb.); Erhard Blum, "Issues and Problems in the Contemporary Debate Regarding the Priestly Writings," in *The Strata of the Priestly Writings: Contemporary Debate and Future Directions*, eds. S. Shechtman and J. S. Baden (Zurich: Theologischer Verlag, 2009), 31–44.

[13] See Christophe Nihan, *From Priestly Torah to Pentateuch*, FAT 2/25 (Tübingen: Mohr Siebeck, 2007), 106–107; Jeffrey Stackert, "The Holiness Legislation and Its Pentateuchal Sources: Revision, Supplementation and Replacement," in *The Strata of Priestly Writings: Contemporary Debate and Future Directions*, eds. S. Shechtman and J. S. Baden (Zurich: Theologischer Verlag, 2009), 187–204 (esp. 187, 189).

[14] See further Roy Gane, "Didactic Logic and the Authorship of Leviticus," in *Current Issues in Priestly and Related Literature: The Legacy of Jacob Milgrom and Beyond*, eds. R. E. Gane and A. Taggar-Cohen (Atlanta, GA: SBL, 2015), 197–221.

strategy requires reading Lev 15 in light of the explicit prohibitions stated in Lev 18:19 and 20:18. Elizabeth W. Goldstein has suggested an intermediate position: "In contrast to Lev 15 (P), which only discourages sex with a menstruating woman because of the immediate cost of ritual impurity, the Holiness Code transforms the act into a sin which causes moral impurity."[15]

Let us examine the laconic reference in Lev 12:2 more closely. Lev 12 compares the parturient in her initial state of pollution to that of the menstruant, which is differentiated from the second stage of "pure blood" when she is prohibited only from the sacred precincts. This two-stage process is correlated with the sex of the offspring:

[2b]When a woman expresses seed and gives birth to a male, she shall be impure seven days; she shall be impure as at the time of her menstrual infirmity . . . [4]She shall remain in a state of pure blood for thirty-three days: she shall not touch any consecrated thing, nor enter the sanctuary until her period of purification is completed. [5]If she bears a female, she shall be impure two weeks as during her menstruation, and she shall remain in a state of pure blood for sixty-six days.

The meaning of the more lenient second stage is explicit: she is banned from contact with the sacred domain, but what is the practical import of the first phase that "she shall be impure as at the time of her menstrual infirmity" (k^e-*niddat-d^ewotha;* 2b)? Two possible interpretations may be suggested:[16]

a. The parturient needed to be secluded even within the domestic sphere, that is, not just banned from the temple;
b. The parturient was prohibited from sexual relations.

Obviously, the latter interpretation (assumed by the Rabbis) relies on a chain of inferences that assume that the menstruant is prohibited in sexual relations, reading Lev 12:2 and Lev 15 in light of Lev 18:19 and 20:18.[17] The former interpretation is ostensibly more careful in its interpretation but yields a radically more stringent view, requiring seclusion

---

[15] *Impurity and Gender in the Hebrew Bible* (Lanham, MD: Lexington Books, 2015), 52.
[16] This import of this expression is "as during the days" of menstrual impurity, referring to the quality, not just the length of the impurity (Milgrom, *Leviticus,* 1:744). If the latter sense were intended, the expression would not add anything to the specification of seven days.
[17] b. *Ḥullin* 31a. For discussion, see Milgrom, *Leviticus,* 1:748–749; Zev Farber, "The Parturient's 'Days of Purity': From Torah to Halacha" (www.thetorah.com/article/the-parturients-days-of-purity-from-torah-to-halacha); accessed 2/12/2020.

within the domestic domain of menstruants and parturients.[18] It finds support in the etymology of *niddah* and its connotations of isolation (e.g., Lamentations 1:8–19).[19] Even according to this view, it is difficult to assume that P permitted sexual relations.

Be that as it may, the key point is that the unavoidable process of gap-filling will have inevitable implications beyond the limited context of a single passage. Responding to Gilder's call for interpretive restraint, the editors of a volume on biblical purity offer the following comment:

> The analysis of the text can only proceed on the basis of what the text provides in its context . . . At the same time, an examination of genre might reveal that the gaps can best be filled by attempting systematic analysis of the broader context. By "the text," after all, we do not necessarily mean the smallest textual unit; the dictum of the Talmudic sages that "the words of the Torah are sparse in one passage and plentiful in another" is often applicable to the priestly writings when studied in their fullest form.[20]

In summary, while several considerations favor a harmonistic reading of these sources, the question of whether Lev 12 and 15 presume a prohibition of sex during menstruation remains contentious. At this point, the ambiguity of the text will be respected, and we will proceed to the next interpretive problem.

CASE STUDY #2: WASHING AFTER POLLUTION

The second topic pertains to washing after pollution. The problem becomes clear upon comparing the rules of male (Lev 15:3–15) and female (25–30) gonorrheics. The purification of each is prescribed as shown in Table 11.1.

In analyzing these two passages, it is important to point out that the intransitive *qal* form of *ṭ-h-r* appears twice in the first verse of each (13, 28) with two distinct usages. The first refers to the cessation of the genital flow, which serves as the starting point for the process of purification; here "purity" refers to the patient being healed from the symptoms of disease. The second refers to the completion of purification, enabling the presentation of sacrificial offerings. Curiously, however, the passage dealing

---

[18] See Avraham Faust and Haya Katz, "The Archaeology of Purity and Impurity: A Case-Study from Tel 'Eton, Israel," *Cambridge Archaeological Journal* 27.1 (2017): 1–27.

[19] See above, p. 219.

[20] Baruch J. Schwartz et al., "Introduction," in *Perspectives on Purity and Purification in the Bible*, eds. David P. Wright et al. (New York: T&T Clark, 2008), 5.

TABLE I I . I *Purification from gonorrhea: Male and female*

Male (vv. 13–15)	Female (vv. 28–30)
[13]When one with a discharge becomes pure (*yithar*) of his discharge, he shall count off seven days for his cleansing, launder his clothes, and bathe his body in fresh water; then he shall be pure (*ve-ṭaher*). [14]On the eighth day he shall take two turtledoves or two pigeons and come before Yhwh at the entrance of the Tent of Meeting and give them to the priest. [15]The priest shall offer them, the one as a sin offering and the other as a burnt offering. Thus the priest shall make expiation on his behalf, for his discharge, before Yhwh.	[28]When she becomes pure (*ṭahara*) of her discharge, she shall count off seven days, and after that she shall be pure (*tiṭhar*). [29]On the eighth day she shall take two turtledoves or two pigeons, and bring them to the priest at the entrance of the Tent of Meeting. [30]The priest shall offer the one as a sin offering and the other as a burnt offering; and the priest shall make expiation on her behalf, for her impure discharge, before Yhwh.

with the male specifies that he launders his clothes and bathes in fresh water, whereas the passage dealing with the female states only that she counts off seven days and is pure (v. 28: *tiṭhar*).

On one hand, it is reasonable to claim that the law of the female is abbreviated and relies on the more detailed instructions for the male. A similar use of *ṭ-h-r* (qal) can be found in Lev 22:4: "No man of Aaron's offspring who has 'leprosy' or a discharge shall eat of the sacred donations until he is clean (*yithar*)," which clearly implies the completion of the purificatory rites mentioned in Lev 14–15. However, one cannot so easily ignore the fact that a requirement of bathing is not mentioned for the menstruant (Lev 15:19) and, even more conspicuously, is not included in the detailed instructions for the purification of a woman following birth. Is the reader expected to infer a bathing a requirement in all of these cases? What is the significance of this omission?

One possibility is to take these passages at face value, as implying that women need not bathe because they are purified automatically by the passage of time.[21] This conclusion seems unlikely for several reasons. In

[21] For example, Nicole Ruane tentatively makes this inference: "The waiting period seems to make her sufficiently ritually clean to bring her offering." See "Bathing, Status and Gender in Priestly Ritual," in *A Question of Sex: Gender and Difference in the Hebrew*

ancient Israel, as well as other cultures, bathing seems to be a minimal requirement of purification.[22] Moreover, additional passages can be found where bathing is omitted but can be inferred from others dealing with similar subject matter.[23] The case for assuming that no washing was necessary would be much stronger if there were a biblical narrative suggesting as much, but none exists. As it turns out, we have a narrative which indicates the very opposite. Indeed, the story of David and Bathsheba divulges (only because it is central to the plot) that Bathsheba washed (*mitqaddešet*) after her menstrual impurity (2 Samuel 11:4; see v. 2),[24] indicating not only the existence of the practice but also the audience's familiarity with it (with no further explanation needed).

Still, the question remains: is it coincidental that the bathing requirement is omitted specifically in the case of females? Judith Romney Wegner offers a valuable new angle on this crux. She pointed out an additional discrepancy between the laws of male and female gonorrheics.

Regarding the male it is written, "On the eighth day he shall take two turtledoves or two pigeons and come before Yhwh at the entrance of the

Bible and Beyond, ed. D. W. Rooke (Sheffield: Sheffield Phoenix Press, 2007), 66–81 (73). See also Zev Farber, "The Purification of a Niddah: The Torah Requirement," www .thetorah.com/article/the-purification-of-a-niddah-the-torah-requirement; my rejoinder: "The Purification of a Niddah: The Legal Responsibility of the Reader," www .thetorah.com/article/the-purification-of-a-niddah-the-legal-responsibility-of-the-reader (both accessed 2/12/2020).

[22] From a cursory inspection of cross-cultural evidence pertaining to menstrual impurity, it can be seen that menstrual pollution was/is removed by washing in Hindu, Zoroastrian, Muslim and apparently ancient Egyptian religions. Regarding Mesopotamia, a check in *CAD* M/2 239–240 for *musukkatu* ("menstruant") brings references to the impurity of water that a menstruant touches or bathes in (admittedly the context isn't entirely clear). The alternative term *urruštu* (*CAD* U/W 248) yields similar references. Regarding ancient Greece, however, Robert Parker does cite an example in which passage of time following intercourse (nightfall) takes the place of washing. See Robert Parker, *Miasma: Pollution and Purification in Early Greek Literature* (Oxford: Clarendon Press, 1983), 74. For the biblical evidence, see following note.

[23] For example: Lev 11:40 versus 17:15 regarding the consumption of an improperly killed clean animal; Lev 11:31 for touching a creeping creature compared with a vessel which must be washed (32); the person who gathers the ashes of the red cow, who is the only one of those involved in preparing the ashes whom the text explicitly requires to launder his clothes (Num 19:10) versus the others involved in preparing the ashes (7–8); note that the requirement to launder implies a more stringent degree of impurity, applied on top of the washing requirement, as can be seen from Lev 15, passim; and Num 31:24 versus 19:19 regarding corpse impurity. See David P. Wright, *The Disposal of Impurity: Elimination Rites in the Bible and in Hittite and Mesopotamian Literature* (Atlanta, GA: Scholars Press, 1987), 185, n. 38, 191, n. 44; Milgrom, *Leviticus*, 1.672.

[24] For the usage of *q-d-š* in reference to purification, see, e.g., Exodus 19:10, and the discussion below in Chapter 12.

Tent of Meeting and give them to the priest" (14). However, the reference to coming before Yhwh is absent in the corresponding instructions for females: "On the eighth day she shall take two turtledoves or two pigeons, and bring them to the priest at the entrance of the Tent of Meeting" (29). Romney Wegner notes a subtler difference: whereas the male "gives" his offering to the priest, the female only "brings" her offering to the priest: "She approaches the entrance, but presumably sets her offering down somewhere outside; unlike her male counterpart, she does not place the birds directly into the hands of the priest."[25] These inferences are buttressed by additional evidence for the partial exclusion of women from cult participation, for example the law of pilgrimages in Deuteronomy 16:16: "Three times a year all your males (*zakurka*) shall appear before Yhwh, your God, in the place that he will choose." Accordingly, the omission of reference to a washing requirement for women may be a direct consequence of their exclusion from the cult: "the priestly system mandates ritual purity only for the performance of cultic acts, i.e., it is required of one who will be either literally or figuratively entering the presence of Yhwh. But, unlike the (male) *zab*, the (female) *zaba* does *not* come symbolically 'before Yhwh,' because as a woman she is ineligible to do so; consequently, *in this context*, her state of cultic purity is irrelevant."[26]

Based on these observations, Wegner postulates that "the disqualification of women . . . from ritual or cultic activities" was based on women's fundamental unfitness to participate and from "male fears of potential cultic contamination by females."[27] According to this logic, there was no reason to specify purification for women, since they were in any case kept at a safe distance from the sanctuary. Yet, these far-reaching conclusions are at odds with the evidence, since P actually requires women to bring offerings on certain occasions following their purification (e.g., Lev 12:6–8; 13:29, 38; 15:29–30).[28] It seems that a more nuanced account is required.

---

[25] "'Coming Before the Lord': Exclusion of Women from the Public Domain of the Israelite Priestly Cult," in *The Book of Leviticus: Composition and Reception*, VTSupp 93, eds. R. Rendtorff and R. A. Kugler (Leiden: Brill, 2003), 457.

[26] Ibid., 458. Hebrew text has been replaced with transcriptions and clarifications.

[27] Ibid., 464–465.

[28] See Mayer S. Gruber, "Women in the Cult According to the Priestly Code," in *Judaic Perspectives on Ancient Israel*, ed. J. Neusner (Philadelphia, PA: Wipf & Stock, 1987), 35–48; Ruane, *Sacrifice and Gender*, 18–39.

There may be an additional consideration at work in limiting women's cult participation, namely a concern with the mingling of the sexes in the context of worship. The HB offers abundant testimony to the possibilities of illicitly mixing cultic work (*'avoda*) with sexual pleasure, from Hosea's references to sacrifice and promiscuity at the *bamot* (Hos 4:13–14) to Deuteronomy's exhortations against using the wages of prostitution to pay for offerings (23:19 [18]).[29] Along these lines, the narrative of the high priest Eli's corrupt sons who "lay with the women who performed tasks at the entrance of the Tent of Meeting" (1 Sam 2:22; NJPS translation) suggests that these concerns were not hypothetical. For this reason, one should not be surprised if P sought to distance women from direct inter-action with the priests. The narrative of the theophany at Sinai (Exodus 19) offers further illustration of this perspective. Following the divine commandment "Go to the people and warn them to stay pure today and tomorrow. Let them wash their clothes" (10), Moses relates the message as follows: "Be ready for the third day: do not go near a woman" (15).[30] As Nicole Ruane points out, this verse "illustrates a difficulty in separating women's personhood from reproductive activity."[31] To summarize this point, one might tentatively suggest that while women's participation was not forbidden outright by P, it was not encouraged. The reason for this tacit discouragement was not women's inferiority per se, but the threat posed by their sexuality as perceived by the male priesthood.

The question of women's bathing was reviewed systematically by Ruane. Fundamentally, she agrees with Wegner that "[t]he omission is far too systematic to be some sort of coincidence."[32] Yet, she is hesitant to draw far-reaching practical distinctions between male and female impurity bearers. She notes that the law of skin disease in the hair in Lev 13:29–34 treats females as equivalent in requiring them to bathe. Furthermore, she questions whether the rules of male and female gonor-rheics are substantially different in their topology, since both bring their sacrifices to the entrance of the Tent of Meeting, though she admits that

---

[29] The previous verse also refers to prostitution, employing the male and female counter-parts *qadesh(a)*, whose etymology has given fuel to widespread speculation. For a relevant discussion, see Karel van der Toorn, "Female Prostitution in Payment of Vows in Ancient Israel," *JBL* 108.2 (1989): 193–205.

[30] Similarly, David reassures Ahimelek, priest of Nob, that his men can partake of sanctified bread "for women have been kept from them always" (1 Sam 21:6). For this passage, see above, p. 215.

[31] *Sacrifice and Gender in Biblical Law* (New York, NY: Cambridge University Press, 2013), 18.

[32] "Bathing," 77.

"the omission of a statement on the woman's presence 'before the Lord,' even if it does not indicate a different cultic act or location, de-emphasizes her relationship with the divine."[33] Throughout her treatment, Ruane wrestles with the ambiguity surrounding the textualization of ritual, wondering whether these distinctions should be attributed to the practical or only the literary level.

These questions pertaining to the requirement of bathing bear implications for the previously discussed question regarding sexual relations with menstruants. In particular, the view that women need not bathe is most plausible according to the assumption that sexual relations with a menstruant were permissible. According to Wegner, the rationale for the omission of reference to women needing to bathe is explained on a basis of their exclusion from the cult. However, if sex were prohibited to menstruants, then they would need to bathe nonetheless before engaging in marital relations. In short, an interpretive decision regarding one of these cruxes will have immediate ramifications for how other ambiguities are resolved.

CASE STUDY #3: WOMEN'S HABITATION IN THE TEMPLE CITY

A third related interpretive question pertains not to the Priestly regulations themselves but to their appropriation in the Temple Scroll from Qumran (second/first century BCE). Column 45 of the scroll sets forth requirements to banish impurity bearers from the temple city. These rules include strictures for semen emission that exceed the comparable sources in Lev 15:16–18 and Deut 23:11–12:

No m[an] who has a nocturnal emission is to enter any part of my temple until he has [com]pleted three days. He shall launder his clothes and bathe on the first day; on the third day he shall launder and bathe; then, after the sun has set, he may enter the temple. And they shall not come into my temple with their *niddah*-impurity and defile it. If a man has intercourse with his wife, he may not enter any part of the temple city where I shall make my name to dwell for three days (45:7–12).

Whereas the comparable biblical laws ascribe a single day of impurity for semen emission, this passage extends this impurity to three days.[34] Among

---

[33] Ibid.

[34] As scholars have noted, the inspiration for this three-day duration is probably Ex 19:15 (cited above) and perhaps also 1 Sam 21:6. See Yigal Yadin, *The Temple Scroll*, 3 vols. (Jerusalem: Israel Exploration Society, 1977–1983), 1:287–289.

the numerous peculiarities of this passage, the important point pertinent to the present discussion is the strange discrepancy between a man who has had a nocturnal emission, who is forbidden to enter "any part of the temple" for three days, and a man who has engaged in sexual intercourse, who is forbidden to enter "any part of the temple city."

In his elaborate published edition of the scroll, Yigal Yadin draws several far-reaching inferences from this discrepancy and through comparison with other scrolls. First, he points out, reasonably enough, that the formulation of the rule of sexual relations implies that sexual intercourse was banned anywhere in the temple city.[35] Jacob Milgrom elaborates that the difference between the two laws suggests that the nocturnal emission took place within the city, whereas sexual relations took place outside.[36] Second, drawing on Josephus' writings on the Essenes, he argues that this ban was "tantamount to ordaining complete celibacy for them."[37] Third, Yadin calls attention to the fact that the Temple Scroll (46:16–18) requires the establishment of "three places to the east of the city, separated from one another, where those with a skin disease, a genital flux, or a [nocturnal] emission shall go." The fact that the scroll makes no comparable requirement for menstruants and other female impurity bearers "proves that doctrine of the sect deemed it necessary to ban women from permanent residence in the Temple city,"[38] and this argument finds corroboration in the War Scroll (1QM 7:3), which bans women and children from the war camp.

These claims have been contested on numerous grounds.[39] While some of these objections can be dismissed,[40] one cannot ignore the Temple Scroll's explicit ban of women from the middle court of the temple (39:7–9; 40:6), which shows that women were allowed in the temple city.

---

[35] Yadin, *Temple Scroll*, 1.288–289.

[36] "Studies in the Temple Scroll," *JBL* 97.4 (1978): 517: "the one who has a nocturnal emission in the city may not enter the temple and the one who has sexual intercourse outside the city may not enter the city."

[37] Yadin, *Temple Scroll*, 1:288.   [38] Ibid., 1:289.

[39] Most systematically, see Sara Japhet, "The Prohibition of the Habitation of Women: The Temple Scroll's Attitude Toward Sexual Impurity and Its Biblical Precedents," *JANES* 22.1 (1993): 69–87; also William Loader, *The Dead Sea Scrolls on Sexuality* (Grand Rapids, MI: Eerdmans Publishing, 2009), 10–27.

[40] For example, addressing the absence of installations for impure women in 46:17, Japhet suggests that a parallel formulation for impure women may have appeared in the lost text at the beginning of 47 ("Prohibition," 77, n. 29). Aside from the speculative nature of this suggestion, it is highly unlikely considering the explicit stipulation of three installations (and no more) in 46:17, especially considering that the comparable law in 48:14–17 deals with impure men and women together.

This point prompted Yadin's qualification, which denied "permanent residence" to women in the temple city, while acknowledging that they were able to visit. More fundamentally, Sara Japhet has argued that Yadin's supposed strictures against women are inconsistent with the rationale of sexual impurity:

> According to the Jewish outlook, which is found in the Bible and preserved in the rabbinic halakhah – and which is also reflected in the Temple Scroll – the cause of ritual pollution in sexual relations is the seminal emission, the source of which is the man; the woman's pollution in sexual relations is only a result of that . . . if the source of the impurity is the man, why should we conclude from this law that the residence of women was forbidden? Logically one should draw the opposite conclusion, which is the prohibition against the permanent habitation of men![41]

While this argument may be *logically* persuasive, it fails to explain the discrepancy in language in the laws of seminal emission (i.e., the distinction between nocturnal emission and sexual relations in 45:7–12), nor does it address the absence of installations for impure women alongside the three places set aside for males who have suffered from skin disease, a flux or seminal emission (46:16–18). Japhet's argument presumes a high degree of gender symmetry underlying the laws of defilement, but the laws themselves are predicated on asymmetry. In fact, the expression "their *niddah*-defilement" in 45:10 appropriates the term for menstrual impurity (*niddah*) in a generalized, nontechnical usage to serve as a superlative for denigrating transgressive behavior, as is found elsewhere in the Qumran corpus.[42] This idiom, situated in male-oriented laws, reveals an underlying misogyny. What are the implications of this tendency for the interpretation of these purity laws?

SYNTHESIS: GENDER ASYMMETRY AND THE ROLE OF THE READER

Before drawing more general conclusions based on the laws of banishment in the Temple Scroll, it is important to recognize some common themes that connect this case with the prior case of the absence of an explicit washing requirement for female impurity bearers in Leviticus. While the

---

[41] "Prohibition," 71–72.
[42] See especially 1QM 13:5, which uses this same expression to describe the wicked behavior of the "Sons of Darkness." The use of *niddah* as a general term for pollution is widespread in Qumran, for example 1QS 11:14–15; 4Q512 29–32:9. For biblical precedents to the condemnatory use of this term, see Lev 20:21; Ezek 7:19–20; Ezra 9:11. See also Goldstein, *Impurity and Gender*, 51–60.

cases are not exactly parallel, they have both challenged modern interpreters to fill gaps in order to understand whether subtle discrepancies in
the formulation of the laws and omissions have practical implications.
Moreover, following the suggestion of Wegner, one may ask whether the
omission of an explicit washing requirement as well as the seeming
absence of permanent residences for women in the temple city in the
Temple Scroll suggest an underlying presumption of limited female
participation in the cult. However, it is significant that the texts in
both cases are sufficiently ambiguous, allowing readings which deny
the existence of any practical implications. In other words, the laws in
Leviticus can very plausibly be understood as *presuming* that women
need to wash, and it is possible (following Japhet) to deny that the
Temple Scroll limited the habitation of women. Considering the fact
that both cases involve purity laws that bear on women's ability to
approach the sacred domain, one conclusion seems certain: these ambiguities are not coincidental!

So what can be learned from these ambiguities? Hypothetically, one
could follow Wegner in her conclusion that the discrepancy between the
formulation of the male and female laws (particularly the omission of
"before Yhwh" for females) "undoubtedly *reflects* the priestly view of
women's ineligibility to enter, still more participate in, the public domain
of the cult."[43] However, this far-reaching conclusion cannot be reconciled
with the evidence. Lev 12 explicitly commands the purified parturient to
bring offerings, as is the case for the purified female gonorrheic (Lev
15:29–30), and the Temple Scroll allows women to enter the temple, as
noted above. A more nuanced conclusion is that these discrepancies
pertain to the shared assumptions of the authors and their presumed
male audiences. One might say that in the tacit contract between author
and reader, women as active participants in the cult faded into the background. Consider, once again, Moses' transmission of the divine message,
intended for the "people" (10): "Be ready for the third day: do not go near
a woman" (15). From this perspective, which is diametrically opposed to
the gender symmetry presumed by Japhet's otherwise logical argument,
these texts (as well as 1 Sam 21:6) suggest that women were perceived
as threats to male participation in the cult from the perspective of the
implied male audiences. A related consideration may pertain to the
presumption of female illiteracy or the exclusion, not necessarily forced,

---

[43] Wegner, "Coming Before the Lord," 357.

of women from the listening or reading audience of the text.[44] Within this societal milieu, only men were assumed to have agency. Women were expected to comply with the basic purity requirements of the law, but this compliance was mediated by their intellectual subordination to men. Unexpected support for this approach comes from ancient Greek sacred laws governing access to temples. Citing an exceptional text which mentions equal purity requirements for both sexes, Robert Parker observes: "This passage shows that, though most of our evidence concerns the purification of a man 'from a woman', there is no difference in the purification that woman requires 'from a man.'"[45] In short, the ambiguities in these texts – Leviticus and the Temple Scroll alike – are better understood as reflecting an implicit exclusion of women from the reading audience than their absolute exclusion from the temple.

CONCLUSION

In summary, gender-sensitive analysis of purity laws reveals ambiguities in the text. Leaving aside the interpretive impulse to bring closure to these points of indeterminacy, the very existence of these ambiguities calls attention to the power structures embedded in gender relations, which in turn shape the modes of formulating the purity laws. At the basis of these laws, one finds an underlying tension between a systematicity which seeks symmetry between the sexes and a subtler asymmetry which subtly marginalizes women. This marginalization may be in part explained by the limitations on literacy and social agency ascribed to women within the sociohistorical context of P (and that of the Temple Scroll's editor), but also as a means by which the male-dominated cult could restrain its carnal impulses by keeping the threat of female sexuality at a safe distance. As has been seen, the silences in these texts are not accidental. By minding these gaps, the careful reader can get a glimpse of a subtle purity discourse that is at the boundary between text and praxis.

---

[44] Indeed, there is no evidence for female scribes in Judea up to and including the Second Temple period, as pointed out by Sidnie White Crawford, "Were There Women at Qumran?" *Biblical Archaeology Review* 46.2 (2020): 48–53.
[45] *Miasma*, 75.

PART III

IMAGES, CODES AND DISCOURSE

12

Contagious Holiness

Though the main focus of this book is pollution, there are several reasons why holiness is indispensable to this discussion. The antinomy between the sacred domain and impurity suggests that these antagonistic categories are inextricably related to one another. For this reason, it seems hardly coincidental that several biblical passages depict a contagious aspect to holiness that is similar to that of pollution, which suggests that there is an additional, positive potential of contagion that needs to be explored. Finally, and most fundamentally, the emphasis of the present work on embodiment as a key to understanding ostensibly "religious" concepts faces its greatest challenge with holiness, which appears to be otherworldly by definition and hence separate from mundane experience. Confronting this challenge, this chapter will examine the various means of conceptualizing holiness in the HB, showing that they are in varying degrees grounded in experience.

TRYING TO GRASP THE SACRED

In many accounts of religion, the domain of the holy is marked by the limits of rationality, defined as the category of beings and forces that is beyond human understanding. For Émile Durkheim, the notion of the sacred was more fundamental than even the worship of supernatural beings and gods, defining religion as "a unified system of beliefs and practices relative to sacred things."¹ While this straightforward definition has appeal, the idea of the sacred is far from self-explanatory.

Firstly, the concept of the sacred poses a fascinating challenge for evolutionary accounts of human behavior. What would lead a hominid to believe in the existence of a realm outside its immediate sensory experience, let alone sacrifice precious time and energy in expressions of awe and dread to entities that belong to this realm? Could such behavior be considered advantageous from a Darwinist perspective – or even rational?² Perhaps the belief in the sacred can only be properly addressed in emotional terms – as an ontological projection of a certain type of extreme emotional experience such as awe or ecstasy. Such an approach was expressed by Rudolf Otto in his emphasis on the sense of the numinous as a feeling which affects the believer, but it has more recently found more strictly psychological and even neurological interpretations in the cognitive science of religions.³

Evolutionary speculations aside, how is it possible for humans to conceptualize and communicate ideas that pertain to a domain that is outside their sensory experience? How does one imagine holiness? As an initial approach to this question, an easy do-it-yourself experiment is to perform an internet search in Google Images. A search for "holiness" elicits a surprising consensus: aside from denominational symbols (such as the cross), the vast majority of pictures involve the sun's rays penetrating a cloudy sky. Remarkably, this imagery was prevalent already in the ancient Near East, not only in Egypt (known for its solar deities) but also in Mesopotamia and even the HB, even though Yhwh was not overtly depicted as a solar deity.⁴ This near-universal characterization of holiness

---

¹ *The Elementary Forms of Religious Life*, trans. K. E. Fields (New York: Free Press, 1995 [1912]), 44. For the purposes of this discussion, the primary interest of Durkheim's treatment of the "sacred" will be his use of this term as a descriptive category cutting across cultural boundaries, leaving aside his ultimate reduction of religious phenomena to social entities. Admittedly, Durkheim's focus on the depersonalized aspect of the sacred was strategic, seeking to achieve his own theoretical aims; nevertheless, his observations remain productive even without relegating theistic religion to a "secondary" stage.
² See, e.g., Richard Sosis and Candace Alcorta, "Signaling, Solidarity, and the Sacred: The Evolution of Religious Behavior," *Evolutionary Anthropology* 12.6 (2003): 264–274.
³ For example: Ann Taves, "'Religious Experience' and the Brain," in *The Evolution of Religion: Studies, Theories, and Critiques*, eds. J. Bulbulia et al. (Santa Margarita, CA: Collins Foundation Press, 2008), 211–218.
⁴ See Mark S. Smith, *An Early History of God* (Grand Rapids, MI: Eerdmans Publishing, 2002), 148–159; for a possible depiction of Yhwh with solar imagery on the tenth/ninth century BCE cult stand from Taanach, see J. Glen Taylor, *Yahweh and the Sun: Biblical and Archaeological Evidence for Sun Worship in Ancient Israel*, JSOTSupp 111 (Sheffield:

invites a cognitive explanation.[5] In fact, the conceptualization of holiness is grounded in embodied experience, which can be explicated in the form of the following two premises:

1) Holiness (divinity) is located in the heavens
2) This otherworldly power expresses itself in the form of emanations of light.

Indeed, ancient Near Eastern literature and iconography identify the gods with astral bodies themselves (sun, moon, planets, etc.), and the HB builds off these traditions. By depicting the gods as living "out there," the ancients were able to create an intuitive dichotomy between this world and the heavenly realm of the gods, though without denying the possibility that the gods could dwell in proximity to their devotees in temples.[6] In late antiquity and especially the Middle Ages, the Jewish conception of the divine become more spiritualized, based on the assertion of God's incorporeality. Accordingly, God was relocated from *outer* space to *inner* space, apprehensible only through contemplation or mystical experience. Though few religiously affiliated people today would expect NASA to find God out there in the universe, the intuitive folk dichotomy between "down here" and "up there" lives on in speech and gesture, with allusions to God usually accompanied by a glance or gesture to the sky.[7] The second aspect of this conceptualization, the manifestation of divine power in the form of radiance, was discussed in the Introduction, so it need not detain us here. This metaphysical aspect finds expression in assertions that holiness can be transferred by contact (see below in the section "Sacred Contagion").

Although these two characteristics of the sacred are combined in the image of light radiating from behind clouds, they can also appear separately as seemingly alternative approaches. These two approaches can be distinguished as seen in Table 12.1.

JSOT Press, 1993), 31–37. More generally, see Beate Pongratz-Leisten, "Reflections on the Translatability of the Notion of Holiness," in *Of God(s), Trees, Kings, and Scholars: Neo-Assyrian and Related Studies in Honour of Simo Parpola*, eds. M. Luukko, S. Svard and R. Mattila (Helsinki: Finnish Oriental Society, 2009), 409–427.

[5] See Chapter 1.

[6] Cf. Edmund R. Leach, *Culture and Communication* (Cambridge: Cambridge University, 1976), 81–84.

[7] See Brian P. Meier et al., "What's 'Up' With God? Vertical Space as a Representation of the Divine," *Journal of Personality and Social Psychology* 93.5 (2007): 699–710.

TABLE 12.1 *Characterizing sacrality*

Power (radiance)	Separateness (heavens)
positive	negative
semantic (grounded)	structural

This schematic representation makes the following distinction: The depiction of sacrality as a force ascribes to it a positive content and hence can be viewed as a semantic characterization, whereas the depiction of sacrality as separation can be viewed as a negative definition (separate from mundane experience) and hence relational (structural) in its foundation.[8]

This distinction between positive and negative characterizations of sacrality can be mapped onto a similar theoretical division offered by William Paden, who makes a crucial distinction between ontological and descriptive accounts of the sacred. Paden seeks to combat the bias in religious studies toward addressing holiness in metaphysical terms, characterized as an otherworldly or supernatural power. To this effect, he finds in Durkheim's treatments of sacrality an alternative approach which focuses more on modes of behavior than their implied metaphysical assumptions. The former tendency, epitomized by Rudolf Otto's influential *The Idea of the Holy*,[9] is characterized by Paden as a "mana model": "In it the sacred is the name for the transcendent reality to which religious experience points and to which it responds."[10] In contrast, an alternative emphasis is no less pervasive in Durkheim's work: "Here sacredness has no content of its own. It is purely relational. It is what is not to be profaned. As such, the term is metaphysically neutral."[11] At first glance, this distinction may appear to correspond to the well-known emic–etic distinction, but it actually can bridge the two perspectives, since emic descriptions may express both ontological and behavioral dimensions of the sacred. Indeed, as will be seen, the biblical terminology of holiness (*q-d-š*) has a wide semantic range and may emphasize either ontological or behavioral distinctions in any particular instance.

---

[8] For the distinction between grounded and structural accounts to meaning, see above, pp. 10ff.

[9] Rudolf Otto, *The Idea of the Holy*, trans. J. W. Harvey (Woking and London: Penguin Books, 1959 [1917]).

[10] "Before 'the Sacred' Became Theological: Rereading the Durkheimian Legacy," *Method and Theory in the Study of Religion* 3.1 (1991): 12.

[11] Ibid., 15.

APPROACHING THE "SACRED" (Q-D-Š) IN THE HEBREW BIBLE

The Hebrew root *q-d-š* is key for the study of holiness, but it exhibits a puzzling array of uses. While some of them clearly express a divine quality, others appear remarkably mundane. The adjectival form *qadoš* takes a clearly ontological sense when used in reference to God as a divine attribute, as in the throne vision of Isaiah, where the heavenly beings declare (Isaiah 6:3): "Holy, holy, holy! Yhwh of legions! The whole world is filled with his glory!" In this context, the attribute *qadoš* expresses the awe and terror experienced by angelic beings beholding a vision of God. Furthermore, building on a venerable tradition stretching back to the Ugaritic texts of the fourteenth century BCE, biblical sources occasionally mention other minor divine beings as *qedošim*, "holy ones." For example, Psalm 89:6–7 reads:

> Your wonders, Yhwh, are praised by the heavens,
> Your faithfulness, too, in the assembly of holy beings (*qedošim*).
> For who in the skies can equal Yhwh, can compare with Yhwh
>   among the sons of God (*bene 'el*).[12]

This usage suggests that the designation *qadoš* pertains specifically to the divine (as opposed to mortal domain). Though ostensibly this use as an attribute of God, or even more precisely – that Yhwh is the quintessential representative of this attribute, was intended as an ontological assertion, it ultimately is little more than a claim of categorical otherness. Hence, it is not surprising that many scholars have taken "separate/set apart" as being the fundamental sense of *q-d-š*.

This impression is reinforced by nontheological uses of *q-d-š*. For example, the prenatal designation of Jeremiah as prophet is described as follows: "Before I created you in the womb, I selected you; Before you were born, I consecrated you (*hiqdaštika*); a prophet concerning the nations I appointed you" (Jeremiah 1:5). Here *q-d-š* parallels *y-d-'* ("know") and *n-t-n* ("appoint") – both general verbs which do not relate specifically to the sacred or cultic domain. A similarly mundane rendering of this verb appears in Joel 1:14: "Solemnize (*qidšu*) a fast, proclaim an assembly."[13]

---

[12] See Simon B. Parker, "Saints קדושים," in *DDD*, eds. K. van der Toorn et al. (Leiden: Brill, 1999), 718–720. The reference to *bene El* in v. 7, rendered "sons of God," also appears to reflect Canaanite traditions, where El designated the head of the pantheon.

[13] NJPS translation. See also 2:15–16; 2 Kings 10:20.

The understanding of *q-d-š* as separateness has profound implications for understanding the central demand of H for Israel to be holy (*qedošim*) in Leviticus 19:2: "You shall be holy (*qedošim*), for I, Yhwh, your God, am holy (*qadoš*)." Does this demand refer to being "holy" or "separate," or are these one and the same idea? Commentators have examined the eclectic list of commandments and prohibitions contained in Lev 19 in order to make sense of this programmatic demand to be like the Deity (*imitatio Dei*). Since many of the requirements are too earthly to pertain to God (e.g., revering parents), some commentators have inferred that imitating Yhwh pertains specifically to moral requirements such as loving one's neighbor.[14] However, this extraction of isolated statements from Lev 19 appears arbitrary and is hardly convincing. Rather, as stressed by Baruch Schwartz, the argument of this text is that just as Yhwh is a singularity in the divine sphere, Israel must make itself unique among nations. This is achieved by distinguishing itself through fulfillment of divine commandments:

Close reading of the texts reminds us that the Israelites are not told to be holy like God; rather they are commanded to be holy *because* He is holy. Their holiness cannot be like His, it can only be analogous. Just as he is "totally Other," completely apart from whatever is not divine, they are told to keep themselves separate, totally apart, from whatever is not Israelite, namely, to keep His laws and commands. Their holiness consists of their loyal obedience to Him.[15]

This understanding finds further support in several H texts where *q-d-š* appears in direct relation to separation (*b-d-l*). The Holiness Code incorporates these two verbs together in the divine exhortations that conclude lists of dietary (Lev 11:44–45) and sexual (20:26) prohibitions. The latter reads: "You shall be *qedošim* to Me, for I, Yhwh, am *qadoš*, and I have set you apart (*'abdil*) from other peoples to be mine." Within the contexts of these two chapters, Lev 11 and 20, the demand to be *qedošim* signifies the demand for self-restraint with respect to the most basic animal drives, calling for selective abstinence from tabooed meats and sexual relations, as will be discussed below in the section "What Is

[14] For example, Baruch Levine writes: "The statement that God is holy means, in effect, that He acts in holy ways: He is just and righteous. Although this interpretation derives from later Jewish tradition, it seems to approximate both the priestly and the prophetic biblical conceptions of holiness" (*Leviticus*, JPS Torah Commentary [Philadelphia, PA: Jewish Publication Society, 1989], 256).
[15] "Israel's Holiness: The Torah Traditions," in *Purity and Holiness: The Heritage of Leviticus*, eds. M. J. H. M. Poorthuis and J. Schwartz (Leiden: Brill, 2000), 57 (his emphasis).

Holiness: Essence or Difference?"[16] Clearly, these formulas are not suggesting a straightforward imitation of the characteristics of the Deity, which is impossible; rather they are a call to be unique and separate from other nations. Accordingly, Israel's holiness is defined by contrast to the image of the Canaanite and Egyptian "Other."

RITUALIZING THE SACRED

This pervasive use of *q-d-š* as designating difference might suggest that Paden's descriptive approach to holiness is more in line with the biblical conception. Ostensibly, it would suggest that the definition of the sacred domain is not a matter of ontology – the divine realm defined in positive, metaphysical terms – but defined rather as an arbitrary product of discourse. This distinction between the mundane and the sacred is materialized – in effect, established – through ritual acts. Along these lines, Jonathan Z. Smith lays the foundation for such an approach with his assertion: "Ritual is, above all, an assertion of difference."[17] This idea was further developed by Catherine Bell in her influential notion of "ritualization," defined as follows:

I will use the term "ritualization" to draw attention to the way in which certain social actions strategically distinguish themselves in relation to other actions. In a very preliminary sense, ritualization is a way of acting that is designed and orchestrated to distinguish and privilege what is being done in comparison to other, usually more quotidian, activities. As such, ritualization is a matter of various culturally specific strategies for setting some activities off from others, for creating and privileging a qualitative distinction between the "sacred" and the "profane," and for ascribing such distinctions to realities thought to transcend the powers of human actors.[18]

In other words, ritualization is a strategy for designating certain agents, objects and practices as intrinsically special and even sacred vis-à-vis mundane activities. This definition, which in its generality is difficult to dispute, seems to imply that it is the ritual activity itself that

---

[16] This rhetorical thrust continues to find expression over a millennium later, when the volume of Maimonides rabbinic legal code dealing with both the topic of forbidden foods and forbidden sexual relations was fittingly entitled "The Book of Holiness" (*Sefer ha-Qeduša*).

[17] *To Take Place: Toward Theory in Ritual* (Chicago, IL: University of Chicago Press, 1987), 109. For the emphasis on arbitrariness, see ibid., 110 (discussed above, p. 116).

[18] Catherine Bell, *Ritual Theory, Ritual Practice* (Oxford: Oxford University Press, 2009), 74.

performatively establishes these privileged relations on a *tabula rasa* of cultural discourse. The biblical usage of *q-d-š* would seem to vindicate such a framework, equating holiness with separateness but without anchoring this distinction in any external criteria except for Yhwh's arbitrary determination. Put differently, the distinction between the sacred and the profane could be viewed as syntax without semantics.[19] Of course, one could argue (correctly) that all holiness in the HB is derivative from that of God, but if God's holiness is itself equated with "otherness," then the entire theological edifice would seem to be anchored in a negative definition, or in the words of Job 26:7: "suspended over nothing."

Yet, building on the insight that the semantics of ritual, like language, are rooted in embodied experience, it is possible to ask how the use of *q-d-š* in ritual contexts in the HB may suggest a positive valence for holiness aside from mere "difference." For example, in preparation for the Sinai revelation, God commands Moses: "Go to the people and have them purify themselves (*qiddaštam*) today and tomorrow and let them wash their clothes" (Exodus 19:19).[20] In most of these instances, *q-d-š* (hitpael/piel) designates purification in preparation for an encounter with the divine realm.[21] When this root is applied to acts of purification (e.g., Ex 19:10; Joshua 3:5), specifically washing and laundering using water, the immediate result is clearly the removal of contaminants. Even when applied to the removal of metaphysical contaminants (e.g., pollution), the act of washing derives its meaning from physical cleansing. By themselves, such acts do not accrue holiness to their recipients, but they do effect a positive transition to a state of preparation for encountering the divine. The use of *q-d-š* in these contexts simultaneously designates the *separation* from impurities and the *consecration* required for the imminent meeting with the divine. As such, many of them would permit a rendering such as "sanctify (oneself)." This ambiguity is also represented in Semitic cognates of *q-d-š*, which seem to privilege either purity

---

[19] In his famous "Chinese Room" thought experiment, John Searle proposes a scenario where a person answers questions in Chinese based on formal rules without understanding what the symbols mean; hence for this person these symbols are syntax without semantics ("Can Computers Think?" in *Philosophy of Mind: Classical and Contemporary Readings*, ed. D. J. Chalmers [New York: Oxford University Press, 2002], 669–675).

[20] See further Ex 19:14, 22; also Num 11:18; Josh 3:5; 7:13; 2 Sam 11:4.

[21] But the purification does not always have cultic significance (e.g., 2 Sam 11:4).

(Akkadian)[22] or holiness (Ugaritic).[23] Leaving aside the moot question of which sense is more original, the existence of this widespread terminological ambiguity attests to the idea that the act of purification, embodied as cleansing, constitutes a transition to a sanctified state.

SACRED CONTAGION

An additional way of depicting holiness which is more explicit in its attribution of a metaphysical character is found in sources which suggest its contagiousness. It is in these sources that Paden's "mana model" is most clearly manifested, in their treatment of holiness as a force that is transmitted by contact. In anthropological discussions from the turn of the twentieth century, contagious sanctity was often touted as a characteristic of "primitive" thought and featured in discussions of taboo.[24] However, the communicability of numinous forces may not be as remote from everyday psychology as was once presumed. A significant body of psychological research has come to acknowledge the existence of positive contagion. In modern consumer culture, this transmission of an invisible essence finds expression in celebrity fetishism, for example the 19,500 British pounds paid for John Lennon's molar.[25] An important observation that emerges from these studies is that the nature of this essence is highly idiosyncratic, varying from the *authenticity* of acquiring an original Picasso painting or brand-name garment to the *energy* or *soul* embodied in a famous musician's instrument. Arguably, these examples offer secular equivalents to the transfer of power to ritual objects and persons in traditional cultures.[26] In any case, the belief in the healing

---

[22] See *CAD* Q 46–47, 146, 320, including the metathesized forms *qašdu/quššudu*.

[23] *DULAT* 694–697. A comparable ambivalence is represented by Hittite *šuppi-*. This ambiguity is characteristic of the terminology of purity in the ANE, where terms such as Sumerian *kug* and Akkadian *ellu* and *ebbu* are used as designations for both purity and holiness, dependent on the context. See above 12ff., and in more detail, Yitzhaq Feder, "The Semantics of Purity in the Ancient Near East: Lexical Meaning as a Projection of Embodied Experience," *JANER* 14.1 (2014): 87–113.

[24] E. E. Evans-Pritchard, *Theories of Primitive Religion* (Oxford: Clarendon Press, 1965), 36–37.

[25] "John Lennon's Tooth Sells for More than $31,000 at Auction," CNN, Nov. 8, 2011, https://edition.cnn.com/2011/11/05/world/europe/uk-lennon-tooth-auction/index.html (accessed 12/4/2019).

[26] Karen V. Fernandez and John L. Lastovicka, "Making Magic: Fetishes in Contemporary Consumption," *Journal of Consumer Research* 38.2 (2011): 278–299; George E. Newman, Gil Diesendruck and Paul Bloom, "Celebrity Contagion and the Value of Objects," *Journal of Consumer Research* 38.2 (2011): 215–228; Julie Y. Huang, Joshua

powers of relics (e.g., the bones of saints) is widespread in the world's cultures and finds a biblical expression in the brief story of a corpse that touched Elisha's bones, and then sprang to life (2 Kgs 13:21). It is important to note that a person who acts in accordance with a presumption of positive contagion may not be able to articulate the metaphysical assumptions underlying his or her behavior. As is the case with contamination appraisals and pollution, positive contagion is an intuitive response which need not be developed into a full-fledged theory or ontology.

While positive contagion shares many of its characteristics with negative contagion, differing in emotional valence, the experiential basis for negative contagion seems to be more substantial due to the tangibility of its negative effects, being associated with concrete elicitors of disgust and fear of infection. For this reason, negative contagion appears to be more salient and widespread.[27] In contrast, the contagiousness of sacred objects is often derived from an intellectual appraisal (belief) that they are derived from a divine or otherworldly source. Still, there exist experiential models for positive contagion, for example electricity in the modern world. For the ancients, the primary model for divine power was the phenomenon of radiance.

Returning to the biblical evidence, Priestly texts repeatedly employ q-d-š in reference to the transfer of a divine quality from Yhwh to the sanctuary, its appurtenances and its personnel. In these contexts, the transfer of sanctity operates in the form of a positive contagion, that is, a transfer of essence.[28] The instructions for building the Tabernacle are accompanied by the promise (Ex 29:43–45):

There I will meet with the Israelites, and it shall be sanctified by my majesty (*niqdašti bikbodi*). I will sanctify (*qiddašti*) the Tent of Meeting and the altar, and I will consecrate Aaron and his sons to serve me as priests. I will abide among the Israelites, and I will be their God.

Here it seems to be the resting of the divine presence on the Tabernacle which constitutes the latter's holiness.[29] More specifically, this presence is

---

M. Ackerman and George E. Newman, "Catching (Up with) Magical Contagion: A Review of Contagion Effects in Consumer Contexts," *Journal of the Association for Consumer Research* 2.4 (2017): 430–443.

[27] Paul Rozin and Edward B. Royzman, "Negativity Bias, Negativity Dominance, and Contagion," *Personality and Social Psychology Review* 5.4 (2001): 296–320.

[28] See Jesper Sorensen, *A Cognitive Theory of Magic* (Lanham, MD: AltaMira Press, 2007), 56.

[29] See Baruch J. Schwartz, *The Holiness Legislation: Studies in the Priestly Code* (Jerusalem: Magnes, 1999), 262 (Hebrew).

manifested in the divine "majesty" (k^ebod): the cloud encompassing the Tabernacle by day and the fire appearing in it by night (Ex 40:34–38).[30] As such, the sanctification of the Tabernacle is not a status distinction dependent exclusively on the mental act of the Israelites viewing it as a site of divine presence, but rather, it finds concrete expression in the k^ebod.

Significantly, the ritual act that enacts the transfer of holiness is by means of the divinely mandated oil of anointment (Ex 30:22–33). This oil is used to consecrate the appurtenances of the Tabernacle, the priestly garments and the priests themselves – Aaron and his sons (Ex 28:41; 40:9–11, 15; Lev 8:10–12; Num 7:1). The fact that oil served as the vehicle for this transfer is not arbitrary, as it relates to the radiant quality of "pure" (*tahor*) oil, which conveys a shining complexion to the skin on which it is rubbed. The relationship between oil and radiance can explain how anointment became a rite of purification and sanctification of people and objects, serving as a rite of passage for emancipated slaves, brides and especially kings.[31] This point is expressed vividly in a prophetic message to Zimri Lim, king of Mari (eighteenth century BCE), which relates anointment to the transfer of divine radiance: "I anointed you with the oil of my luminosity, nobody will offer resist[ance] to you" (*šamnam ša namrīrūtīya apšuškāma mamman ana pānīka ul izz[iz]*).[32] Within the context of Israelite kingship, anointment serves as the consummate rite of divine election, epitomized by the prophet Samuel's anointment of the adolescent Saul: "Samuel took a flask of oil and poured it on Saul's head and kissed him, and said, 'Yhwh herewith anoints you as the chosen one

---

[30] For discussion, see Michael Hundley, *Keeping Heaven on Earth: Safeguarding the Divine Presence in the Priestly Tabernacle*, FAT 2/50 (Tübingen: Mohr Siebeck, 2011), 39–52. Compare also the light radiating from Moses' face, which served as a manifestation of divine influence (Ex 34:29–35), requiring him to wear a veil.

[31] See Meir Malul, *Studies in Mesopotamian Legal Symbolism*, AOAT 221 (Kevelaer: Butzon & Becker, 1988), 40–51; Ilya Yakubovich, "Were Hittite Kings Divinely Anointed? A Palaic Invocation to the Sun-God and Its Significance for Hittite Religion," *JANER* 5.1 (2005): 122–135; Amir Gilan and Alice Mouton, "The Enthronement of the Hittite King as a Royal Rite of Passage," in *Life, Death, and Coming of Age in Antiquity: Individual Rites of Passage in the Ancient Near East and Its Surroundings*, eds. A. Mouton and J. Patrier (Leuven: Peeters, 2014).

[32] See Martti Nissinen, *Prophets and Prophecy in the Ancient Near East*, WAW 12 (Atlanta, GA: Society of Biblical Literature 2003), 22. Jean-Marie Durand has argued to derive the term *namrīrūtu* in this passage as derived from the root *m-r-r* ("bitter"), but the accepted translation (*n-m-r*) enjoys robust support from the lexical evidence (*CAD* N/1 237–238; see GAG §55p for interpreting the base *namrīr-* as a reduplicated form) and fits the present context. Cf. " Le mythologème du combat entre le Dieu de l'Orage et la Mer en Mésopotamie," *MARI* 7 (1993): 41–61 (thanks to Kilian Moreau for the reference).

over his inheritance'" (1 Sam 10:1). Finally, in the ritual for the purification of the "leper" in Lev 14, anointment serves to reincorporate the
healed patient into the community. The sevenfold sprinkling of oil "before
Yhwh" (v. 16) serves as the focal point around which the ritual is structured and serves to establish a channel of influence between God, the oil
and the patient. Here the anointment rite effects a transfer of radiance and
thereby sanctifies the patient, enabling him to dwell in the camp where the
divine presence resides.[33]

The most explicit expression of contagious holiness in Priestly texts
would seem to be in statements that "anything (*kol*) that touches ... will
be made holy" (*yiqdaš*), referring to contact with sacred furniture or
offerings (Ex 29:37; 30:26–29; Lev 6:11, 20).[34] Admittedly, not all commentators accept these formulas as evidence for sacred contagion. The
Rabbis (followed by Rashi) promoted a legalistic rendering of these formulas, explaining that even a disqualified offering that is brought on the
altar attains sacrificial (holy) status and cannot be removed. R. Joseph ben
Isaac Bekhor Shor (twelfth century), however, suggests a more essentialist
account. Though initially accepting the rabbinic interpretation, he then
ventures a more elaborate account of the sanctity transfer: "And one
might say, that after the altar is sanctified by anointment, one who touches
it is anointed by it, for one who touches an anointed object is himself
anointed."[35]

Lest these discrepancies in attitude regarding sacred contagion be taken
as relatively late disputes between medieval biblical commentators, this
topic appears to be a bone of contention already in the biblical period,
specifically the exilic and early post-exilic periods. On one hand, the
prophet-priest Ezekiel refers repeatedly to the threat of spreading the
holiness of the temple offerings to the laity. This concern governs his
systematic distancing of laypeople from the inner court of the temple, as
well as his requirement that the priests change their clothing before exiting
the court: "When they go out to the outer court – the outer court where the
people are – they shall remove the vestments in which they minister and
shall deposit them in the sacred chambers; they shall put on other

[33] See Frank. H. Gorman, *The Ideology of Ritual: Space, Time and Status in the Priestly Theology* (Sheffield: JSOT Press, 1990), 151–181; for the centrality of this anointment in the literary structure of the passage, see Jacob Milgrom, *Leviticus*, AB, 3 vols. (New York, NY: Doubleday, 1991–2000), 1.846–860.
[34] See Haran, *Temples*, 175–181; Milgrom, *Leviticus*, 1:443–456, who argues compellingly for rendering *kol* "anything" rather than "anyone" in these contexts.
[35] Commentary on Ex 29:37 (my translation).

garments, lest they consecrate (v^e-*lo' yeqadd^e$šu$) the people with their vestments" (Ezek 44:19).[36]

A more limited view of contagious sanctity is expressed by Haggai, who poses the following rhetorical question to the priests (Hag 2:12–13):

"If a man is carrying sacrificial flesh in a fold of his garment, and with that fold touches bread, stew, wine, oil, or any other food, will the latter become holy?" The priests answered, "No." Haggai continued, "If someone defiled by a *nepeš* touches any of these, will it be defiled?" And the priests responded, "Yes."

This interchange presumes that the sanctity cannot be transmitted by means of the garment, though it seems to tacitly imply that direct contact would convey the sanctity both to the priest and to the food items in question. In contrast, death pollution is assumed to be transmitted via the garment to the food items.[37]

Returning to the formula in P, a particularly intriguing passage appears to deal with sancta contagion in the cooking of the sin offering (Lev 6:18–23):

[18]Speak to Aaron and his sons thus: this is the law for the sin offering. The sin offering shall be slaughtered before Yhwh, at the place where the burnt offering is slaughtered; it is most holy. [19]The priest who offers it as a sin offering shall consume it; it shall be eaten in a holy place, in the court of the Tent of Meeting. [20]All that touch its flesh will be consecrated, and if its blood spatters on clothing, that which was spattered shall be laundered in a sacred area. [21]An earthenware vessel in which it was boiled will be broken, and if it was boiled in a bronze vessel, it will be scoured and rinsed with water. [22]Any male among the priests may eat it; it is most holy. [23]Any sin offering whose blood was brought into the Tent of Meeting to make expiation in the sanctuary will not be eaten, it shall be consumed in fire.

This passage seems to deal with the transfer of sanctity from the sin offering (bearing the status of a most holy offering) to vessels and garments which come into contact with its flesh and blood. The fact that the passage outlines the need to cleanse these vessels and even destroy earthenware vessels (which do not allow purification) might suggest that the sin offering is defiling, perhaps because it absorbs the sin of the person bringing the offering.[38] Yet, the sevenfold reference to its sanctity

---

[36] See also 42:14; 46:20; Milgrom, *Leviticus*, 1:446–456.

[37] Milgrom, *Leviticus*, 1:450; for further discussion of this passage, see Mignon R. Jacobs, *The Books of Haggai and Malachi*, NICOT (Grand Rapids, MI: Eerdaman's Publishing, 2017), 97–104.

[38] See David P. Wright, *The Disposal of Impurity: Elimination Rites in the Bible and in Hittite and Mesopotamian Literature* (Atlanta, GA: Scholars Press, 1987), 96, 129–131; see also Milgrom, *Leviticus*, 1.403–406; Yitzhaq Feder, *Blood Expiation in Hittite and Biblical Ritual: Origins, Context and Meaning* (Atlanta, GA: SBL, 2011), 71–73.

indicates that the author had a different concern. Accordingly, some have suggested that these cleansing rites constitute desacralization, that is, to remove the potentially dangerous holiness conveyed to these objects.[39]

But since one might assume that to achieve or transmit holiness would constitute a positive state, it may be asked: Why would it be necessary to remove sanctity from objects? Following an idea which was fashionable in early-twentieth-century anthropology, some scholars have cited this passage as evidence for the ambivalence of the sacred, being at the same time awesome and dangerous, mentioning it together with narratives like Lev 10:1–2 and 2 Sam 6:6–8.[40] However, a more modest interpretation seems warranted. As understood by the Rabbis, the primary concern expressed in this passage is that the leftover meat or blood will become disqualified (cf. Lev 7:15–18) and disqualify any future offerings prepared in these vessels.[41] Similarly, James Watts argues,

> This rule does not necessarily presuppose that the pots have contracted either holiness or impurity from the offerings. The concern is rather that they must be washed to remove the sacred substance from them, probably because all the meat should be eaten or disposed of … In that case, dirty pots containing spoiled meat would invalidate the offerings (7:18).[42]

In short, this passage is consistent with P's moderate view, which acknowledges sacred contagion but limits it to vessels and clothing that directly touched sancta. More specifically, the cleansing rites described in Lev 6:18–23 do not refer specifically to the removal of sanctity per se but

---

Whereas Wright's view is predicated on the assumption that the purificatory requirements relate specifically to the sin offering, the traditional rabbinic view assumed that these stringencies applied to all of the "most holy" offerings (see m. *Zeb.* ch. 11; b. *Zeb.* 93b–98b). Along these lines, David Hoffmann offered an alternative explanation why these prescriptions appear in the pericope of the sin offering, and not that of the gift offering, where the principle of "all that touches … will be sanctified" (6:11) initially appears, namely because the gift offering could be baked without use of vessels (*Das Buch Leviticus*, vol. 1 [Berlin: Poppelauer, 1905], 238–240).

[39] For example, William Robertson Smith writes: "The flesh of the Hebrew sin-offering, which is holy in the first degree, conveys a taboo to everyone who touches it, and if a drop of the blood falls on a garment, this must be washed, i.e., the sanctity must be washed out, in a holy place, while the earthen pot in which the sacrifice is sodden must be broken, as in the case where dead vermin falls in a vessel and renders it unclean" (*Lectures on the Religion of the Semites* [New York, NY: Ktav Publishing, 1969 (1927)], 451).

[40] Milgrom, *Leviticus*, 1.405, 454.

[41] See b. 'Avoda Zara 76a; Hoffmann, *Das Buch Leviticus*, 238–240; Levine, *Leviticus*, 40; cf. Milgrom, *Leviticus*, 1.405.

[42] James W. Watts, *Leviticus 1–10, Historical Commentary of the Old Testament* (Leuven: Peeters, 2013), 407–408.

rather to the traces of the sanctified meat as imbued into the vessel. Here the contagiousness of the holiness takes a concrete form in the taste of the sacred meat.

Yet, how can this notion of sacred contagion be reconciled with the different approach articulated by H, which associates holiness first and foremost with obedience to divine commandments? Are these perspectives contradictory?

WHAT IS HOLINESS: ESSENCE OR DIFFERENCE?

Here it will be helpful to return to Paden's theoretical distinction between ontological and behavioristic approaches to sanctity. In particular, by challenging the disproportionate scholarly interest in "mana-type" accounts of holiness, Paden sought to call attention to a no-less-significant type of discourse in which the language of sacrality is used to police societal norms:

> Thus, where sacrality connotes inviolable order rather than numinous power-objects, a significantly different polarity between sacrality and profanity is formed. In the mana model, the sacred is the superhuman "other" and the profane is the mundane or natural, the secular zone "outside the temple" (*pro+fanum*). But in the context of sacred order, or the second model, the profane is not the mundane but the violative and transgressive.[43]

This insight can potentially shed light on the distinct emphases between different layers of the Priestly Source. Specifically, Paden's distinction captures the grammatical difference between the adjectival form *ḥol* ("mundane"), which is neutral in its connotations, and the causative verbal form *ḥ-l-l* (piel), which refers to the desecration of holy entities. The latter form appears sixteen times in Lev 18–22 (H) compared with no instances in Lev 1–16 (P).[44] These warnings against desecration which accompany prohibitions are the mirror image of the positive emphasis on holiness expressed in these same chapters. As such, the prohibitions establish the boundaries of the sacred order and constitute the rhetorical core of the Holiness Code. The focus of these statements is to define the lines of distinction between priests and lay Israelites on one hand and between Israel and other nations on the other.[45]

---

[43] "Sacred Order," *Method & Theory in the Study of Religion* 12.1–4 (2000): 209.

[44] 18:21; 19:8, 12, 29; 20:3; 21:4, 6, 9, 12, 15, 23; 22:2, 9, 15, 32. This emphasis is likewise pervasive in Ezekiel, where *ḥ-l-l* appears no less than thirty times.

[45] Saul M. Olyan, *Rites and Rank* (Princeton, NJ: Princeton University Press, 2000), 35–37.

At first glance, the Holiness Code seems to represent a radical departure from the essentialist conception of holiness implied by P. In a striking departure from P's myopic focus on the cult, H emphasizes how the fulfillment of divine commandments serves as the means for achieving holiness.[46] This tendency is particularly striking in the law that one must tie tassels on the four corners of a garment as a reminder of the commandments:

> Speak to the Israelite people and instruct them to make for themselves fringes on the corners of their garments throughout the ages; let them attach a cord of blue to the fringe at each corner. That shall be your fringe; look at it and recall all the commandments of Yhwh and observe them, so that you do not follow your heart and eyes in your lustful urge. Thus you shall be reminded to observe all my commandments and to be holy (*qedošim*) to your God (Num 15:38–40).[47]

According to this passage, the blue cord on the fringes of the garment serves as a reminder of the divine commandments, presented as the medium by which Israelites are to achieve holiness.

In other H texts within Leviticus, holiness is defined by prohibitions. As mentioned above, the holiness of lay Israelites is achieved by abstaining from impure foods (Lev 11:44–45), "For I, Yhwh, am your God: you shall sanctify yourselves and be holy, for I am holy. You shall not defile your spirits through any swarming thing that moves upon the earth." So too abstinence from proscribed sexual behaviors: "So you shall set apart the pure beast from the impure, the impure bird from the pure . . . You shall be holy to me, for I, Yhwh, am holy, and I have set you apart from other peoples to be mine" (20:25–26). A similar sentiment informs Lev 18, which frames the sex laws by the categorical demand that the Israelites distinguish their behavior from the licentiousness of the indigenous inhabitants of Canaan, which had caused the land to vomit them out (1–4, 24–30). In these instances, H sets forth holiness as the key concept for defining Israelite identity, but in a context where holiness is understood in behavioral terms, tantamount to distinctiveness itself, which is clearly to be distinguished from the ontological, contagious holiness associated with the cult as represented in P.

---

[46] Israel Knohl, *The Sanctuary of Silence: The Priestly Torah and the Holiness School* (Winona Lake, IN: Eisenbrauns, 2007 [1995]), 180–186. Similarly: Milgrom, *Leviticus,* 2:1717–1719.

[47] The affinity of this passage (and Num 15 in its entirety) with the style of H has been noted since the nineteenth century. See Knohl, *Sanctuary of Silence,* 186; Christophe Nihan, *From Priestly Torah to Pentateuch,* FAT 2/25 (Tübingen: Mohr Siebeck, 2007), 570, who nevertheless treats H-style passages in Numbers as distinct from H.

Such evidence might suggest that H is subversively resisting P's emphasis on the cult by asserting that holiness is not the exclusive privilege of the priesthood. For example, Jacob Milgrom argues that H "breaks down the barrier between the priesthood and the laity."[48] However, closer examination suggests that H aims to expand the scope of holiness without undermining the elite status of the cult. Hence, H makes a subtle distinction between the priests, who are inherently *qedošim* (Lev 21), and other Israelites, who need to actively strive for holiness via the commandments (Lev 19:2).[49] Accordingly, the final form of the Priestly literature represents a dual conception of holiness: (1) an essentialist conception that is characterized by the inherent holiness of the Aaronide priesthood and ritualized by the transfer of divine radiance through anointment with the divinely prescribed oil, and (2) a performative conception that is applied to the whole Israelite nation, for whom holiness is acquired by following the divine commandments.

Returning to Paden's analytic distinction between a metaphysical ("mana") and a descriptive behavioristic model of holiness, it can now be stated that the Priestly source (in its final form) reflects a deliberate integration of these two approaches – each delegated to a particular context. The conceptualization of holiness as it relates to the cult (P) is based on an essentialist conception whereby holiness can operate according to principles of contagion, represented in rites of anointment performed on sanctified objects and on Aaron's sons themselves, the priesthood.[50] Alongside this essentialist conception, H offers a separate track to Israelite laypeople for achieving holiness: performance of commandments and especially abstinence from the degrading dietary and sexual practices of other nations. By observing this behavioral code, Israelites can distinguish themselves from those other nations, attaining a holiness that is not contagious. This clear distinction between the innate

---

[48] *Leviticus*, 2.1714–1719 (1714). Knohl likewise perceives a "disagreement" between P, for whom "holiness, which results from God's presence, is restricted to the cultic enclosure" and H, for whom "the holiness of God expands beyond the Sanctuary to encompass the settlements of the entire congregation of Israel, in whose midst God dwells" (*Sanctuary of Silence*, 185). For discussion of this last point, see Yitzhaq Feder, "The Wilderness Camp Paradigm in the Holiness Source and the Temple Scroll: From Purity Laws to Cult Politics," *JAJ* 5.3 (2014): 294, 307–308.

[49] Knohl, *Sanctuary of Silence*, 183, n. 43.

[50] Closer inspection reveals that some of the sources that seem to be part of P and reflect the sanctity of the cult reflect H's style (e.g., Ex 29:43–45; see Knohl, *Sanctuary*, 65), reinforcing the conclusion here that these approaches are differences of emphasis but not actual contradictions. So already Schwartz, *Holiness Legislation*, 262.

holiness of the Aaronide priesthood and the contingent holiness of the laity may explain in part why P implicitly rejects the idea expressed in Ezek 40–48 that holiness can be conveyed to persons by contact, and reserves contagious sanctity to objects. This attitude regarding the (non-)communicability of holiness would then serve as an inviolable boundary between Aaronide priesthood and the laity. As such, the behavioral model of holiness is the mirror image of H's emphasis on moral pollution, which together advance an inclusive program of divine service without compromising the preeminence of sacrificial worship.

CONCLUSION

In conclusion, the usage of the root q-d-$š$ in the HB – and even within the Priestly source – exhibits an ambivalence between ontological and behavioral conceptions of sanctity. These distinct models are both embodied – each in its own way. The ontological conception associated with the cult is based on the rite of anointment concretizing a transfer of numinous force, comparable to the prevalence of radiance as the key experiential image for holiness throughout the ancient Near East. The behavioral extension of holiness to lay persons emphasized in the Holiness Code is most explicit in its restrictions on the carnal drives, whereby lay Israelites attain holiness by avoiding indulgence in forbidden flesh, whether gustatory or sexual.

Ultimately, metaphysical and behavioristic approaches to the sacred are inextricably tied to one another. As even Paden acknowledges, it is difficult to assume a commitment to separating the sacred from the common in behavior without a presumption of an ontological difference between the two. Nevertheless, the fact that the domain of the sacred lies beyond the limits of mundane experience makes it dependent on ritualistic distinctions to be made real. Along these lines, the concrete imagery of radiance (numinous power) and the heavens (separateness) provided the semantic scaffolding – the embodied grounding – by which the structural distinction between sacred and mundane could take hold. Thus, through this dual model of holiness, the most transcendent of religious intuitions is translated into concrete experience and the categorically other is made imminent.

13

Conclusion: Naturalizing a Religious Concept

The central claim of this book has been that the biblical notion of *ṭum'ah* is rooted in embodied experience. Closely related to disgust, it is more specifically to be identified with the experience of contagion as manifested in multiple domains of life, each type according to its own rules and ramifications. Even extensions of defilement discourse which emerge in biblical and Second Temple Period Jewish sources, including those more remote from the physiological causes of impurity, can be traced back to the various schemas of embodied existence.

TRACING THE HISTORY OF BIBLICAL POLLUTION

The ability to reconstruct the historical development of this discourse in ancient Israel is a unique capacity provided by ancient textual sources which span hundreds of years, enabling a "longitudinal study" that is not available either to anthropologists or psychologists working only within contemporary contexts. This perspective has enabled us to appreciate the dynamic and fluid aspects of pollution. Looking back at the evidence surveyed in previous chapters, two main tendencies can be identified that are complementary.

The first, evaluated in Chapters 2–8, pertains to the role of pollution as a folk-biological concept, particularly as it relates to disease (Chapters 2–6) and the soul (Chapters 7–8). A dominant tendency represented in the Priestly Source was that of limiting the concern with physiological sources of pollution and restricting their impact to the sacred domain, seeing them as no longer posing a mortal threat to individuals. The main impetus for this tendency was to eliminate the practice of healing rites, which were apparently perceived to be ineffectual. This subversive program also involved severing the conventional link between sickness and sin, since the latter was inextricably tied to expiatory healing rites. These developments had far-reaching implications for the understanding of the causation of disease, perhaps largely unintended, allowing for the emergence of a proto-naturalistic notion of disease as an *amoral* occurrence, not necessarily the result of divine punishment

In parallel to this tendency, we have examined in Chapters 9–12 how *ṭum'ah* was progressively appropriated into socio-moral discourse. This latter tendency, evident in the attribution of impurity to bloodshed and idolatry, is most pronounced in relation to the sexual domain (Chapter 9). As was argued, the emergence of these social implications of purity can be traced to two distinct mechanisms:

1) purity praxis – the social ramifications and distinctions emerging as natural outgrowths of fear and repulsion from pollution; and
2) purity language – the deliberate and novel appropriation of purity terminology for rhetorical purposes.

As was seen especially in the subsequent chapters, the expressions of pollution in purity praxis is inextricably related to gender attitudes, many of these essentialist (Chapter 11), and the position of women in ancient Israelite society (Chapter 12). The rhetorical extension of purity language is manifested in the biblical discourse on idolatry and intermarriage. Despite the fact that these appropriations are clearly distinct from the immediate physiological sources of impurity, they nevertheless employ images based in embodied experience.

By tracing the trajectories of *ṭum'ah* in the biblical sources in a historical progression, it has become apparent that these two tendencies are interrelated. Specifically, the diminishing concern with physiological pollution cleared the way for an expanding emphasis on socio-moral pollution. This change of emphasis is most saliently expressed in H's depiction of land impurity caused by moral pollution. This expansive notion of pollution is consistent with H's inclusive vision of holiness. Due to the limitation of ritual (physiological) impurity to the cultic domain, corresponding to the central sanctuary, it was crucial to provide an alternative track for achieving holiness that was available to all Israelites throughout the land. This aim was to be achieved positively by the fulfillment of commandments, and negatively by abstaining from behaviors which caused moral pollution.

NATURALIZING POLLUTION

The present work has sought to show how the seemingly mystical or otherworldly concept of impurity is firmly rooted in human experience. This claim is consistent with the broader emphasis in the cognitive science of religions on naturalizing religious belief.[1] Such an approach could be used to "debunk" religion for someone so inclined, showing that these ostensibly "religious" intuitions (as human products) can be traced back to concrete experiential foundations. At the same time, it is important to recognize that ancient Israel's understanding of its own religious concepts was to a large degree naturalistic, constituting an attempt to make sense of experience by means of causal explanations.

The present study may suggest a middle ground between naturalistic-evolutionary and cultural-symbolic accounts.[2] Within the context of the sociobiology debate of the late twentieth century, one was forced to choose (so it seemed) between the blank-slate model of human nature ascribed to the social sciences and the genetic determinism attributed to evolutionary psychologists by their opponents.[3] Formulated in this manner, the question at hand was whether human culture is merely window dressing for the same biologically determined drives and behaviors that control other animals or whether the unique gifts of language and culture have enabled humans to create their own behavioral and intellectual worlds with no constraints other than their imagination. In short, this dichotomy amounts to biological determinism versus cultural relativism. Now that the smoke has settled, it can be readily admitted that both sides are oversimplifications.[4]

---

[1] See Leonardo Abasciano, *An Unnatural History of Religions* (London: Bloomsbury, 2019).

[2] In this pursuit, I have been preceded by: Andreas de Block and Stefaan E. Cuypers, "Why Darwinians Should Not Be Afraid of Mary Douglas – and Vice Versa: The Case of Disgust," *Philosophy of the Social Sciences* 42.4 (2012): 459–488; Thomas Kazen, "Levels of Explanation for Ideas of Impurity: Why Structuralist and Symbolic Models Often Fail While Evolutionary and Cognitive Models Succeed," *JAJ* 9.1 (2018): 75–100. I find the latter account more satisfying due to its more critical evaluation of symbolic approaches.

[3] For a critique of the "standard social science model," see John Tooby and Leda Cosmides, *The Adapted Mind: Evolutionary Psychology and the Generation of Culture* (New York: Oxford University Press, 1992); Steven Pinker, *The Blank Slate: The Modern Denial of Human Nature* (New York, NY: Viking, 2002); for the accusation of genetic determinism, Richard Lewontin, *Biology as Ideology: The Doctrine of DNA* (Concord, ON: Anansi, 2002).

[4] For the sociobiology debate, see Ullica Segerstråle, *Defenders of the Truth: The Sociobiology Debate* (Oxford: Oxford University Press, 2000); Kevin N. Laland and

In this book, I have aimed to understand the development of defilement discourse in ancient Israel as a product of an interaction between two types of processes:

1) "bottom-up" processes, in which embodied experience provides the materials for social codes and cultural discourse; and
2) "top-down" processes, in which culture shapes attitudes regarding embodied experience.

This model can go a long way toward reconciling the aforementioned tension between biology and culture. Furthermore, it offers a framework for reexamining a whole slew of dichotomies that have appeared in different disciplinary contexts but ultimately boil down to similar tensions, as seen in Table 13.1.

I will not attempt to elucidate each of these examples in detail, but merely to point out the common theme. In all of these oppositions, one side stresses how the world impresses itself on human cultural concepts and codes, while the other views these as resulting from theoretical constructs imposed on experience. While these parallels may appear to be roughly similar, further inspection reveals that some of these examples pertain to a native (emic) perspective, whereas others pertain to an analytic (etic) perspective. In other words, they seem to reflect two separate questions that should not be confused:

1) Do the subjects (i.e., the "natives") interpret their categories, laws, and so on, as based on essentialist causes?
2) Are cultural products such as language structured by biology and experience or are they freely constructed by the mind?

While it is important not to confuse these two perspectives, there is considerable overlap between them. As has been seen in the previous chapters, just as a strict binary opposition between biology and culture is unsustainable for analytic discourse, so too the folk biology of ancient Israel occupied a middle ground between experientially grounded concepts and linguistically shaped discourse.

In Chapter 6, I argued that biblical *ṭum'ah* can be viewed as an invisible causal force (Tier 2) within the context of the ancient Israelites' indigenous understanding of "nature," equated with regularity of experience. Within this emic view of nature, it is possible to understand

Gillian R. Brown, *Sense and Nonsense: Evolutionary Perspectives on Human Behaviour* (New York, NY: Oxford University Press, 2011).

how pollution relates to other entities and forces pertaining to this unseen, metaphysical domain. For example, Chapter 7 exhibited how impure foods defile (*ṭimme'*) the *nepeš*, while Chapter 8 reversed these roles, showing how the *nepeš* can defile people and objects when separating from the body at the time of death. Within this framework, it can be

TABLE 13.1 *The problem of essentialism across disciplines*

Discipline	Question	Dichotomy	
Philosophy	Are categories natural kinds or arbitrary groupings shaped by language?[1]	realism	nominalism
Sociology	Is group membership based on inherent characteristics (e.g., race, caste) or a sociopolitical construct?[2]	essentialism	social-constructionism
Law	Does law conform to a natural order or is it an arbitrary expression of authority?[3]	essentialism	formalism/ positivism
Semiotics	Is the relation between form and meaning of signs determined by nature or convention?[4]	natural signs	conventional signs

[1] E.g., Ian Hacking, "A Tradition of Natural Kinds," *Philosophical Studies* 61.1–2 (1991): 109–126, in which Hacking writes: "The nominalist 'left' says that all kinds are human, or at any rate, there are no kinds in nature. The realist 'right' says that there are indeed natural kinds, and that human kinds – at any rate those susceptible of systematic study – are among them" (109). See also the pertinent discussion within an ancient Mesopotamian context, Francesca Rochberg, *Before Nature: Cuneiform Knowledge and the History of Science* (Chicago, IL: University of Chicago Press, 2016), 61–102.

[2] Pnina Werbner, "Essentialising Essentialism, Essentialising Silence: Ambivalence and Multiplicity in the Constructions of Racism and Ethnicity," in *Debating Cultural Hybridity: Multi-Cultural Identities and the Politics of Anti-Racism*, eds. P. Werbner and T. Modood (London: Zed Books, 1997), 226–254; Ramaswami Mahalingam, "Essentialism, Power, and the Representation of Social Categories: A Folk Sociology Perspective," *Human Development* 50.6 (2007): 300–319.

[3] For an application of this distinction to Second Temple Judaism, see Aryeh Amihay, *Theory and Practice in Essene Law* (Oxford: Oxford University Press, 2017), 19–30, with refs.

[4] See Winfried Nöth, *Handbook of Semiotics* (Bloomington, IN: Indiana University Press, 1990), 107–113.

seen that such causal concepts pertaining to invisible forces originate from and derive their validity through their reference to the regularities of perceptible experience (e.g., the spread of odors, infection, etc.).

Yet, it was argued, there is a higher causal level (Tier 3) that pertains to divine control. As noted, the reflective belief in gods is made possible by language, more specifically the ability to create a narrative to explain experience, including cosmological and theological theories. While this observation is intended on the etic level, it is striking that a similar view is made explicit within ancient Near Eastern sources, including the HB, namely that the divine control over the cosmos is mediated by language. Basing her analysis on Mesopotamian divinatory literature, Francesca Rochberg elucidates how its implicit ontology differs from the modern Western conception of nature:

> In the cuneiform world, making correspondences, connections, and relations through semantic and orthographic association, number schemes, and so on, were the expression of a different orientation to the world, not physicalistic (or materialistic) in nature ... Indeed the very term *physical phenomena* implies, via etymology of the word *physical* from Greek *phusis,* its identity within nature. In the cuneiform world it was the effect of divine will manifested in omens that pervaded the visible realms of the cosmos, the terrestrial and the celestial.[5]

The decipherment of omens was understood to be a decoding of divine messages written onto the fabric of the phenomenal world: "Omen divination therefore evinces a fundamental anthropomorphism, where what we call nature is perceived as divine speech, matter turned expressive, meaning materialized in the world of phenomena."[6] This perspective is represented by the Mesopotamian notion of the constellations as a "heavenly writing" (*šiṭir šamê*) that the gods inscribed on the heavens.[7] A similar conception informs the Priestly account of creation in Genesis 1, in which the cosmos is created by divine speech: "And God said: 'Let there be ...,' and there was ... "

This type of emic discourse, which views language as the tool for creating and manipulating reality, serves as a fitting model for understanding the capability of cultural discourse to shape the raw materials of embodied experience. To a large degree, it parallels the view of modern

---

[5] *Before Nature,* 165–166 (her emphasis).   [6] Ibid., 170.

[7] Likewise *šiṭirti šamāmī* and *šiṭir burūmê* ("writing of the firmament"). See *CAD* Š/2 144, 146 and Francesca Rochberg, *The Heavenly Writing: Divination, Horoscopy and Astronomy in Mesopotamian Culture* (Cambridge: Cambridge University Press, 2004), 1–4.

culture theorists who emphasize the seeming unlimited freedom by which linguistically mediated cultural discourse can shape reality.

However, as has been seen, this capability did not emerge from within a vacuum. Even ostensibly abstract concepts such as purity, pollution and holiness reveal, upon closer scrutiny, an evolutionary process from images to codes to discourse. This boot-strapping process, by which abstract discourse could emerge from concrete images, may be contrasted with intellectualist accounts, such as those proposed by Mary Douglas and her followers, who treated abstract concepts as a priori givens to be signified by the concrete signifiers of pollution regulations. The fallacy of the latter approach, stated briefly, is its implicit assumption that these abstract categories (like Platonic ideas) could exist apart from the concrete images used to represent them. In contrast, I have sought, borrowing a provocative formulation of Marcel Merleau-Ponty, "to see rationality in a historical perspective which it set itself on principle to avoid, to seek a philosophy which explains the upsurge of rationality in a world not of its making."[8] In other words, the foregoing analysis has sought to emphasize the role of lived experience as an indispensable precondition for the emergence of abstract, symbolic discourse. Through this process, the flesh has become word.

THE FUTURE OF THE EMBODIED MIND

The present study strikes at the heart of what is the essence of being human. Are we divine sparks from on high, as certain religious traditions promote? Or are we sophisticated symbol-manipulating computers, a view that was once fashionable among cognitive scientists? Or simply primates with delusions of grandeur?

The recognition of the bottom-up and top-down processes that shape purity discourse makes possible a middle ground between two diametrically opposed academic approaches to human culture:

Reductionism: explaining human-level phenomena in terms of more basic causes, specifically by understanding culture as a product of biology, shaped by evolutionary pressures;[9]

---

[8] *Phenomenology of Perception*, trans. C. Smith (London: Routledge, 2002 [1958]), 65–66.
[9] For a helpful discussion of "reductionism" and its perceived threat to humanistic study, see Edward Slingerland, "Who's Afraid of Reductionism? The Study of Religion in the Age of Cognitive Science," *JAAR* 76.2 (2008): 375–411.

Constructionism: viewing human-level phenomena as the freely gener-
ated products of culture, mediated by language.

As intimated above, the latter perspective, championed in the name of
critical theory, bears more than a superficial resemblance to the medieval
theological concept of creation *ex nihilo* ("from nothingness"), whereby
the world was assumed to be a product of the mind of God, realized
through creative utterances.[10] However, in the disenchanted worldview
of modern science, this perspective has been stood on its head. In the
beginning, there was matter. Mind is reduced to neurons firing in the
brain. The shocking implications of this perspective are articulated by
Edward Slingerland as follows:

This means that our thoughts and behavior are, at least in principle, as predetermined and predictable as any other physical process. It also means that the self as
we ordinarily understand it – as a disembodied something, soul or spirit or mind,
caused by nothing other than itself – is nothing more than an illusion created by the
workings of our embodied brain.[11]

Accordingly, there is no room for metaphysical concepts such as pollution
or souls, raising the question of why people entertain these delusionary
notions in the first place. The implicit assumption informing such inquiries
is "that anyone who actually thinks that un-physical realities exist is under
the thrall of a superstitious, primitive, and irrational devotion to an
outdated dualistic ontology."[12]

Yet, recognizing that these metaphysical concepts are based to a great
extent on empirical observation undermines such temptations to
"debunk" them. A more productive strategy is to identify the correspondences between indigenous concepts and those of Western science.
A similar view was advocated with practical implications by the medical

---

[10] Actually, this pervasive idea of creation *ex nihilo* reflects a misreading (perhaps deliberate) of the first verse of Genesis: "In the beginning God created the heaven and the earth"
(KJV; so also m. *Abot* 5:1: "With ten utterances the world was created ... "). Note the
different implications in the more grammatically correct NJPS translation (so also Rashi
and Ibn Ezra): "When God began to create heaven and earth – the earth being unformed
and void, with darkness over the surface of the deep and a wind from God sweeping over
the water ... " For further discussion, see Jon D. Levenson, *Creation and the Persistence
of Evil* (Princeton, NJ: Princeton University Press, 1985), 3–25.
[11] "Who's Afraid," 383. See also Julien Musolino, *The Soul Fallacy* (Amherst, NY:
Prometheus Books, 2015).
[12] Richard Shweder, "The Metaphysical Realities of the Unphysical Sciences: Or Why
Vertical Integration Seems Unrealistic to Ontological Pluralists," in *Creating
Consilience: Integrating the Sciences and the Humanities*, eds. E. Slingerland and
M. Collard (Oxford: Oxford University Press, 2012), 60.

anthropologist Edward Green in his argument that pollution beliefs are "naturalistic" and ultimately compatible with Western notions of infectious disease. Arguing that the diseases associated with impurity "tend not to be interpreted supernaturally, but rather belong to an interpretive system that is essentially rational, empirically based, promotive of good health, and not very different from Western biomedicine in important ways," Green suggests that public health officials are best advised to work within indigenous frameworks to the extent possible rather than deny their validity.[13] Viewed from the perspective of cultural evolution, it may be argued that the perpetuation of pollution beliefs can largely be attributed to their correspondence to experience (in this case, infection) as well as their utility in pathogen avoidance.[14]

In conclusion, the present study has argued that in the discourse on pollution in the HB, embodied experience and symbolic culture are deeply entangled. The key point here is that the artificial boundaries between academic disciplines are poorly equipped to capture the synthetic nature of the human mind: it is the *embodied foundations of mind* that distinguish human thought from that of computers and forms of artificial intelligence whose symbolic systems operate in isolation from experience.[15] On the other hand, it is the *potential to establish symbolic concepts* from the immediate perceptions of the senses that enables the abstract cognition that distinguishes humans from other primates. Stated differently, the approximately 95 percent of shared DNA between chimpanzees and humans may serve as proof for our evolutionary heritage, but it proves simultaneously that genes are not destiny. Alongside the biophysical causality of bodies, it is necessary to acknowledge the causal power of ideas, as transmitted through the symbolic repertoire of culture.[16] Accordingly, only a deeply *consilient* approach that appreciates

---

[13] *Indigenous Theories of Contagious Disease* (Walnut Creek, CA: AltaMira, 1999), 16.

[14] See further Yitzhaq Feder, "Contamination Appraisals, Pollution Beliefs and the Role of Cultural Inheritance in Shaping Disease Avoidance Behavior," *Cognitive Science* 40.6 (2016): 1561–1585.

[15] This point pertains specifically to symbolically driven artificial intelligence (AI), sometimes labeled "Good Old-Fashioned Artificial Intelligence," to be contrasted with more recent trends in AI which seek to incorporate principles of embodied cognition, e.g., Ron Chrisley, "Embodied Artificial Intelligence," *Artificial Intelligence* 149.1 (2003): 131–150.

[16] This idea is not original. An early-twentieth-century version was outlined by Ernst Cassirer, *An Essay on Man: An Introduction to a Philosophy of Human Culture* (New Haven, CT: Yale University Press, 1944). More recent versions include Merlin Donald, *Origins of the Modern Mind: Three Stages in the Evolution of Culture and Cognition* (Cambridge, MA: Harvard University Press, 1991); Terrance W. Deacon,

the complementary roles of biology and culture wields the potential to offer a satisfying account of phenomena such as pollution.[17] My hope is that once straw men are laid to rest, it will be possible to move from the contentiousness of sociobiology to new directions of "super-humanistic" investigation.

Completing this book under the shadow of the coronavirus pandemic, it has become clear that much can be learned from the experience of disease. In particular, bodies, which are taken for granted in times of health, suddenly become noticed in times of sickness. By analogy, it is hoped that the present investigation of contagion has shed light on the role of bodies in their indispensable role in mediating discourse. However, the bodies that emerge are not merely physiological entities, but rather themselves products of a reciprocal process through which "nature" and "culture" are inextricably intertwined. These bodies have a history, shaped by patterns of practical and linguistic sense-making that extend into the indefinite past, through the earliest literate civilizations into prehistory. Future study of the embodied mind will need to engage this history.

The Symbolic Species: The Co-Evolution of Language and the Brain (New York: W. W. Norton, 1997); Eva Jablonka and Marion J. Lamb, *Evolution in Four Dimensions* (Cambridge, MA: MIT Press, 2005), 193–232; and many others.

[17] Edward Slingerland, *What Science Offers the Humanities* (Cambridge: Cambridge University Press, 2012); Edward Slingerland and Mark Collard (eds.), *Creating Consilience: Integrating the Sciences and the Humanities* (Oxford: Oxford University Press, 2012).

Works Cited

Aartun, Kjell. "Studien zum Gesetz über den grossen Versöhnungstag Lv 16 mit Varianten. Ein ritualgeschichtlicher Beitrag." *Studia Theologica* 34.1 (1980): 73–109.

Abasciano, Leonardo. *An Unnatural History of Religions*. London: Bloomsbury, 2019.

Aberle, David F. "Navaho." In *Matrilineal Kinship*, edited by D. M. Schneider and K. Gough, 96–201. Berkeley, CA: University of California, 1974.

Achenbach, Reinhard. "Verunreinigung durch die Berührung Toter: Zum Ursprung einer alisraelitischen Vorstellung." In *Tod und Jenseits im alten Israel in seiner Umwelt*, edited by A. Berlejung and B. Janowski, 347–369. FAT 64. Tübingen: Mohr Siebeck, 2009.

Ahern, Emily M. *The Cult of the Dead in a Chinese Village*. Stanford, CA: Stanford University Press, 1973.

Albertz, Rainer and Rudiger Schmitt. *Family and Household Religion in Ancient Israel and the Levant*. Winona Lake, IN: Eisenbrauns, 2012.

Alfrink, Bern. "L'expression שכב עם אבותיו." *OTS* 2 (1943): 106–118.
"L'expression נאסף אל עמיו." *OTS* 5 (1948): 118–131.

Amihay, Aryeh. *Theory and Practice in Essene Law*. Oxford: Oxford University Press, 2017.

Amit, Yaira. *Hidden Polemics in the Hebrew Bible*, translated by J. Chipman. Leiden: Brill, 2000.

Anderson, Gary. *Sin: A History*. New Haven, CT: Yale University Press, 2009.

Anthes-Frey, Henrike. *Unheilsmächte und Schutzgenien, Antiwesen und Grenzgänger: Vorstellungen von "Dämonen" im alten Israel*. OBO 227. Göttingen: Vandenhoeck-Ruprecht, 2007.

Arrizabalaga, Jon, John Henderson and Roger French. *The Great Pox: The French Disease in Renaissance Europe*. New Haven, CT: Yale University Press, 1997.

Artemov, Nikita. "Belief in Family Reunion in the Afterlife in the Ancient Near East and Mediterranean." In *La famille dans le Proche-Orient ancien: réalités, symbolismes, et images: Proceedings of the 55th Rencontre Assyriologique Internationale at Paris 6–9 July 2009*, edited by L. Marti, 27–41. Winona Lake, IN: Eisenbrauns, 2014.

Assmann, Jan. *Death and Salvation in Ancient Egypt,* translated by D. Lorton. Ithaca, NY: Cornell University Press, 2005.

Avalos, Hector. *Illness and Health Care in the Ancient Near East: The Role of the Temple in Greece, Mesopotamia and Israel.* Atlanta, GA: Scholars Press, 1995.

Baden, Joel S. and Candida R. Moss. "The Origins and Interpretation of ṣāraʿat in Leviticus 13–14." *JBL* 130.4 (2011): 643–653.

Badour, Christal L., Matthew T. Feldner, Kimberly A. Babson, Heidemarie Blumenthal and Courtney E. Dutton. "Disgust, Mental Contamination, and Posttraumatic Stress: Unique Relations Following Sexual Versus Non-Sexual Assault." *Journal of Anxiety Disorder* 27.1 (2013): 155–162.

Barnes, Michael H. *Stages of Thought: The Co-Evolution of Religious Thought and Science.* Oxford: Oxford University Press, 2000.

Barr, James. *The Garden of Eden and the Hope of Immortality.* Minneapolis, MN: Fortress Press, 1992.

"Scope and Problems in the Semantics of Classical Hebrew." *ZAH* 6.1 (1993): 3–14.

"Semantics and Biblical Theology – A Contribution to the Discussion." In *Congress Volume: Uppsala 1971,* edited by P. A. H. de Boer, 11–19. VTSupp 22. Leiden: Brill, 1972.

The Semantics of Biblical Language. London: Oxford University, 1961.

Barrett, Justin L. and Jonathan A. Lanman. "The Science of Religious Beliefs." *Religion* 38.2 (2008): 109–124.

Barrett, Louise. "The Evolution of Cognition: A 4E Perspective." In *The Oxford Handbook of 4E Cognition,* edited by A. Newen, L. de Bruin and S. Gallagher, 719–734. Oxford: Oxford University Press, 2018.

Barsalou, Lawrence. "Grounded Cognition." *Annual Review of Psychology* 59 (2008): 617–645.

"Grounding Symbolic Operations in the Brain's Modal Systems." In *Embodied Grounding: Social, Cognitive, Affective and Neuroscientific Approaches,* edited by G. R. Semin and E. R. Smith, 9–42. Cambridge: Cambridge University Press, 2009.

"Perceptual Symbol Systems." *Behavior and Brain Sciences* 22 (1999): 577–660.

Bateson, Gregory. *Steps to an Ecology of Mind.* Chicago, IL: University of Chicago Press, 1972.

Bauer, Andrew J., and Marcel A. Just. "Neural Representations of Concept Knowledge." In *Oxford Handbook of Neurolinguistics,* edited by G. I. de Zubicaray and N. O. Schiller, 518–547. Oxford: Oxford University Press, 2019.

Bear, Mark F., Barry W. Connors and Michael A. Paradiso. *Neuroscience: Exploring the Brain.* Philadelphia, PA: Lippincott Williams & Wilkins, 2007.

Beckman, G. *Hittite Birth Rituals.* StBoT 29. Wiesbaden: Harrasowitz, 1983.

Hittite Diplomatic Texts. WAW 7. Atlanta, GA: Scholars Press, 1999.

Bell, Catherine. *Ritual Theory, Ritual Practice.* Oxford: Oxford University Press, 2009.

Bendann, Effie. *Death Customs: An Analytical Study of Burial Rites*. London: K. Paul, 1930.

Ben-Hayyim, Zev. "Word-Studies IV." *Tarbiz* 50 (1980): 192–208 (in Hebrew).

Berlejung, Angelika and Bernd Janowski. *Tod und Jenseits im alten Israel in seiner Umwelt*. FAT 64. Tübingen: Mohr Siebeck, 2009.

Berquist, Jon L. *Controlling Corporeality: The Body and the Household in Ancient Israel*. Piscataway, NJ: Rutgers University Press, 2002.

Best, Elsdon. "Notes on the Art of War: Part II." *Journal of the Polynesian Society* 11 (1902): 47–75.

Blair, Judit M. *De-Demonising the Old Testament: An Investigation of Azazel, Lilith, Deber, Qeteb and Reshef in the Hebrew Bible*. FAT 2. Tübingen: Mohr Siebeck, 2009.

Blidstein, Moshe. *Purity, Community, and Ritual in Early Christian Literature*. Oxford: Oxford University Press, 2017.

Bloch-Smith, Elizabeth. *Judahite Burial Practices and Beliefs about the Dead*. JSOTSupp 123. Sheffield: JSOT Press, 1992.

Bloom, Paul. *Descartes' Baby*. New York: Basic Books, 2004.

Blum, Erhard. "Issues and Problems in the Contemporary Debate Regarding the Priestly Writings." In *The Strata of the Priestly Writings: Contemporary Debate and Future Directions*, edited by S. Shechtman and J. S. Baden, 31–44. Zurich: Theologischer Verlag, 2009.

Böck, Barbara. "Gilgamesh's Dreams of Enkidu." *Bibliotheca Orientalis* 71.5–6 (2014): 664–672.

Bóid, Iain Ruairidh mac Mhanain. *Principles of Samaritan Halachah*. Studies in Judaism in Late Antiquity 38. Leiden: Brill, 1989.

Borger, R. "ŠurpuII, III, IV, und VIII in 'Partitur.'" In *Wisdom Gods and Literature: Studies in Assyriology in Honour of W. G. Lambert*, edited by A. R. George and I. L. Finkel, 15–90. Winona Lake, IN: Eisenbrauns, 2000.

Bottéro, Alain. "Consumption by Semen Loss in India and Elsewhere." *Culture, Medicine and Psychiatry* 15.3 (1991): 303–320.

Brand, Miriam T. *Evil Within and Without: The Source of Sin and Its Nature as Portrayed in Second Temple Literature*. Göttingen: Vandenhoeck & Ruprecht, 2013.

Bremmer, Jan. *The Early Greek Concept of the Soul*. Princeton, NJ: Princeton University Press, 1983.

Brenner, Athalya. *The Intercourse of Knowledge: On Gendering Desire and "Sexuality" in the Hebrew Bible*. Leiden: Brill, 1997.

"Pornoprophetics Revisited: Some Additional Reflections." *JSOT* 70 (1996): 63–86.

Broida, Marian W. *Forestalling Doom: "Apotropaic Intercession" in the Hebrew Bible and the Ancient Near East*. AOAT 417. Münster: Ugarit-Verlag, 2015.

Büchler, Adolph. *Studies in Sin and Atonement in the Rabbinic Literature of the First Century*. New York: Ktav, 1967.

Buckley, Thomas and Alma Gottlieb. "A Critical Appraisal of Theories of Menstrual Symbolism." In *Blood Magic: The Anthropology of Menstruation*, edited by T. Buckley and A. Gottlieb, 3–53. Berkeley, CA: University of California Press, 1988.

Burkert, Walter. *Creation of the Sacred: Tracks of Biology in Early Religions.* Cambridge, MA: Harvard University Press, 1996.

Buttenwieser, Moses. "Blood Revenge and Burial Rites in Ancient Israel." *JAOS* 39 (1919): 303–321.

Caplice, Richard. *The Akkadian Namburbi Texts: An Introduction.* SANE 1/1. Los Angeles: Undena, 1974.

"Namburbi Texts in the British Museum V." *OrNS* 40 (1971): 133–183.

Carey, Susan. *The Origin of Concepts.* Oxford: Oxford University, 2009.

Cassirer, Ernst. *An Essay on Man: An Introduction to a Philosophy of Human Culture.* New Haven, CT: Yale University Press, 1944.

Chan, Kai Qin, Rob W. Holland, Ruud van Loon, Roy Arts and Ad van Knippenberg. "Disgust and Fear Lower Olfactory Threshold." *Emotion* 16.5 (2016): 740–749.

Chapman, Hanah A. and Adam K. Anderson. "Things Rank and Gross in Nature: A Review and Synthesis of Moral Disgust." *Psychological Bulletin* 139.2 (2013): 300–327.

"Trait Physical Disgust Is Related to Moral Judgments Outside of the Purity Domain." *Emotion* 14.2 (2014): 341–348.

Chavel, Simeon. *Oracular Law and Priestly Historiography in the Torah.* FAT 2/71. Tübingen: Mohr Siebeck, 2014.

Chrisley, Ron. "Embodied Artificial Intelligence." *Artificial Intelligence* 149.1 (2003): 131–150.

Clark, Andy. *Being There: Putting Brain, Body and World Together Again.* Cambridge, MA: MIT Press, 1997.

Classen, Constance. "The Odor of the Other: Olfactory Symbolism and Cultural Categories." *Ethos* 20.2 (1992): 133–166.

Claus, David B. *Toward the Soul: An Inquiry into the Meaning of ψυχή Before Plato.* New Haven, CT/London: Yale University Press, 1981.

Cogan, Morton. "A Note on Disinterment in Jeremiah." In *Gratz College Anniversary Volume*, edited by I. D. Passow and S. T. Lachs, 61–83. Philadelphia, PA: Gratz College, 1971.

Cohen, Andrew C. *Death Rituals, Ideology, and the Development of Early Mesopotamian Kingship.* Leiden: Brill, 2005.

Cohen, Chaim. "More Examples of 'False Friends': Regular Meanings of Words in Modern Hebrew Which Originated Erroneously." *Language Studies* 11–12 (2008): 173–198 (in Hebrew).

Cohen, David S. "Keeping Men Men and Women Down: Sex Segregation, Anti-Essentialism, and Masculinity." *Harvard Journal of Law and Gender* 33 (2010): 509–553.

Cohen, Shai J. D. *The Beginnings of Jewishness: Boundaries, Varieties, Uncertainties.* Berkeley, CA: University of California Press, 1999.

Cohen, Yoram. *The Scribes and Scholars of the City of Emar in the Late Bronze Age.* Winona Lake, IN: Eisenbrauns, 2009.

Collins, Billie Jean. "The First Soldiers' Oath (1.66)." *CoS* 2: 165–166.

"Necromancy, Fertility and the Dark Earth: The Use of Ritual Pits in Hittite Cult." In *Magic and Ritual in the Ancient World*, edited by P. Mirecki and M. Meyer, 224–241. Leiden: Brill, 2002.

"Purifying a House: A Ritual for the Infernal Deities (1.68)." *CoS* 1: 168–171.

Colombetti, Giovanna. "Enacting Affectivity." In *The Oxford Handbook of 4E Cognition*, edited by A. Newen, L. de Bruin and S. Gallagher, 571–588. Oxford: Oxford University Press, 2018.

The Feeling Body: Affective Science Meets the Enactive Mind. Cambridge, MA: MIT Press, 2014.

Conczorowski, B. "All the Same as Ezra? Conceptual Differences between the Texts of Intermarriage in Genesis, Deuteronomy 7 and Ezra." In *Mixed Marriages: Intermarriage and Group Identity in the Second Temple Period*, edited by C. Frevel, 90–98. New York: T&T Clark, 2011.

Conrad, Lawrence. "A Ninth-Century Muslim Scholar's Discussion of Contagion." In *Contagion: Perspectives from Pre-Modern Societies*, edited by L. I Conrad and D. Wujastyk, 163–178. Aldershot: Ashgate, 2000.

Cooper, Jerrold S. "Sumerian and Akkadian." In *The World's Writing Systems*, edited by P. T. Daniels and W. Bright, 37–57. New York: Oxford University, 1996.

Cooper, John W. *Body, Soul, and Life Everlasting: Biblical Anthropology and the Monism-Dualism Debate*. Grand Rapids, MI: Eerdmans, 1989.

Corbin, Alain. *The Foul and the Fragrant: Odor and French Social Imagination*. Cambridge, MA: Harvard University Press, 1986.

Couto-Ferreira, Erica and Agnès Garcia-Ventura. "Engendering Purity and Impurity in Assyriological Studies: A Historiographical Overview." *Gender & History* 25.3 (2013): 513–528.

Crawford, Sidnie White. "Were There Women at Qumran?" *Biblical Archaeology Review* 46.2 (2020): 48–53.

Croft, William. "The Role of Domains in the Interpretation of Metaphors and Metonymies." In *Metaphor and Metonymy in Comparison and Contrast*, edited by R. Dirven and R. Pörings, 161–205. Berlin: de Gruyter, 2003.

Crofts, Tracey and Julie Fisher. "Menstrual Hygiene in Ugandan Schools: An Investigation of Low-Cost Sanitary Pads." *Journal of Water, Sanitation and Hygiene for Development* 2.1 (2012): 50–58.

Cunningham, Andrew. "Transforming Plague: The Laboratory and the Identity of Infectious Disease." In *The Laboratory Revolution in Medicine*, edited by A. Cunningham and P. Williams, 209–244. Cambridge: Cambridge University Press, 1992.

Cunningham, Graham. *Deliver Me from Evil: Mesopotamian Incantations 2500–1500 B. C*. Rome: Editrice Pontificio Instituto Biblico, 1997.

Curry, Oliver S. "Who's Afraid of the Naturalistic Fallacy?" *Evolutionary Psychology* 4.1 (2006): 234–247.

Curtis, Valerie. *Don't Look, Don't Touch, Don't Eat: The Science Behind Repulsion*. Oxford: Oxford University Press, 2013.

Curtis, Valerie, Mícheál de Barra and Robert Aunger. "Disgust as an Adaptive System for Disease Avoidance Behavior." *Philosophical Transactions of the Royal Society B: Biological Sciences* 366 (2011): 389–401.

Cranz, Isabel. *Atonement and Purification*. FAT 2/92. Tübingen: Mohr Siebeck, 2017.

D'Andrade, Roy G. "Schemas as Motivation." In *Human Motives and Cultural Models*, edited by R. G. D'Andrade and C. Strauss, 23–44. Cambridge: Cambridge University Press, 1992.

Darby, Eran. *Interpreting Judean Pillar Figurines: Gender and Empire in Judean Apotropaic Ritual*. FAT 2/69. Tübingen: Mohr Siebeck, 2014.

Darwin, Charles. *The Expression of the Emotions in Man and Animals*. Chicago, IL: University of Chicago Press, 1965 [1872].

Das, Rahul Peter. "Notions of 'Contagion' in Classical Indian Medical Texts." In *Contagion: Perspectives from Pre-Modern Societies*, edited by L. I. Conrad and D. Wujastyk, 55–78. Aldershot: Ashgate, 2000.

Deacon, Terrance W. *The Symbolic Species: The Co-Evolution of Language and the Brain*. New York, NY: W. W. Norton, 1997.

De Block, Andreas and Cuypers, Stefaan E. "Why Darwinians Should Not Be Afraid of Mary Douglas – And Vice Versa: The Case of Disgust." *Philosophy of the Social Sciences* 42.4 (2012): 459–488.

de Jong, Peter J., Mark van Overveld and Charmaine Borg. "Giving in to Arousal or Staying Stuck in Disgust? Disgust-Based Mechanisms in Sex and Sexual Dysfunction." *Journal of Sex Research* 50.3–4 (2013): 247–262.

Demaitre, Luke. *Leprosy in Premodern Medicine*. Baltimore, MD: Johns Hopkins University Press, 2007.

Desjarlais, Robert R. *Body and Emotion: The Aesthetics of Illness and Healing in the Nepal Himalayas*. Philadelphia, PA: University of Pennsylvania, 1992.

Diesendruck, Gil and Lital Haber. "God's Categories: The Effect of Religiosity on Children's Teleological and Essentialist Beliefs about Categories." *Cognition* 110.1 (2009): 100–114.

Diethelm, Michel. "*Næpæš als Leichnam?*" *ZAH* 7 (1974): 81–84.

Dietrich, Jan. *Kollektive Schuld und Haftung: Religions- und rechtsgeschichtliche Studien zum Sündenkuhritus des Deuteronomiums und zu verwandten Texten*. Tübingen: Mohr Siebeck, 2010.

Dinari, Yedidya. "Customs Related to the Impurity of the Menstruant: Their Origin and Development." *Tarbiz* 49 (1979–1980): 302–324 (in Hebrew).

Donald, Merlin. *Origins of the Modern Mind: Three Stages in the Evolution of Culture and Cognition*. Cambridge, MA: Harvard University Press, 1991.

Dor, Daniel. *The Instruction of Imagination: Language as a Social Communication Technology*. Oxford: Oxford University Press, 2015.

Douek, Ellis. "Ancient and Contemporary Management in a Disease of Unknown Aetiology." In *Disease in Babylonia*, edited by I. J. Finkel and M. J. Geller, 215–218. Leiden: Brill, 2007.

Douglas, Mary. *In the Wilderness: The Doctrine of Defilement in the Book of Numbers*. Sheffield: JSOT Press, 1993.

Jacob's Tears: The Priestly Work of Reconciliation. Oxford: Oxford University Press, 2004.

Purity and Danger: An Analysis of the Concepts of Pollution and Taboo. Routledge: London, 1992 [1966].

Dreyfus, Herbert L. *What Computers Still Can't Do: A Critique of Artificial Reason*. Cambridge, MA: MIT Press, 1992.

Dumont, Louis. *Homo Hierarchicus: The Caste System and Its Implications*, translated by M. Sainsbury, L. Dumont and B. Gulati. Chicago, IL: University of Chicago Press, 1970.

Durand, Jean-Marie. "Cuneiform Script." In *A History of Writing*, edited by A. M. Christin, 20–32. Paris: Flammarion, 2002.

"Le mythologème du combat entre le Dieu de l'Orage et la Mer en Mésopotamie." *MARI* 7 (1993): 41–61.

"Trois études de Mari." *MARI* 3 (1984): 127–180.

Durkheim, E. *The Elementary Forms of Religious Life*, translated by K. E. Fields. New York, NY: Free Press, 1995 [1912].

Earle, William James. "Skulls, Causality, and Belief." *Philosophy of the Social Sciences* 15.3 (1985): 305–311.

Ehrlich, Arnold. *Randglossen zur hebräischen Bibel*, vol. 2. Leipzig: J. C. Hinrichs, 1909.

Eichrodt, Walther. *Theology of the Old Testament*, vol. 2, OTL, translated by J. A. Baker. London: SCM Press, 1967.

Eilberg-Schwartz, Howard. *The Savage in Judaism: An Anthropology of Israelite Religion and Ancient Judaism*. Bloomington, IN: Indiana University Press, 1990.

Elias, Norbert. *The Civilizing Process*, translated by E. Jephcott. Malden, MA: Blackwell, 2000.

Elliger, Karl. *Leviticus*. HAT. Tübingen: Mohr, 1966.

Erbele-Küster, Dorothea. *Body, Gender and Purity in Leviticus 12 and 15*. London: T&T Clark, 2017.

Evans-Pritchard, E. E. *Theories of Primitive Religion*. Oxford: Clarendon Press, 1965.

Witchcraft, Oracles and Magic among the Azande. Oxford: Clarendon Press, 1976.

Fairbrother, Nicole and Stanley Rachman. "Feelings of Mental Pollution Subsequent to Sexual Assault." *Behaviour Research and Therapy* 42.2 (2004): 173–189.

Farber, Walther. "How to Marry a Disease: Epidemics, Contagion, and a Magic Ritual against the 'Hand of a Ghost.'" In *Magic and Rationality in Ancient Near Eastern and Greco-Roman Medicine*, edited by H. F. J. Horstmanshoff and M. Stol, 117–132. Leiden: Brill, 2004.

Farber, Zev. "The Parturient's 'Days of Purity': From Torah to Halacha." *The Torah*. www.thetorah.com/article/the-parturients-days-of-purity-from-torah-to-halacha (accessed 2/12/2020)

"The Purification of a Niddah: The Torah Requirement." *The Torah*. www .thetorah.com/article/the-purification-of-a-niddah-the-torah-requirement (accessed 2/20/2020)

Fardon, Richard. *Mary Douglas: An Intellectual Biography*. London/New York, NY: Routledge, 2001.

Faust, Avraham and Haya Katz. "The Archaeology of Purity and Impurity: A Case-Study from Tel 'Eton, Israel." *Cambridge Archaeological Journal* 27.1 (2017): 1–27.

Feder, Yitzhaq. "The Aniconic Tradition, Deuteronomy 4 and the Politics of Israelite Identity." *JBL* 132.2 (2013): 251–274.

"Behind the Scenes of a Priestly Polemic: Leviticus 14 and Its Extra-Biblical Parallels." *JHS* 15.4 (2015): 1–26. https://doi.org/10.5508/jhs.2015.v15.a4

Blood Expiation in Hittite and Biblical Ritual: Origins, Context and Meaning. Atlanta, GA: SBL, 2011.

"Contamination Appraisals, Pollution Beliefs and the Role of Cultural Inheritance in Shaping Disease Avoidance Behavior." *Cognitive Science* 40.6 (2016): 1561–1585.

"Defilement and Moral Discourse in the Hebrew Bible: An Evolutionary Framework." *Journal of Cognitive Historiography* 3 (2016): 170–172.

"Defilement, Disgust and Disease: The Experiential Basis for Akkadian and Hittite Terms for Pollution." *JAOS* 136.1 (2016): 99–116.

"The Defilement of Dina: Uncontrolled Passions, Textual Violence and the Search for Moral Foundations." *Biblical Interpretation* 24.3 (2016): 281–309.

"The Mechanics of Retribution in Hittite, Mesopotamian and Biblical Texts." *JANER* 10.2 (2010): 127–135.

"The Polemic Regarding Skin Disease in 4QMMT." *DSD* 19.1 (2012): 55–70.

"The Purification of a Niddah: The Legal Responsibility of the Reader." *The Torah.* www.thetorah.com/article/the-purification-of-a-niddah-the-legal-responsibility-of-the-reader (accessed 2/20/2020).

"The Semantics of Purity in the Ancient Near East: Lexical Meaning as a Projection of Embodied Experience." *JANER* 14.1 (2014): 87–113.

"The Wilderness Camp Paradigm in the Holiness Source and the Temple Scroll: From Purity Laws to Cult Politics." *JAJ* 5.3 (2014): 290–310.

Feldman Barrett, Lisa. "Are Emotions Natural Kinds?" *Perspectives on Psychological Science* 1.1 (2006): 28–58.

Fernandez, Karen V. and John L. Lastovicka. "Making Magic: Fetishes in Contemporary Consumption." *Journal of Consumer Research* 38.2 (2011): 278–299.

Finkel, Irving L. "Magic and Medicine at Meskene." *NABU* (1999): 28–30.

Fishbane, Michael A. "Biblical Colophons, Textual Criticism and Legal Analogies." *Catholic Biblical Quarterly* 42.4 (1980): 438–449.

Fleischman, Diana S., Lisa D. Hamilton, Daniel M. T. Fessler and Cindy M. Meston. "Disgust Versus Lust: Exploring the Interactions of Disgust and Fear with Sexual Arousal in Women." *PLOS ONE* 10 (2015)// e0118151. DOI: https://doi.org/10.1371/journal.pone.0118151

Fletcher, Adele. "Sanctity, Power, and the 'Impure Sacred': Analyzing Maori Comments of *Tapu* and *Noa* in Early Documentary Sources." *History of Religions* 47.1 (2007/2008): 51–74.

Fleming, Daniel E. "The Integration of Household and Family Religion." In *Household and Family Religion in Antiquity*, edited by J. Bodel and S. M. Olyan, 37–59. Malden, MA: Blackwell, 2008.

Time at Emar: The Cultic Calendar and the Rituals from the Diviner's House. Winona Lake, IN: Eisenbrauns, 2000.

Fokkelman, Jan P. *Narrative Art and Poetry in the Books of Samuel. Volume 2: The Crossing Fates.* Assen/Maastricht: Van Gorcum, 1986.

Ford, James N. "The Ugaritic Letter RS 18.038 (KTU² 2.39) and the Meaning of the Term *spr* 'lapis lazuli' (= BH sappīr 'lapis lazuli')." *UF* 40 (2008): 277–338.

Frazer, James. *The Golden Bough: A Study in Magic and Religion*, 1 vol. abridged edition, New York: Macmillan, 1952 [1922].

"On Certain Burial Customs as Illustrative of the Primitive Theory of the Soul." *Journal of the Anthropological Institute of Great Britain and Ireland* 15 (1886): 63–104.

Frazer, James and Theodor Gaster. *Myth, Legend and Custom in the Old Testament*. New York, NY: Harper & Row, 1969.

Freeman, Walter J. *How Brains Make Up Their Minds*. New York, NY: Columbia University Press, 2000.

Frevel, Christian. "Purity Conceptions in the Book of Numbers in Context." In *Purity and the Forming of Religious Traditions in the Ancient Mediterranean and Ancient Judaism*, edited by C. Frevel and C. Nihan, 369–411. Leiden: Brill, 2013.

"'Separate Yourself from the Gentiles' (Jubilees 22:16); Intermarriage in the Book of *Jubilees*." In *Mixed Marriages: Intermarriage and Group Identity in the Second Temple Period*, edited by C. Frevel, 220–250. New York: T&T Clark, 2011.

"Struggling with the Vitality of Corpses: Understanding the Rationale of the Ritual in Numbers 19." In *Les vivants et leur morts*, edited by J.-M. Durand, T. Römer and J. Hutzli, 199–226. OBO 257. Fribourg/Göttingen: Academic Press/Vandenhoeck & Ruprecht, 2012.

Frymer-Kensky, Tikva. *The Judicial Ordeal in the Ancient Near East*. Diss., Yale University, 1977.

"Pollution, Purification and Purgation in Biblical Israel." In *The Word of the Lord Shall Go Forth: Essays in Honor of David Noel Freedman in Celebration of his Sixtieth Birthday*, edited by C. L. Meyers and M. O'Connor, 399–414. Winona Lake, IN: Eisenbrauns, 1983.

Gadotti, Alhena. *Gilgamesh, Enkidu and the Netherworld and the Sumerian Gilgamesh Cycle*. Berlin: de Gruyter, 2014.

Gallagher, Shaun and Daniel Hutto. "Understanding Others Through Primary Interaction and Narrative Practice." In *The Shared Mind: Perspectives on Intersubjectivity*, edited by J. Zlatev, T. P. Racine, C. Sinha and E. Itkonen, 17–38. Amsterdam: John Benjamins, 2008.

Gane, Roy. *Cult and Character: Purification Offerings, Day of Atonement, and Theodicy*. Winona Lake, IN: Eisenbrauns, 2005.

"Didactic Logic and the Authorship of Leviticus." In *Current Issues in Priestly and Related Literature: The Legacy of Jacob Milgrom and Beyond*, edited by R. E. Gane and A. Taggar-Cohen, 197–221. Atlanta, GA: SBL, 2015.

"The Function of the Nazirite's Concluding Purification Offering." In *Perspectives on Purity and Purification in the Bible*, edited by N. S. Meshel, J. Stackert, D. P. Wright and B. J. Schwartz, 9–17. New York, NY: T&T Clark, 2008.

Ganzel, Tova. "The Transformation of Pentateuchal Descriptions of Idolatry." In *Transforming Visions: Transformations of Text, Tradition, and Theology in*

Ezekiel, edited by W. A. Tooman and M. A. Lyons, 33–49. Eugene, OR: Pickwick, 2009.

Geller, Markham J. *Ancient Babylonian Medicine: Theory and Practice*. Malden, MA: Wiley: Blackwell, 2010.

Evil Demons. Canonical Utukkū Lemnūtu *Incantations*. SAACT 5. Helsinki: Neo-Assyrian Text Corpus Project, 2007.

Forerunners to Udug-Hul: Sumerian Exorcistic Incantations. FAOS 12. Wiesbaden: Harrasowitz, 1985.

"Review of Joann Scurlock, Sourcebook for Ancient Mesopotamian Medicine." *JSS* 63.1 (2018): 259–264.

"Review of N. Heessel, Divinatorische Texte II: Opferschau-Omina." *AfO* 53 (2016): 201–208.

"The Šurpu Incantations and Lev. V. 1–5." *JSS* 25.2 (1980): 181–192.

Gelman, Susan. *The Essential Child: Origins of Essentialism in Everyday Thought*. Oxford: Oxford University Press, 2003.

George, Andrew. *The Babylonian Gilgamesh Epic: Introduction, Critical Edition and Cuneiform Texts*, vol. 1. Oxford: Oxford University Press, 2003.

Gesundheit, Simon. *Three Times a Year: Studies of Festival Legislation in the Pentateuch*. FAT 2/82. Tübingen: Mohr Siebeck, 2012.

Gibbs, Raymond W., Jr. *Embodiment and Cognitive Science*. Cambridge: Cambridge University Press, 2006.

Gilan, Amir and Alice Mouton. "The Enthronement of the Hittite King as a Royal Rite of Passage." In *Life, Death, and Coming of Age in Antiquity: Individual Rites of Passage in the Ancient Near East and Its Surroundings*, edited by A. Mouton and J. Patrier, 97–115. Leuven: Peeters, 2014.

Gilders, William K. *Blood Ritual in the Hebrew Bible: Meaning and Power*. Baltimore, MD: Johns Hopkins University, 2004.

Giner-Sorolla, Roger. *Judging Passions: Moral Emotions in Persons and Groups*. London: Psychology Press, 2013.

Glickman, Franklin S. "Lepra, Psora, Psoriasis." *Journal of the American Academy of Dermatology* 14.5 (1986): 863–866.

Goldstein, Elizabeth W. *Impurity and Gender in the Hebrew Bible*. Lanham, MD: Lexington Books, 2015.

Good, Byron J. *Magic, Rationality, and Experience: An Anthropological Perspective*. Cambridge: Cambridge University Press, 1994.

Goodall, Jane. *The Chimpanzees of Gombe: Patterns of Behavior*. Cambridge, MA: Belknap Press of Harvard University Press, 1986.

In the Shadow of Man. Boston, MA: Houghton Mifflin Co, 1971.

"Social Rejection, Exclusion, and Shunning Among the Gombe Chimpanzees." *Ethology and Sociobiology* 7.3–4 (1986): 227–36.

Goodnick Westenholz, Joan and Ilona Zsolnay. "Categorizing Men and Masculinity in Sumer." In *Being a Man: Negotiating Ancient Constructs of Masculinity*, edited by I. Zsolnay, 12–41. London: Routledge, 2017.

Gorman, Frank H. *The Ideology of Ritual: Space, Time and Status in the Priestly Theology*, 151–181. Sheffield: JSOT Press, 1990.

Gould, Stephen J. *Rocks of Ages: Science and Religion in the Fullness of Life.* New York, NY: Ballantine Books, 1999.

Gourévitch, Danielle. "Peut-on employer le mot *d'infection* dans les traductions françaises de textes latins?" *Mémoires du Centre Jean Palerne* 5 (1984): 49–52.

Grady, Joseph. "Primary Metaphors as Inputs to Conceptual Integration." *Journal of Pragmatics* 37.10 (2005): 1595–1614.

Grady, Joseph and Christopher Johnson. "Converging Evidence for the Notions of Subscene and Primary Scene." In *Metaphor and Metonymy in Comparison and Contrast*, edited by R. Dirven and R. Pörings, 533–555. Berlin: De Gruyter, 2003.

Graham, Jesse, Jonathan Haidt, Matt Motyl, Peter Meindl, Carol Iskiwitch and Marlon Mooijman. "Moral Foundations Theory: On the Advantages of Moral Pluralism over Moral Monism." In *Atlas of Moral Psychology*, edited by K. Gray and J. Graham, 211–222. New York: Guilford Press, 2018.

Green, Edward. *Indigenous Theories of Contagious Disease*. Walnut Creek, CA: AltaMira, 1999.

Greenberg, Moshe. "The Etymology of נדה 'Menstrual Impurity.'" In *Solving Riddles and Untying Knots: Biblical, Epigraphic, and Semitic studies in Honor of Jonas C. Greenfield*, edited by Z. Zevit, S. Gitin and M. Sokoloff, 69–78. Winona Lake: Eisenbrauns, 1995.

Ezekiel 1–20. AB. New York, NY: Doubleday, 1983.

Greenstein, Edward L. "Biblical Law." In *Back to the Sources: Reading the Classic Jewish Texts*, edited by B.W. Holz, 83–104. New York, NY: Summit, 1984.

Griffiths, Paul E. *What Emotions Really Are*. Chicago, IL: University of Chicago Press, 1997.

Grmek, Mirko D. *Diseases in the Ancient Greek World*, translated by M. and L. Muellner. Baltimore, MD: Johns Hopkins University Press, 1989.

"Les vicissitudes des notions d'infection, de contagion, et de germe dans la médecine antique." In *Textes médicaux latins antiques (Mémoires 5)*, edited by G. Sabbah, 53–66. St. Etienne: Centre Jean Palerne, 1984.

Gruber, Mayer S. "Women in the Cult According to the Priestly Code." In *Judaic Perspectives on Ancient Israel*, edited by J. Neusner, 35–48. Philadelphia, PA: Wipf & Stock, 1987.

Hacking, Ian. "A Tradition of Natural Kinds." *Philosophical Studies* 61.1–2 (1991): 109–126.

Haidt, Jonathan. "The Emotional Dog and Its Rational Tail: A Social Intuitionist Approach to Moral Judgment." *Psychological Review* 108.4 (2001): 814–834.

The Righteous Mind. New York: Pantheon Books, 2012.

Haidt, Jonathan and Clark R. McCauley. "Disgust." In *Handbook of Emotions*, edited by M. Lewis, J. M. Haviland-Jones and L. F. Barrett, 3rd ed., 757–776. New York, NY: Guilford Press, 2008.

Halina, Marta, Federico Rossano and Michael Tomasello. "The Ontogenetic Ritualization of Bonobo Gestures." *Animal Cognition* 16.4 (2013): 653–666.

Hallo, William H. "Disturbing the Dead." In *Minḥah le-Naḥum: Biblical and Other Studies Presented to Nahum M. Sarna in Honour of His 70th Birthday*.

JSOTS 154, edited by M. Brettler and M. Fishbane, 183–192. Sheffield: JSOT Press, 1993.

Hallpike, Christopher R. *The Foundations of Primitive Thought.* Oxford: Clarendon Press, 1979.

Haran, M. *Temple and Temple Service in Ancient Israel.* Winona Lake, IN: Eisenbrauns, 1985.

Haslam, Nick, Brock Bastian, Paul Bain and Yoshihisa Kashima. "Psychological Essentialism, Implicit Theories, and Intergroup Relations." *Group Processes and Intergroup Relations* 9.1 (2006): 63–76.

Have, Henk ten. "Knowledge and Practice in European Medicine: The Case of Infectious Diseases." In *The Growth of Medical Knowledge*, edited by H. ten Have et al., 15–40. Dordrecht: Springer, 1990.

Hayes, Christina. *Gentile Impurities and Jewish Identities: Intermarriage and Conversation from the Bible to the Talmud.* New York, NY: Oxford University Press, 2002.

Hayes, Christopher B., *Death in the Iron Age II and in First Isaiah.* FAT 79. Tübingen: Mohr Siebeck, 2011.

Healy, Margaret. "Anxious and Fatal Contacts: Taming the Contagious Touch." In *Sensible Flesh: On Touch in Early Modern Culture*, edited by E. D. Harvey, 22–38. Philadelphia, PA: University of Pennsylvania, 2003.

Heimpel, Wolfgang. *Letters to the King of Mari.* Winona Lake, IN: Eisenbrauns, 2003.

Heinrich, Joseph J., Steven J. Heine and Ara Norenzayan. "The Weirdest People in the World." *Behavioral and Brain Sciences* 33.2–3 (2010): 61–83.

Herdt, Gilbert. *The Sambia: Ritual and Gender in New Guinea.* Fort Worth, TX: Harcourt Brace Jovanovich College Publishers, 1987.

Herdt, Gilbert H. and Fitz J. P. Poole. "'Sexual Antagonism': The Intellectual History of a Concept in New Guinea Anthropology." *Social Analysis: The International Journal of Anthropology* 12 (1982): 3–28.

Hertz, Robert. *Death and the Right Hand*, translated by R. Needham and C. Needham. Aberdeen: Cohen & West, 1960 [1907–1909].

Hiebert, Paul. "Karma and Other Explanation Traditions in a South Indian Village." In *Karma: An Anthropological Inquiry*, edited by C. F. Keyes and E. V. Daniel, 119–130. Berkeley, CA: University of California Press, 1983.

Hieke, Thomas. "Die Unreinheit der Leiche nach der Tora." In *The Human Body in Death and Resurrection*, edited by T. Nicklas, F. V. Reiterer and J. Verheyden, 43–65. Berlin: de Gruyter, 2009.

Hirschfeld, Lawrence A. *Race in the Making.* Cambridge: MIT Press, 1996.

Hoffmann, D. *Das Buch Leviticus*, vol. 2. Berlin: Poppelauer, 1906.

Hoffner, Harry A. "Paskuwatti's Ritual Against Sexual Impotence (CTH 406)." *Aula Orientalis* 5 (1987): 271–287.

"Second Millennium Antecedents to the Hebrew 'Ôb." *JBL* 86.4 (1967): 385–401.

"Symbols for Masculinity and Femininity." *JBL* 85.3 (1966): 326–334.

Houston, Walter. *Purity and Monotheism: Clean and Unclean Animals in Biblical Law.* JSOTSupp 140. Sheffield: JSOT Press, 1993.

Huang, Julie Y., Joshua M. Ackerman and George E. Newman. "Catching (Up with) Magical Contagion: A Review of Contagion Effects in Consumer

Contexts." *Journal of the Association for Consumer Research* 2.4 (2017): 430–443.

Hugh, Lindsay. "Death-Pollution and Funerals in the City of Rome." In *Death and Disease in the Ancient City*, edited by V. M. Hope and E. Marshall, 152–172. London: Routledge, 2000.

Hulse, E. V. "The Nature of Biblical 'Leprosy' and the Use of Alternative Medical Terms in Modern Translations of the Bible." *PEQ* 107.2 (1975): 87–105.

Hume, David. *An Enquiry Concerning the Principles of Morals*, edited by T. L. Beauchamp. Oxford: Oxford University Press, 1998 [1751].

A Treatise of Human Nature, edited by P. H. Niditch. Oxford: Oxford University Press, 1978 [1739].

Hundley, Michael. *Keeping Heaven on Earth: Safeguarding the Divine Presence in the Priestly Tabernacle*. FAT 2/50. Tübingen: Mohr Siebeck, 2011.

Hutto, Daniel. "Why I Believe in Contentless Beliefs." In *New Essays on Belief: Structure, Constitution and Content*, edited by N. Nottelmann, 55–74. Basingstoke: Palgrave, 2013.

Isac, Moshe and Stanley Schneider. "Some Psychological Reactions of Rape Victims." *Medicine and Law* 11.3–4 (1992): 303–308.

Ishikawa, Ryotaro, Eiji Shimizu and Osamu Kobori. "Unwanted Sexual Experiences and Cognitive Appraisals That Evoke Mental Contamination." *Behavioural and Cognitive Psychotherapy* 43.1 (2015): 74–88.

Jablonka, Eva and Marion J. Lamb. *Evolution in Four Dimensions*. Cambridge, MA: MIT Press, 2005.

Jacob, Amber. "Demotic Pharmacology: An Overview of the Demotic Medical Manuscripts in the Papyrus Carlsberg Collection." In *Parlare la medicina: fra lingue e culture, nello spazio e nel tempo*, edited by N. Reggiani and F. Bertonazzi, 57–79. Milan: La Monnier Università, 2018.

Jacobs, Mignon R. *The Books of Haggai and Malachi*. NICOT. Grand Rapids, MI: Eerdaman's Publishing, 2017.

Jackson, Michael. *Paths Toward a Clearing: Radical Empiricism and Ethnographic Inquiry*. Bloomingfield, IN: University of Indiana Press, 1989.

Japhet, Sara. "The Prohibition of the Habitation of Women: The Temple Scroll's Attitude Toward Sexual Impurity and Its Biblical Precedents." *JANES* 22.1 (1993): 69–87.

Jaques, Margaret. *Le vocabulaire des sentiments dans les textes sumériens*. AOAT 332. Münster: Ugarit Verlag, 2006.

Mon dieu qu'ai-je fait?: les diĝir-šà-dab(5)-ba et la piété privée en Mésopotami. OBO 273, 330–332. Fribourg/Göttingen: Academic Press/Vandenhoeck & Ruprecht, 2015.

Jarcho, Saul. *The Concept of Contagion: In Medicine, Literature, and Religion*. Malabar, FL: Krieger Publishing, 2000.

Jenni, Ernst. *Das hebräische Pi'el*. Zurich: EVZ-Verlag, 1968.

Jeon, Jaeyoung. "Two Laws in the Sotah Passage (Num. v 11–31)." *VT* 57.2 (2007): 181–207.

Jindo, Job. "Toward a Poetics of the Biblical Mind: Language, Culture and Cognition." *VT* 59.2 (2009): 222–243.

Johnston, Sarah I. *Restless Dead: Encounters Between the Living and the Dead in Ancient Greece*. Berkeley, CA: University of California Press, 2013.

Jones, W. H. S. *Hippocrates*. Loeb, vol. 2. Cambridge, MA: Harvard University Press, 1923.

Jouanna, Jacques. *Greek Medicine from Hippocrates to Galen: Selected Papers*, translated by N. Allies. Leiden: Brill, 2012.

Kaddari, Menahem Zevi. *A Dictionary of Biblical Hebrew*. Ramat-Gan: Bar-Ilan University, 2006 (Hebrew).

Kamlah, Jens. "Grab und Begräbnis in Israel/Juda: Materielle Befunde, Jenheitsvorstellungen und die Frage des Totenkultes." In *Tod und Jenseits im alten Israel in seiner Umwelt*. FAT 64, edited by A. Berlejung and B. Janowski, 257–298. Tübingen: Mohr Siebeck, 2009.

Katz, Dina. "The Naked Soul: Deliberations on a Popular Theme." In *Gazing on the Deep, Studies in Honor of Tzvi Abusch*, edited by J. Stackert, B. Nevling Porter and D. P. Wright, 107–120. Winona Lake, IN: Eisenbrauns, 2010.

Kaufmann, Yehezkel. *The Religion of Israel*, translated by M. Greenberg. Chicago, IL: University of Chicago, 1960.

Kavaliers, Martin, Klaus-Peter Ossenkopp and Elena Choleris. "Social Neuroscience of Disgust." *Genes, Brain and Behavior* 18.1 (2019): e12508. DOI: 10.1111/gbb.12508.

Kazen, Thomas. "Dirt and Disgust: Body and Morality in Biblical Purity Laws." In *Perspectives on Purity and Purification in the Bible*, edited by N. S. Meshel, J. Stackert, D. P. Wright and B. J. Schwartz, 43–64. New York, NY: T&T Clark, 2008.

"Explaining Discrepancies in the Purity Laws on Discharges." *RB* 14.3 (2007): 348–371.

"Impurity, Ritual, and Emotion: A Psycho-Biological Approach." In *Issues of Impurity in Early Judaism*, 13–40. Winona Lake, IN: Eisenbrauns, 2010.

Jesus and Purity Halakhah. Stockholm: Almqvist & Wiksell, 2002.

"Levels of Explanation for Ideas of Impurity: Why Structuralist and Symbolic Models Often Fail While Evolutionary and Cognitive Models Succeed." *JAJ* 9.1 (2018): 75–100.

"Purity and Persia." In *Current Issues in Priestly and Related Literature: The Legacy of Jacob Milgrom and Beyond*, edited by R. E. Gane and A. Taggar-Cohen, 435–462. Atlanta, GA: SBL, 2015.

"The Role of Disgust in Priestly Purity Law: Insights from Conceptual Metaphor and Blending Theories." *Journal of Law, Religion and State* 3.1 (2014): 62–92.

Keller, Sharon Ruth. "Egyptian Letters to the Dead in Relation to the Old Testament and Other Near Eastern Sources." PhD diss., New York University, 1989.

Kelly, Daniel. *Yuck! The Nature and Moral Significance of Disgust*. Cambridge, MA: MIT Press, 2011.

Keltner, Dacher, Jonathan Haidt and Michelle N. Shiota. "Social Functionalism and the Evolution of Emotions." In *Evolution and Social Psychology*, edited by M. Schaller, J. A. Simpson and D. T. Kenrick, 115–142. New York, NY: Psychology Press, 2006.

Kimmel, M. "The Arc from the Body to Culture: How Affect, Proprioception, Kinesthesia, and Perceptual Imagery Shape Cultural Knowledge (and vice versa)." *Integral Review* 9.2 (2013): 300–348.

"Culture Regained: Situated and Compound Image Schemas." In *From Perception to Meaning: Image Schemas in Cognitive Linguistics*, edited by B. Hampe, 285–312. Berlin: de Gruyter, 2005.

"Properties of Cultural Embodiment: Lessons from the Anthropology of the Body." In *Body, Language and Mind. Volume 2: Sociocultural Situatedness*, edited by T. Ziemke, J. Zlatev and R. M. Frank, 77–108. Berlin: de Gruyter, 2008.

King, Leonard W. *Babylonian Boundary-Stones and Memorial Tablets in the British Museum*. London: Longmans & Co., 1912.

King, Philip J. and Lawrence E. Stager. *Life in Biblical Israel*. Louisville, KY: Westminster John Knox Press, 2001.

Kitz, Ann Marie. *Cursed Are You! The Phenomenology of Cursing in Cuneiform and Hebrew Texts*. Winona Lake, IN: Eisenbrauns, 2014.

Klawans, Jonathan. *Impurity and Sin in Ancient Judaism*. New York, NY: Oxford University Press, 2000.

Kleiman, Arthur. *The Illness Narratives: Suffering, Healing, and the Human Condition*. New York, NY: Basic Books, 1988.

Klein, Jacob. "Leprosy and Lepers in Mesopotamian Literature." *Korot* 21 (2011–2012): 9–24 (in Hebrew).

Knowles, Kelly, Charmaine Borg and Bunmi O. Olatunji. "Disgust, Disease, and Disorder: Impurity as a Mechanism for Psychopathology." In *Purity and Danger Now: New Perspectives*, edited by R. Duschinsky, S. Schnall and D. Weiss, 103–120. New York, NY: Routledge, 2017.

Koehler, Ludwig and Walter Baumgartner. *Lexicon in Veteris Testament Libros*. Leiden: Brill, 1958.

Koller, Aaron. "Pornography or Theology? The Legal Background, Psychological Realism, and Theological Import of Ezekiel 16." *CBQ* 79.3 (2017): 402–421.

Knohl, Israel. *Sanctuary of Silence: The Priestly Torah and the Holiness School*. Winona Lake, IN: Eisenbrauns, 2007 [1995].

Kolnai, Aurel. *On Disgust*. Chicago and La Salle, IL: Open Court, 2004 [1929].

Krüger, Annette. "Auf dem Weg 'zu den Vätern': Zur Tradition der alttestamentlischen Sterbenotizen." In *Tod und Jenseits im alten Israel in seiner Umwelt*, edited by A. Berlejung and B. Janowski, 137–150. FAT 64. Tübingen: Mohr Siebeck, 2009.

Kugel, James L. *The Great Shift: Encountering God in Biblical Times*. Boston, MA: Houghton Mifflin Harcourt, 2017.

In the Valley of the Shadow: On the Foundations of Religious Belief. New York, NY: Free Press, 2011.

Kühn, Dagmar. *Totengedenken bei den Nabatäern und im Alten Testament*. AOAT 311. Münster: Ugarit-Verlag, 2005.

Lakoff, George. "The Neural Theory of Metaphor." In *The Cambridge Handbook of Metaphor and Thought*, edited by R. Gibbs, 17–38. Cambridge: Cambridge University Press, 2009.

Woman, Fire and Dangerous Things: What Categories Reveal About the Mind.
   Chicago, IL: University of Chicago Press, 1987.
Lam, Joseph. *Patterns of Sin in the Hebrew Bible.* Oxford: Oxford University
   Press, 2016.
Lambert, Wilfred G. and Alan R. Millard. *Atra-Ḥasis: The Babylonian Story of
   the Flood.* Oxford: Clarendon Press, 1969.
   "DINGIR.ŠÀ.DIB.BA Incantations." *JNES* 33.3 (1974): 267–322.
Laland, Kevin N. and Gillian R. Brown. *Sense and Nonsense: Evolutionary
   Perspectives on Human Behaviour.* New York, NY: Oxford University
   Press, 2011.
Landy, Justin F. and Geoffrey P. Goodwin. "Does Incidental Disgust Amplify
   Moral Disgust? A Meta-analytic Review of Experimental Evidence."
   Perspectives on Psychological Science 10.4 (2015): 518–536.
Langacker, Ronald W. *Cognitive Linguistics: A Basic Introduction.* New York,
   NY: Oxford University Press, 2008.
Langness, Lewis L. "Discussion." *Social Analysis: The International Journal of
   Anthropology* 12 (1982): 79–82.
Lauinger, Jacob. "Esarhaddon's Succession Treaty at Tel Tayinat: Edition and
   Commentary." *JCS* 64 (2012): 87–123.
Leach, Edmund R. *Culture and Communication.* Cambridge: Cambridge
   University, 1976.
Leakey, Louis. *The Southern Kikuyu Before 1903*, vol. 3. London: Academic
   Press, 1977.
Legare, Christine H. "The Coexistence of Natural and Supernatural Explanations
   Across Cultures and Development." *Child Development* 83.3 (2012): 779–793.
Lemos, Tracy M. "Where There Is Dirt, Is There System? Revisiting Biblical Purity
   Constructions." *JSOT* 37.3 (2013): 265–294.
Levavi Feinstein, Eve. *Sexual Pollution in the Hebrew Bible.* Oxford: Oxford
   University Press, 2014.
Levenson, Jon D. *Creation and the Persistence of Evil.* Princeton, NJ: Princeton
   University Press, 1985.
Levine, Baruch A. *In the Presence of the Lord.* Leiden: Brill, 1974.
   Leviticus. JPS Torah Commentary. Philadelphia, PA: Jewish Publication
   Society, 1989.
   Numbers 1–20. AB. New York, NY: Doubleday, 1993.
Lewis, Theodore J. "How Far Can Texts Take Us? Evaluating Textual Sources for
   Reconstructing Ancient Israelite Beliefs about the Dead." In *Sacred Time,
   Sacred Place: Archaeology and the Religion of Israel*, edited by B. M. Gittlen,
   169–217. Winona Lake, IN: Eisenbrauns, 2002.
Lewontin, Richard. *Biology as Ideology: The Doctrine of DNA.* Concord, ON:
   Anansi, 2002.
Licht, Jacob. *A Commentary on the Book of Numbers*, vol. 1–3. Jerusalem:
   Magnes, 1985 (in Hebrew).
   "Nefesh." In *Encyclopaedia Biblica*, vol. 5. Jerusalem: Mossad Bialik, 1968 (in
   Hebrew).
Lloyd, Geoffrey E. R. *Demystifying Mentalities.* Cambridge: Cambridge
   University Press, 1990.

Magic, Reason and Experience. Cambridge: Cambridge University Press, 1979.

Loader, William. *The Dead Sea Scrolls on Sexuality.* Grand Rapids, MI: Eerdmans Publishing, 2009.

Löhnert, Anne and Annette Zgoll. "Schutzgott." In *Reallexikon der Assyriologie und vorderasiatischen Archaologie* vol. 12, 311–314. Berlin: De Gruyter, 2009–2011.

Lonie, Iain M. *The Hippocratic Treatises "On Generation," "On the Nature of the Child," "Diseases IV": A Commentary.* Ars Medica 7. Berlin: De Gruyter, 1981.

Maccoby, H. *Ritual and Morality: The Ritual Purity System and Its Place in Ancient Judaism.* Cambridge: Cambridge University Press, 1999.

Magonet, Jonathan. "'But If It Is a Girl She Is Unclean for Twice Seven Days....': The Riddle of Leviticus 12.5." In *Reading Leviticus: A Conversation with Mary Douglas*, edited by J. F. A. Sawyer, 144–152. JSOTSup 227. Sheffield: Sheffield Academic Press, 1996.

Mahalingam, Ramaswami. "Essentialism, Power, and the Representation of Social Categories: A Folk Sociology Perspective." *Human Development* 50.6 (2007): 300–319.

Mahon, Thérèse and Maria Fernandes. "Menstrual Hygiene in South Asia: A Neglected Issue for WASH (Water, Sanitation and Hygiene) Programmes." *Gender & Development* 18.1 (2010): 99–113.

Malinowski, Bronislaw. *Magic, Science and Religion and Other Essays.* Glencoe, IL: Free Press, 1948.

Malul, Meir. "David's Curse of Joab and the Social Significance of mḥzyq bplk." *Aula Orientalis* 10 (1992): 49–67.

Knowledge, Control and Sex: Studies in Biblical Thought, Culture and Worldview. Tel Aviv/Jaffa: Archaeological Center Publication, 2002.

Studies in Mesopotamian Legal Symbolism. AOAT 221. Kevelaer: Butzon & Becker, 1988.

Mandler, Jean M. *Foundations of Mind: Origins of Conceptual Thought.* Oxford: Oxford University, 2004.

Mansen, Frances Dora. "Desecrated Covenant, Deprived Burial: Threats of Non-Burial in the Hebrew Bible." PhD diss., Boston University, 2014.

Marshall, Eireann. "Death and Disease in Cyrene." In *Death and Disease in the Ancient City*, edited by V. M. Hope and E. Marshall, 8–23. London: Routledge, 2000.

Maul, Stefan M. "Die 'Lösung vom Bann': Überlegungen zu altorientalischen Konzeptionen von Krankheit und Heilkunst." In *Magic and Rationality in Ancient Near Eastern and Greco-Roman Medicine*, edited by H. F. J. Horstmanshoff and M. Stol, 79–95. Leiden: Brill, 2004.

Zukunftsbewältigung. BF 18. Mainz: Zabern, 1994.

Mayer, Werner R. "Ein neues Königsritual gegen feindliche Bedrohung." *Orientalia NS* 57 (1988): 145–164.

McCarter, Kyle P. "The Royal Steward Inscription." *CoS* 2.54: 180.

"The Sarcophagus Inscription of Tabnit, King of Sidon." *CoS* 2.56: 181.

Meggitt, Mervyn J. "Male–Female Relationships in the Highlands of Australian New Guinea." *American Anthropologist* 66.4 (1964): 204–224.

Meier, Brian P., David J. Hauser, Michael D. Robinson, Chris Kelland Friesen and Katie Schjeldahl. "What's 'Up' With God? Vertical Space as a Representation of the Divine." *Journal of Personality and Social Psychology* 93.5 (2007): 699–710.

Meigs, Anna S. *Food, Sex, and Pollution: A New Guinea Religion.* New Brunswick, NJ: Rutgers University Press, 1988.

"A Papuan Perspective on Pollution." *Man* 13.2 (1978): 304–318.

Meier, Samuel. "House Fungus: Mesopotamia and Israel (Lev 14: 33–53)." *RevBib* 96.2 (1989): 182–192.

Merleau-Ponty, Marcel. *Phenomenology of Perception*, translated by C. Smith. London: Routledge, 2002 [1958].

Merritt, Michele. "Dismantling Standard Cognitive Science: It's Time the Dog Has Its Day." *Biological Philosophy* 30.6 (2015): 811–829.

Meshel, Naphtali S. "Food for Thought: Systems of Categorization in Leviticus 11." *HTR* 101.2 (2008): 203–229.

"Pure, Impure, Permitted, Prohibited: A Study of Classification Systems in P." In *Perspectives on Purity and Purification in the Bible*, edited by N. S. Meshel, J. Stackert, D. P. Wright and B. J. Schwartz, 32–42. New York, NY: T&T Clark, 2008.

Meyer, Melissa. *Thicker Than Water: The Origins of Blood as Symbol and Ritual.* New York, NY: Routledge, 2005.

Michalowski, Piotr. "Origin." In *The World's Writing Systems*, edited by P. T. Daniels and W. Bright, 33–36. New York, NY: Oxford University, 1996.

Michael, B. *Keeping Heaven on Earth: Safeguarding the Divine Presence in the Priestly Tabernacle.* FAT II/50. Tübingen: Mohr Siebeck, 2011.

Milgrom, Jacob. *Leviticus.* AB, 3 vols. New York, NY: Doubleday, 1991–2000.

"Once Again, the Expiatory Sacrifices." *JBL* 116.4 (1997): 697–699.

"Sin-Offering or Purification-Offering." *VT* 21.2 (1971): 237–239.

"Studies in the Temple Scroll." *JBL* 97.4 (1978): 501–523.

Miller, Jared L. "Paskuwatti's Ritual: Remedy for Impotence or Antidote to Homosexuality?" *JANER* 10.1 (2010): 83–89.

Millikan, Ruth Garrett. *Beyond Concepts.* Oxford: Oxford University Press, 2017.

Murdock, George P. *Theories of Illness.* Pittsburgh, PA: University of Pittsburgh Press, 1980.

Muriuki, Godfrey. *The Southern Kikuyu Before 1903*, vol. 3. London: Academic Press, 1977.

Musolino, Julien. *The Soul Fallacy.* Amherst, NY: Prometheus Books, 2015.

Nabi, Robin L. "The Theoretical Versus the Lay Meaning of Disgust: Implications for Emotion Research." *Cognition and Emotion* 16.5 (2002): 695–703.

Needham, Rodney. *Belief, Language and Experience.* Blackwell: Oxford, 1972.

"Skulls and Causality." *Man* 11.1 (1976): 71–88.

Nemeroff, Carol and Paul Rozin. "The Contagion Concept in Adult Thinking in the United States: Transmission of Germs and Interpersonal Influence." *Ethos* 22.2 (1994): 158–186.

"The Makings of the Magical Mind: The Nature and Function of Sympathetic Magical Thinking." In *Imagining the Impossible: Magical, Scientific and*

Religious Thinking in Children, edited by K. S. Rosengren, C. N. Johnson and P. L. Harris, 1–34. Cambridge: Cambridge University Press, 2000.

"Sympathetic Magical Thinking: The Contagion and Similarity 'Heuristics.'" In *Heuristics and Biases: The Psychology of Intuitive Judgment*, edited by T. Gilovich, D. W. Griffin and D. Kahneman, 201–216. Cambridge: Cambridge University Press, 2002.

Neuberg, Steven, T. Kenrick Douglas and Mark Schaller. "Human Threat Management Systems: Self-Protection and Disease Avoidance." *Neuroscience and Biobehavioral Reviews* 35.4 (2011): 1042–1051.

Neufeld, E. "The Earliest Document of a Case of Contagious Disease in Mesopotamia (Mari Tablet *ARM* X, 129)." *JANES* 18.1 (1986): 53–66.

Neusner, Jacob. *The Mishnaic System of Uncleanness: Its Context and History*. Vol. 22 of *A History of the Mishnaic Law of Impurities*. Leiden: Brill, 1977.

Pesiqta deRab Kahana: An Analytical Translation, vol. 1. Atlanta, GA: Scholars Press, 1987.

Newman, George E., Gil Diesendruck and Paul Bloom. "Celebrity Contagion and the Value of Objects." *Journal of Consumer Research* 38.2 (2011): 215–228.

Ngubane, Harriet. *Body and Mind in Zulu Medicine*. London: Academic Press, 1977.

Nichols, Shaun. "On the Genealogy of Norms: A Case for the Role of Emotion in Cultural Evolution." *Philosophy of Science* 69.2 (2002): 234–255.

Niehr, Herbert. "The Changed Status of the Dead in Yehud." In *Yahwism After the Exile: Perspectives on Israelite Religion in the Persian Era*, edited by R. Albertz and B. Becking, 136–155. Assen: Royal Van Gorcum, 2003.

Nihan, Christophe. *From Priestly Torah to Pentateuch*. FAT 2/25. Tübingen: Mohr Siebeck, 2007.

"The Laws About Clean and Unclean Animals in Leviticus and Deuteronomy and Their Place in the Formation of the Pentateuch." In *The Pentateuch: International Perspectives on Current Research*, edited by T. B. Dozeman, K. Schmid and B. J. Schwartz, 401–432. Tübingen: Mohr Siebeck, 2011.

"La polémique contre le culte des ancêtres dans la Bible Hébraïque: Origines et Fonctions." In *Les vivants et leur morts*. OBO 257, edited by J.-M. Durand, T. Römer and J. Hutzli, 139–173. Fribourg/Göttingen: Academic Press/Vandenhoeck & Ruprecht, 2012.

"The Priestly Laws of Numbers, the Holiness Legislation, and the Pentateuch." In *Torah and the Book of Numbers*, edited by C. Frevel, T. Pola and A. Schart, 109–137. FAT 2/ 62. Tübingen: Mohr Siebeck, 2013.

Nissinen, Martti. *Prophets and Prophecy in the Ancient Near East*. WAW 12. Atlanta, GA: Society of Biblical Literature 2003.

Noam, Vered. "Ritual Impurity in Tannaitic Literature: Two Opposing Perspectives." *JAJ* 1.1 (2010): 65–103.

Noth, M. *Exodus: A Commentary*, OTL, translated by J. E. Anderson. London: SCM Press, 1965.

Leviticus: A Commentary, OTL, translated by J. E. Anderson. London: SCM Press, 1965.

Nöth, Winfried. *Handbook of Semiotics*. Bloomington, IN: Indiana University Press, 1990.

Nutton, Vivian. "Did the Greeks Have a Word for It?" In *Contagion: Perspectives from Pre-Modern Societies*, edited by L. I. Conrad and D. Wujastyk, 137–162. Aldershot: Ashgate, 2000.

"The Seeds of Disease: An Explanation of Contagion and Infection from the Greeks to the Renaissance." *Medical History* 27.1 (1983): 1–24.

Oaten, Megan, Richard J. Stevenson and Trevor I. Case. "Disease Avoidance as a Functional Basis for Stigmatization." *Philosophical Transactions of the Royal Society B* 366 (2011): 3433–3452.

"Disgust as a Disease Avoidance Mechanism: A Review and Model." *Psychological Bulletin* 135.2 (2009): 303–332.

Oatley, Keith and Philip Johnson-Laird. "Towards a Cognitive Theory of Emotions." *Cognition and Emotion* 1.1 (1987): 29–50.

Olatunji, Bunmi O., Craig Ebesutani, Jonathan Haidt and Chad N. Sawchuk. "Specificity of Disgust Domains in the Prediction of Contamination Anxiety and Avoidance: A Multimodal Examination." *Behavior Therapy* 45.4 (2014): 469–481.

Olyan, Saul M. *Biblical Mourning: Ritual and Social Dimensions*. Oxford: Oxford University Press, 2004.

Disability in the Hebrew Bible: Interpreting Mental and Physical Differences. Cambridge: Cambridge University Press, 2008.

Rites and Rank. Princeton, NJ: Princeton University Press, 2000

"Some Neglected Aspects of Israelite Interment Ideology." *JBL* 124.4 (2005): 603–616.

Orlinsky, Harry M. "The Hebrew Root *škb*." *JBL* 63.1 (1944): 19–44.

Otten, Heinrich. "Eine Beschwörung der Unterirdischen aus Boğazköy." *ZA* 54 (1961), 114–157.

Otto, Rudolf. *The Idea of the Holy*, translated by J. W. Harvey. Woking and London: Penguin Books, 1959 (1917).

Paden, William E. "Before 'The Sacred' Became Theological: Rereading the Durkheimian Legacy." *Method & Theory in the Study of Religion* 3.1 (1991): 10–23.

"Sacred Order." *Method & Theory in the Study of Religion* 12.1–4 (2000): 207–225.

di Paolo, Ezequiel A., Elana C. Cuffari and Hanna de Jaegher. *Linguistic Bodies: The Continuity Between Life and Language*. Cambridge, MA: MIT Press, 2018.

Pardee, Dennis. "A New Aramaic Inscription from Zincirli." *BASOR* 356.1 (2009): 51–71.

Parker, Robert. *Miasma: Pollution and Purification in Early Greek Religion*. Oxford: Clarendon Press, 1983.

Parker, Simon B. "Saints קדושים." *DDD*: 718–720.

Paschen, Wilfried. *Rein und Unrein: Untersuchung zur biblischen Wortgeschichte*. Munich: Kösel-Verlag, 1970.

Peled, Ilan. "Expelling the Demon of Effeminacy: Anniwiyani's Ritual and the Question of Homosexuality in Hittite Thought." *JANER* 10.1 (2010): 69–81.

Perler, Dominik and Ulrich Rudolph. *Occasionalismus: Theorien der Kausalität im arabisch-islamischen und im europäischen Denken.* Göttingen: Vandenhoeck & Ruprecht, 2000.

Pfälzner, Peter, H. Niehr, E. Pernicka and A. Wissing (eds.). *(Re-)Constructing Funerary Rituals in the Ancient Near East.* Wiesbaden: Harrasowitz, 2012.

Pinker, Steven. *The Blank Slate: The Modern Denial of Human Nature.* New York, NY: Viking, 2002.

Pongratz-Leisten, Beate. "Reflections on the Translatability of the Notion of Holiness." In *Of God(s), Trees, Kings, and Scholars: Neo-Assyrian and Related Studies in Honour of Simo Parpola*, edited by M. Luukko, S. Svard and R. Mattila, 409–427. Helsinki: Finnish Oriental Society, 2009.

Prinz, Jesse. *The Emotional Construction of Morals.* Oxford: Oxford University Press, 2007.

Propp, William H. C. *Exodus 1–18*, AB. New York, NY: Doubleday, 1999. *Exodus 19–40*, AB. New York, NY: Doubleday, 2006.

Pulvermüller, Friedemann. "Brain Embodiment of Category-Specific Semantic Memory Circuits." In *Embodied Grounding: Social, Cognitive, Affective and Neuroscientific Approaches*, edited by G. R. Semin and E. R. Smith, 71–97. Cambridge: Cambridge University Press, 2009.

Qimron, Elisha. *The Temple Scroll: A Critical Edition with Extensive Reconstructions.* Beer Sheva-Jerusalem, 1996.

Ranking, W. H. "Observations on Spermatorrhœa; or the Involuntary Discharge of the Seminal Fluid." *Provincial Medical Journal and Retrospect of the Medical Sciences* 7.159 (1843): 26–29.

Rapp, Alexander Michael. "Comprehension of Metaphors and Idioms: An Updated Meta-analysis of Functional Magnetic Resonance Imaging Studies." In *Oxford Handbook of Neurolinguistics*, edited by G. I. de Zubicaray and N. O. Schiller, 710–735. Oxford: Oxford University Press, 2019.

Reid, T. and D. R. Brookes. *Thomas Reid, an Inquiry into the Human Mind on the Principles of Common Mind.* Edinburgh: Edinburgh University Press, 1997.

Reiner, Erica. *Šurpu: A Collection of Sumerian and Akkadian Incantations.* AoF Beiheft 11. Osnabrück: Biblio Verlag, 1970.

Reventlow, Henning G. "Krankheit – ein Makel an heiliger Vollkommenheit. Das Urteil altisraelitischer Priester in Leviticus 13 in seinem Kontext." In *Studies on Ritual and Society in the Ancient Near East: Tartuer Symposien 1998–2004*, edited by T. R. Kämmerer, 282–290. Berlin: de Gruyter, 2007.

Rhyder, Julia. *Centralizing the Cult.* FAT 134. Tübingen: Mohr Siebeck, 2019.

Ricoeur, Paul. *The Symbolism of Evil*, translated by E. Buchanan. Boston, MA: Beacon Press, 1967.

Richardson, Seth. "Death and Dismemberment in Mesopotamia: Discorporation Between the Body and the Body Politic." In *Performing Death: Social Analyses of Funerary Traditions in the Ancient Near East and Mediterranean*, edited by N. Laneri, 189–208. OIS 3. Chicago, IL: Oriental Institute, 2007.

Robinson, Joanne-Marie. *"Blood Is Thicker Than Water": Non-Royal Consanguineous Marriage in Ancient Egypt.* Oxford: Archaeopress, 2020.

Rochberg, Francesca. *Before Nature: Cuneiform Knowledge and the History of Science*. Chicago, IL: University of Chicago Press, 2016.

The Heavenly Writing: Divination, Horoscopy and Astronomy in Mesopotamian Culture. Cambridge: Cambridge University Press, 2004.

Rohde, Erwin. *Psyche: The Cult of Souls and Belief in Immortality Among the Greeks*, translated by W. B. Hillis. New York, NY: Harcourt Brace, 1925 (1897).

Rosen, Ralph M. and Ineke Sluiter (eds.). *Andreia: Studies in Manliness and Courage in Classical Antiquity*. Leiden: Brill, 2003.

Roth, Martha. *Law Collections from Mesopotamia and Asia Minor*, 2nd ed. Atlanta, GA: SBL, 1997.

Royzman, Edward B., Pavel Atanasov, Justin F. Landy, Amanda Parks and Andrew Gepty. "CAD or MAD? Anger (Not Disgust) as the Predominant Response to Pathogen-Free Violations of the Divinity Code." *Emotion* 14.5 (2014): 892–907.

Royzman, Edward B. and John Sabini. "Something It Takes to Be an Emotion: The Interesting Case of Disgust." *Journal for the Theory of Social Behaviour* 31.1 (2001): 29–59.

Rozin, Paul and April E. Fallon. "A Perspective on Disgust." *Psychological Review* 94.1 (1987): 23–41.

Rozin, Paul, Jonathan Haidt and Clark R. McCauley. "Disgust." In *Handbook of Emotions*, edited by M. Lewis, J. M. Haviland-Jones and L. F. Barrett, 3rd ed., 757–776. New York, NY: Guilford Press, 2008.

Rozin, Paul and Carol Nemeroff. "Sympathetic Magical Thinking: The Contagion and Similarity 'Heuristics.'" In *Heuristics and Biases: The Psychology of Intuitive Judgment*, edited by T. Gilovich, D. W. Griffin and D. Kahneman, 201–216. Cambridge: Cambridge University Press, 2002.

Rozin, Paul, Carol Nemeroff, Matthew Horowitz, Bonnie Gordon and Wendy Voet. "The Borders of the Self: Contamination Sensitivity and Potency of the Body Apertures and Other Body Parts." *Journal of Research in Personality* 29.3 (1995): 318–340.

Rozin, Paul and Edward B. Royzman. "Negativity Bias, Negativity Dominance, and Contagion." *Personality and Social Psychology Review* 5.4 (2001): 296–320.

Ruane, Nicole. "Bathing, Status and Gender in Priestly Ritual." In *A Question of Sex: Gender and Difference in the Hebrew Bible and Beyond*, edited by D. W. Rooke, 66–81. Sheffield: Sheffield Phoenix Press, 2007.

Sacrifice and Gender in Biblical Law. New York, NY: Cambridge University Press, 2013.

Russell, James A. "Core Affect and the Psychological Construction of Emotion." *Psychological Review* 110.1 (2003): 145–172.

Russell, Sophie and Roger Giner-Sorolla. "Bodily Moral Disgust: What It Is, How It Is Different from Anger, and Why It Is an Unreasoned Emotion." *Psychological Bulletin* 139.2 (2013): 328–351.

Salin, Sylvia. "When Disease 'Touches,' 'Hits,' or 'Seizes' in Assyro-Babylonian Medicine." *Kaskal* 12 (2015): 319–336.

Samuelson, Sue. "The Cooties Complex." *Western Folklore* 39.3 (1980): 198–210.

Sanders, Seth L. "The Appetites of the Dead: West Semitic Linguistic and Ritual Aspects of the KTMW Stele." *BASOR* 369.1 (2013): 35–55.

"Naming the Dead: Funerary Writing and Historical Change in Iron Age Levant." *Maarav* 19.1–2 (2012): 11–36.

Saussure, Ferdinand de. *Course in General Linguistics*, translated by W. Baskin. London: Peter Owen, 1959.

Schaller, Mark and Justin H. Park. "The Behavioral Immune System (and Why It Matters)." *Current Directions in Psychological Science* 20.2 (2011): 99–103.

Schaper, Joachim. "Elements of a History of the Soul in North-West Semitic Texts: npš/nbš in the Hebrew Bible and the Katumuwa Inscription." *VT* 70.1: 156–176.

Schenker, Adrian. "Once Again, the Expiatory Sacrifices." *JBL* 116.4 (1997): 697–699.

Recht und Kult im Alten Testament: achtzehn Studien. OBO 172. Freiburg: Universitätsverlag, 2000 (1990).

Schiffman, Lawrence. *Sectarian Law in the Dead Sea Scrolls: Courts, Testimony and the Penal Code.* Chico, CA: Scholars Press, 1983.

Schmidt, Brian B. *Israel's Beneficent Dead: Ancestor Cult and Necromancy in Ancient Israelite Religion and Tradition.* FAT 11. Tübingen: Mohr Siebeck, 1996.

"The Social Matrix of Early Judean Magic and Divination: From 'Top Down' or 'Bottom Up.'" In *Beyond Hatti: A Tribute to Gary Beckman*, edited by B. J. Collins and P. Michalowski, 279–294. Atlanta, GA: Lockwood Press, 2013.

Schmitt, Rudiger. *Magie im Alten Testament.* AOAT 313. Münster: Ugarit Verlag, 2004.

Schnall, Simone, Jonathan Haidt, Gerald L. Clore and Alexander H. Jordan. "Disgust as Embodied Moral Judgment." *Personality and Social Psychology Bulletin* 34.8 (2008): 1096–1109.

Schwartz, Baruch J. "The Bearing of Sin in the Priestly Literature." In *Pomegranates and Golden Bells: Studies in Biblical, Jewish and Near Eastern Ritual, Law, and Literature in Honor of Jacob Milgrom*, edited by D. P. Wright, D. N. Freedman and A. Hurvitz, 3–21. Winona Lake, IN: Eisenbrauns, 1995.

The Holiness Legislation: Studies in the Priestly Code. Jerusalem: Magnes, 1999 (in Hebrew).

"Israel's Holiness: The Torah Traditions." In *Purity and Holiness: The Heritage of Leviticus*, edited by M. J. H. M. Poorthuis and J. Schwartz, 47–59. Leiden: Brill, 2000.

Schwemer, Daniel. "Akkadische Texte des 2. und 1. Jt. V. Chr. 2: Therapeutische Texte." *TUAT* 5: 41–45 (2.2.2).

Scorgie, Fiona, Jennifer Foster, Jonathan Stadler et al. "'Bitten by Shyness': Menstrual Hygiene Management, Sanitation, and the Quest for Privacy in South Africa." *Medical Anthropology* 35.2 (2016): 161–176.

Scurlock, JoAnn. "Baby-Snatching Demons, Restless Souls and the Dangers of Childbirth: Medico-Magical Means of Dealing with Some of the Perils of Motherhood in Ancient Mesopotamia." *Incognita* 2 (1991): 135–183.

Magico-Medical Means of Treating Ghost-Induced Disease in Ancient Mesopotamia. Ancient Magic and Divination 3. Leiden: Brill, 2006.

Sourcebook for Ancient Mesopotamian Medicine. WAW 36. Atlanta, GA: SBL, 2014.

"'Supernatural' Causes: The Moon God Sîn (4.88G): Leprosy." *CoS* 4: 291–293.

"Translating Transfers in Ancient Mesopotamia." In *Magic and Ritual in the Ancient World*, edited by P. Mirecki and M. Meyer, 209–223. Leiden: Brill, 2002.

Scurlock, JoAnn and Burton R. Andersen. *Diagnoses in Assyrian and Babylonian Medicine.* Urbana and Chicago, IL: University of Illinois Press, 2005.

Searle, John. "Can Computers Think?" In *Philosophy of Mind: Classical and Contemporary Readings*, edited by D. J. Chalmers, 669–675. New York: Oxford University Press, 2002.

Segerstråle, Ullica. *Defenders of the Truth: The Sociobiology Debate.* Oxford: Oxford University Press, 2000.

Semin, Gün R. and Eliot R. Smith. "Introducing Embodied Grounding." In *Embodied Grounding: Social, Cognitive, Affective and Neuroscientific Approaches*, edited by G. R. Semin and E. R. Smith, 1–5. Cambridge: Cambridge University Press, 2009.

Seow, Choon Leong. *Job 1–21: Interpretation and Commentary.* Grand Rapids, MI: Eerdmans, 2013.

Shemesh, Aharon. "4Q271.3: A Key to Sectarian Matrimonial Law." *JJS* 49.2 (1998): 244–253.

"Rebuke, Warning and Obligation to Testify – In Judean Desert Writings and Rabbinic Halakha." *Tarbiz* 66 (1997) 149–168 (in Hebrew).

Shemesh, Yael. "'I Find Woman More Bitter Than Death' (Ecclesiastes 7:26): Is There Misogyny in the Bible?" *Shnaton* 19 (2009): 77–104 (in Hebrew).

Shiloh, Yigal. "A Group of Hebrew Bullae from the City of David." *IEJ* 36.1/2 (1986): 16–38.

Shupak, Nili. "'An Abomination to the Egyptians': New Light on an Old Problem." In *Marbeh Hokmah: Studies in the Bible and the Ancient Near East in Loving Memory of Victor Avigdor Hurowitz*, edited by S. Yona, E. L. Greenstein, M. I. Gruber, P. Machinist and S. Paul, 271*–294*. Winona Lake, IN: Eisenbrauns, 2015 (in Hebrew).

Shweder, Richard A. "Ghost Busters in Anthropology." In *Human Motives and Cultural Models*, edited by R. G. D'Andrade and C. Strauss, 45–58. Cambridge: Cambridge University Press, 1992.

"The Metaphysical Realities of the Unphysical Sciences: Or Why Vertical Integration Seems Unrealistic to Ontological Pluralists." In *Creating Consilience: Integrating the Sciences and the Humanities*, edited by E. Slingerland and M. Collard, 56–73. Oxford: Oxford University Press, 2012.

Sigrist, H. E. *A History of Medicine*, vol. 1. New York, NY: Oxford University Press, 1951.

Simon, Zsolt. "Why Did Paškuwatti's Patient Fail in the Marital Bed?" In *Fortune and Misfortune in the Ancient Near East: Proceedings of the 60th Rencontre Assyriologique Internationale at Warsaw 21–25 July 2014*, edited by

O. Drewnowska and M. Sandowicz, 97–103. Winona Lake, IN: Eisenbrauns, 2016.

Singer, Itamar. *Hittite Prayers*. WAW 11. Atlanta, GA: Society of Biblical Literature, 2002.

Sklar, J. *Sin, Impurity, Sacrifice, Atonement: The Priestly Conceptions*. Sheffield: Sheffield Phoenix Press, 2005.

Slanski, Kathryn E. *The Babylonian Entitlement narûs (kudurrus)*. ASOR Books 9. Boston, MA: American Schools of Oriental Research, 2003

Slingerland, Edward. *What Science Offers the Humanities*. Cambridge: Cambridge University Press, 2008.

"Who's Afraid of Reductionism? The Study of Religion in the Age of Cognitive Science." *JAAR* 76.2 (2008): 375–411.

Slingerland, Edward and Mark Collard (eds.). *Creating Consilience: Integrating the Sciences and the Humanities*. Oxford: Oxford University Press, 2012.

Smith, Jonathan Z. "Manna, Mana, Everywhere and /-/-/." In *Relating Religion: Essays in the Study of Religion*, 117–144. Chicago, IL: University of Chicago Press, 2004.

To Take Place: Toward Theory in Ritual. Chicago, IL: University of Chicago Press, 1987.

Smith, Mark S. *An Early History of God*. Grand Rapids, MI: Eerdmans Publishing, 2002.

Smith, Virginia. *Clean: A History of Personal Hygiene and Purity*. Oxford: Oxford University, 2007.

Smith, William Robertson. *Lectures on the Religion of the Semites*. New York: Ktav Publishing, 1969 (1927).

Smoak, Jeremy D. "May YHWH Bless You and Keep You from Evil: The Rhetorical Argument of Ketef Hinnom Amulet I and the Form of the Prayers for Deliverance in the Psalms." *JANER* 12.2 (2012): 202–236.

The Priestly Blessing in Inscription and Scripture. Oxford: Oxford University Press, 2016.

Sokoloff, Michael. *A Dictionary of Jewish Babylonian Aramaic*. Ramat Gan: Bar-Ilan University, 2002.

Solomon, Jon. "Thucydides and the Recognition of Contagion." *Maia* 37 (1985): 121–123.

Sorensen, Jesper. *A Cognitive Theory of Magic*. Lanham, MD: AltaMira Press, 2007.

Sosis, Richard and Candace Alcorta. "Signaling, Solidarity, and the Sacred: The Evolution of Religious Behavior." *Evolutionary Anthropology* 12.6 (2003): 264–274.

Southwood, Katherine E. *Ethnicity and the Intermarriage Crisis in Ezra 9–10*. Oxford: Oxford University, 2012.

Sperber, Dan. "Intuitive and Reflective Beliefs." *Mind and Language* 12.1 (1997): 67–83.

Rethinking Symbolism, translated by A. L. Morton. Cambridge: Cambridge University Press, 1975.

Spronk, Klaas. *Beatific Afterlife in Ancient Israel and the Ancient Near East*. AOAT 219. Kevelear/Neukirchen: Verlag Butzon & Bercker, 1986.

Stackert, Jeffrey. "The Holiness Legislation and Its Pentateuchal Sources: Revision, Supplementation and Replacement." In *The Strata of Priestly Writings*, edited by S. Shechtman and J. S. Baden, 187–204. Zurich: Theologischer Verlag, 2009.

Starr, Ivan. *Queries to the Sungod*. SAA 4. Helsinki: Neo-Assyrian Text Corpus Project, 1990.

Staubli, Thomas. "Disgusting Deeds and Disgusting Gods: Ethnic and Ethical Constructions of Disgust in the Hebrew Bible." *HeBAI* 6 (2017): 457–487.

"Feces: The Primary Disgust Elicitor in the Hebrew Bible and in the Ancient Near East." In *Sounding Sensory Profiles in the Ancient Near East*, edited by A. Schellenberg and T. Krüger, 119–144. Atlanta, GA: SBL Press, 2019.

Staubli, Thomas and Silvia Schroer. *Body Symbolism in the Body*, translated by L. Maloney. Collegeville, MN: Liturgical Press, 2001.

Stavrakopoulou, Francesca. *Land of Our Fathers: The Role of Ancestor Veneration in Biblical Law Claims*. New York, NY: T&T Clark, 2010.

Stearns, Justin K. *Infectious Ideas: Contagion in Premodern Islamic and Christian Thought in the Western Mediterranean*. Baltimore, MD: Johns Hopkins University Press, 2011.

Steiner, Richard C. *Disembodied Souls: The Nefesh in Israel and Kindred Spirits in the Ancient Near East, with an Appendix on the Katumuwa Inscription*. Atlanta, GA: SBL Press, 2015.

Steinert, Ulrike. *Aspekte des Menschseins im Alten Mesopotamien: Eine Studie zu Person und Identität im 2. und 1. Jt. v. Chr.* Leiden: Brill, 2012.

Stol, Marten. *Birth in Babylonia and the Bible: Its Mediterranean Setting*. CM 14. Gröningen: Styx, 2000.

"Leprosy: New Light from Greek and Babylonian Sources." *Jaarbericht van het Vooraziatisch-Egyptisch Genootschap* (*Ex Oriente Lux*) 30 (1989): 22–31.

Strauß, Rita. *Reinigungsrituale aus Kizzuwatna*. Berlin: de Gruyter, 2006.

Sudhoff, Karl. "Επαφή der Aussatz?" *Sudhoffs Archiv für Geschichte der Medizin* 21 (1929): 204–206.

Sur, Piyali. "Women, Bodies and Discourse on Rape." *Indian Journal of Social and Natural Sciences* 4 (2015): 40–48.

Suriano, Mathew J. "Breaking Bread with the Dead: Katumuwa's Stele, Hosea 9:4, and the Early History of the Soul." *JAOS* 134.3 (2014): 385–405.

A History of Death in the Hebrew Bible. Oxford: Oxford University Press, 2018.

Taggar-Cohen, Ada. *Hittite Priesthood*. Texte der Hethiter 26. Heidelberg: Winter, 2006.

Tambiah, Stanley J. *Culture, Thought and Social Action: An Anthropological Perspective*. Cambridge, MA: Harvard University Press, 1985.

Magic, Science, Religion, and the Scope of Rationality. Cambridge, UK: Cambridge University Press, 1990.

Taves, Ann. "'Religious Experience' and the Brain." In *The Evolution of Religion: Studies, Theories, and Critiques*, edited by J. Bulbulia, R. Sosis, E. Harris, R. Genet, C. Genet and K. Wyman, 211–218. Santa Margarita, CA: Collins Foundation Press, 2008.

Taylor, J. Glen. *Yahweh and the Sun: Biblical and Archaeological Evidence for Sun Worship in Ancient Israel.* JSOTSupp 111. Sheffield: JSOT Press, 1993.

Teinz, Katharina. "How to Become an Ancestor – Some Thoughts." In *(Re-) Constructing Funerary Rituals in the Ancient Near East,* edited by P. Pfälzner, H. Niehr, E. Pernicka and A. Wissing, 235–243. Wiesbaden: Harrasowitz, 2012.

Temkin, Owsei. "An Historical Analysis of the Concept of Infection." In *The Double Face of Janus and Other Essays in the History of Medicine.* Baltimore, MD: Johns Hopkins Press, 1977 [1953].

Thiessen, Matthew. "The Legislation of Leviticus 12 in Light of Ancient Embryology." *VT* 68.2 (2018): 297–319.

"Luke 2:22, Leviticus 12, and Parturient Impurity." *Novum Testamentum* 54.1 (2012): 16–29.

Tigay, Jeffrey H. *Deuteronomy.* JPS Torah Commentary. Philadelphia, PA: JPS, 1996.

Deuteronomy: Introduction and Commentary, vol. 2. Mikra Leyisra'el. Tel Aviv/Jerusalem: Magnes, 2016 (in Hebrew).

Tigay, Jeffrey H. and Alan P. Millard. "Seals and Seal Impressions" (Hebrew). *CoS* 2.70.O: 200.

Tomasello, Michael. *A Natural History of Human Thinking.* Cambridge, MA; Harvard University Press, 2014.

The Origins of Human Communication. Cambridge, MA: MIT Press, 2008.

"Two Hypotheses about Primate Cognition." In *The Evolution of Cognition,* edited by C. Heyes and L. Huber, 165–183. Cambridge, MA: MIT Press, 2000.

Tooby, John and Leda Cosmides. *The Adapted Mind: Evolutionary Psychology and the Generation of Culture.* New York, NY: Oxford University Press, 1992.

van der Toorn, Karel. "Family Religion in Second Millennium West Asia (Mesopotamia, Emar, Nuzi)." In *Household and Family Religion in Antiquity,* edited by J. Bodel and S. M. Olyan, 20–36. Malden, MA: Blackwell, 2008.

"Female Prostitution in Payment of Vows in Ancient Israel." *JBL* 108.2 (1989): 193–205.

Sin and Sanction in Israel and Mesopotamia: A Comparative Study. Assen: Van Gorcum, 1985.

Touati, François-Olivier. "Contagion and Leprosy: Myth, Ideas and Evolution in Medieval Minds and Societies." In *Contagion: Perspectives from Pre-Modern Societies,* edited by L. I. Conrad and D. Wujastyk, 179–202. Aldershot: Ashgate, 2000.

Trible, Phyllis. *God and the Rhetoric of Sexuality.* OBT. Philadelphia, PA: Fortress, 1978.

Triebel, Lothar. *Jenseitshoffnung in Wort und Stein: Nefesch und pyramidales Grabmal als Phänomene antiken jüdischen Bestattungswesens im Kontext der Nachbarkulturen.* Leiden: Brill, 2004.

Tropper, Josef. *Die Inschriften von Zincirli.* ALASP 6. Münster: Ugarit-Verlag, 1993.

Tsukimoto, Akio. "By the Hand of Madi-Dagan, the Scribe and *Apkallu*-Priest' – A Medical Text from the Middle Euphrates Region." In *Priests and Officials in the Ancient Near East*, edited by K. Watanabe, 187–200. Heidelberg: Winter, 1999.

Turnbull, Colin. *The Mountain People.* New York, NY: Simon & Schuster, 1972.

Upashe, Shivaleela P., Tesfalidet Tekelab and Jalane Mekonnen. "Assessment of Knowledge and Practice of Menstrual Hygiene Among High School Girls in Western Ethiopia." *BMC Women's Health* 15.1, 84 (2015): DOI: https://doi.org/10.1186/s12905-015-0245-7.

Valeri, Valerio. *The Forest of Taboos: Morality, Hunting, and Identity among the Huaulu of the Moluccas.* Madison, WI: University of Wisconsin, 2000.

Veijola, Timo. "'Fluch des Totengeistes ist der Aufgehängte' (Dtn 21, 23)." *UF* 32 (2000): 643–653.

Violi, Patrizia. "Beyond the Body: Towards a Full Embodied Semiosis." In *Body, Language and Mind. Volume 2: Sociocultural Situatedness*, edited by R. M. Frank, T. Ziemke, J. Zlatev and R. M. Frank, 66–71. Berlin: de Gruyter, 2008.

Meaning and Experience, translated by J. Carden. Bloomington, IN: Indiana University Press, 2001.

Wagner, Roy. "Taboo." In *Encyclopedia of Religion*, vol. 14, edited by M. Eliade, 233–236. New York, NY: Macmillan, 1987.

Waltke, Bruce K. and Michael O'Connor. *An Introduction to Biblical Hebrew Syntax.* Winona Lake, IN: Eisenbrauns, 1990.

Watanabe, Kazuko. "Die literarische Überlieferung eines babylonisch-assyrischen Fluchthemas mit Anrufung des Mondgottes Sîn." *Acta Sumerologica* 6 (1984): 99–119.

Watson, James L. "Of Flesh and Bones: The Management of Death Pollution in Cantonese Society." In *Death and the Regeneration of Life*, edited by M. Bloch and J. Parry, 155–186. Cambridge: Cambridge University Press, 1982.

Watts, James W. *Leviticus 1–10, Historical Commentary of the Old Testament.* Leuven: Peeters, 2013.

Wegner, Romney. "'Coming Before the Lord': Exclusion of Women from the Public Domain of the Israelite Priestly Cult." In *The Book of Leviticus: Composition and Reception*, edited by R. Rendtorff and R. A. Kugler, 451–465. VTSupp 93. Leiden: Brill, 2003.

Weiss, Karen G. "Too Ashamed to Report: Deconstructing the Shame of Sexual Victimization." *Feminist Criminology* 5.3 (2010): 286–310.

Weiss, I. M. *Sifra with Rabad's Commentary.* New York: OM, 1946.

Wenham, Gordon J. *The Book of Leviticus.* NICOT, Grand Rapids, MI: Eerdmans, 1979.

"Why Does Sexual Intercourse Defile (Lev 15, 18)?" *ZAW* 95.3 (1983): 432–434.

Wenning, Robert. "No Cult of the Dead." In *(Re-)Constructing Funerary Rituals in the Ancient Near East*, edited by P. Pfälzner H. Niehr, E. Pernicka and A. Wissing, 291–300. QSS 1. Wiesbaden: Harrasowitz, 2012.

Werbner, Pnina. "Essentialising Essentialism, Essentialising Silence: Ambivalence and Multiplicity in the Constructions of Racism and Ethnicity." In *Debating Cultural Hybridity: Multi-Cultural Identities and the Politics of Anti-Racism*, edited by P. Werbner and T. Modood, 226–254. London: Zed Books, 1997.

West, Colin and Chen-Bo Zhong. "Moral Cleansing." *Current Opinion in Psychology* 6 (2015): 211–215.

Westbrook, Raymond. *Studies in Biblical and Cuneiform Law*. Paris: J. Gabalda, 1988.

Westenholz, Aage. "*berūtum, damtum*, and Old Akkadian KI. GAL: Burial of Dead Enemies in Ancient Mesopotamia." *AfO* 23 (1970): 27–31.

Westenholz, Aage and Ulla Koch-Westenholz. "Enkidu – The Noble Savage?" In *Wisdom, Gods and Literature: Studies in Assyriology in Honour of W. G. Lambert*, edited by A. R. George and I. L. Finkel, 437–452. Winona Lake, IN: Eisenbrauns, 2000.

Whitekettle, Richard. "All Creatures Great and Small: Intermediate Level Taxa in Israelite Zoological Thought." *SJOT* 16.2 (2002): 163–183.

"Levitical Thought and the Female Reproductive Cycle: Wombs, Wellsprings, and the Primeval World." *VT* 46.3 (1996): 376–391.

"Leviticus 15.18 Reconsidered: Chiasm, Spatial Structure and the Body." *JSOT* 49 (1991): 31–45.

"A Study in Scarlet: The Physiology and Treatment of Blood, Breath and Fish in Ancient Israel." *JBL* 135.4 (2016): 685–704.

Whorf, Benjamin Lee. *Language, Thought and Reality*, edited by J. B. Carroll. Cambridge, MA: MIT Press, 1956.

Williams, Raymond. *Keywords*. Oxford: Oxford University Press, 1983.

Wilson, J. V. Kinnier. "Leprosy in Ancient Mesopotamia." *RA* 60.1 (1966): 47–58.

Wilson, Edward O. *Consilience: The Unity of Knowledge*. New York, NY: Alfred Knopf, 1998.

Sociobiology: The New Synthesis. Cambridge, MA: Belknap Press, 2000 (1975).

Wittgenstein, Ludwig. *Philosophical Investigations*, translated by G. E. M. Anscombe, P. M. S. Hacker and J. Schulte. Chichester: Wiley-Blackwell, 2009.

Remarks on Frazer's Golden Bough, edited by R. Rhees, translated by A. C. Miles. Gringley-on-the-Hill: Doncaster, 1991.

van Wolde, Ellen. *Reframing Biblical Studies: When Language and Text Meet Culture, Cognition and Context*. Winona Lake, IN: Eisenbrauns, 2009.

Wootton, David. *Bad Medicine: Doctors Doing Harm Since Hippocrates*. Oxford: Oxford University Press, 2006.

Wright, David P. "Clean and Unclean [OT]." In *Anchor Bible Dictionary*. New York, NY: Doubleday, 1992, 6: 729–741.

Creating God's Law: How the Covenant Code of the Bible Used and Revised the Laws of Hammurabi. Oxford, UK: Oxford University Press, 2009.

The Disposal of Impurity: Elimination Rites in the Bible and in Hittite and Mesopotamian Literature. Atlanta, GA: Scholars Press, 1987.

"The Spectrum of Priestly Impurity." In *Priesthood and Cult in Ancient Israel*, edited by G. A. Anderson and S. M. Olyan, 150–181. JSOTSup 125. Sheffield: JSOT Press, 1991.

Wright, David P., Baruch J. Schwartz, Jeffrey Stackert and Naphtali S. Meshel. "Introduction." In *Perspectives on Purity and Purification in the Bible*, edited by N. S. Meshel, J. Stackert, D. P. Wright and B. J. Schwartz, 1–5. New York, NY: T&T Clark, 2008.

Yadin, Yigal. *The Temple Scroll.* 3 vols. Jerusalem: Israel Exploration Society, 1977–1983.

Yakubovich, Ilya. "Were Hittite Kings Divinely Anointed? A Palaic Invocation to the Sun-God and Its Significance for Hittite Religion." *JANER* 5.1 (2005): 122–135.

Zhong, Chen-Bo and Katie Liljenquist. "Washing Away Your Sins: Threatened Morality and Physical Cleansing." *Science* 313 (2006): 1451–1452.

Zimmerli, Walther. "Die Eigenart der prophetischen Rede des Ezechiel." *ZAW* 66 (1954): 1–26.

Zlatev, Jordan. "Embodiment, Language and Mimesis." In *Body, Language and Mind. Volume 1: Embodiment*, edited by T. Ziemke, J. Zlatev and R. M. Frank, 297–337. Berlin: de Gruyter, 2007.

Zucconi, Laura M. *Can No Physician Be Found? The Influence of Religion on Medical Pluralism in Ancient Egypt, Mesopotamia and Israel.* Diss, University of California, San Diego, 2005.

Index of Biblical Sources

Index of Selected Ancient Near Eastern Sources

Index of Rabbinic and Second Temple
Literature Sources

Subject Index

promiscuity, 178, 184, 189, 191, 192, 200, 202, 234

sin
as a cause of disease, 49, 67, 89, 91–106, 111, 124

sin offering (ḫaṭṭ'at), 49, 95–106, 118, 255–256

soul, 131–144, 154, 162, 164, 201, 261, 265, 268
and death pollution, 145–171

stain, 39, 47, 51–52, 54, 55, 56, 67, 121, 137, 161, 163, 164, 170, 185, 188, 189, 191, 206, 207

Šurpu incantations, 29, 41, 43, 94, 99, 111, 273

symbolic interpretations, 6, 32, 33, 146, 156, 176, 177, 193, 197, 222

touch, ix, 37, 41, 42, 64, 65–68, 75, 93, 94, 181

ṭum'ah, 7, 8, 28, 29, 30, 32, 35, 43, 52, 53, 54, 59, 69, 74, 76, 90, 118, 131, 147, 155, 170, 176, 189, 201, 261, 262, 264

Wittgenstein, Ludwig, 8, 30, 115

For EU product safety concerns, contact us at Calle de José Abascal, 56–1°, 28003 Madrid, Spain or eugpsr@cambridge.org.

www.ingramcontent.com/pod-product-compliance
Ingram Content Group UK Ltd.
Pitfield, Milton Keynes, MK11 3LW, UK
UKHW010249140625
459647UK00013BA/1745